Nigeria and the Nation-State

Nigeria and the Nation-State

Rethinking Diplomacy with the Postcolonial World

Revised Edition

John Campbell

ROWMAN & LITTLEFIELD
Lanham • Boulder • New York • London

Executive Acquisitions Editor: Michael Kerns
Assistant Editor: Elizabeth Von Buhr
Sales and Marketing Inquiries: textbooks@rowman.com

Published by Rowman & Littlefield
An imprint of The Rowman & Littlefield Publishing Group, Inc.
4501 Forbes Boulevard, Suite 200, Lanham, Maryland 20706
www.rowman.com

86-90 Paul Street, London EC2A 4NE

British Library Cataloguing in Publication Information available

Library of Congress Cataloging-in-Publication Data

Names: Campbell, John, 1944- author.
Title: Nigeria and the nation-state : rethinking diplomacy with the postcolonial world / John Campbell.
Description: Revised edition. | Lanham : Rowman & Littlefield, 2025. | Includes bibliographical references and index.
Identifiers: LCCN 2024028970 (print) | LCCN 2024028971 (ebook) | ISBN 9798881803094 (hardcover) | ISBN 9781538197806 (paperback) | ISBN 9781538197813 (epub)
Subjects: LCSH: Nigeria—Foreign relations. | Nigeria—Politics and government.
Classification: LCC DT515.62 .C34 2025 (print) | LCC DT515.62 (ebook) | DDC 966.9—dc23/eng/20240627
LC record available at https://lccn.loc.gov/2024028970
LC ebook record available at https://lccn.loc.gov/2024028971

Contents

Preface to the Revised Edition

Why an updated edition of a book about Nigeria that was published as recently as 2020? Since the first edition was published, there have been national elections; a new president, Bola Tinubu, assumed office; and the alienation of Nigerians from their government and the system it embodies has continued. In many parts of the country, personal security is in free fall. Yet, despite the current grim outlook, whether we acknowledge it or not, the growth of Nigeria's importance to the United States and to the world has only accelerated. With its already huge and rapidly growing population—estimated to become the third largest in the world by the end of the century—Nigeria is only going to become more, not less, important.[1] Hence the need for a better understanding of the "Giant of Africa" to which an updated edition may contribute.

US policy remains mired in the illusion that Nigeria is a conventional nation-state, and that we should relate to it as we do other nation-states. Under President Biden official policy is much the same as it was under President Trump and their predecessors, with wishful thinking that Nigeria is evolving into a Western-style democracy combined with inattention to complicated developments, and both too often underpinned by ignorance. With only a few exceptions, US administrations from Eisenhower to Biden have given Nigeria's rulers (whether military or ostensibly civilian) a pass on human rights and democracy, too often because it was the easiest thing to do. Differences of approach by successive Washington administrations are mostly of style rather than substance.

Since the establishment of bilateral relations in 1960, our preconceptions and ignorance of a complex polity have inhibited our understanding of how Nigeria works. We have ignored how Nigeria's history, including the slave trade, colonial rule, and a generation of postindependence military leadership have distorted what we presumed to be a modern, democratic state. We largely ignore new developments, such as a parallel Muslim and Christian revival that now shapes politics and the influence of traditional rulers,

Pentecostal preachers, and Islamic marabouts[2] that is unrecognized by the formal, Westphalian Nigerian state. Accordingly, our diplomacy is too often ineffective, with official Americans and Nigerians talking past each other about topics that are largely irrelevant to a productive bilateral relationship. Too often, US policy initiatives are irrelevant to those Nigerians in control. More effective US diplomacy requires a reassessment of who US diplomats should talk to, what they should focus on, and how they should assess what they hear.

In America, the 2020 Black Lives Matter demonstrations, ignited by the police murder of George Floyd, have made clear to many Americans that systemic racial oppression did not end with emancipation, the Civil Rights Act, or even the election of America's first Black president. Similarly, this book argues that the systemic exploitation and misrule of Nigerians did not end with independence, the civil war, or even the return to civilian-led democratic forms, if not their substance. It aims to inspire a rethink with respect to our own, secular, post-Enlightenment preconceptions and assumptions about how other countries ought to function, especially postcolonial states, in Africa and elsewhere. As we have learned in Vietnam, Afghanistan, and Iraq, the consequences for misunderstanding the internal dynamics of a country can be disastrous. Nigeria's experience where public life is infused with religion and enchantment[3] is not necessarily predictive of other states, but its example provides important lessons for understanding how other postcolonial, multiethnic, developing countries function, and how outsiders—corporations, NGOs, and other governments—can best interact with Nigeria. Hence, this book may be relevant to other countries and continents.

* * *

In June 2004, I presented my credentials to Nigeria's civilian president Olusegun Obasanjo as President George W. Bush's ambassador extraordinary and plenipotentiary, the fifteenth American envoy in the then forty-four years since Nigeria's independence. At the ceremony, I inspected a guard of honor, signed various documents, and handed over President Bush's letters recalling my predecessor and appointing me. There then followed a polite, nonsubstantive conversation among the president, the foreign minister, and me. In a ceremony nearly identical to mine, Joseph Palmer II had presented his credentials to the new Nigerian government as the first US ambassador to Nigeria three days after the country celebrated its independence on October 1, 1960. Also a career foreign service officer, he had been appointed by President Dwight Eisenhower.

Ambassadorial credentials ceremonies such as these reflect the conventional diplomatic and legal principles and practices governing relations among states, many of which were codified at the 1648 Congress of Westphalia ending the Thirty Years' War (1618–48) and the dawn of the Enlightenment and secularism. That meeting of European crowned heads and their representatives formalized the principles and vocabulary of the modern nation-state system, including a common understanding of such concepts as sovereignty, equality under international law of all states big or small, the sanctity of national boundaries, the recognition of individual citizenship, and the role and authorities of diplomats—altogether the Westphalian system. The acknowledgment at Westphalia that the crown determined the religion of the people put paid to the principle of universal religious truth. Those concepts evolved out of the Middle Ages, the Renaissance, the Reformation, and the Enlightenment were peculiarly European in origin. They have proved to be an ill fit for many postcolonial, multiethnic states characterized by the persistence of traditional cosmologies, strong tribal identities, weak national identity, and widespread popular alienation from their governments.

But, however artificial and arbitrary they may now seem in African and other non-European contexts, the continent's newly independent states, as elsewhere, adopted these Westphalian concepts and definitions. In doing so they reflected both their history of colonial occupation and the continued European and American domination of the international system in the era of decolonization. As a practical matter, their new leaderships had no alternative way to engage with the rest of the world, including the institutional financial system upon which they thought economic development depended. Hence, as is the case of other US ambassadors, Joseph Palmer and I were the American president's personal representative to the host country's head of state, with his presumed authority and the "state" both defined in the traditional, Westphalian sense.

The African independence wave accelerated during the last year of the Eisenhower administration, though it left intact the Portuguese and Spanish tropical empires and apartheid South Africa. Insofar as the Eisenhower administration paid attention to Africa, it was in the context of the Cold War, colored by the residue of colonialism, and the emerging chaos in the former Belgian Congo. By the time I arrived in Abuja as ambassador, almost half a century later, Congo had marginalized itself, and the European tropical empires, apartheid South Africa, and the Cold War were all long gone, over time subsequently to be replaced by American fraught relations with a resurgent China and Vladimir Putin's post-Soviet Russia. In my instructions, President Bush through Secretary of State Colin Powell charged me with working to strengthen the bilateral relationship by encouraging security cooperation, especially through Nigerian participation in multilateral peacekeeping, facilitating closer economic ties, and supporting Nigeria's democratic trajectory. Despite the end of colonialism, and based on the assumption that

Nigeria was a conventional nation-state, these have been the broad policy goals of Democratic and Republican administrations since Nigeria became independent.

There will be little that is new in this book to many Nigerians, who are often the fiercest critics of their country's leadership and are chagrined by the failure of postindependence Nigeria to reach its potential. Writers Chinua Achebe, Ken Saro-Wiwa, and Wole Soyinka, among many others, have dissected "the trouble with Nigeria."[4] So, too, have academics, both Nigerian and Western. But, all too often, foreign government policymakers, media, business, representatives of nongovernmental organizations, and others new to Nigeria are slow to make use of insights and expertise that point in directions different from Westphalian assumptions. A case in point: Richard Joseph's seminal work on Nigerian governance—to which this book owes an intellectual debt—appeared in 1987 and a lively academic discussion of "prebendalism," its core idea, continues right up to the present, though mostly in academic rather than policy circles.[5]

The essence of prebendalism and its associated neopatrimonialism is the privatization and exploitation of public resources by those who control the government and its bureaucracy.[6] By origin, "prebendal" refers to Anglican and Roman Catholic clergy assigned to cathedrals that were entitled to a share of the foundation's income by virtue of their position—not as a return for the services they might or might not perform. The income itself is called a "prebend" and the recipient is called a "prebendary." In the Nigerian context, prebendal describes the behavior of elites that access and share the government's oil revenue, not because of their services to the state, but because they are *entitled* to do so, by tradition, force, or chicanery. There is the expectation that prebendal beneficiaries will share their prebend with their patrons and their clients. This relationship, in which patrons distribute wealth to their clients, is often described as neopatrimonial.[7] Hence, prebendalism is intimately related to the neopatrimonial patronage-clientage organization of Nigerian society. Prebendal behavior is most salient among elites, but its spirit and that of neopatrimonialism extends throughout. A policeman at a checkpoint is salaried. But because he controls the checkpoint, he is *entitled* to ask for a bribe, and does so: "What do you have for me today?" He is expected to share a portion of the bribe he receives with his boss or patron and with subordinates and family. The system is partly a product of poverty: the policeman at the checkpoint may not have received his official salary for months, and, if he had, it would be too small to support a family. So, his bribe is part of a system of workarounds. This system of entitlements and sharing is unregulated except by various local customs and religious sensibilities and wide open to abuse. The three leading presidential candidates in 2023, Bola Tinubu (the putative victor), Atiku Abubakar, and Peter Obi, were all products of, and operated within, this prebendal and patrimonial system. There is little room for the concepts of patriotism, public service, and individual subordination to the common good as governance ideals. Hence, the argument here is that Nigeria is a prebendal, neopatrimonial state—one not one based on the Western concepts enshrined at the Congress of Westphalia. And successive Washington administrations have failed to recognize that reality and shape policy accordingly.

PERSONAL NOTE AND A CONFESSION

By background, I am neither an academic nor an Africanist. Instead, I spent most of my professional career as a US foreign service officer, a diplomat. I knew nothing firsthand about Africa until the US Department of State quixotically transferred me from Geneva to Lagos in 1988. Hence, my understanding of Africa was based initially on two diplomatic assignments in Nigeria totaling six years and one in South Africa of three years, rather than on conventional academic pursuits. Like my peers, I uncritically accepted a Westphalian, secular view of developing states and saw their foreign relationships as shaped by the accepted, Western-derived rules of diplomacy.

I served as political counselor at the American embassy, then in Lagos, from January 1988 to July 1990, during a period of military rule.[8] During the thirty months I was in Nigeria the first time, I visited twenty of Nigeria's then twenty-one states.[9] I met Nigerians of every station and profession, from the sultan of Sokoto and Nigeria's two resident Roman Catholic cardinals in the country (there was a third living in Rome) to academics, farmers, fishermen, journalists, and shopkeepers. I built on those contacts when I returned to Nigeria as ambassador from 2004 to 2007 and maintained many of them during frequent visits to Nigeria during my subsequent time at the Council on Foreign Relations (2009–21).

In the period between my two Nigeria sojourns, I held a variety of assignments in Washington, including service as dean of the State Department's language school. I was the political counselor in Pretoria from 1993 to 1996, during South Africa's transition from apartheid to "nonracial" democracy. Nevertheless, such is the importance of Nigeria to Africa and the United States that I kept returning to it, even if it was not the primary focus of what I was doing. Going back to Nigeria in 2004 as ambassador was a bit like going home. After my mission to Nigeria concluded in 2007, I continued to study Nigeria and Africa as a visiting professor at the University of Wisconsin–Madison, and later as a senior fellow for Africa at the Council on Foreign Relations. Up to 2020, I served as a member of the executive board of the American University of Nigeria.

When I arrived in Lagos the first time in 1988, I had assumed that diplomatic relations with Nigeria would be not so very different from those with other secular, Westphalian nation-states. That was partially true. On the one hand, much embassy work is routine, requiring no deep understanding of how a country really works. There are visa applications to be adjudicated; American citizen marriages, births, and deaths to be registered; Americans in jail to be visited; appointments for Washington-based visitors to be made; and the host of administrative requirements simply to keep the doors open at what was often the largest American diplomatic mission in Africa. On the other hand, knowledge of how a country really works is crucial for the effective management of the political and economic dimensions of the bilateral relationship. It is also necessary if an embassy is to tell effectively America's story, its "public diplomacy." Diplomacy can promote a better understanding of American values and perceptions on issues of mutual concern in the host country. Through diplomatic contact-building and reporting, an embassy also should enhance Washington's understanding of its host country. Diplomats need to understand what makes their interlocutors tick if they are to be effective representatives of any US administration.

I only slowly became aware that the relations between Nigerians and their government were different from the relationship between citizens and their government in France and Switzerland, where I had served previously, and in the United States. Among much else, the cosmology was shaped by the spirit world and far from Western secularism. There seemed to be structures of religious authority that often commanded deeper loyalty than the government of Nigeria and its capital, Abuja.[10] Tribes tended to be more important than national identification. Traditional rulers and institutions, whose power was based on custom rather than on statute of the European model, exercised informal or extralegal power. Hundreds of traditional rulers in Nigeria, among them the sultan of Sokoto, the shehu of Bornu, the oba of Benin, and the ooni of Ife, appeared to exercise authority parallel to that of the formal state and in some cases nearly its equal. The same was true of Christian Pentecostal preachers and Islamic imams and marabouts.

Bitten by the Nigeria bug in 1988, I was fascinated with the richness of its culture, but I was increasingly aware of the superficiality of our comprehension of its political and social arrangements, a shortcoming that reduced the quality of my reporting on political dynamics. But, I also sensed that understanding Nigeria was more important than Washington too often allowed for. Given its size, Nigeria would increasingly influence developments in Africa and beyond in the coming decades in ways sometimes difficult to predict. Subsequently serving in Pretoria and Cape Town, I was often looking over my shoulder at Nigeria. From that perspective, South Africa's national identity, its leadership, and its institutions of government seemed so much stronger despite all of the country's racial and class divisions: unlike most Nigerians, South Africans *knew* they were South African, though race and tribe were also an important part of their identity.

In 2004 when I took up my duties as ambassador, already to be seen were the challenges to Nigeria posed by a demographic boom and resulting youth bulge, too-rapid urbanization, degradation of the environment, the consequences of climate change, the deterioration of personal security caused by crime and insurrection, and a false economic boom tied to oil prices that fizzled out when international demand declined. At the Council, I came to see that Nigeria's challenges, if unusually salient, are shared by other states in Africa and elsewhere. The Nigerian economic and political system, based on oil and patronage, worked primarily for the benefit of a narrow elite and provided a measure of relative stability. But, in 2005, it began to break down with a new round of the perennial insurgency in the oil patch. By 2020, stability, such as it was, had come under assault in all corners of the country: insurrections in the northeast and the oil patch, violence in the middle of the country, and crime nationwide. These conflicts, in turn, were driven by factors beyond the control of a weak government and the largely predatory political elites. The elections of 2023 marked a breakdown of an elite, political consensus that had fostered a degree of stability by the alternation of presidential power between the north and the south, Christian and Muslim. This political arrangement had been fostered by the two predominate political parties controlled by competing and cooperating elites. In 2023, both parties ran Muslim candidates, even though it was the turn of the Christian south for the presidency, reflecting the breakdown of an elite consensus that had usually bridged ethnic and religious divides. Though the victor, Bola Tinubu, was the candidate of one of the establishment parties, the election saw a third-party Christian candidate, Peter Obi, come in third. Of concern for Nigeria's democratic trajectory, only 27 percent of registered voters submitted ballots.

The current round of poor security, if with deep historical roots, was not a reality for most Nigerians until as recently as 2005 and after. In 1989, three female officers from the American embassy, then in Lagos, set out in an embassy car with a driver for a familiarization visit to northern Nigeria—now the heartland of radical, jihadist Islam—that lasted some days. They traveled with no security personnel, nor did they need any. In 2004, when I returned to Nigeria, I could still travel throughout the country with only the normal security provided an ambassador. After 2005, however, the insurgency precluded my travel to parts of the Delta and limited that of other embassy officers. Since 2011, the terrorism associated with Boko Haram and its mutations and jihadist successors, ethnic and religious conflict in the middle belt, incipient insurgency in the Delta, and a nationwide crime wave have together precluded official embassy travel throughout the country without special, often elaborate, security arrangements.

Subsequent to my foreign service career, my years at the Council on Foreign Relations provided a special opportunity to see Nigeria in a wider Africa context and move beyond Westphalian assumptions. Reading and talking to a wide range of Nigerians and others in the fifteen years since I served as ambassador has led to the conclusion that rather than a Westphalian state, Nigeria was a prebendal and neopatrimonial political entity that requires a different approach to diplomacy. That is the theme of this book.

Acknowledgments

Both editions of this book are dedicated to the memory of two Africanists who deeply appreciated Nigeria and its importance to the United States and shaped my understanding of Africa's giant. A consummate diplomat, Ambassador Princeton Nathan Lyman served as, among other positions, USAID mission director in Ethiopia, US ambassador to Nigeria and later to South Africa, and presidential special envoy to Sudan. He was also the first to hold the Ralph Bunche Chair for Africa Policy Studies at the Council on Foreign Relations, the chair that I held until my retirement in 2021. He was a mentor to me throughout my Foreign Service career, during which I had the privilege of working for him twice, as his political counselor in Nigeria and later in South Africa. Professor Jean Frances Herskovits, daughter of the pioneering American Africanist Melville Herskovits, was an academic whose involvement with Nigeria dated from independence in 1960. An active member of the Council on Foreign Relations throughout her career, she deeply influenced a generation of scholars and American diplomats. I was privileged to be among them. For me, she was a bridge between academia and diplomacy.

I am grateful to the Council on Foreign Relations (CFR) for its support and encouragement of my effort to understand how Nigeria works and to convey what I hope is a deeper understanding to a nonspecialist audience, especially those in the public and private sectors shaping the American relationship with Nigeria. I also hope this will further our collective understanding of how other postcolonial states work.

With respect to the first edition, of which this is an update, President Richard N. Haass and Senior Vice President and Director of Studies James M. Lindsay helped refine and focus the book, reviewing drafts and providing invaluable criticism and suggestions. I benefited from the help of the David Rockefeller Studies Program staff, particularly Shannon O'Neil, Janine Hill, Patricia Dorff, Amy Baker, Shira Schwartz, and Christina Wehrmann. My thanks also to Irina Faskianos's National Program and Outreach team, particularly Krista Zegura and Oliva Cayoux, for organizing meetings with CFR members in Chicago and Boston to discuss early drafts. I am grateful to Richard Joseph, who chaired the Chicago session, and Pearl Robinson, who chaired the one in Boston. I am also grateful to Paul Lubeck and Peter Lewis, who organized a seminar session around chapters at the School for Advanced International Studies (SAIS) at John Hopkins University. My thanks, too, to the CFR library staff, especially Connie Stagnaro and Monique Libby, and to Will Morrow in CFR graphics. I would also like to thank the Global Communications and Media outreach team. I greatly benefited from conversations with Council colleagues, especially Tom Bollyky on public health in Africa, Alice Hill on climate change, and Shannon O'Neil on Mexican parallels with Nigeria.

Constance Freeman, Jacob Olupona, and Terry Pflaumer were generous in their time to provide feedback on specific chapters but also the themes of the book's first edition. I am grateful to Benjamin Arah and three anonymous reviewers who provided valuable criticism and insights. Their time and patience have made this a better book.

The first edition was my third book published by Rowman & Littlefield. I greatly value our relationship, now nearly a decade old. A special thanks to editor Susan McEachern, copyeditor Katelyn Turner, and the rest of their team. At Rowman & Littlefield, I am grateful to editors Michael Kerns and Janice Braunstein for shepherding this updated edition to publication.

My thanks to colleagues who continue to be involved after they moved on to greener pastures. I am grateful to Asch Harwood and Charlotte Renfield-Miller, who run the Nigeria Security Tracker and whose data informs the book, and also Asch for his interpretation of statistics and sensitivity to the challenge of quantifying Nigeria. Allen Grane worked with me on the proposal for this book and has since provided helpful guidance on military issues and defense cooperation, always making himself available to chat. Interns at CFR have been an invaluable "cloud of witnesses." I salute Tareian King, Alvin Young, Neil Edwards, Elizabeth Munn, Adam Valavanis, Nolan Quinn, Ayobami Egunyomi, and Rachael Sullivan for their work at all stages of this project.

A work of interpretation and analysis is always dependent on many others. Judy Asuni, Pauline and Ray Baker, Johnnie Carson, Jonathan Chanis, Herman J. Cohen, Richard Joseph, Deidre Le Pen, A. Carl LeVan, Katherine Marshall, and John Paden all taught me much. The work of Wale Adebanwi, Sara Chayes, Nic Cheeseman, Stephen Ellis, Abdulbasit Kassim, Ebenezer Obadare, Jacob Olupona, Matthew Page, Max Siollun, Alexander Thurston, Patrick Ukata, Olufemi Vaughn, and Jacob Zenn expanded my thinking. Conversations with Bukola Ademola Adelehin, Yodi Alakija, Lauren Ploch Blanchard, Judd Devermont, Jackie Ferris, Michelle Gavin, Nate Haken,

Nathan Hosler and the members of the Nigeria Working Group, Mike Jobbins, Chris Kwaja, J. Peter Pham, Geoff Porter, and Katie Smith helped refine my thinking.

Throughout my time at CFR, I greatly valued the research and analysis of numerous other organizations, including the Africa Center for Strategic Studies, Afrobarometer, Amnesty International, the Atlantic Council, the Berkley Center for Religion, Peace, and World Affairs, the Brookings Institution, the Carnegie Endowment for International Peace, the Center for Strategic and International Studies, Fund for Peace, Human Rights Watch, International Crisis Group, International Republican Institute, Open Society, the Pew Research Center, National Democratic Institute, National Endowment for Democracy, SAIS, Search for Common Ground, Socioeconomic Rights and Accountability Project (Nigeria), the US Institute of Peace, and the Woodrow Wilson Center for International Scholars.

With respect to this revised edition, I have particularly benefited from conversation with Ebenezer Obadare, now at the Council on Foreign Relations, and the work of Michelle Gavin, my successor as Ralph Bunche Senior Fellow; Anthony Carroll, with his deep understanding of Nigerian economics; and John Charlton, who has been personally engaged with Nigeria over a lifetime and is the hub of a network of international scholars and observers. For technical assistance with this edition, I am also indebted to Jack McCaslin, Nolan Quinn, and Alice Hawfield.

Those who have so patiently provided me with help and advice do not necessarily agree with my conclusions, and the responsibility for the interpretations and judgments in this book is mine.

Writing a book is like going on a pilgrimage. You have an idea about where you want to end up, but not necessarily how you will get there, what you will learn along the way, or how the journey will change you. In writing the first edition this book, Jack McCaslin, then my research associate, helped me find my way. A meticulous researcher, a trenchant critic, and a careful editor, he was indispensable to completing the journey. His organizational skills are formidable, as is his energy. He was there from the start, the first conversations about the shape a book might take, and he was there at the end with his (as ever) thoughtful criticism of the selected bibliography. He even designed the book jacket. Throughout the pilgrimage, he encouraged rigorous thinking and clear drafting. Not least, he was also good company.

Author's Note

One difficulty with discussing Nigeria's history is how often the formal nomenclature of the whole and of its constituent parts changes. Starting in 1914, the "beginning" of Nigeria, the British called it the Colony and Protectorate of Nigeria. Following internal, British-led constitutional changes, it became the Federation of Nigeria in 1954. In 1960, it gained independence as a dominion but kept this name. In 1963, after it abandoned dominion status, it became the Federal Republic of Nigeria. Despite the many changes to government since, it retains this formal title today.

Under the British, Nigeria was divided into three regions, the Northern, the Western, and the Eastern. These regions were retained upon independence, with a fourth, the Midwestern, added in 1963. In 1967, during the Nigerian civil war, the Federal Military Government abolished the regions and replaced them with states, twelve then, later nineteen, and thirty-six now. In addition, the Federal Capital Territory of Abuja has a special status not unlike Washington, DC, in the United States.

In the book, I refer to the north, east, west, and south of the country. The first three geographical designations roughly approximate the old regions. However, nearly half of the old Northern region is now called the middle belt. Accordingly, when I capitalize the name of a region (e.g., the Northern Region), I am referring to the British-created region that existed at the beginning of the Nigerian civil war. If it is not capitalized—the north—I am referring to a geographical area that does not have defined boundaries.

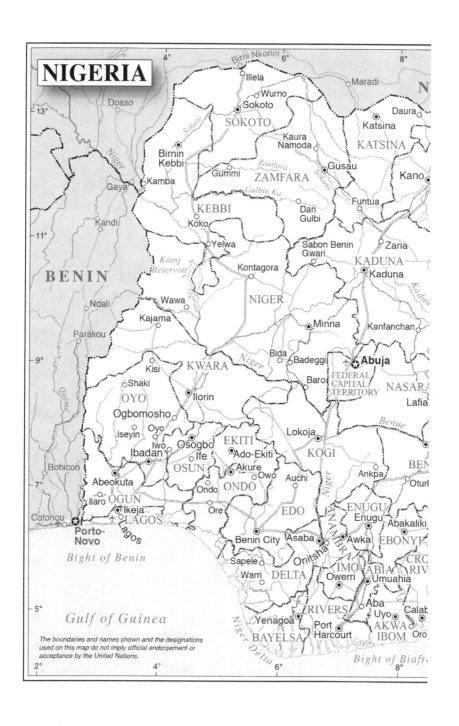

NIGERIA

Birni Nkonni

Illela

Dosso

Wurno

Sokoto

Maradi

SOKOTO

Daura

Katsina

KATSINA

Kaura
Namoda

Birnin
Kebbi

Gummi

Zamfara

Gusau

Kano

Kamba

ZAMFARA

Gaya

Gulbin Ka

KEBBI

Dan
Gulbi

Funtua

Kandi

Koko

Sabon Benin
Gwari

Zaria

Yelwa

Kontagora

KADUNA

Kaduna

Kainj
Reservoir

BENIN

Ndali

Wawa

NIGER

Kajama

Minna

Kanfanchan

Parakou

Bida

Badeggi

Abuja

Kisi

KWARA

Baro

FEDERAL
CAPITAL
TERRITORY

NASAR

Shaki

Ilorin

Lafia

OYO

Ogbomosho

Iseyin

Oyo

Lokoja

Benue

Iwo

Osogbo

EKITI

Ibadan

Ife

Ado-Ekiti

KOGI

BE

OSUN

Akure

Ankpa

Oturl

Abeokuta

Ondo

ONDO

Owo

Auchi

Ilaro

OGUN

Ore

EDO

ENUGU

Cotonou

Ikeja

LAGOS

Enugu

Abakaliki

Porto-
Novo

Benin City

Asaba

Awka

EBONYI

CRC
RIV

Bight of Benin

Sapele

Onitsha

IMO

ABIA

Warri

DELTA

Owerri

Umuahia

RIVERS

Aba

Uyo

Calab

Gulf of Guinea

Yenagoa

Port
Harcourt

AKWA
IBOM

Oro

The boundaries and names shown and the designations
used on this map do not imply official endorsement or
acceptance by the United Nations.

BAYELSA

Bight of Biafr

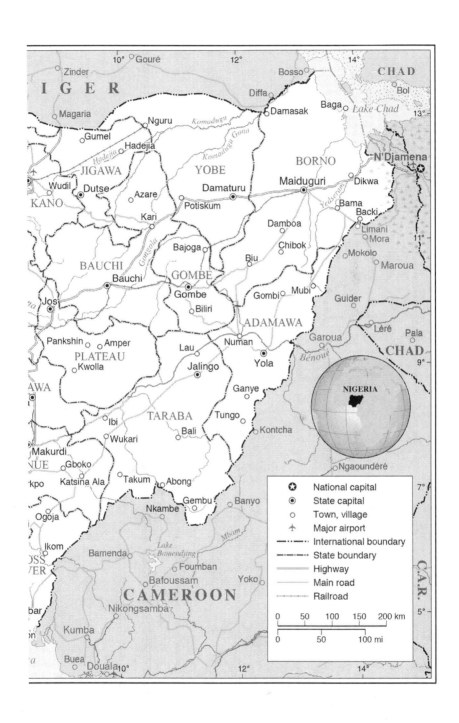

10° Gouré   12°   Bosso   CHAD
Zinder   Diffa   Bol
I G E R   Damasak Baga Lake Chad 13°
Magaria   Nguru Komudugu
Gumel   Hadejia   Komadugu Gana
JIGAWA   Hadejia   BORNO   N'Djamena
Wudil Dutse   Azare YOBE   Maiduguri   Dikwa
KANO   Damaturu   Bama
Kari   Potiskum   Backi
                        Damboa   Limani
        Bajoga   Chibok   Mora   11°
BAUCHI   Biu   Mokolo
  Bauchi   GOMBE   Maroua
Jos   Gombe   Gombi Mubi   Guider
        Biliri   ADAMAWA   Léré   Pala
Pankshin Amper   Lau Numan Garoua   CHAD
PLATEAU   Jalingo   Yola Bénoué   9°
Kwolla   Ganye
AWA   Tungo   NIGERIA
      Ibi TARABA   Kontcha
Makurdi Wukari   Bali
NUE Gboko   Abong   Ngaoundéré
kpo Katsina Ala Takum
Ogoja   Gembu   Banyo
    Nkambe
Ikom   Lake
OSS Bamenda Bamendjing   Yoko   C.A.R.
VER   Foumban
    Bafoussam
bar CAMEROON
  Nikongsamba
Kumba
Buea
Douala 10°   12°   14°

✪	National capital
⊙	State capital
○	Town, village
✈	Major airport
–·–·–	International boundary
–··–··–	State boundary
═══	Highway
——	Main road
+++	Railroad

0   50   100   150   200 km
0   50   100 mi

Timeline of Nigerian Political History

1804	Usman Dan Fodio establishes the Sokoto caliphate following his jihad in what would become northern Nigeria.
1861	British annex Lagos.
1888	Brazil abolishes slavery. Some Yoruba slaves in Brazil return to Nigeria, primarily Lagos.
1903	British conquer and occupy the Sokoto caliphate.
1914	Amalgamation of northern and southern Nigeria. Indirect rule begins.
1951	First-ever election in the Eastern, Northern, and Western regions, marking the beginning of "Native Administration." Indirect rule ends.
1960	Independence as a British-style democracy, Queen Elizabeth II is head of state within the Commonwealth, Tafawa Balewa is the prime minister.
1963	Nnamdi Azikiwe becomes head of state.
1966	Igbo military coup led by J. T. Aguiyi-Ironsi in January against "Muslim and northern dominated civilian government," killing Prime Minister Balewa and Premier of the Northern Region Ahmadu Bello. A few months later, a countercoup led primarily by northern military officers overthrows and kills Aguiyi-Ironsi. Yakubu Gowon, a thirty-one-year-old lieutenant colonel, becomes head of state.
1967	Biafra declares independence in July, led by Lieutenant Colonel Ojukwu.
1967–70	Nigerian Civil War (Biafra War). Biafra is defeated in January 1970.
1975	Gowon ousted in bloodless coup led by Joe Garba, Olusegun Obasanjo, and Murtala Muhammed (who goes on to become military chief of state) after he appears to back away from his stated commitment to restore civilian government.
1976	Muhammed assassinated in a Lagos "go-slow" (traffic jam) during a botched coup attempt, and the military council appoints Obasanjo to succeed him.
1979	Obasanjo orchestrates a return to civilian rule and multiparty elections are held under a new, US-style (presidential, federal) constitution. Shehu Shagari, a secondary-school science teacher, elected president, marking the beginning of the Second Republic.
1983	Shagari reelected with 47.5 percent of the vote in rigged elections, but four months later, Major General Muhammadu Buhari overthrows Shagari in a military coup, bringing the Second Republic to an end.
1985	General Ibrahim Babangida overthrows Buhari in a bloodless coup.

1990   After a failed junior-officer coup, General Babangida moves the govern-
        ment to the unfinished new capital of Abuja.
1993   Elections won by Moshood Abiola, marking the beginning of the very brief
        Third Republic. The results are annulled by General Babangida, who
        subsequently steps down as military chief of state and is replaced by
        General Sani Abacha, who turns Nigeria into an international pariah.
1995   Environmental activist in the Delta Ken Saro-Wiwa, as well as eight other
        fellow members of the Ogoni ethnic group, are executed after a sham
        trial. They are known as the "Ogoni Nine" and symbolize Abacha's
        repression.
1998   Sani Abacha dies under mysterious circumstances. Power shifts to General
        Abdulsalami Abubakar.
1998–99 Following a deal between military and civilian elites, Abubakar holds elec-
        tions and ends the period of military rule.
1999   Olusegun Obasanjo elected president, marking the beginning of the Fourth
        Republic. The transition establishes an unofficial "bargain" between
        northerners and southerners ensuring that the presidency rotates every
        eight years between the north and south. Related bargain between the
        military and civilian leaders, promising to protect military access to
        wealth in exchange for noninterference in politics.
2003   Obasanjo reelected, defeating opposition candidate Muhammadu Buhari.
        The elections are rigged, but 70 percent of voters participate, the highest
        to date.
2007   Umaru Yar'Adua is elected president, defeating opposition candidate
        Muhammadu Buhari. Obasanjo wanted to run for a third term, but his
        efforts to amend the constitution fail in 2006. Blocked, he handpicks
        Yar'Adua, not a political heavyweight.
2009   Boko Haram, led by founder Muhammad Yusuf, riots. Hundreds are
        killed, including Yusuf while he is in police custody. The group goes
        underground.
2010   President Yar'Adua dies in office. Vice President Goodluck Jonathan
        becomes president.
2011   Goodluck Jonathan wins presidential elections widely considered to be
        rigged.
2015   Muhammadu Buhari defeats Jonathan and becomes president.
2019   President Buhari wins reelection against former vice president Atiku
        Abubakar in elections widely regarded as rigged.
2023   National Elections: Bola Tinubu, former governor of Lagos state, defeats
        Atiku Abubakar, a former vice president, and Peter Obi, the only
        Christian candidate, for the presidency.

Introduction

The relationship with my people, the Nigerian people, is very good. My relationship with the rulers has always been problematic.

—Chinua Achebe[1]

Up to now, Americans have largely avoided in Africa the mistakes they made in Afghanistan, Iraq, and Vietnam. That is not the result of new wisdom but rather because Africa has been of only marginal concern to successive Washington administrations, and Nigeria has not been the subject of US foreign policy initiatives of the first rank. However, the era of American neglect is ending, driven not least by demography, security issues, and optimistic anticipation of a more extensive economic relationship. Africa's population is now double that of North America, and a rapidly growing percentage of Africans are moving to cities. The seemingly huge African market, despite the relative poverty of its consumers, is of increasing interest to foreign investors. But such rapid population growth combined with urbanization at breakneck speed, if not properly managed, could represent a threat to the health, prosperity, and security of many Africans—with serious implications for Europe and even North America. For example, two of the most horrific diseases to emerge in the twentieth century, HIV/AIDS and Ebola, "jumped" from animals—bushmeat and bats—to humans as the African rain forest was compromised by population pressure. Worldwide, there is no reason to think that the era of new diseases is over. A new coronavirus, COVID-19, caused a global pandemic with massive political, social, and economic disruption worldwide. Meanwhile, African migration continues to increase as undocumented migrants flee violence, hunger, and poverty, often crossing the Mediterranean to reach Europe.[2]

Insecurity in Nigeria and the Sahel is as ubiquitous as poverty, and contributes to it. Radical jihadist movements seek to destroy the corrupt, secular states in the region, replace them with an Islamic polity, and potentially establish a base from which to attack the West, as al-Qaeda did from Afghanistan. The Niger Delta—Nigeria's oil patch—faces a separate, low-level insurgency;

conflict over water and land with ethnic and religious dimensions continues in the middle belt, and there is a nationwide wave of kidnapping and murder that is likely to intensify if the country falls into recession. The question is not *whether* international involvement in Nigeria and Africa increases, it is under what terms and how.

A purpose of this book is to warn Americans and their partners against making the same conceptual mistakes in Africa that they did during wars in Afghanistan, Iraq, and Vietnam. Africa is complex, and its politics are highly local. It does not lend itself to the good-versus-evil analytical dichotomy that distorted policy in those three wars. A close study of Nigeria reveals profound tensions between the Nigerian state and its people—the "nation"—as well as tensions among its many ethnicities. Nigeria's experience is not necessarily predictive of other states, but its example can provide important lessons for understanding how other postcolonial, multiethnic, developing countries function, and how outsiders—corporations, NGOs, and other governments—can best interact with them.

Nigeria is one of the most culturally diverse countries in the world. Its population comprises hundreds of ethnic groups, most with their own language and culture.[3] Nigerians have moved across Africa and the world, with large and influential diaspora communities in South Africa, the United Kingdom, the United States, and China.[4] Nigeria is where Christianity and Islam meet, divided more or less equally between the two world religions, neither of which can claim to hold a decisive majority.[5] While the Nigerian state is nominally secular, traditional rulers and institutions incorporate both secular and religious authority, a reason why they remain so powerful. Further, Nigerians are intensely religious, more so than Americans, themselves considered the most devout in the developed world.[6] Evil, Satan, magic, mystery, the ancestors, and the spirit world are influential in daily life. In such a spirit- and faith-infused country, a fundamental cleavage exists between the predominately Muslim north, which is poor, and a mostly Christian south, which is also poor, if less so.[7]

Like other postcolonial states, Nigeria has modern elements that overlay traditions and customs with precolonial and colonial roots. A weak national identity and underdeveloped and eroding state structures facilitate the elite cartel's exploitation of the national wealth for private purposes. Nigeria defines itself as a federal state, that is, the central government in theory shares power with states. But the appearance of Nigeria's federal system and constitution is misleading. The reality is that political power has been concentrated in the central government, as it is in certain other ostensibly "federal" states such as Pakistan or Ethiopia. In Nigeria, the state is seemingly everywhere, from police checkpoints to hospitals to schools (all three too often of poor quality). There is a tax collection system, along with a full range of government agencies such as a foreign ministry, a diplomatic service, and even a space agency. But if the form is familiar, the substance is often absent. As in many other African countries, to fill the void between aspiration and reality, the ever-resilient develop workarounds often involving family, religion, and ethnicity, often greased by corruption. This dynamic is especially clear in Nigeria.

Much of Nigeria's international heft has come from its oil. In 2021, Nigeria ranked sixth among the Organization of Petroleum Exporting Countries (OPEC).[8] Its oil production was big enough that any significant variation in it could move world energy markets. But Nigeria is not an oil-rich state comparable to the Gulf emirates or even Angola, now Africa's largest oil producer but with a population of less than thirty million.[9] Nigeria's population is too large and its total oil revenue is too small. Even if the oil revenue could be equally distributed to all Nigerians, the increase in individual income would not be transformative. Yet, the federal government remains highly dependent on oil revenue, even as traditional rulers, often with precolonial roots, do not.[10] Oil's continued centrality to the Nigerian government, however, has been thrown into question with the collapse of international oil prices and the 2019–2023 coronavirus pandemic. By 2023, oil prices had largely recovered, though they remained volatile.

Depending on world commodity prices, Nigeria's economy is the continent's largest or second largest after South Africa according to conventional economic measurements, and the economy of just one state out of thirty-six, Lagos, is estimated to be larger than Kenya's.[11] There is a cornucopia of other resources, ranging from coal to gold to good soil for agriculture, but a generation of easy money from oil has left much of that potential unexploited. As oil corralled most domestic and international investment, public monopolies for power, telephones, and transport built and maintained only a fraction of the infrastructure Nigeria required. Nigeria, with its two hundred plus millions, generates about the same amount of electricity through the national grid as the city of Edinburgh, with a population of 482,000.[12] In a workaround, companies must rely on their own diesel generators to provide a reliable source of electricity, but these are costly. Nevertheless, under the right circumstances, economic progress can be remarkable. In 1999, in a country of then 120 million people, the public telephone monopoly could provide only 450,000 landlines.[13] After the Nigerian government liberalized telecommunications, some 80 percent of Nigeria's population gained access to mobile phones.[14]

Political leaders fully recognize that the federal government depends too much on oil revenue, but the economic diversification of a country as large, poor, and insecure as Nigeria is fraught with challenges. Put simply, for a generation Nigeria suffered from the natural resource curse. According to Jeffrey Frankel, "Countries endowed with natural resources more often develop social structures in which autocratic or corrupt political elites finance themselves through physical control of the natural resources."[15] Not only does an abundance of natural resources not guarantee economic and social development, this can actually inhibit it. At independence the breadbasket of West Africa, Nigeria is now a net importer of food, and in 2019, it overtook India as home to the largest absolute number of people living in extreme poverty despite having a sixth of India's population.[16] "I am convinced that Nigeria would have been a more highly developed country without the oil," said Nigerian Nobel laureate Wole Soyinka. "I wished we'd never smelled the fumes of petroleum."[17]

The past weighs heavily on Nigeria. The territory that encompasses modern Nigeria was politically unified only in 1914 by the British for their bureaucratic and fiscal convenience, and it became independent in 1960 as part of a wave of European decolonization of sub-Saharan Africa. There is no shared national myth or narrative that unites all Nigerians across ethnic and religious divisions, nor was there an ethnically unified independence movement. Those opposed to colonialism and British rule had an outlook that was pan-African and opposed to racism rather than specifically Nigerian, and independence-era electoral politics was organized by ethnicity.

Nigeria's history as an independent state is checkered with coups, counter-coups, a civil war, and military governments; it is now experiencing its fourth, and thus far its longest, experiment in the form if not the substance of democracy. Such a history has left the country fractured—religiously, ethnically, and generationally. A social contract between the government and the governed is still rudimentary, and few pay direct taxes. Nigeria's elites, be they religious, business, military, or tribal, head patronage networks. Most of their wealth and influence directly or indirectly is based on their prebendal access to the profits from the sale of government-owned oil. Perhaps 80 percent of oil earnings end up in the hands of an estimated 1 percent of the population.[18] Elites include those who run Nigeria's economy and public life at all levels, not just formal officeholders and other politicians. Indeed, "godfathers" traditionally manipulate politics without holding office themselves. Pentecostal preachers have become a significant part of the ruling elite, largely without themselves holding office.

Since the return to civilian rule in 1999 after a generation of military rule, continuity has been more characteristic of Nigeria than change, despite mounting challenges to the current political system and the security downward spiral. Corruption remains deeply embedded in all aspects of public and private life.[19] Absent a positive state presence in most of daily life, people turn to kin, religious structures, and ethnic groups for security, justice, and to secure their livelihoods. Operating outside the bounds of the state, much of this activity is technically illegal.[20] But Nigerians do not have much of a choice.

Such is Nigeria, an amalgamation of ethnicities, organized into a federal structure, but one effectively run by a cartel of elites who compete and cooperate for their share of state wealth and are largely alienated from the rest of the population. Prebendal and neopatrimonial behavior evolved out of Nigeria's colonial history and has been shaped by relations among its multiple ethnicities and by the response of the elites to colonial masters. After the 1967–70 civil war, military governments functioned outside the constraints of law, magnifying the scale of corruption, itself a consequence of prebendal and neopatrimonial behavior. Many of the beneficiaries of military rule became spectacularly rich while leaving millions of Nigerians mired in poverty. Prebendalism prefers a weak state, but one strong enough to negotiate with international oil companies, collect the revenue from oil, and provide the venue and the means by which elites can distribute it, or "share the cake," as Nigerians say. The state exists primarily to enrich those who have captured it, not to provide services for its people.

Despite these shortcomings, prebendal and neopatrimonial behavior provided a measure of stability in the aftermath of military rule. It is closely related to what Nigerians call "Federal Character," a principle that ensured that national wealth, the "cake," was "cut," or distributed, across elites of different regions, ethnicities, religions, and levels of government. The elites justify such a system as the means to keep an otherwise fractious country together. Governors, increasingly joined by Pentecostal preachers, are the current linchpins of the system, receiving and controlling state and local allocations of revenue, though there is little transparency as to how these allocations are spent and distributed. The same is true of how the president spends much of the revenue allocated to the federal government.[21] The benefits of such a system were perhaps clearest during the administration of President Olusegun Obasanjo, from 1999 to 2007. It provided a measure of stability in a dangerous period that saw the end of military rule and the fraught transition to the forms of civilian democracy. But if the system has been central to preserving the territorial integrity of Nigeria, there has been little or no accountability as to how the stewards of Nigeria's survival used this wealth. With insurrections and conflicts involving ethnicity, land use, and religion, together with the rise of banditry and other forms of criminality, especially kidnapping and cattle rustling, and the collapse of international oil prices, that stability is now under siege. In the elections of 2023, the informal arrangement among elites by which the presidency alternated between the Muslim north and Christian south broke down when the two major political parties each nominated a Muslim candidate as a result of political maneuvering devoid of principle. That led to a third major candidate, Peter Obi, a Christian, who garnered almost one-third of the vote. Still, an old-school politician, former Lagos state governor Bola Tinubu, eked out a victory.

Since the time of British colonial rule, no government's writ has run throughout the country, though it came closest during the generation of military rule. Rather, it is restricted to islands of authority, an archipelago in a sea of spaces controlled by elements other than formal government, such as traditional, religious, or criminal leaders.[22] The most important such islands are Abuja, the Lagos-Ibadan corridor, Port Harcourt in the oil patch, and most of the state capitals. These urban islands are also the modern economy's footholds. Nevertheless, deindustrialization, rapid urbanization, and desertification are challenging government authority even where it is strongest.

Despite all its troubles and criminal-inflected governance, Nigeria has long been of particular importance to its African neighbors, the major western European states, and the United States. It is a matter of either history (it is part of Britain's imperial legacy), commerce (European and American oil companies were heavily invested), or Nigeria's regional influence (Nigeria dominates the diplomacy and politics of West Africa). Accordingly, the United Kingdom, China, the European Union, the African Union, and the Economic Community of West African States engage with Nigeria. Often overlooked in Washington, they have been joined by Turkey, the Gulf States, Israel, Japan, Russia, and Iran.

For many years the United States imported large quantities of Nigerian oil and gas, often in excess of one million barrels a day. Nigeria's oil was of strategic importance to the United States, and successive Nigerian administrations assured Washington that should there be an interruption in the Middle East oil flow, Nigeria would do what it could to increase production. For their part, successive Washington administrations valued this political assurance and accordingly were predisposed to give a pass on human rights, democracy, and the rule of law to whatever government functioned in Lagos and subsequently Abuja. Now, the US produces much of the oil it consumes and imports almost none from Nigeria. Nevertheless, giving Nigeria a pass continued to be the theme in the aftermath of the flawed 2023 elections where the Biden administration chose to look the other way at fraud and irregularities, as had its predecessors.

Nigeria's importance to the world has been based on more than oil, a reason why Washington continues to look the other way at Abuja's governance and human rights failings. Nigeria has historically been a major participant in United Nations, African Union (AU), and regional peacekeeping missions, especially where other countries could not, or more often would not, be present. It has been one of the largest suppliers of peacekeepers on the continent and supports, both politically and financially, regional security and economic organizations, especially the Economic Community of West African States

(ECOWAS). Even before the 1999 transition to civilian governance, Nigeria led the fight against West Africa's military coup culture and has stood up for democratic norms despite its own domestic shortcomings, notably in Sierra Leone, Liberia, Ivory Coast, and the Gambia. Nigeria has also been the largest supplier of peacekeepers to Darfur and was an integral part of the successful peacekeeping mission in Liberia, helping that country move forward after a brutal civil war. Of late, however, Nigeria's international role has been in recession as it is increasingly bedeviled by insurrections and unrest at home. A consequence has been a decline in Nigeria's influence in African and in wider international fora, such as the United Nations or the World Trade Organization.

However, Nigeria's diplomatic activism, and its international influence, reached its highpoint during the administration of Olusegun Obasanjo (1999–2007). Since then, Nigeria's international role has receded as it has been increasingly bedeviled by domestic unrest across the country, jihadist insurrection associated with Boko Haram in the north, and weak presidential leadership. In part because it was the headquarters and principal funder of the Economic Community of West African States (ECOWAS), Nigerian prestige has declined with that organization's failure to roll back military coups in Burkina Faso, Mali, and Niger in 2023. Nigeria's influence in Africa and in wider internal fora, such as the United Nations, the Africa Union, and the World Trade Organization is in decline. However, the country's sheer size makes it unlikely that this decline will be permanent.

Nigeria is big, important, and troubled. As in other postcolonial countries, formal authority is fragmented, with only the illusion of a government presence in many parts of the country. The elite cartel shaped by prebendalism has stymied the country's socioeconomic development. Elites need the state as a venue to access wealth, but they keep it so weak that it does not inhibit them. A consequence of that weakness is a profound lack of government legitimacy among its own people; in the 2023 presidential elections, only 23 percent of registered voters cast their ballots.

Hence, rather than a nation-state, Nigeria is better described as a "prebendal archipelago." The label is a mouthful. Nevertheless, it fits. Though it is not a nation-state, neither has it been a failed state because it successfully distributed national oil wealth to national elites; this is what it was supposed to do. Whether the state can continue to do so given the challenges it faces remains to be seen. For most Nigerians the state provides little, and they in turn have little loyalty to it. Alienation is a common theme among the insurrections that are undermining the state.

A challenge for policymakers, diplomats, and foreign corporations is how to maintain a relationship with an increasingly weak and absent government and a fracturing political system, to identify those areas where cooperation is still possible, and those issues where outsiders may have a positive impact. For example, expanded US military cooperation with the Nigerian army has been stymied by the latter's human rights abuses, which are not likely to ameliorate anytime soon. Does shared concern about Islamist, jihadist penetration of the Sahel outweigh the manifest human rights abuses of the Nigerian security services? Does US identification with those human rights abusers damage the American image among Nigerians over the long term? (After all, the present political dispensation is unlikely to last forever.) What will be the consequences for US security interests or US advocacy of gay rights in Nigeria where homophobia is one of the few sources of national unity? There are similar dilemmas in, say, Pakistan and the Democratic Republic of the Congo, where American strategic and economic interest can sometimes clash with democratic values. We Americans must decide what our interests are and then pick our battles. This requires thinking about Nigeria as something other than the familiar nation-state. If US approaches to the Giant of Africa and involvement in West Africa are better grounded in this reality, the interests of both countries will be better served. At the same time, for most Americans, respect for human rights and the rule of law are central to what US policy should be. No Washington administration can altogether sweep them aside.

Much of Africa and the developing world faces the challenges of climate change, a youth bulge, and economies too dependent on extractive industries. Poverty is often rampant even in the face of positive economic growth statistics that fail to capture the reality for most people outside a small elite that is part of the modern economy. Many of these countries are characterized by fragmented societies held together by prebendalism with poor political leadership and weak institutions. In many, government authority does not extend throughout the country. Nigeria is a veritable case study of prebendal, patrimonial governance with official authority confined to an archipelago in a sea of spaces that it does not govern. No two countries are the same, but Nigeria's experience is instructive. Its prebendalism resembles that of the Democratic Republic of the Congo, Cameroon, and Zimbabwe; its archipelago of government authority resembles those of Pakistan, Iraq, and Afghanistan before Taliban victory. The weakness of national identity is seen everywhere from Africa to the Middle East to Asia. Hence, a book about Nigeria's realities and challenges is also a book about the challenges facing much of the world.

Four broad themes run throughout the book: First, Nigeria's current challenges were not inevitable, but they nevertheless have deep historical roots that stretch back to the colonial and precolonial periods, and exceptionally poor leadership has not helped; second, the goal of Nigeria's distinctive political culture is the increase and preservation of elite wealth and privileges; third, that political culture is now under assault, and what the outcome will be is unclear; fourth, Nigeria is too big and too important to ignore.

While this book hopes to expand our collective understanding of political organization beyond the one-size-fits-all nation-state, its focus is on Nigeria. It argues that Nigeria's present reality, rather than our assumptions about what a state is merely by virtue of its existence on a map, should be the starting point for US foreign policy. Rather than a nation-state as defined by the Congress of Westphalia, Nigeria is a prebendal archipelago. It is a collection of numerous languages, histories, and cultures not yet united, governed by a weak state in conjunction with other power structures in the context of vast patronage networks, fundamentally funded by oil.

Where is Nigeria going? It could break up, it could restructure itself into a genuine federal and democratic republic, or it could continue to limp along as an elite playground largely irrelevant to most of its citizens. The most desirable outcome, in my view, is the independence-era vision of a democratic, prosperous, multiethnic state. That vision, called the Nigeria Project, continues to animate Nigerian democrats.

Seemingly so full of optimism at independence in 1960, with predictions that it would soon become Africa's superpower—there was even talk of acquiring nuclear weapons as late as the early 2000s—Nigeria has disappointed many of its citizens by what seems to be its chronic inability to fulfill its promise. Nevertheless, individual Nigerians consistently demonstrate resilience and ingenious workarounds, and it is from them that change must ultimately come. Nigeria's friends can support a democratic trajectory, but only on the margins. The future of Nigeria is up to Nigerians.

Chapter 1

The Origins of Nigeria

History is to a large extent the selective emphasis of events from a national point of view. . . . The essence of colonial history is the demonstration of the massive importance of the European "intervention" in Africa.

—Peter Ekeh[1]

HISTORY HAS NOT BEEN KIND

As with other postcolonial states, understanding of contemporary Nigeria must start with its history. Nigerian governance and its present dysfunction have deep historical roots that frame and limit its options going forward. And this history has not been kind. Modern Nigeria is the result of British amalgamation into a single state of disparate territories with no shared language, culture, or religion; subsequent British failure to lay the groundwork for a modern, democratic state; followed by military rule postindependence. The consequences of this complicated history are often poorly understood and underappreciated by outside observers as well as by Nigeria's current political elites. Hence the justification for this romp through hundreds of years of the history of what has become Nigeria. This chapter explores the precolonial and colonial origins of Nigeria, the civil war, the coming of military rule, and the transition to ostensibly democratic governance.

The British colonial system preserved, modified, or destroyed many precolonial identities, belief systems, and traditional authorities. Moreover, British rule is associated with "modernization." The term familiarly refers to a cluster of behaviors and values that promote economic development, improved public health, and advanced technologies based on science, all of which Africans came to want. But the term also refers to the resulting transformation of individual and social values, including a shift of emphasis from the collective

11

(including family, village, or ethnic group) to the individual, a process that, however, remains far from complete.

British justification for their colonial rule was not static; it shifted during the interwar years and World War II from the early twentieth century's "civilizing mission" (especially ending the slave trade and cannibalism and promoting trade) to a "modernization paradigm" that looked toward the eventual creation of a democratic state following the Western model.[2]

While the British quite literally put Nigeria on the map, they did little to foster loyalty to it. Indeed, the very concept of a "nation" is a European, postmedieval construct, and the notion of creating nations, as the British eventually claimed they were doing in Nigeria, is profoundly imperialistic and Eurocentric. It implies that Africa was a tabula rasa on which the British and other Europeans could impose their will without reference to the people who lived there.[3]

Among the peoples of Nigeria old identities persisted that today often command stronger loyalties than does the Nigerian state. Postindependence military rule promoted lawlessness—the military governments were literally above the law, as often was the ostensibly civilian Obasanjo administration—and opened the gates to wholesale looting of the state of a magnitude far beyond that of the precolonial and colonial eras.

THE PRECOLONIAL PERIOD

In the eighteenth century, the Scottish philosopher and historian David Hume wrote, "I am apt to suspect the Negroes . . . to be naturally inferior to the whites. There never was a civilized nation of any other complexion than white."[4] H. R. Trevor-Roper—denizen of Britain's post–World War II intellectual and social establishment; Master of Peterhouse, University of Cambridge; Regius Professor of Modern History at Oxford; a life member of the House of Lords; and a historian, essayist, and regular media commentator—argued in 1965 that Africa had no history prior to European exploration and colonization. He said, "There is only the history of Europeans in Africa. The rest is darkness," its past the "unedifying gyrations of barbarous tribes in picturesque but irrelevant corners of the globe."[5] Trevor-Roper reflected long-held European views of Africa and peoples of color. During the period after World War II, this outlook was common. It was shaped by the Cold War and decolonization in the context of persistent if largely unexamined and slowly waning white racism.

Racist Roots

The roots of European and American racism reflected by Hume and Trevor-Roper, each in his own way, are deep, going back a least as far as the Portuguese contact with West Africa in the fifteenth century. In the nineteenth century, French aristocrat Joseph Arthur de Gobineau provided a "modern," "science-based" explanation of the alleged racial inferiority of Africans, which was deeply influential at the time and still persists on the European and American white supremacist margins. Written in 1853, his essay *The Inequality of Human Races* became the basis for European and American labeling of nonwhite races as "primitive" and "savage" and justified their need to be "civilized" by the white race. That way of thinking provided a central, usually unspoken, justification for the colonial enterprise in Africa. His essay, which includes a common misreading of Charles Darwin's ideas on natural selection, argued that the "civilized" societies of Europe were a mark of European racial supremacy. He outlined what he believed to be a racial hierarchy of achievement, with whites at the top and Blacks at the bottom.[6] It should go without saying that since the days of Gobineau, the scientific community has definitively demonstrated that there is no "science" behind his theories. Nevertheless, if marginal now, a form of white supremacy was intrinsic to most Europeans or Americans in contact with Africa until the mid-twentieth century. Like their European counterparts elsewhere in Africa, the British involved with Nigeria, its colonization and its subsequent decolonization, were nearly all racist white supremacists, to a greater or lesser extent. That did not preclude among the best of them a genuine concern for the Africans that they ruled, especially among the district officers that had the greatest contact with the indigenous population. Moreover, by the 1930s, the policy of the British Colonial Office was to frown on overt racism, though in practice it persisted throughout the colonial period. Even so, Nigeria was spared many of the consequences of white racism simply because it never was a country of white settlement, unlike Algeria, Angola, Kenya, Zimbabwe, or South Africa. Indeed, throughout the colonial period, few Nigerians ever saw a European.

The contributions of Africans ranging from Nelson Mandela to Desmond Tutu to Kofi Annan have demolished Hume, just as more than a generation of study of African history has proven Trevor-Roper wrong. Using techniques that were unknown to Hume or new to Trevor-Roper, including linguistics, the critical use of oral tradition, biological and genetic sources, archology, archaeology, and the new discovery and critical use of documents, scholars show that Africa's precolonial history is far more compelling than "the unedifying gyration of barbarous tribes." Instead of consigning Africa to darkness as Hume and Trevor-Roper and their contemporaries did, the challenge is to comprehend the complexity of its history and how it shapes the present.

A Continuum

The history of Africa, as elsewhere, is a continuum stretching back thousands of years. For example, the Iron Age Nok people appeared ca. 1500 BC and disappeared ca. 500 AD; they left behind superb terra-cotta sculptures and influenced, in ways not yet fully explored, their successors. Of more immediate significance for modern Nigeria during the European Middle Ages and Early Modern periods were numerous kingdoms and empires in the West African Sahel and along the coast of the Gulf of Guinea. They are remembered today with pride. Profits from gold mining; trade, including slaves; agriculture; and stock-raising were the foundation for African empires. Wealth could be acquired only in limited ways, absent mechanized production. Hence, warfare that fed slavery and the slave trade was a constant in West Africa.[7]

The largest empires were in the Sahel, abutting the trans-Saharan trade routes for a millennium, and along the coast, where well-organized kingdoms traded with Europeans beginning in the fifteenth century. In terms of culture, most of them were influenced by the Islam of the Middle East, a market for the trans-Saharan trade and the export of slaves, gold, copper, and salt.

But, modern myths associated with these empires have not promoted a specifically Nigerian national identity. Instead, myth and memory of ancient empires promote ethnic, religious, or pan-African mentalities among Nigerian and other African intellectuals. Memories of ancient empires have reinforced ethnic or religious identities rather than one that was specifically Nigerian, which, after all, is an identity created by the British.

Even the term "precolonial Nigeria" is misleading (see map 1.1). "Nigeria" as a geographic, cultural, historical, or political entity did not exist in any sense before the British created it. There are no mountain ranges, rivers, or deserts that obviously indicate where one political territory should end and where another should begin. There was no equivalent to Louis XIV's "natural boundaries" of France, the territories encompassed by the Rhine, the Alps, the Mediterranean, the Pyrenees, and the Atlantic. What is now Nigeria was not under the rule of a single emperor, nor did its constituent kings, emirs, sultans, and chiefs ever form a territory-encompassing political alliance or entity. While trade existed within the present-day borders, it also extended well beyond.

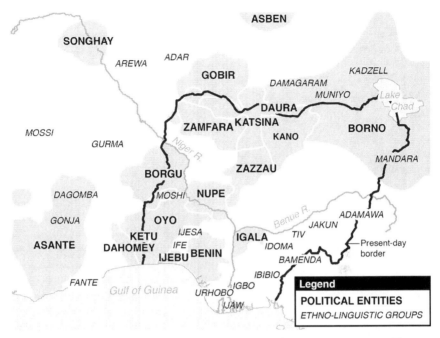

Map 1.1 Sokoto Caliphate, Borno Empire, and Yoruba States ca. 1840 with map of present-day Nigerian borders superimposed. *Source*: Henry B. Lovejoy, African Diaspora Maps, Ltd.

SLAVERY AND THE SLAVE TRADE

Rather than precious metals such as gold in the Ashanti Empire or copper elsewhere, slaves appear to have been the primary commodity traded by Africans beyond the village level in the territories that now make up Nigeria. They were a source of domestic labor and their sale paid for imported European goods increasingly desired by elites. Their capture and sale were a means by which kingdoms and empires organized themselves. John Hawkins, an English commander against the 1588 Spanish Armada, sold slaves captured from Spanish vessels sailing from Africa to the Caribbean and South America at immense profit. He showed the way for the transatlantic slave trade. By the middle of the eighteenth century, the British had dislodged their Portuguese, Dutch, and French competitors and dominated the transatlantic trade. But, by the early nineteenth century, the British antislavery movement, with its origins in the late eighteenth-century evangelical and Methodist religious revival, became a powerful force in British domestic politics. Britain subsequently abolished its participation in the slave trade in 1803 and ended slavery throughout its empire in 1833. Once the largest slaver, Britain's antislavery movement became a crusade that contributed directly to British occupation of Lagos in 1860 and spurred British conquest of the slave empires in the north.

Slavery was an important part of African Islamic society. In fact, the trans-Saharan slave trade lasted longer than the transatlantic. It was largely in the hands of Arabs and Ottoman Turks based in the then-Turkish colonies of Libya and Morocco. It was the basis of the prosperity of such Muslim African empires as the Sultanate of Sokoto.

Religion provided the primary distinction between who could be a slave and who could not. Once introduced into what is now northern Nigeria by Fulani migrants in the eleventh century, Islam became an elite, urban religion, with little penetration into the countryside even by the seventeenth century. There appears to have been a certain ambivalence among Muslims about mass conversions, as only "pagans" could be enslaved. Conversion to Islam provided immunity to slavery, at least in theory in most schools of Islamic theology.[8] (Christian slavers faced a similar, religious dilemma in the transatlantic slave trade.) The Fulani pushed south and southwest in search of land and, through military conquest, acquired slaves from the Hausa, Oyo, and Kanem-Borno kingdoms.[9]

By the nineteenth century and British occupation of Nigeria, the two most important Islamic empires were the caliphate of Sokoto and the dominions of the shehu of Borno. The caliphate was a consequence of a wave of reforms that sought to purge alleged African elements from Islam led by the sultan of Sokoto, Usman Dan Fodio, in 1806. It was predominately Fulani in ethnicity and Hausa in language. Usman Dan Fodio started the process by which a new Hausa–Fulani ethnic identity merged with an Islamic religious identity.[10] His jihad largely conquered what is now northern Nigeria, except Borno, which was an older kingdom and predominately Kanuri in ethnicity and language. By the nineteenth century, both empires were culturally highly sophisticated. At the time the British defeated the caliphate in 1903, Sokoto was judged to be the largest slave empire remaining in the world. After the caliphate's defeat, Borno accepted British rule as all but inevitable. The British abolished only some of the formal authorities of the Sokoto caliphate and the Borno empire and retained the titles and the courts of the sultan, the shehu, and their subordinate emirs, which continue today.

An estimated twelve to fifteen million Africans, mostly from West Africa and Angola, were captured and sold to the Western Hemisphere during the four hundred years the Atlantic slave trade was active.[11] An estimated additional nine million slaves were sold to North Africa and the Middle East over a longer period, between the ninth and nineteenth centuries.[12] Slaves that stayed in West Africa, while usually at the bottom of the social pyramid, had certain rights and privileges that North American chattel slaves did not. In some ways, they resembled a caste, rather than solely a species of property to be bought and sold as any other commodity. For example, in the empires that adjoined the Sahara, slaves might be civil servants as well as soldiers, in a way reminiscent of slavery within the Ottoman Empire.

Slaves and the slave trade became increasingly transactional and monetized over time, as the trans-Saharan and Atlantic slave trades expanded and as the tastes of African elites grew for European goods, especially weapons and alcohol. (According to an Ibo interlocutor of the author's, by the eighteenth century French brandy had a sacramental role among some coastal peoples.)

The British found it relatively easy to end the Atlantic slave trade but more difficult with respect to the diffuse and entrenched intra-Sahel and trans-Saharan trade. In one form or another, a derivative of the slave trade persists into the twenty-first century through sex trafficking, the exploitation of migrants, and forced domestic servants.

African slave-catchers and middlemen played an essential role in both slave trades. In effect, Africans controlled the wholesale portion of the trade, Europeans and Arabs the much smaller retail of slaves for export out of Africa. In the north, the slave trade was predominately organized by Muslims; along the coast of the Gulf of Guinea, middlemen practiced traditional African religions of varying degrees of sophistication, sometimes with a Christian overlay. European slave traders were nominally Christian. Islam, Christianity, and indigenous religions supported slavery as intrinsic to the human condition. (European slave forts sometimes had Christian chapels within them.)

For both slave trades, indigenous slave-catchers procured slaves through violence, often at the village level and, with the participation or connivance of local chiefs, sold their victims to African middlemen, who in turn sold them to other middlemen and ultimately to European and Arab transatlantic and trans-Saharan traders, usually in small numbers.

European traders often remain off the coast for long periods to assembly a cargo necessary for the voyage to be profitable. Aboard the vessels, disease could be rampant, exacerbated by bad food and water. Though hard figures are lacking, the mortality rates for both victims of the slave trade and for the enslavers were high. For the trans-Saharan slave trade, Arab merchants established entrepôts on the edge of the Sahara where they assembled caravans for crossing the Sahara. Casualties were probably higher for the trans-Saharan trade than the transatlantic because of the rigors of crossing the Sahara on foot.[13]

In northern Nigeria, the slave trade had ethnic and religious dimensions, the consequences of which shape instability in the region today. Slave-catchers and slave traders were usually Muslim and Fulani. They were a horse and herder culture. They preyed on small tribes that practiced traditional religion and were agriculturally based. When they moved beyond traditional religion in the twentieth century, these minority tribes usually embraced Christianity, not least because it was not the religion of the Fulani slavers. Much of the violence in the region today occurs because ethnic, religious, and land-use boundaries overlap: Muslim Fulani herdsmen confront non-Muslim, often Christian, farmers from smaller ethnic groups, just as they did during the epoch of slavery.

Europeans had explored and traded along the West African coast since the fifteenth century, but before the nineteenth century, they had little contact with the interior or the Sahel. Instead, middlemen procured slaves from the interior and marched them to the coast for the Atlantic trade.[14] European maps of what is now Nigeria were largely blank except for coastal slave trading posts. An exception was the Kingdom of Benin, one of the most sophisticated kingdoms of West Africa that dates back to the eleventh century. With its capital at Edo (now Benin City in present-day Nigeria), it established a trading relationship with the Portuguese after 1485 that was one between equals. There was even a short-lived, Portuguese-sponsored Roman Catholic mission. Benin was strong enough and well organized enough that it was able to abolish the slave trade with Europeans, though it retained it domestically. It produced magnificent works of "bronze" (in reality brass), and after the British sacked and looted Edo in 1897, many of the works of art found their way into American and European art museums, where they influenced Western artists such as Pablo Picasso and ignited popular interest in African art.

Throughout the slave trade epoch, African empires and kingdoms often had powerful militaries. Europeans enjoyed no overarching technical and military advantage over African empires before the nineteenth century, a reason why Africans could corral European slave traders into seaside fortifications. In southern Africa, a Zulu military force defeated a well-equipped British fighting force as late as 1879 at the Battle of Isandlwana. Even later, in 1896, an army led by King Menelik II of Ethiopia defeated an Italian invasion at the Battle of Adwa, using a hodgepodge of stockpiled rifles and guns accumulated over time or provided by Italy's European rivals.

However, the military triumphs in Isandlwana and Adwa were exceptions. The technological balance would quickly favor Europeans later in the nineteenth century. Hilaire Belloc wrote his notorious jibe in 1898:

> Whatever happens
> We have the Gatling gun,
> And they have not.[15]

By the time Belloc was writing, European technological and military supremacy over Africans was almost absolute. With the exception of Ethiopia, Europeans were able to carve up the African continent as they pleased at the

Berlin Conference (1884–85) and without reference to indigenous peoples, surviving empires, or kingdoms.

BRITISH RULE BEGINS

The British created the state of Nigeria. They did not, could not, and had no sustained interest in developing a nation until World War II and later. Before the mid-nineteenth century, the lack of a malarial prophylaxis and the strength of African states precluded much European settlement. European slave stations on the coast existed on the sufferance of local rulers. Though the British had dominated the eighteenth-century slave trade, the formal British administration of extensive territory that would eventually become Nigeria began only with occupation of Lagos in 1861. Their stated purpose was to protect missionaries, their converts, and trade in a period when endemic civil wars were causing traditional Yoruba governance to break down. British expansion in the south involved their humanitarian desire to suppress the slave trade and alleged cannibalism, greed for tradeable goods, and opportunities for investment.[16] European capital eventually developed a large palm oil industry and, subsequently, mining, especially of coal.[17]

The British occupation of northern Nigeria, on the other hand, was part of a more coherent imperial strategy, though it was also driven by slave-trade abolitionists. The British needed to keep the French and Germans from expanding in the mid-Sahel region. (Kamerun, present-day Cameroon, was a German colony and base before World War I; between the Franco-Prussian War and 1914, France created a huge empire consisting of French West Africa, French Equatorial Africa, and Ivory Coast.) The Ottoman Empire also attempted unsuccessfully to press south into Borno after it was largely expelled from the Balkans in late nineteenth-century wars with Russia.[18] Its ambitions were blocked by the three Western colonial powers and by the Ottomans' shift of focus to telegraph and railway construction in the Hijaz, which would connect Damascus to Mecca. By 1903, with its conquest of the Sokoto Caliphate and shehu of Borno, the British dominated all the territory that would become present-day Nigeria and organized it into two separate protectorates.

There were differing proposals in the Colonial Office for how to organize what became Nigeria, including its division into a number of separate colonies. However, in 1914, the Liberal government of H. H. Asquith opted to create a single colony by amalgamating the Colony and Protectorate of Southern Nigeria (itself an earlier amalgamation of the Royal Colony of Lagos with the Protectorate of Southern Nigeria) with the Northern Nigeria Protectorate. Legally, Secretary of State for the Colonies Lewis Harcourt amalgamated

Nigeria through an order-in-council. Lord Lugard, the pre-1914 governor of both the southern and northern protectorates and subsequently the first governor-general of the united colony, drove the amalgamation process, and he and his wife, Lady Flora Shaw Lugard, a former colonial editor of the *Times* and the highest-paid female journalist of her time, may be considered the creators of the Nigerian state. In what was to become a pattern, the views of a strong-willed governor prevailed against other views within the Colonial Office.[19]

Much like the 1884 Berlin Conference where the European powers carved up Africa, the amalgamation of myriad peoples into one country went forward without any pretense of consultation with those who were about to become Nigerians. There existed indigenous assemblies and councils with which the British authorities could have consulted, but at the swaggering, high-water mark of colonial imperialism, it would never have occurred to any British colonial administrator to do so. The British seem to have given little forethought to the enduring implications of amalgamation.

A case in point: the amalgamation of those territories into Nigeria was an administrative convenience. Lugard described the amalgamation in marital terms:

> What we often call the Northern Protectorate of Nigeria today can be better described as the poor husband whilst its southern counterpart can be fairly described as the rich wife or the woman of substance and means. A forced union of marriage between the two will undoubtedly result in peace, prosperity and marital bliss for both husband and wife for many years to come. It is my prayer that that union will last forever.[20]

He expected to fund British administration in the north with revenue from a south that was integrating slowly into the world economy. But even among British sympathizers of imperialism at the time of amalgamation, there were forebodings. Malcolm Hailey, an expert on British governance in India and Africa, characterized Nigeria as "perhaps the most artificial of the many administrative units created in the course of the European occupation of Africa."[21] Margery Perham, an Oxford academic, noted Africanist, and Lugard's biographer, described Nigeria as an "arbitrary block."[22]

THE BRITISH COLONY OF NIGERIA

Having occupied and amalgamated Nigeria, what were the British to do with it? After the slave trade was outlawed internationally and before Nigeria became a major hydrocarbon producer in the last quarter of the twentieth century, there were no huge fortunes for Europeans to make in Nigeria, unlike in Britain's Indian empire. Economically, Nigeria was less developed than the nearby Gold Coast (British) or Ivory Coast (French). The few Europeans in Nigeria were primarily soldiers, administrators, missionaries, and traders. At the end of their tours of duty or expiration of their contracts, Europeans just went home. On the other hand, Lebanese, Chinese, and Indian immigrants established longer-term communities and were prominent in both the wholesale and retail trade during the colonial period, though not to the same extent as elsewhere in West Africa. Altogether they were a tiny part of the population and never became a distinctive caste as they did in east Africa, though the British administration privileged them over Africans. Pressure from the small number of whites and other racial minorities for self-government such as occurred in Rhodesia (later Zimbabwe) was weak and easily ignored. Moreover, for the British, Nigerian self-government would have meant Black government. In the racist early twentieth century, that reality made unthinkable any potential British effort to move Nigeria along the path followed by Canada, Australia, New Zealand, or South Africa, the so-called "white dominions." That would start to change only slowly just before the beginning of World War II. Meanwhile, Nigeria remained part of the "Tropical Empire."

Nevertheless, after troops from Britain's African colonies participated in World War I, the British increasingly justified their rule of Nigeria as laying the foundations for a modern state that would someday emerge, presumably in subordinate partnership with the United Kingdom. But they had no sense of urgency about that process.[23] Margery Perham, who traveled widely in Nigeria in the 1930s, observed, "There was an atmosphere of almost unlimited time in which to carry on the task, regarded then as hardly begun, of building a new Nigeria from the bottom up."[24]

The British occupation was central to the process of "modernization." The short colonial period transformed the lives of some Nigerians through the study and application of modern science, the use of new technologies, and modern medicine. Monetization of economic life greatly increased consumption, and participation in a global economy affected especially residents of Lagos and other large cities. Modernization even included the introduction of new concepts of time and of calendar dating that seeped into the rural areas.[25] Nevertheless, large areas of the country, especially in the north, remained little touched.

During the colonial period, the overriding concern of the British administration was to maintain order; develop a subordinate, native administration; suppress the slave trade; and end cannibalism and other practices they regarded as barbaric—all at no expense to the home exchequer. These goals were probably more important than the economic relationship. Flora Shaw had reported extensively in the *Times* on allegedly ubiquitous cannibalism, human sacrifice, and trial by ordeal in southern Nigeria, all of which were anathema to British sensibilities but also likely exaggerated by the British media. Christian missionaries were also a primary driver of British colonialism in Nigeria. The protection of them and their converts was a goal of the British occupation of Lagos and eventually all of Yorubaland in the mid-nineteenth century. (Christian missionaries were not necessarily European. The Anglican Church, nominally Nigeria's largest, for example, was established by non-white missionaries based in Sierra Leone, not England, and led by a Yoruba, Bishop Samuel Crowther.) The great numerical expansion of Christianity dates only from the postindependence period, but it had its roots in the nineteenth century.

For the British officers and officials stationed in Nigeria, the emirate north was more attractive than other parts of the country. It was a horse culture organized according to an easily understood hierarchy, and its Islam was more familiar to British colonial officials, some of whom had served in the Indian empire, than the multiple gods of the south. (Similarly, in India, British colonial officials often favored Muslims over Hindus, with their multiple gods.) But the British posture locally was more than sentiment. They were protective of Islam in the north, seeing its preservation as essential if they were to govern through indigenous institutions on the cheap. Further, until the end of Britain's Indian empire (which included what is now the Union of India, Pakistan, and Bangladesh) in 1947, the British Empire was the largest Muslim entity in the world.[26] Colonial officials were aware that what happened in northern Nigeria could have deleterious consequences in their Indian empire, with its Muslim millions.

The British Treasury's goal was usually achieved: Nigeria was to be governed as cheaply as possible, relying on local resources. Governance and security were to be funded entirely by Nigeria, mostly through customs and excise taxes. The amalgamation of northern and southern Nigeria created a single fiscal unit, which streamlined this funding approach. Customs and excise taxes from the south, where trade had long been significant, subsidized the costs of administration in the north, where there was relatively little. And the budget paperwork would be simplified, an attraction for British officials who thought themselves to be overworked.[27] While this made sense to the handful of colonial bureaucrats, little changed for newly minted "Nigerians."

Despite unifying their two protectorates, the British did little else to fuse together the disparate regions. British Nigeria never commanded popular loyalty from its indigenous people. Nevertheless, certain colonial superficialities have endured. Nigerian judges still wear wigs, bowler hats are part of "native" dress in the south and east, and there is the preference for tea rather than coffee.

The British imposed English as the official language in the southern part of the country, though it was spoken by few. In the north, Hausa remained the official language. At independence, Nigeria retained English as the only official language and extended it to the north, largely because, in a country with some 350 languages, it belonged to no one. For those who mastered it, it provided access to the larger world, unlike other indigenous languages, such as Urdu and Hindi, which are not used in international economic activity. Christian missionaries established British-style primary and secondary schools except (with a handful of exceptions) in the emirate north. British education, particularly its focus on modern science and technology, as well as an emerging capitalist economy in the southern and western parts of the country overtook, compromised, or transformed traditional religion, culture, and governance. Southern graduates dominated journalism, filling the small number of government jobs open to them, and eventually led the agitation for self-rule and independence. But European "modern" ways of thinking did not altogether displace the traditional. Elements of each often existed, and still exist, side by side in individuals as well as communities. The great Nigerian novelist of the late colonial and early independence era, Chinua Achebe, chronicled the ragged and incomplete reality for a Western audience in his novel *Things Fall Apart*, published in 1959.

In the north, however, the British set out to preserve the region's medieval emirate civilization, though purged of slavery and some of the barbarous punishments associated with sharia—but not sharia itself. They discouraged Christian missionary activity and schools in most of the region, lest it upset the hierarchical and seemingly stable Islamic societies.[28] As a consequence, modernization was late, slow, and far less transformative than in the south. The few exceptions were certain towns associated with railway construction, notably Kaduna, which was also the British administrative capital of the north. By 1960, the north had an estimated forty-one formal schools, compared to 842 in the south.[29] British administrators knew what they were doing—forgoing potentially destabilizing modernization to preserve a centuries-old political structure through which they could govern on the cheap.

BRITISH INDIRECT RULE

From the final defeat of Sokoto in 1903 until just before World War II, British policy was to preserve precolonial social organization whenever possible. The British saw "detribalization" and urbanization as destabilizing. They fostered traditional rulers. They doubted that the economy and the small number of modern-sector jobs open to Nigerians could absorb large numbers of the Western-educated, hence they established few institutions of higher education.

To a greater or lesser extent, the British applied indirect rule nationwide. At its most basic, this was governance through indigenous surrogates, reminiscent of parts of their Indian empire, the so-called "princely states," which retained their maharajas. Moses Ochonu distinguishes between two different types of indirect rule, both practiced by the British in Nigeria and both based on the Native Authority Ordinance of 1916, which established indigenous, or "native," administration for Nigeria.[30] The more common was the use of local elites as intermediaries between the British and the local population. In the north, they ruled through the traditional emirate system, which included a political hierarchy and system of Islamic law and justice.

In other cases, the British either created elites that they tried to invest with authority or they imported members of an ethnic group not hitherto present in a particular area to administer it. For example, in parts of the middle belt, the British used Fulani, who were not indigenous to the region, as proxy rulers. These Muslim Fulani proxies attempted to replicate the emirate system, alienating many of the small tribes that had existed outside of Islamic culture. In the south, the British invented local "traditional rulers," commonly called "warrant chiefs," and created a more centralized system of governance than had been characteristic of the highly decentralized traditional authority structures. Warrant chiefs had little popular legitimacy. They, in turn, showed little accountability to the people they ostensibly served, or to their British masters.[31]

In theory, if remote in practice, the British saw indirect rule as a preliminary and temporary step toward the creation of a modern Nigerian state that would follow the model of most of Europe's nation-states. Western education was to be the instrument that would modernize the indigenous population, but this would be a long-term process. In the meantime, the British would govern through indigenous elites and institutions at virtually no cost to the British taxpayer.

British support for indirect rule along with the justification for the larger imperial enterprise collapsed during the 1930s and World War II in the face of fascism. At Whitehall and among British colonial officials indirect rule was succeeded by the ideal of democratic nation-building. Detribalization, education, and indigenous participation in governance became the watchwords. In fact, only a tiny minority of indigenous Nigerians were able to benefit from the limited educational opportunities and adopted for themselves the British understanding of modernization. Literate in English, they became the spokesmen for indigenous grievances against the colonial system. Accordingly, many British colonial figures were suspicious of them, maintaining that they were devoted solely to their self-interest.[32] Nevertheless, Western-educated

Nigerians, in many ways, inherited Nigeria once the British left, and they increasingly came to resemble their predecessors in their relations with the mass of the population. But their adopted Western mentality isolated them from the mass of the Nigerian population that remained outside that foreign value system. Elite modernization accounts in part for the isolation of many Nigerians from their government and even from the concept of Nigeria as a nation.

The British occupation of Lagos in 1861 happened not long after Commodore Perry's expeditions to Tokyo Bay of 1853 and 1854. But Japan's subsequent modernization experience was very different from Nigeria's. In the case of the former, the process was controlled by indigenous elites who borrowed the technical innovations of the West while protecting traditional Japanese culture and affirming the divine nature of the emperor. Hence, modernization did not isolate most Japanese from their traditions and their elites. Unlike Nigeria, Japan already had a common culture, language, a sense of shared history, and a very strong national identity. In other words, Japan was a nation with a state. By contrast, in Nigeria, with no prior common culture or identity, modernization was introduced and led by a colonial power and its local collaborators, Nigeria was a state but not a nation.

Early on, British and other observers saw indirect rule as riddled with corruption, which they defined as the abuse of power for personal benefit. They had little or no understanding of the complexities of the relationships that they defined as "corrupt." Indeed, "corruption" was often their excuse for the removal of traditional rulers whose behavior they thought was inimical to their rule. Native administration, they complained, was suborned by secret societies, and traditional gift-giving helped contribute to ubiquitous payment of bribes. There were never enough British administrators to oversee indirect rule or to impose British styles or values of governance. Moreover, too often those indigenous elites essential to British rule had little credibility with the people they were supposed to administer. Hence, the emergence of a two-tiered ethic: it was good, even laudatory to defraud governing institutions and powers for the benefit of one's own family, ethnic group, or religion, while scrupulous honesty characterized one's private life. For example, when a 1962 official tribunal investigated corruption in the Western Region, its premier, Obafemi Awolowo, was arrested in the presence of a large crowd of supporters, who "wanted Awo to take a lot more public funds for himself as he was their son and his money was their money."[33]

Racism and segregation contributed to the British lack of understanding of the peoples of its Nigerian empire. British officials practiced residential segregation as an outgrowth of indirect rule. They did not live among Nigerians (except for servants and other dependents) but rather in Government Reserved Areas (GRAs). These were made up of government-owned houses to which officials were assigned according to rank and function. The houses were of high quality and paid for by taxes levied on Nigerians. As such, they engendered some resentment among indigenous elites. They were usually geographically separated from Nigerian towns. Initially, it was British medical officers who made the argument for segregation. They were concerned that African children were often the hosts for malaria, and that a way to protect highly vulnerable Europeans was by isolating them from the indigenous population through residential segregation. They also cited the need to guard against the spread of plague and yellow fever, both of which caused epidemics in the Indian empire early in the twentieth century. British officials apparently did not seriously consider eliminating malaria from the indigenous population, presumably because either they did not know how to do it or were unwilling to use the necessary resources. Instead, the focus was on protecting British officials and their dependents. The concept of segregating Europeans from Africans was supported by Lord Lugard as an aspect of indirect rule. In 1915 he wrote, "A great native city . . . lives its life as its forefathers did and is little affected by progress. Such a community has no desire for municipal improvement. It neither appreciates nor desires clean water, sanitation, or good roads or streets."[34]

Most colonial governors of Nigeria opposed formal residential segregation as potentially exacerbating race relations, but they were overruled by the Colonial Office in London following the advice of medical officers. During the period of British rule, in effect, GRAs resulted in racial segregation. But GRA segregation was based on government office and function, not race (even if it amounted to much the same thing). Efforts to establish legally mandated residential segregation based on race in Nigeria such as existed in South Africa or the American South foundered over the opposition of the governors and even more so its impracticality in a country where whites were rare.[35]

With their high quality, GRAs became popular residential areas after independence for the new, indigenous elites that had been shaped by the values and practices of colonialism. As was the case under colonialism, the political leaders of postindependence Nigeria lived apart from the people they ostensibly governed. As Nigeria's independence leaders took power, they quite literally replaced the colonial officials, moving into the GRAs formerly occupied by the British. GRAs are still being built to accommodate government officials today, despite the irrelevance of their original purpose. Such segregation became a symbol of their aloofness and contributes to the isolation of Nigerian elites from the mass of the population that persists to this day.

For all its apparent faults now, the British were proud of indirect rule at the time. In a report to the Colonial Office in 1939, Bernard Bourdillion, governor-general from 1935 to 1943, stated that there was the potential to build "a sound, united state," because indirect rule resulted in the "least possible breach with the past" and there was little "dislocation of tradition and familiar methods of administration."[36] At the heart of British governance of Nigeria was a fundamental inconsistency: if their footprint was light, the traditional societies that they ruled would somehow "organically" follow the European path to nationhood. Despite periodic lip service to this ideal, the British authorities in London, Lagos, and the later northern administrative capital of Kaduna showed little practical concern about creating a viable, integrated state, which, ostensibly, was their goal.

Twilight of the British in Nigeria

Nevertheless, the colonial period was not static, neither for the British nor for Nigerians. Despite pressure from the tiny, westernized middle class, Nigerian participation in governance was minimal until the 1950s, toward the end of the colonial period. After World War I, in which a significant number of Nigerians fought in the British forces, a few Nigerians were appointed to office, but the British and apparently most Nigerians saw self-government and eventual independence as generations away. Rather than working to create an independent nation, especially during the interwar years, the few activist Nigerians tended to be anticolonial, antiracist in their focus, and influenced by African American thinkers. They were more concerned about confronting racism than achieving independence. Though World War II, in which even larger numbers of Nigerians fought for the British, accelerated the growth of anticolonial sentiment, it never was as strong or focused as it was elsewhere in the empire, such as India or the Gold Coast.

Nevertheless, throughout the colonial period, there were Nigerian protests against the colonial system. Radical newspapers and broadsheets appeared even before the 1914 amalgamation and continued until independence in 1960. They are in some ways the ancestors of Nigeria's relatively free press today. There was labor unrest that accelerated after each of the world wars. For example, in 1929, Igbo women staged a major demonstration, now called the "women's war" or the "Aba riots" against indirect rule and the introduction of new taxes. It started as a local protest but morphed into a regional one. A 1945 general strike paralyzed the economy. Ostensibly over wages that had been frozen during the war while the cost of living soared, it soon incorporated a host of other grievances. As the number of Nigerians with a European education increased, so, too, did their pressure on the British for more spending on infrastructure and for self-governance. In 1937, there were 288,000 enrolled in primary schools; by 1960 they had increased to 1.4 million. In 1939, there were twenty-three Nigerians in the senior civil service; by 1960, there were 2,600.[37]

British views on Nigerian governance also evolved. As the number of literate Nigerians grew, the warrant chiefs that the British appointed in the south were sometimes less educated than their subjects. Before and after World War II, British officials increasingly questioned the lack of democracy and implicit racism in the colonial system. By 1939, many in the Colonial Office had concluded that indirect rule should be set aside. Proposals for its replacement included reform and institutionalization of the chiefs to increase literate Nigerian participation in their own government, which would evolve toward the Westminster, parliamentary representative system. Still, the new British approach as late as the 1950s was reform, not independence.[38]

Reform of governance and eventual independence involved a push-pull dynamic between the British and Nigerian nationalists. Modern Nigerian writers tend to see the movement toward independence as the British response to nationalist agitation, including strikes. Yet compared to the national movements in Algeria, Kenya, the Gold Coast, or the anti-apartheid movement in South Africa (an anticolonial movement of a special type), the Nigerian nationalist and independence movements were small in scale and were primarily driven by pan-African and ethnic inspiration. If the British had wished to hold on to Nigeria in 1960, they almost certainly could have done so.

WHAT OF THE FRENCH? AN ALTERNATIVE COLONIALISM

The British approach to its tropical African empire was different from that of the French. The French goal was to turn the peoples of their colonies into Black Frenchmen and Frenchwomen. That was their *mission civilisatrice*. Unlike the British, at least in theory, the French goal was not to midwife an African modern state. It was to turn its empire into departments of France, as it had done in coastal Algeria and Senegal. Hence, an African who spoke perfect French, benefited from a French education, and self-identified as French *was* French. Such a personage could (though rarely did) sit in the French National Assembly. He could even marry a (white) French woman without public censure among the French elites, at least in theory and sometimes in practice. Léopold Senghor, a member of the French National Assembly, a drafter of the constitution of the Fifth Republic, and eventually president of independent Senegal, is a celebrated example of an African-become-French-become-African personality. Another is Houphouët-Boigny, who was elected to the French National Assembly, held French ministerial posts, and became the first president of Côte d'Ivoire. However, the number of Africans that became French was always minuscule.[39]

Like Britain's, France's African possessions were part of an empire that stretched around the world. For example, the expatriate community in French west and equatorial Africa included many from Lebanon, which was under direct French control between the world wars. The Lebanese presence in the French possessions was more salient than the Chinese, Lebanese, and Indian communities together in Nigeria. Today, business ties between France and its African possessions appear stronger than those between the United Kingdom and its former African territories.[40]

The French were less overtly racist than the British, and though interracial marriage was frowned on in conservative circles, it was not illegal as it was in most of the British Empire.[41] Furthermore, there is no African equivalent to Senghor and Houphouët-Boigny from Britain's African empire.[42] To be "British" meant to be white. A resident of Nigeria who spoke perfect English and benefited from a British education and served in the British or later in the Nigerian army remained African from a British perspective. But from the perspective of this hypothetical African, he (the colonial-era Nigerian army was all male) likely saw himself as a member of a particular family, clan, religion, or ethnic group, rather than a subject of the British colony. What Nigerian national identity did develop did so primarily during the independence era and in the military, among journalists and secondary-school teachers, and among those educated abroad.

Part of the reason for the differences between the British and French approaches was the purpose of colonization. For the British, it was driven by security concerns for the empire as a whole, trade, investment, and the humanitarian impulse that was widespread in British society. For the French, the security of the metropole was primary. Colonies were to be a means to balance France's relative decline in the face of the growing demographic and industrial power of Germany. Hence the French colonial expansion after their defeat in the Franco-Prussian War of 1870–71 and the renewed focus on the African empire after France's severe demographic losses from World War I. The French used troops from their African colonies to occupy the Rhineland in 1918, which the Germans regarded as a deliberate humiliation.[43] During World War II, Charles de Gaulle insisted that "France" continue in its African colonies even if the homeland was occupied by the Germans. In August 1940, Chad and its Black governor (of Caribbean origin) provided de Gaulle and the Free French with their first, exclusive military launching pad against the Nazis. In 1944, a regiment from Chad participated in the liberation of Strasbourg. Though smaller in population and less wealthy, the French empire in Africa was and still is much more important to Paris than the African portions of the British Empire were to London. As one British high commissioner to Nigeria said, "We have done pitifully less than we could have done to help our former colonies along. Whatever one may say about the French (and who does not), at least they have done better for their ex-colonies than we have."[44]

The End of the Empire

After the end of World War II, some British political leaders, notably prime ministers Clement Attlee, Winston Churchill, and Anthony Eden, saw the continuation of empire as essential to the maintenance of great power status, along with possession of nuclear weapons. After the end of Britain's Indian empire in 1947, however, British elite sentiment turned slowly against what it regarded as the burdens of imperialism. This change of sentiment accelerated after the British, French, and Israeli failure in 1956 to overthrow Abdul Gamal Nasser in Egypt. In the British business community and among some in the Conservative Party, there was the view that the commercial advantages of empire could be preserved without the complications and expense of colonial governance. (The opposition Labour Party had long questioned the advantages of empire.) The humanitarian impulse shifted from the official sphere that had encouraged colonies to suppress slavery to nongovernmental organizations that often were hostile to colonialism as a matter of principle. In post–World War II austerity Britain, there was the mood that empire was simply too expensive for the country's reduced circumstances. The always weak idealistic underpinnings of imperialism had almost entirely dissipated. The end of the British Empire was not so much the result of domestic anticolonialism as it was a lack of will by the British political class to keep it going. Though leaders like Churchill and even Queen Elizabeth wished to see the empire continue, they could not find a critical mass of elites sympathetic to this cause. The spirit of empire had been broken by two world wars.[45] Moreover, the successful test in 1952 of a nuclear weapon made the United Kingdom the third member of the nuclear club, seen at the time as a guarantee of continued great power status, making continuation of empire less important.

The British decision to wind down their African empire was prompted by agitation in the Gold Coast, which became independent Ghana in 1957. Proindependence rioting in the Gold Coast, always regarded as the most-developed British colony in West Africa, led by Kwame Nkrumah and incompetently handled by the local British authorities, unnerved the Colonial Office and the Eden and Macmillan governments. Further, the Battle of Algiers began in 1956 between the Algerian National Liberation Front and the French Algerian authorities. Its guerilla warfare wrought wholesale carnage that was captured by international media.

The British, then, moved Nigeria to independence for reasons that extended beyond the largely local agitation for the end of colonialism. Successive British governments were generally concerned about the potential for a colonial war such as the French fought in Vietnam and Algeria, even though there was no realistic near-term prospect of one in Nigeria. Westminster also recognized that the Soviet Union could exploit colonial discontent, though there was little evidence of Moscow fishing in Nigerian waters. Nevertheless, the Macmillan government hastily attempted to establish constitutional structures to which it could grant independence. However, in Nigeria, no independence movement with truly national support and scope had emerged, and the passage to independence did not play a transformative role in nation-building such as it had in Algeria, Kenya, or India.[46] Independence-era politics were organized around the rival interests of the Yoruba, Igbo, and Hausa-Fulani and smaller ethnic groups rather than by a national vision. What held them together was not a vision of a Nigerian nation but rather opposition to colonialism and racism. In northern, emirate Nigeria, there was resistance to independence; northern elites were generally satisfied with indirect rule, which largely preserved their status and power. Both could be better preserved if ultimate government authority was in faraway London rather than nearer-at-hand Lagos.

If the British established few institutions—and virtually none that were nationwide—the notable exception was the Nigerian military. The Colonial Office founded the Royal West African Frontier Force (RWAFF) in 1900 to garrison its West African possessions: Nigeria, the Gold Coast, Sierra Leone, and the Gambia. It was the force Lord Lugard used to conquer the Sultanate of Sokoto. After the conquest of the north, the Colonial Office was spurred by concern about possible French or German expansion in the Sahel rather than domestic insurrection. The RWAFF saw action against the Germans during World War I in Cameroon and in East Africa. During World War II, in addition to operations in Africa, the RWAFF fought in Burma. Nigeria was by far the largest contributor of troops to the RWAFF, and the Nigerian brigades were mostly stationed in the north. By the end of the colonial period, Hausa was the lingua franca, though the force was multiethnic. In 1956, the Nigeria regiments in the RWAFF were transferred from the Colonial Office to the Nigerian government. At independence in 1960, they became the Nigerian army. For many years the army retained a northern and Hausa coloration. Despite being predominately Muslim, it remained a secular institution. After independence, as virtually the only national institution, the military regarded itself as the ultimate guarantor of the Nigerian state and thereby justified its coups against ineffectual civilian and military leadership.

With respect to internal law and order, the British regarded Nigeria as generally law-abiding, with the notable exception of what they saw as ubiquitous corruption in native governance. They established a northern and southern constabulary, which were the antecedents of the present national police service. Domestic policing, however, was largely the responsibility of local authorities under indirect rule but ended at independence. Hence, Nigeria currently has no local police force, but rather a national gendarmerie, controlled by the federal government. Compared with the army, the police have always been underfunded, undertrained, and viewed with greater popular dislike.

THE BRITISH LEGACY

What is the bottom line of British rule in Nigeria? British administrators made little attempt to impose a common language, uniform administration, or a national educational or legal system that applied to all. "There was thus no central representative institution which could have become an instrument for inculcating a sense of Nigerian unity."[47] Instead, the British recognized multiple regimes of formal and informal law that persist today: the formal, written legal code based on British common law; Islamic law (sharia), some of which was written; and customary law that varied from ethnic group to ethnic group.[48] The British did not harmonize or coordinate these varying legal systems.

The British largely ruled the north and south of Nigeria as separate entities, with separate lieutenant governors and colonial bureaucracies, despite amalgamation.[49] Moreover, the administrators of the two regions typically met only annually. Snobbery within the British Colonial Service between the two regions was widespread: British officials in the north, with its horse culture and colorful emirs, looked down on their southern colleagues as desk-bound bureaucrats working in a hot and steamy climate among farmers, fishermen, ex-cannibals, and ex–slave traders. (Such officials tended to overlook northern involvement in the trans-Saharan slave trade.) British officials in the north often purchased their own horses and as late as the 1950s used them for home-to-office transportation. From the perspective of northern British officials, their colleagues in the south "took their first gin-and-tonic of the evening a good thirty minutes too early."[50] (The British official *Handbook of Health in the Tropics*, issued in 1956, advised the avoidance of alcohol before 6 p.m.)[51] Yet Chinua Achebe recalled the nutsandbolts of British administration as relatively efficient and free of corruption.[52] Colonial administrators themselves, if not the Nigerians over whom they presided, were also free of the tribalism (if not of racism) that so disfigures postindependence administrations.[53]

But the longer it lasted, British rule within each region tended to reinforce more parochial interests and identities. The Sokoto caliphate, one of the preeminent institutions of Muslim rule in the north, survives today. In the south, where precolonial administrative systems were less developed, the British reluctantly intervened more directly. Even in the south, there were differences in the extent to which the British needed to create new administrative structures; the Yoruba in the west had more-developed administrative structures than groups in the east. Hence, there was more indirect rule in Yorubaland than in Igboland.[54]

Indirect rule was a failure in terms of promoting modernization and state-building according to the European model, though it did keep down the costs of administration. Under indirect rule, Western education was not a priority and there was never remotely enough investment by churches and other charities in education to transform deeply entrenched traditional societies in most areas. The reform initiative dating from the 1930s that looked to build a democratic state over many years through detribalization and education was also a failure. The first university-level institution was established in 1948 in Ibadan, some eighty miles north of Lagos, as a subsidiary of the University of London, fully thirty-four years after amalgamation and eighty-six years after the British first colonized Lagos, and only twelve years before independence. It became fully independent as the University of Ibadan after independence. Earlier in the twentieth century the British did establish secondary boarding schools, designed to teach the children of elites the Western skills necessary for indirect rule. For example, the British established Kings College in Lagos in 1909 and Barewa College in Zaria in 1921, both secular institutions designed to cater to the children of elites.[55]

Ultimately, British investments were never sufficient to establish formal governmental institutions run by indigenous university-educated and independent civil servants, as foreseen by colonial reformers. Although it is estimated that there were approximately fifty thousand Nigerian civil servants performing routine tasks in the colonial administration by 1945, almost none of them had a university education. The British established only a few small, underfunded facilities to train public servants. The British administration opened a medical college in 1930 and Yaba Higher College in 1934. Admission to these two colleges was very limited. From 1934 to 1944, the largest entering class numbered only thirty-six. In addition, a few hundred Nigerians studied in the United Kingdom or the United States during this period. By the early 1950s, out of a population of thirty to forty million, 31,000 Nigerians had completed Western-style secondary school, and only an estimated one thousand had completed Western-style university education.[56] British officials often denigrated them as "mission boys," disliking that with a Western education they could—and did—talk back. Still, their influence would soon be outsized. Graduates of these schools would later become prominent business and political leaders, the heirs to the British after the end of the colonial era.

Otherwise, education was largely left to schools founded and operated by Christian missionary societies in the south, which were generally of high quality and followed a standard British curriculum, while traditional Islamic institutions in the north focused on the study and memorization of the Koran. In 1947, only 66,000 were attending primary school in the north, 240,000 in the west, and 320,000 in the east. Enrollment in secondary schools was even more limited—only ten thousand students were enrolled nation-wide. Christian institutions made little conscious effort to incorporate tradi-tional, indigenous values into their curriculum, though in a few cases they encouraged "tribal loyalty," further reinforcing ethnic, religious, and regional differences, Nigerians in the south had greater access to education, limited though it was, which both gave them a larger role in the colonial administra-tion as civil servants and allowed them to pursue more lucrative careers than residents of the north. This, in turn, heightened tensions among the regions. Despite their lofty rhetoric, the overall effect of British administrative policies, spanning government, the judiciary, and education, was to promote regional and parochial identities rather than a national one. If education was to be the vector by which the British would prepare Nigerians to take over the state imposed on them, that policy failed because, like so many other aspects of British governance, it was overambitious and underresourced.

British Nigeria was short-lived, from amalgamation on January 1, 1914, to Independence Day, October 1, 1960, less than forty-seven years.[57] In fact, since 2007, Nigeria has been an independent state longer than it was an amalgamated British colony. Among British soldiers and officials stationed in Nigeria, independence was a distant chimera as late as the 1950s. The British then abruptly brought Nigeria to independence—not because of the strength of local agitation or in response to the overwhelming demands of a powerful national independence movement, but because Britain had lost confidence in the entire colonial enterprise and determined to withdraw from many parts of the world as fast as possible.[58] The British left behind a parliamentary form of government that had no indigenous roots and little popular buy-in beyond some of the late colonial-era Nigerian elites, a common trend among postco-lonial states in sub-Saharan Africa.[59]

Much more important than short-lived political structures, British policy toward religion, particularly the free rein it gave to Christian mission edu-cation in the southern half of the country; the preservation of the Islamic emirates; and the growing, uncontrolled economic linkages with the outside world combined to unleash a revolution.[60] But it was one that was incomplete as the British had done too little to create a modern nation-state. Still, the British were the primary, if unwitting, vector for the modernism that trans-formed some among the diverse peoples of Nigeria. The British proved to be more important to Nigeria than Nigeria was to the British.

INDEPENDENCE, SECESSION, AND CIVIL WAR

Failure of the Parliamentary Interlude

By 1960, the parameters of modern Nigeria were set. Precolonial identities continued, while national identity was weak. Ethnicity, clan, and family, soon to be joined by religion after independence, mattered more to Nigerians than the young Nigerian state. Consequently, independence was not primarily the result of a unifying national struggle but rather Britain's reading of its own short-term interests largely without reference to Nigerians themselves.

Indirect rule largely preserved emirate culture in the north. Elsewhere, British conquest led to the destruction of many indigenous institutions and relationships. The clearing away of much of tradition opened the way for the south and east's acceptance of Christianity, Western education, and modernization. Indirect rule had the unintended consequence of inhibiting modernization and economic development in the north. Hence, few though they were, Western-educated southerners came to dominate the modern economy and the civil service, fostering deep suspicion from northern Islamic leaders. The stage was set for the current bifurcation of Nigeria between the poor north and the less-poor south. Even so, and despite the efforts of missionaries, Western education in the south and east was available to only a small percentage of elites. Those who received it were cut off from the still-dominant traditional society. In the north, traditional Islamic education continued; with its focus on memorization of sacred scriptures, it ill-prepared its graduates to participate in the modern world, and few did.

At independence, indigenous politicians inherited Nigeria. They were tiny in number, mostly Western-educated, and viewed themselves as part of the modern world, but their political power was primarily based on their ethnic identity and connections. Because they benefited from it personally, they supported the independence settlement. By and large, they did little to promote the common good of most Nigerians. (Awolowo was an exception, but his progressive measures were limited to the Yoruba-dominated part of the country that he dominated politically.) During the postindependence period, each of the three major ethnic groups in Nigeria more or less dominated one of the country's three (briefly, four) regions established by the British (Western, Northern, and Eastern), and each threatened secession at one time or another. But only leaders of the Eastern Region, predominately Igbo, actually acted on this threat.

Coups

The secession of Biafra followed two calamitous coups. The first, in January 1966, led by "junior" officers (they were majors) destroyed the first postindependence civilian government and led to the murders of Prime Minister Abubakar Balewa and Sardana of Sokoto Ahmadu Bello, the premier of the Northern Region, both of whom were regarded as founding fathers of independent Nigeria. Numerous other politicians and military officers were killed, mostly Muslims from the north. The president, Nnamdi Azikiwe, was out of the country on vacation. In the ensuing chaos, the head of the army, General Johnson Aguiyi-Ironsi, wrested control of the coup in the south, while Colonel Emeka Ojukwu ended it in the north. Ironsi suspended the constitution and established a military government. He appointed his fellow Igbo, Ojukwu, as military governor of the Eastern Region.

Though the coup was ostensibly a response to corruption rather than an ethnic grab for power, a number of the coup makers, including General Ironsi, were Igbos, and in the aftermath several Igbo military officers not associated with the coup were promoted. The Igbo majors that perpetrated the coup in the first place were not prosecuted. Hence, the coup was widely perceived as an Igbo effort to wrest control of the government from the northern Muslims that had dominated it since independence. Six months later, in July, there was a second coup, led by Murtala Muhammed and Theophilus Danjuma, which killed Ironsi and established a military government dominated by northerners. This second coup was even bloodier than the first, with many Igbo military officers murdered.

Associated with the second coup was a major pogrom against Christians that lasted several months. It took place primarily in the north, was often led by the military, and its victims were mostly Igbo. In its intensity, if not scale, the pogrom recalls the Rwanda genocide of 1994.[61] By September most of the Igbos in the north were dead or had fled to their homeland in the Eastern Region. Meanwhile, in the Christian parts of the country, there were pogroms against northern Muslims; those that survived fled to the Northern Region. The stage was set for Ojukwu's declaration of the Eastern Region's independence as Biafra.

Civil War

Though the predominately Igbo areas of southeast Nigeria, the core of Biafra, are overwhelmingly Christian and mostly Roman Catholic, the Biafran leadership presented the conflict initially in ethnic terms, as a battle between Igbos and Hausa-Fulani directly related to the preceding anti-Igbo pogrom in the north. By the end of 1967, Biafra was reduced to a fifth of its original size, and Ojukwu looked for international support to stave off defeat. With the help of a New York–based public relations firm, his regime transformed the conflict from an ethnic struggle into one between Christians and Muslims. His effort proved highly effective. Media helped elevate the war in public consciousness in the United States and Europe. The Pope became involved, and Christian charities supplied humanitarian aid, in which weapons were sometimes smuggled. Western television discovered the conflict and exploited it, often in terms of a struggle between Christianity and Islam.[62] Ojukwu's strategy became a self-fulfilling prophecy, as Muslim Koranic schools in Biafra, few though they were, and Christian missionary schools outside of Biafra, were targeted and destroyed by one side or the other because of their religious affiliation.[63] In some ways, the exaggerated religious polarization in Nigeria today is a descendent of that manufactured during the civil war. Politicians' manipulation of religious identities has since become an old song in Nigeria. Altogether, it took nearly three years for federal forces to defeat and reincorporate Biafra back into Nigeria, in what is "one of the deadliest events in African history."[64]

Incomplete Reconciliation

At the time, it was widely expected that the federal victors would massacre the Igbo. Instead, President Yakubu Gowon instituted a policy of "no victor, no vanquished" to promote national reconciliation. The discipline of federal troops proved to be better than anticipated, physical reconstruction and national reconciliation took place remarkably quickly, and the Igbo resumed a position in national life.

National reconciliation appeared to proceed more quickly than in the United States after the Civil War. But, by the 1898 Spanish-American War, secessionist sentiment in the American South was well and truly dead, if not loyalty to the Lost Cause and belief in states' rights. In Nigeria, sentiment for "Biafra" persists today, almost half a century after the war ended, albeit probably among only a minority of Igbos. Nevertheless, such are the twists and turns of Nigerian politics that President Shagari pardoned Ojukwu, restoring his military pension. When Ojukwu died in 2012, the Jonathan administration accorded him a state funeral.[65]

The end of the civil war coincided with a huge increase in oil production that led to almost unimaginable revenue flows to the government and facilitated physical reconstruction. Still, many Igbos believe that in the aftermath of the civil war, there is in effect a glass ceiling in Nigerian life through which they cannot break. No Igbo has been chief of state since the civil war.

THE MEN ON HORSEBACK AND
INCOMPLETE DEMOCRACY[66]

The coups and the civil war promoted the militarization of governance. With the exception of a four-year civilian interregnum under a weak president, the military directly ruled Nigeria from 1966 to 1999. Over time, the military eroded the independence of the civil service, and it diverted funding (such as it was) from education into other areas that were obscure, such as private pockets. With almost unimaginable wealth from petrochemical production after 1970, the new elites, military officers and businessmen, enriched themselves. The government remained weak, starved of revenue, and lacked capacity even for systematic repression.

With the death under suspicious circumstances of Nigeria's last military chief of state, Sani Abacha, in 1998, the elites concluded that they could best preserve their position by restoring the country to nominally civilian rule. Military and civilian power brokers reached a bargain whereby the military's access to wealth was preserved so long as it stayed out of politics.[67] They reached an informal agreement whereby the presidency would rotate between north and south (in effect, between Muslims and Christians), and a president would be restricted to two terms. This arrangement was called "zoning" or "power shift" and it remained in effect through the 2019 elections but ended in those of 2023, largely because of the personal ambition of the leading presidential candidates.[68] In 1998, power brokers chose Olusegun Obasanjo, a former general and former military chief of state, as their presidential candidate and subsequently ensured his election.

If nominally a civilian, Obasanjo's style was that of a military ruler, which he had been from 1976 to 1979. He ignored court decisions that he did not like and parliament tried to impeach him and failed on numerous occasions. But when he tried to change the constitution to allow him to run for a third term, he was blocked by an elite consensus against what appeared to be "a president for life." Thwarted, he secured the election of Umaru Yar'Adua, the brother of his deputy when he was military chief of state. Yar'Adua was ill and died in office. His successor was his vice president, Goodluck Jonathan, who was elected in his own right in 2011. In 2015, however, he was defeated by Muhammadu Buhari, the first time an opposition candidate became president through the ballot box. Buhari was reelected in 2019. Buhari did not seek to overturn the constitutional prohibition of a presidential third term and did not run for the presidency in 2023. Victorious in the elections of 2023 was Bola Tinubu, an elderly, old-line warhorse antipathetic to fundamental change.

Since 1999, Nigeria has been a civilian democracy, albeit one often led by former military leaders. Most Nigerians have benefited little if at all from governance. Accordingly, participation in elections has steadily declined; in 2023, only 27 percent of registered voters actually cast ballots.

Chapter 2

Nigerians

There are no "Nigerians" in the same sense as there are "English" or "Welsh" or "French." The word Nigeria is merely a distinctive appellation to distinguish those who live within the boundaries of Nigeria from those who do not.

—Obafemi Awolowo[1]

At independence, some Nigerians and their international friends predicted that their country would soon become a superpower—a multiethnic, democratic republic based on the rule of law and protection of human rights that would give Black people a seat at the highest international table. They called that vision the "Nigeria Project." It was not a manifesto; it was rather a way of thinking about nation-building, of achieving national unity. Implicit in it is a close and trusting relationship between the government and the Nigerian people. In 1960, Nnamdi Azikiwe said in London:

> The essence of the Nigeria project is captured by an exchange between Azikiwe and the Sardauna. Azikiwe said, "Let us forget our differences." To which the Sardauna replied, "No, let us understand our differences. I am a Muslim and a northerner. You are a Christian and an Easterner. By understanding our differences, we can build unity in our country."[2]

The reality has been different. Nigeria has been racked by coups, military governments, ongoing insurrections, and escalating corruption. Corralled by a tiny elite, abundant wealth from oil has not been used for economic and social development, which in some ways has actually moved backward. The undisputed leader of the Africa Union and the Economic Community of West African States during the 1999–2007 administration of President Olusegun Obasanjo, Nigeria's international influence is now in decline as it considers closing embassies abroad and struggles with multiple domestic

41

insurrections. President Tinubu struggles to assert his international leadership as ECOWAS tries to respond to military coups, the latest being in Niger in August 2023. Nigerians lament that their country has failed to reach its potential. In May 2019, then–Central Bank governor Godwin Emefiele, in testimony before the Nigerian senate said that over the past fifty years, "the country has receded."[3] Many of the educated under the age of forty have little faith in Nigeria's future and try to immigrate to Australia, Canada, the United Kingdom, and the United States.[4]

The presidential elections of 2023 followed a familiar pattern. The victor, Bola Tinubu, is a septuagenarian former governor of Lagos state with business interests that in the past appeared to be dubious. The runner-up, Atiku Abubakar, also a septuagenarian, was President Obsanjo's vice president and made an immense fortune in the oil services industry with alleged connections to convicted criminal former US Congressman William Jefferson. The third candidate, Peter Obi, was the only Christian candidate and was some twenty years or more younger than Tinubu and Atiku. The media darling in the West and the candidate of the westernized elite in Lagos and Abuja, he did not have the national organization and alliances necessary to win in Nigeria.[5]

What happened? Chinua Achebe, perhaps Africa's most celebrated author, speaks for many: "The trouble with Nigeria is simply and squarely a failure of leadership. There is basically nothing wrong with the Nigerian character. There is nothing wrong with the Nigerian land or climate or water or air or anything else."[6] Achebe's comment raises the question of why Nigerian leadership is so poor. After all, with at least 220 million people today, Nigeria has produced outstanding leaders in areas other than governance. In terms of education and income level, the Nigerian diaspora is one of the more successful immigrant groups in the United States. Rather than Nigerian leaders being less skilled and more venal than others, perhaps part of the answer is that poor leadership is a consequence of the country's weak sense of national identity, poorly developed institutions of government, and a feeble culture of the rule of law.[7]

These deficiencies are primarily the result of history, not merely of the personal inadequacies of the leadership class. They are at the root of the pervasive absence of individual patriotism and public-spiritedness that is often a crucial ingredient of good governance. Yet it is with this leadership that diplomats, nongovernmental organizations, and the foreign trade and investment community interacts. This chapter and the subsequent one look at Nigeria from the perspective of the admittedly abstract but nevertheless instructive concepts of "nation" and "state."

NATION AND STATE

Why start with the concept of nation-state? Because it has long been a primary organizing principle for the conduct of international relations. Hence, American policymakers and diplomats routinely, and somewhat uncritically, view Nigeria through the lens of a nation-state framework and base their policies and expectations on that presumption. Under those circumstances, too often American and Nigerian interlocutors talk past each other. There is a specialized, academic literature written by and for political scientists and other academics that seeks to define nation and state with precision.[8] A skim milk derivative of that often-dense academic work guides policymaker thinking; the problem is not so much with the definitions as with their uncritical application to Nigeria. For our purposes (and for those of most policymakers), a nation is defined as "an imagined political community . . . beyond which lie other nations."[9] Nation refers to a group of people that are similar in language, ethnicity, history, culture, or shared values in relation to other groups of people. Nations define themselves by their differences from other nations. Hence Americans see themselves as different from Canadians, even though the two peoples share strong similarities. A state, on the other hand, can be thought of as the physical and political manifestation of a nation, an apparatus to organize and protect members of such a community.[10] The American state is the United States of America with Washington, DC, as its seat of government; the Canadian state is the Dominion of Canada with its capital at Ottawa.

A state can exist before the nation it ultimately embodies. The notable American historian Jill Lepore shows that the thirteen colonies established a state, the "united States of America," with "united" being lowercase, before there was a collective national identity. The "united States of America" was a political union of thirteen sovereign entities, stretching from Georgia to New Hampshire, each of which commanded primary allegiance from its citizens.[11] Indeed, Lepore dates the emergence of the language of American nationalism only from the 1830s, two generations after independence.[12] The converse may also be true. A nation can also exist before it creates a state. Germany and Italy were nations—people of a shared language, culture, and history that recognized that they shared a common nationality—long before they were unified into states during the nineteenth century.

By the nineteenth century, the uniting of all peoples belonging to the same nation into a single state was a respectable goal of statecraft, as the campaigns for the unification of Germany and Italy demonstrate. In the twentieth century the Nazi government justified German occupation of the Sudetenland in 1938 as the incorporation of the Sudeten Germans, part of the German nation, into the German state. Or, later, Russia occupied Ukrainian Crimea in 2014 to incorporate territory occupied by ethnic Russians into the Russian state. And in the war he started in 2022 against the democratic government in Kiev, Putin insists that Ukrainians are Russians. The converse was also true; a state could expel those who were part of a different nation. The victorious allies after World War II freely accepted the Polish expulsion of those same Sudeten Germans who found themselves inside Poland's redrawn national borders, thereby ridding that country of "foreign" nationals.

The state has become the basic unit of international relations. American diplomats and policymakers interact with the Nigerian state, largely in its capital, Abuja, and not with the abstract Nigerian "nation." The point is that US foreign policy takes as a starting point the assumption that most states that are not tyrannies or multiethnic empires (both applied to the Soviet Union) are populated by a coherent nation, that is, by a people sharing a common identity and, to some extent, loyalty to a government that is empowered by them. "Nation" and "state" are often all but interchangeable terms, and American policymakers and diplomats often uncritically apply those concepts to any multicultural country. For them, every African state is presumed to be a nation, and they assume that those within such a state will identify themselves as part of the same nation. Where loyalty to the state is absent and violence is ubiquitous, diplomats and policymakers will dismiss them as "failed states," such as the Central African Republic, South Sudan, or Somalia. But there is a gray area that separates nation-states and failed states that describes Nigeria and others better than either extreme.

NIGERIA'S COLONIAL EXPERIENCE

The previous chapter shows that history stacked the deck against postindependence Nigeria, particularly with respect to achieving a sense of national identity and patriotism.[13] Shared myths, or narratives, and their attached symbols would seem to be essential to a sense of nationhood. But a widely accepted, unifying story of Nigeria does not exist. Lacking such a narrative, national symbols, such as the flag and the national anthem, have little meaning for many Nigerians. The British, not Africans, created Nigeria, and as colonial administrators, they had little interest in promoting any sense of Nigerian national identity, let alone patriotism.[14] While there was an official effort to encourage pride in the British Empire and its monarchy, the spirit of British rule until the interwar years was divide, conquer, and extract. The current popularity among elites of Nigeria's membership in the Commonwealth of Nations may echo if faintly those efforts on behalf of an imperial identity, though tabloid coverage of the royal family is probably more important to the Commonwealth's popularity. As with so many of its other endeavors in its African tropical possessions, British efforts to transform Nigerians into willing subjects of the British Empire were quixotic, underfunded, and unsuccessful. There was nothing commensurate with the French effort—though also shallow, in practice if not in theory—to transform its African subjects into French citizens through cultural assimilation. For the deeply racist British, subjects of their tropical empire remained the "other," as shown by the oft-quoted adage "the natives are restless tonight."[15] The distinguished American academic Helen Epstein puts it succinctly: "A nation is not only a list of laws, a treasury, a road network, and an army. It is a shared identity and feeling. This is what the British and other colonial powers failed to create."[16]

If the British could not, would not, and did not create a Nigerian nation, how did Nigerians fare? Independence movements can be important foundations of national identity by forging closer ties in the face of a common enemy. This was true of the American Revolutionary War; when it started, those favoring independence were perhaps a third of the population; when it was over, nearly everybody was in favor (those who did not had left, or kept quiet).[17] But in Nigeria, as mentioned in the previous chapter, independence was largely driven by the British for reasons that were external to Nigeria. There were colonial-era strikes, usually over wages, but they lacked an overt national framework. Fundamentally, Nigerian opposition to colonialism was an intellectual, literary, and journalistic enterprise rather than one that involved mass mobilization of people across ethnic divisions.[18] Advocates for independence often were pan-Africans rather than pro-Nigerians. There was no "war of liberation" that might have forged a sense of national identity and created a shared national story, such as in Algeria or Kenya. There are no national martyrs, such as Nathan Hale, hero and martyr of the American Revolution ("I only regret that I have but one life to lose for my country").[19] There is no widely accepted Nigerian equivalent to the American myth of the heroic Founding Fathers or Valley Forge or of popular patriotic songs such as "Yankee Doodle." No Nigerian political leader has been "the Father of the Country," as was George Washington. Indeed, among many Muslims there is dislike of all national symbols, such as a pledge of allegiance to the flag or the national anthem, as promoting idolatry of the secular state, which is contrary to their strict monotheism.

Nevertheless, the past does not foreclose the possibility that a national identity may develop with time, as happened so clearly in the United States. The experience of Nigeria fighting a civil war and its elites holding together through insurrections, economic depression, and a transition from military rule to incomplete civilian democracy may provide the basis for future, stronger national identity. But not yet.

WHO ARE NIGERIANS?

Based on polling data comparing sixteen sub-Saharan African nations, Nigerians have the lowest ranking of self-identification with the state.[20] For most Nigerians, their loyalty is to their family, their religion, and their ethnic group. Of course, in most countries around the world, citizens are not exclusively loyal to the state, but this fact does not preclude a strong sense of national identity. In one sphere, Americans are loyal to their families and, many of them, to their religion. In another sphere, they are loyal to the American nation-state. Rarely is there conflict between them, in part, because the American state has historically been careful to respect the boundary between personal and public life. For example, the concept of conscientious objection to military service respects the state's recognition of religious loyalty. The principle that close family members may not be compelled to testify against each other in courts of law is an example of state respect for family loyalty. In Nigeria, however, the notion of parallel loyalties is much less developed, and, after all, it is not to the state that Nigerians turn in times of need but rather their families, religion, or ethnic group.

Polling data and abundant anecdotal evidence testifies that for most Nigerians, loyalty to their families is paramount. Family is almost always multigenerational and characterized by many children, but it is also highly variable, depending on religion, ethnic group, and circumstance.[21] In the urban and predominately Christian south, women average two to three children.[22] In the Islamic north, in parts of Yorubaland, and among certain ethnic groups and "big men," fathers with multiple wives may have more than twenty children.[23] The family provides for a Nigerian in old age, an important spur to having large numbers of children, and old age comes early. The average life expectancy among Nigerian men is only 53.7 years and among women it is 55.4, both of which are among the lowest in Africa.[24] Hence, loyalty to the family is almost always stronger than loyalty to the state. A Nigerian will choose to advance his family members at the expense of the state if he or she has the opportunity. Providing for children and strengthening the family is a major motivation for corruption. Indeed, within the local political and economic context, what outsiders would view as illegal behavior is normalized to the point that it is no longer viewed as corruption. Amid the absence or neglect of state authority, families are relatively autonomous and form an informal political economy sometimes called the "economy of affection." In this informal setting, individuals rely on kinship, community, religion, or other affinities to survive.[25]

"THE MOST RELIGIOUS PEOPLE IN THE WORLD"

From a secular, American perspective, the most important reality for many Nigerians and other Africans is spiritual, not material. Many Nigerians live in an enchanted universe. Causation of events is determined by higher powers, divine or satanic. Reuben Abati's musings in a 2016 article in a Lagos newspaper are illustrative. He is a highly distinguished journalist and was the press spokesman for President Goodluck Jonathan:

> When presidents make mistakes they are probably victims of a force higher than what we can imagine. Every student of Aso Villa [the presidential official residence] would readily admit that when people get in there, they actually become something else. They act like they are under a spell. . . . I am therefore convinced that there is an evil spell enveloping this country. We need to rescue Nigeria from the forces of darkness. Aso Villa should be converted into a spiritual museum, and abandoned.[26]

Abati is by no means alone. Responding to his article, Ben Agande, a journalist from a different newspaper, wrote:

> Since president Babangida . . . subsequent occupants of the sprawling edifice [Aso Villa] have brought spirituality to bear on their stay in the office. From General Sani Abacha to Abdulsalami Abubakar to Olusegun Obasanjo to Umaru Yar'Adua down to the present occupant, Muhammadu Buhari, these occupants have had to carry out spiritual cleaning of the place before moving in with their families and hordes of aides.[27]

If Abati and Agande seem to channel seventeenth-century Salem, Massachusetts, and its witch trials, in other ways Nigeria is a part of the world familiar to contemporary Americans. Nollywood, Nigeria's indigenous film industry, has enormous influence on the continent and increasingly around the world.[28] Cell phone use is ubiquitous, and there were 116 million Nigerians—over half the population—accessing the internet in March 2019, for example.[29] In the Lagos-Ibadan corridor, the capital Abuja, and sporadically elsewhere, there are the familiar financial and business services that are available in major cities around the world. Nevertheless, while information technology and financial services are starting to power the modern sectors of the economy, Nigeria still lags behind South Africa and even Kenya. As for formal politics at the national level, Nigeria has been on a modestly positive democratic trajectory since the end of military rule in 1999, but it is far from certain that progress can be sustained: the quality and credibility of the 2019 national elections were a step backward from those of 2015, while those of 2023 were worse than those of 2019.

Like the family with which it is intertwined, religion for most Nigerians is a far more compelling focus of loyalty than the state. Nigerians like to say that they are the world's most religious people, and the happiest.[30] The basis of that happiness appears to be the hope that religion supplies.[31] Among Nigerians, whether they adhere to Christianity, Islam, the traditional gods, or all three as some do, the next life and the dead are close at hand. Ancestor worship is widespread; ancestors are typically consulted about almost anything of importance. So, too, at some places are traditional gods at shrines. Religious leaders, ranging from cardinals to Pentecostal preachers to imams and mallams to soothsayers and marabouts are powerful figures in their communities. Personal loyalty to family, religion, and ethnic group by and large puts space between the individual and the Nigerian state, especially as there is little sense of nationality to mediate between them. Many Nigerians, especially among northern Muslims, are intensely loyal to Islam, their families, and their traditional ruler while largely ignoring the state altogether. Religion in the north is more integrated into traditional political institutions than in the south chiefly because northern institutions were less impacted by colonial rule and are supported by deeper historical roots. Hence the appeal of "One North, One People," which is "the notion of a unified Islamic region with Arab influence and ties."[32] The quality of loyalty to an ethnic group varies. While in the Islamic north, loyalty to religion may supersede loyalty even to family, among the Yoruba, loyalty to family usually comes first, followed by ethnic group. Yoruba religion is an intrinsic element in Yoruba identity, and the two together may supersede loyalty to either Christianity or Islam, both of which are "imported" religions.

Emirate Islam in northern Nigeria traditionally makes no distinction between secular and religious authority. Hence, many northern Nigerian Muslims reject the concept of a secular state, or even Nigerian nationality. For its part, the postindependence secular state in theory does not recognize the authority of Islam as a valid alternative to its own. That attitude feeds the implacable hostility to Abuja that is widespread within northern Islam—not just among jihadist radicals. The British reinforced the emirate amalgamation of secular and religious authority through indirect rule. As was discussed in the previous chapter, they kept in place the sultan, the shehu, and the emirs that exercised both religious and secular authority. Colonial officials tried, with considerable success from their perspective, to rule from behind the scenes and were rewarded for this approach by the relative lack of interest in independence in the north in 1960.

Among Christians there is also little distinction between secular and religious authority, Religious leaders actively intervene in political life. For example, in the 2015 national elections, the primate of the Church of Nigeria-Anglican Communion, nominally the largest denomination in the country, instructed the bishops to ensure that their flocks voted for fellow Christian Goodluck Jonathan for president, rather than the Muslim Muhammadu Buhari. Buhari's vice president, Yemi Osinbajo, was a Pentecostal preacher who described himself as "on loan" from the church.[33] Blatant clerical interference in politics is common and regarded as righteous, and politicians regard the support of religious leaders as essential to electoral victory.[34] For many, misfortune, political and otherwise, is ascribed to the will of God—or the machinations of Satan.[35]

Some scholars see the emergence of national identity in the seventeenth and eighteen century in Europe as essentially a replacement for religion: the rise of national identity reflected, among other things, the decline of the universal church, brought on at least in part by the reformation, modern science, and secularism.[36] Nigeria is in the midst of a religious revival among both Christians and Muslims. A genuinely secular outlook is rare. It may be argued that few Nigerians need a substitute for religion, which, whether Christianity or Islam or worship of the traditional gods, dominates daily Nigerian life.

Members of ethnic groups in Nigeria usually share a specific cultural and linguistic identity and a common myth intertwined with a common religion, often linked to a particular place.[37] The Hausa-Fulani, Yoruba, and Igbo resemble in many ways large nations that lack a state.[38] Though they are to be found all over the country, they are identified with a specific geographic area, a homeland. The Hausa-Fulani (about seventy million) are probably more populous than South Africans, and the Yoruba and Igbo are both about as numerous as Angolans. Lacking the international recognition and formal administrative apparatus of a sovereign state, nevertheless, they often command greater popular respect than those of Nigeria's secular institutions. When ethnic groups constitute a large share of the population, a nation is often challenged to form a unified national culture and identity.[39]

Though the three all have precolonial origins, the expression of their identities has evolved and, in some ways, grown in significance, under the pressures of colonialism and modernization as Africa has become part of the global economy. They have a strong sense of difference and separation from other peoples. There has always been some intermarriage among the three, though there is anecdotal evidence that it is declining. Compared to these big three, other ethnic groups are small, sometimes represented by little more than a collection of villages. Yet others still, in particular the Kanuri (4.9 million), Tiv (4.9 million), Ijaw (3.6 million), and the Ibibo (about 3.6 million), are large enough and distinctive enough to also resemble a small nation similar to the Welsh in the United Kingdom (3 million) or the Catalans in Spain (8 million).[40] The existence of dominant ethnic groups curtails the cultures and voices of the smaller groups to be incorporated. In contrast, states with numerous but smaller ethnic groups often have a stronger sense of national identity. Citizens of Tanzania, for example, identify more with their nation than do the citizens of other sub-Saharan African states; its largest ethnic group comprises only 12 percent of the population.[41]

Nigerian ethnic groups usually have a hierarchy of traditional rulers, and many have birthed cultural and quasi-political organizations to advance their specific interests against their rivals and the secular state. Some even field armed militias that on occasion fight the state, other militias, or, as is the case in the Niger Delta, agents of international oil companies. By and large, the federal government in Abuja is not strong enough to disarm them. Among the Hausa-Fulani hierarchy, at the top it is the sultan of Sokoto; among the Kanuri, the shehu of Borno; and among the Tiv, the tor tiv. The Yoruba have at least two supreme authority figures: the ooni of Ife and the alaafin of Oyo. By contrast, the Igbo, historically politically decentralized, have never had a hierarchy of traditional rulers.[42]

Ethnicities and their associated organizations claim historical or even divine legitimacy. But in many cases they owe their being to the colonial experience. As one historian put it, "Igbos had to be convinced that they were Igbos," though they had no manifest connections to other fellow Igbos, and the term Yoruba "was popularized by Church Missionary Society leaders during the nineteenth century who were anxious to produce a Bible in a uniform language" for the warring Yoruba city-states.[43] According to another, "Everyone recognizes that the notion of 'being Nigerian' is a new kind of conception. But it would seem that the notion of 'being a Yoruba' is not very much older."[44] Hence, today's unified ethnic groups, whose leaders tend to ground their legitimacy in history, often have roots not much deeper than those of Nigeria itself. Nevertheless, whatever the historical reality, the legend of a divine or ancient ethnic origin has a powerful hold.[45]

Nigeria's largest ethnic groups tend to dominate specific states. The Yoruba dominate Ekiti, Kogi, Kwara, Lagos, Ogun, Ondo, Osun, and Oyo states. The Igbo dominate Abia, Anambra, Ebonyi, Enugu, and Imo states. The Hausa-Fulani dominate Bauchi, Jigawa, Kaduna, Kano, Katsina, Kebbi, Niger, Sokoto, and Zamfara states. Thus, the three largest ethnic groups dominate twenty-two of the thirty-six states, almost two-thirds. The smaller Ijaw dominate an additional four: Akwa Ibom, Bayelsa, Delta, and Rivers. The Kanuri predominate in Adamawa, Borno, and Yobe. Altogether twenty-nine of Nigeria's thirty-six states are dominated by a specific ethnic group, essentially creating an ethnic federalism that inherently contradicts the values of a unified, multiethnic, secular state.

Nigeria's borders do not restrict the distribution of different ethnic groups—respectively, large numbers of Hausa-Fulani, Kanuri, and Yoruba reside in Niger, Cameroon, and Benin, for example. Individual Igbos freely migrate the world over; they are probably the largest component of the

Nigerian community in the United States. They are said to be 40 percent of the population of Lagos, ostensibly a Yoruba city in historically Yoruba territory. As a result of the transatlantic slave trade, there is a large Yoruba population in Brazil with which the ooni of Ife is in regular contact.[46] The Fulani, a traditionally nomadic people, are to be found all over the Sahel, which straddles Africa east to west along the southern edge of the Sahara Desert.

It may be that, in geographical areas where ethnic identities are the same, similar, or at least nonthreatened, a space can be created for a national identity to have meaning. A study of two Hausa-speaking Fulani villages, one on the Nigerian side of the border, the other on the Nigerien side, showed that the strongest identities were with Islam and the local village.[47] National identity, however, was stronger than ethnic identity in a venue where a single ethnic group, the Fulani, was dominant on both sides of the border and unchallenged by ethnic rivals. Even so, in the two villages the strongest identity remained religion, not nationality.

Each ethnic group has its own language, making Nigeria a veritable Tower of Babel. The multiplicity of languages illustrates the sheer scale of diversity within Nigeria and the challenges of creating a sense of national community. Nigeria's 350 or so languages are divided among three of the six major language families in Africa: Niger-Congo, Afro-Asiatic, and Nilo-Saharan. For comparison, Europe is made up almost entirely of languages in one language family, Indo-European. In Nigeria, the postindependence solution to such a degree of diversity has been to make English the only legal language and the language of government. Postindependence India followed the same strategy for largely the same reasons; only after decades of independence did the Indian government move to make Hindi the national language and with only limited success. Because it belonged to no specific ethnic group, English could therefore belong to all. But for most Nigerians, the government—and its language—intruded little on their daily lives.

Spoken language is one manifestation of elite isolation from most Nigerians that inhibits the development of national identity. The language of government was and still is English; it is the language of the political classes. But for only about 11 percent of Nigeria's population is it the primary language spoken at home.[48] A credible estimate is that only about half of Nigeria's population understands and speaks even a little English.[49]

Under the British, English had been the official language in the south, Hausa in the north. Independence-era Nigerian politicians argued that English, as the sole legal language, would promote national unity, so they expanded its legal status nationwide. It is tempting to compare the role played by the English language in contemporary Nigeria to that of Latin in medieval and early-modern Europe. Both languages existed alongside indigenous languages, and both were the languages of academia, religion, business, and diplomacy. Except in a few places, Latin was never the language of the household, and neither is English in most Nigerian households today. In Europe, starting as early as the fourteenth century in England, vernacular languages spread across the continent through mass communication, especially the printing press, rapidly superseding Latin, which by the twenty-first century had become a dead language, except within parts of the legal profession in some countries and the Roman Catholic Church.[50]

The supplanting of Latin by the modern European languages promoted a specific national identity: being English or French or German was identified with speaking those languages, and they supplanted the concept of a universal Latin "Christendom" of the Middle Ages. In Nigeria today, English is the language of elites and business, but its number of speakers is growing only slowly if at all. Most Nigerians still use their indigenous languages in daily life. Indeed, the use of English by elites may have the ironic consequence of inhibiting the growth of Nigerian national identity. Pidgin, an indigenous language spoken across ethnic groups with roots in English just as French has roots in Latin, is expanding rapidly.[51] In 2017, the BBC launched a Pidgin-language news service.

With an abundance of ethnic groups and languages and multiple religions, a sense of shared values has been slow to develop among Nigerians. The importance of religion is, indeed, an overarching value.[52] But adherents are divided between Islam and Christianity, and the undergirding component of traditional religion is largely formally ignored by elites and the secular state even if it is often deeply influential with respect to the struggle for power.[53] Hence, the importance of religion has thus far has not promoted an "imagined community" that bridges the country's myriad divisions. It is not clear that those educated and relatively wealthy residents of Lagos or members of the diaspora that self-identify as Nigerian represent the future of the country. Instead, Nigeria the country has within it Hausa-Fulanis, Igbos, Ijaws, Yorubas, Tivs, and Itsekiris; it has Protestants, Pentecostals, and Catholics; it has Shias, Salafis, Sufis, and Sunnis; and it has followers of Odudwa, Chukwu, and Mammy Wata.[54] This diversity does not preclude a shared identity, but a coherent, unified nation of Nigeria remains an aspiration, and not one whose attainment is inevitable.

AN INDEPENDENT NATION

If the British created Nigeria, their stay in West Africa was but an episode. The inadequacies of the short-lived British administration should not overshadow the fact that the postindependence political leadership has largely failed the Nigerian people. Following independence, civil war, and the oil boom, a voraciously corrupt elite cartel, national in scope but not in loyalty, has become increasingly isolated from the mass of the population, producing no heroes. Simply put, the state provides few or no services for most Nigerians. Too many Nigerians appear to regard it as an agency of exploitation, not much different from the colonial regime, only now with Nigerians in positions once held by the British.

After World War II, Nnamdi Azikiwe, an Igbo, led the largest, though not truly a mass anticolonial movement, and he was later the first president of independent Nigeria. A journalist and a highly successful newspaper owner, he founded the National Council of Nigeria and the Cameroons with Herbert Macaulay, who is often regarded by contemporary Nigerians as the intellectual founder of Nigerian nationalism.[55] Macaulay first cut his teeth fighting against racism well before amalgamation in 1914. Obafemi Awolowo, also the founder and owner of a major newspaper, was the most powerful Yoruba politician during the independence and postindependence era. The most powerful northern politician was Sir Ahmadu Bello, sardauna of Sokoto. But he was never an enthusiast for independence, fearing domination by the Christian south should the British no longer underwrite the privileged position of the Islamic establishment.[56]

Aside from their opposition to colonialism and racism, Nigeria's ostensible founding fathers all shared an intense loyalty to their respective regions and ethnic groups and, as such, were never able to develop a truly national following. Instead, the sardauna remained a Hausa-Fulani, Awolowo a Yoruba, and Azikiwe an Igbo. They also represented the two world religions. The sardauna was Muslim, Awolowo an Anglican Christian, and Azikiwe self-identified as a Christian. (He was associated with the National Church of Nigeria and Cameroons, a hybrid of Christianity and traditional African religion closely tied to his political movement, which was predominately Igbo.)[57] All three were skeptical at various points in their careers about even the possibility of a Nigerian sense of national identity. The sardauna characterized Nigeria as "a misalliance of people, who are . . . of the same racial stock, but with different language, historical background, and in fact distinct territory and distinct cultural and political identity."[58] He was skeptical about the benefits that independence would bring the Hausa-Fulani. Awolowo famously said, "Nigeria is not a nation. It is a mere geographical expression."[59] And Azikiwe, when he supported the secession of Biafra, said, "It is better that we disintegrate in peace and not in pieces."[60]

Countries at all levels of development have also faced the challenges of building a national identity and a common political culture across ethnic, linguistic, and religious divisions. A look at Ghana, Tanzania, and India provides a point of comparison for Nigeria's trajectory, including their responses to similar challenges. The three were all parts of the British Empire and secured their independence within the same time frame: India in 1947, Ghana in 1957, Nigeria in 1960, and Tanzania in 1961. Switzerland and Canada are highly developed, highly successful twenty-first-century countries that have managed well the factors that might have pulled them apart. Finally, the transformation of Britain's thirteen American colonies into the United States highlights the difficulties of nation-building even when the objective circumstances were more favorable than Nigeria's. "Nations are not merely multicolored patches in the atlas," wrote Wole Soyinka. "They answer to some internal logic and historic coherence, and an evolved tradition of managing incompatibilities."[61]

DIVERGENT PATHS: GHANA AND NIGERIA

Ghana provides an instructive comparison with Nigeria, especially with respect to the role of ethnicity and the influence of leadership. Though far smaller in population and territory, it is also a former British possession on the Gulf of Guinea. It shares with Nigeria the distortions of the slave trade, borders drawn in London, Paris, and Berlin, and colonial rule based on racist assumptions. After independence, both countries were characterized by civilian corruption, coups, and periods of military rule. Military rulers in both countries came from small ethnic groups, not the major ones. In Ghana, the 1979 coup led by Flight Lieutenant Jerry Rawlings publicly executed at least three hundred members of the political class, usually for "corruption." Subsequently, however, in both countries the military withdrew and civilian governance was reestablished. In both countries the opposition over the past decade has come to power through elections.

Despite the similarities, in many ways Ghana is more developed than Nigeria. It certainly has better human development statistics.[62] A possible explanation for this gap in development is that Ghana's sense of national identity appears stronger and more widespread than in Nigeria.[63] In part, this derives from Ghana's and Nigeria's differing approaches to nation-building following independence. Ghana's elite developed a single, dominant nationalist movement, fostering a sense of unifying purpose and national identity.[64] This contrasts with Nigeria's ethnically grounded independence movements, which produced three major political parties, each representing a major ethnic group.

Nigeria lacked a nationwide independence movement, and only one among the founding fathers, Nnamdi Azikiwe, promoted, and then only for a time, a national vision. In 1967, of course, he as an Igbo supported the Biafra secessionist movement. The contrast with Ghana is striking: Kwame Nkrumah was the leader of the independence movement and subsequently chief of state from 1957 to 1966. His reputation has been tarred by his close ties to the Soviet Union during the Cold War, advocacy of "scientific Marxism" despite a Presbyterian background, and personal corruption, including his alleged possession of a solid-gold bedstead. But he played a major role in freeing Ghana from overweening tribalism. So, too, did Jerry Rawlings, who dominated Ghanaian political life far longer, from 1979 to 2001. With a Scottish father and an African mother, he, too, did not pander to ethnic identities. By contrast, Nigeria's first generation of politicians was largely defined by ethnicity.

The Gold Coast (as Ghana was called in the colonial period) was, like Nigeria, a center of pan-African thinking. Kwame Nkrumah was strongly influenced by Jamaica-born, longtime US resident Marcus Garvey, the founder of the Universal Negro Improvement Association and organizer of the American "back to Africa" movement. Garvey founded a shipping company, the Black Star Line, to facilitate diaspora travel to Africa; the black star on the current Ghanaian flag deliberately recalls Garvey.[65] Nkrumah spent a decade in the United States, earning degrees from Lincoln University and the University of Pennsylvania, which Nigeria's Nnamdi Azikiwe also attended. (The two became friends.)[66] Nkrumah was also influenced by W. E. B. Du Bois, perhaps the most prominent African American intellectual of his era as well as an American Trotskyist then active in New York's Harlem. Nevertheless, Nkrumah's conversion to "scientific Marxism" likely owed more to its opposition to racism and colonialism than to its economic and political theory.

In the aftermath of World War II, indigenous Gold Coast businessmen organized in 1947 the country's first political party, the United Gold Coast Convention (UGCC). The party called for independence as early as possible. Despite their concerns about his Trotskyist sympathies, party organizers hired Nkrumah to be, in effect, the party's salaried general secretary. There were serious riots and boycotts of foreign traders beginning in 1948 (though any UGCC role in the unrest has not been definitively established). In any event, by 1949, Nkrumah had broken with the UGCC and formed his own, more radical political party, the Convention People's Party (CPP). In 1950, he led a general strike over the slow pace of progress toward independence. Nkrumah was arrested and jailed, but the CPP still swept the elections of 1951, which were the first in Africa without a suffrage income requirement. That vote demonstrated the potency of Nkrumah's pan-African, socialist, and independence message.[67] Released from jail, Nkrumah thereupon became, in effect at once and later in title, the prime minister and led the movement and negotiations for independence, which was achieved in 1957.

Nkrumah presented himself as a pan-African and national leader, not an ethnic chief. All his political life he was a strong pan-Africanist and is counted as one of the founders of the Organization of African Unity (OAU). For Nkrumah, pan-Africanism and Ghanaian nationalism were mutually supportive and reenforcing. Unlike Nigerian political parties, the UGCC and the CPP were national in reach. Kwame Nkrumah energized a mass movement for independence that bridged ethnic differences. His advocacy of socialism and nationalism appealed to the mass electorate in Ghana across ethnic lines.

In 1966, Nkrumah and his government were overthrown by a coup orchestrated by the military and the police, with the alleged support of American intelligence services, which were deeply suspicious of his ties to the Eastern Bloc at the height of the Cold War. The subsequent military government reoriented Ghana away from the Soviet Union and toward the West.

Nkrumah and Jerry Rawlings both minimized ethnicity. Hence, unlike in Nigeria, there was a liberation struggle against British colonialism that transcended ethnic, religious, and regional divisions. It is a source of national pride today that Ghana was the first colonial tropical territory to win its independence. Nkrumah's and Rawlings's opposition to tribalism highlights the importance of leadership. Other Ghanaian politicians might well have taken the country down a different road.

INDIRECTLY RULED: INDIA AND NIGERIA

A glance at the independence-era Indian leadership also highlights the lack of a national vision among their Nigerian equivalents. British colonial thinking often yoked the African tropical empire to India. Throughout the colonial period, those British concerned with Nigeria were often looking over their shoulders at their Indian empire. With respect to health policy affecting whites, for example, Nigeria and the Colonial Office followed India's lead. However, among the British, service in India conferred higher status than service in West Africa.

The Indian and Nigerian colonies were both huge and multiethnic, and split, if unevenly in India's case, between two major religions. But Britain's Indian empire was socially and economically far more developed than its tropical empire, as illustrated by the more extensive railway network, more vibrant newspapers, more numerous educational institutions, and the presence of profitable manufacturing. Hence, unlike Nigeria, it was a significant source of British imperial wealth. Indeed, India was central to the British Empire while Nigeria was marginal. The British had been there since 1667, when Bombay was part of Catherine of Braganza's dowry when she married Charles II.[68] Almost three hundred years later, the British withdrew from their Indian empire, following popular agitation for independence that became progressively more widespread and was characterized by strikes, riots, and even a pro-Japanese political movement during World War II. Independence for India had support in some British circles from the interwar years, especially within the Labour Party, which formed the first post–World War II government. Despite the horrors of the partition of the old empire between the new India and Pakistan, the independence movement and its dislocations promoted a national vision in both India and Pakistan.

Demands for the end of British rule started earlier in India and were much more deep-rooted than in West Africa. Moreover, during the independence period, there was no Nigerian equivalent of Mahatma Gandhi, Jawaharlal Nehru, and Muhammed Ali Jinnah, leaders of the movement for India's independence and partition. Gandhi and Nehru had a vision that would incorporate India's multitude of ethnicities and religions into one united, democratic, secular state. Jinnah's vision was more parochial: he sought a place in the sun for India's Muslim minority.[69] (In that sense he was reminiscent of Awolowo or the sardauna.) Unlike the Nigerian anticolonial leadership, all three were able to electrify the Hindu and Muslim masses with a compelling vision of the future. Awolowo's and Azikiwe's appeal was usually limited to their specific ethnic group.

MAKING TANZANIA

Tanzania, like Nigeria, is ethnically, linguistically, and religiously diverse and was once under British rule.[70] Its language policy is an alternative to Nigeria's in the effort to promote national identity. Like Nigeria, its population is divided. By some estimates the country comprises some 120 ethnic groups and languages. Its people are about two-thirds Christian and one-third Muslim. But unlike Nigeria, Tanzania substituted Swahili for English as its national language in 1960. The adoption of Swahili as lingua franca and as an aspirational national language required a concerted effort by national leaders to set an example by using it, and concrete policies to teach it. In 1962, its president, Julius Nyerere, addressed the national assembly of the newly independent state of Tanganyika (Tanzania's name before merger with Zanzibar in 1963) in Swahili, signaling to the country, and the world, the primacy of this African language.[71] In 2015, the Tanzanian government finally completed the process by making Swahili the language of instruction in primary school. English remains the language of instruction from secondary school through university.

Tanzanian politicians often use Swahili in parliament, though sometimes they switch back and forth with English. Swahili has indeed become the language of politics. For other parts of life, Tanzanians continued to use local languages, or, when it comes to international business and the higher courts,

English.[72] Nevertheless, the significance of giving Tanzanians the ability to communicate effectively with each other across ethnic and linguistic lines in the political space should not be minimized. Julius Nyerere, the independence leader as well as the first president of Tanzania, used Swahili across the country to promote the unity of a country with more than a hundred different languages.[73]

Julius Nyerere had advantages that the postcolonial Nigerian leadership lacked. That Nyerere was a member of the Zanaki ethnic group, one of the smallest in Tanzania, probably made it easier for him to push for a Tanzania that transcended ethnicity, language, and religion, and not simply elevate his own ethnic group, as so many independence-era Nigerian leaders had sought to do.[74] Tanzanian leadership in general has been stronger and more national in orientation than in Nigeria. Therefore, Nyerere did not face long-established ethnic political networks, and unlike Nigeria's founding fathers, he did not inherit a state already deeply divided by ethnicity and religion.[75] Further, Tanzania's elites have historically been less rapacious, in part because of the strong leadership of Julius Nyerere and his establishment of a variety of Afro-socialism. It helped, too, that Tanzania was not then blessed (or plagued) with the oil or mineral riches that fueled corruption in Nigeria.

DIVERSITY WORKS: SWITZERLAND AND CANADA

Linguistic and cultural unity is by no means essential to a sense of common nationhood, as Switzerland and Canada show. Switzerland has four official languages: French, German, Italian, and Romansch. Its population is divided between Protestants and Catholics, with Protestants further divided into a number of denominations. Catholics are also divided, between traditionalists and the theologically conservative on the one hand, and the more liberal or "modern" on the other. But, as has been said, if the Swiss disagree on language and religion, they agree on everything else—especially that they are all Swiss. French, German, Italian, and Romansch speakers recognize each other as Swiss, not as Germans, French, or Italians, despite the language they speak.[76] This unity is expressed in a national narrative, contemporary shared experience, and by symbols. These include the flag, practices such as universal national service, and also by a perceived shared history articulated by a commonly understood narrative, such as "six hundred years of armed neutrality."

Canada is divided between Anglophone and Francophone speakers, with the latter historically resenting the former because they were assumed to be better educated, wealthier, and more "modern." Historically, English speakers identified with the British Empire, French speakers with France and Roman Catholicism. The indigenous peoples—now called First Nations—following generations of marginalization currently participate in a renewed, vibrant Canadian national narrative despite their greater poverty and poorer social statistics compared to the rest of Canadians. Following the dissolution of the British Empire, the decline of France and the French language on the world stage, and of Catholicism in most Western countries in the face of secularism, these traditional identities have withered, creating the space for a now-flourishing, distinctive Canadian identity, expressed by a new national flag replacing a generation ago the British Union Jack and a popular national anthem replacing "God Save the Queen."

French president Charles de Gaulle's "Vive le Quebec libre" of 1967 no longer resonates among Canadian Francophones as it once did. With legislation that established equality between the two languages, economic changes that reduced economic disparity among speakers from the two language groups, and immigration from many other parts of the world, Canadian identity has become a strong social construct based on ideas, the shared values of democracy, tolerance, strong respect for human rights and the rule of law, and good government, rather than the old identities of language, religion, and ethnicity.[77]

It might be objected that Canada and Switzerland cannot in any way be compared to Nigeria. The first two have among the highest incomes and best social statistics in the world. Nigeria is one of the world's poorest countries with among the worst social statistics. Switzerland is medieval in origin, French Canadians date from the seventeenth century, English Canadians from the eighteenth, and Canada today is a major recipient of immigrants from all over the world, Nigeria included. Canada honors its indigenous people, though their social statistics are the poorest of the groups that make up the Canadian "salade." Nigeria was created only in 1914 and exports people, rather than receiving them. Yet all three, ostensibly, are democracies conducted according to the rule of law with memberships in various international organizations, chief among them the United Nations. The point here is that linguistic and cultural diversity do not preclude a strong sense of national identity if properly managed with good leadership and if blessed by history.

THIRTEEN NATIONS INTO ONE: THE UNITED STATES

Created by the British with little thought given to religious, cultural, and historical differences of its inhabitants, Nigeria's challenges to building a stronger national identity are formidable, but not insurmountable. Nigerians exposed to Western education or travel often use the United States as the measure against which to evaluate Nigeria. It is instructive to look at the challenges faced by other former British colonies, as some Nigerians do, this time to North America where thirteen fractious colonies transformed themselves into a single political entity and ultimately into a nation-state.

The thirteen colonies then may have had a stronger basis for unity than Nigeria does now, and in the end the process succeeded. But it still took many years and a devastating civil war to achieve the reality—rather than just the rhetoric—of a unified nation-state. From the first, the individual colonies commanded the deepest loyalty from their citizens. But they managed to transform themselves into the United States by reducing their differences and strengthening their similarities. "If we do not hang together, we shall surely hang separately," Benjamin Franklin allegedly said during the crucible of national identity, the War of the American Revolution.

Unlike Nigeria, however, the thirteen colonies shared a common language, a common culture, a common form of governance, and a common religion. Of the signers of the Declaration of Independence, all but one, a Roman Catholic, were Protestant Christians and all were of European descent. More than half were Anglican, 23 percent were Congregationalist, 21 percent were Presbyterian, and 2 percent were Unitarian. English was the first language of every one of the signers of the Declaration of Independence and the Constitution. Even the domestic architecture of the colonies was cut from the same cloth, with differences being largely the result of availability of building materials. The two oldest universities, Harvard and William & Mary, were six hundred miles apart but operated on the basis of shared British cultural assumptions and religious practice, and they followed similar curricula. Slavery, later the greatest threat to national cohesion, was legal and present in every one of the thirteen colonies, and New York was second only to Charleston in the number of enslaved residents in 1776.[78] Nearly universal among the elites of all the colonies was the belief that westward expansion at the expense of Native Americans was ordained by God.

The American road to independence was evidently different than Nigeria's. The armed struggle for independence from Britain lasted almost a decade and brought together hitherto disparate elites. The initiative for American independence was unambiguously American. The elites in most of the thirteen colonies drove the independence movement and fought a war successfully against what was then the most powerful military force in the world. After independence, the United States successfully fought continuous wars with Native Americans, stood down Republican and Napoleonic France, doubled its territory with the Louisiana Purchase, and believed it won the 1812 war against the British.

During the independence and postindependence periods, the level of American political leadership was exceptionally high. For the first forty years of independence, from 1789 to 1829, the presidents were George Washington, John Adams, Thomas Jefferson, James Madison, James Monroe, and John Quincy Adams. Well educated, sharing a common vision of the United States despite political differences, and personally uncorrupt, they provided exceptional leadership that was inclusive of white males from all parts of the country, and they are remembered and extolled even today. (At the time, people of African descent, Native Americans, and most women were usually excluded from public life in the United States and Europe.) Local and state governments shared authority with the federal government, most of the time precluding "winner-take-all" politics. Finally, on a per capita basis, the thirteen colonies were already among the wealthiest territories in the world by 1700 (always excepting Native Americans and slaves, who constituted a large percentage of the settled population, but not a majority), with extremes of rich and poor but an ethos of equality of opportunity and the promise of free land in the west for those willing to pull up stakes.

Nevertheless, even with all of these advantages for nation-building, the United States was unable to address peacefully its most divisive issue—slavery—which in turn exacerbated the relationship among the states and between them and the federal government. It was only Union victory in the Civil War, which lasted from 1861 to 1865, that legally ended slavery and established the preeminence of the United States over the individual states and their identities. As late as 1861, before fighting started, Virginia's Robert E. Lee, an officer in the United States Army, declined to command a Union army by saying, "I look upon secession as anarchy. If I owned the four millions of slaves in the South, I would sacrifice them all to the Union; but how can I draw my sword upon Virginia, my native State?"[79] For Lee and many other Americans, loyalty to one's state took precedence over loyalty to the federal government. The tension between the states and the federal government became a proxy for a more fundamental disagreement over slavery. There was enormous cost. The Civil War left an estimated 750,000 dead, about 10 percent of those eligible to fight and almost 2.5 percent of the total population.[80] Subsequent Reconstruction amendments to the Constitution abolished slavery and established as a matter of law the preeminence of the United States over the individual states. The postwar political arrangements failed, however, to address the poverty of freed slaves, and the marginalization of their descendants, though diminishing, continues today. But the triumph of the national government solidified American nationalism. By the mid-twentieth century so pervasive had American national identity become that Lyndon B. Johnson, Robert E. Lee's fellow Southerner, himself from a state that had attempted to secede a century earlier, and later president from 1963 to 1969, said, "I am an American, a Texan, and a Democrat, in that order."[81]

WORK IN PROGRESS

Building a nation is hard work. It requires a beneficent history, talented leaders, and a compelling vision. Nigeria has lacked the first two, and the buy-in of elites to the third, the Nigeria Project, has been limited. The deck appears stacked against Nigeria, though there are some Nigerian spaces that are naturally national. Perhaps most obvious is the national news media, where journalists and consumers are more inclined to think about the country as a whole. Nollywood, Nigeria's indigenous film industry, is perhaps the most influential in promoting Nigerian national identity. It produces films and TV shows that cater to an Africa-wide audience. The industry is among the strongest and most inclusive symbols of Nigeria within the international community, even though it is dominated by a single ethnic group, the Yoruba, and is centered in Lagos. Finally, Nigeria's national football (soccer) team, the Super Eagles, routinely generates excitement and national enthusiasm every time it plays. Expatriate Nigerians who return home from the United States or the United Kingdom have often shed or minimized their ethnic identities in favor of their Nigerian one. This may reflect the irrelevance of their inherited ethnic identities to their new lives. The Americans and the British among whom they lived have at least heard of Nigeria, if not, say, the Yoruba. Similarly, Nigerians that marry outside their ethnic group often adopt a Nigerian national identity. So, too, do those of mixed race. Nigerian national identity can grow from such roots.

In Nigeria, for Western-educated participants in the modern economy, a sense of Nigerian identity may supersede extended family, ethnic group, clan, or religion. It is from them that the most biting criticism of state dysfunction comes. This group regularly fields a handful of "good government" candidates at each national presidential election. They garner a small percentage of votes. Prominent in the media, academia, the civil service, the medical and legal professions, and parts of the business world, Nigerians with a strong sense of national identity appear to outsiders to be more numerous and more influential than they really are. Too often they are the principal interlocutors of diplomats and policymakers, and thus skew outsiders' perspectives. For now, an underdeveloped sense of national identity accompanied by little patriotism underpins a weak and dysfunctional state. This leaves the field largely clear for elites to "share the cake" among themselves with little resistance and without reference to the vast majority of the population. A weak national identity facilitates the weaponizing of ethnic or religious differences by unscrupulous political figures pursuing a narrow agenda.

Chapter 3

The State of Nigeria

From the implementation of Indirect Rule until today, much of the routine law-breaking by state officials that has gone under the general name corruption has come to constitute the fabric of the state itself.

—Stephen Ellis[1]

The United States conducts its diplomatic relations with the Nigerian state, not with that abstraction, the Nigerian nation. A state is concrete, a nation, abstract. For our purposes, a state is a territory with mostly defined boundaries and with a government that has, among other things, a monopoly on the use of violence in that territory and a set of political institutions that regulate and enforce its power.[2] It is expected to provide services, of which the most important is security, for the people it governs. In this way, "state" is often used as a proxy for "government," though state is a more expansive concept. But just as the application of nation to Nigeria is misleading, so too is the application of this positive conception of a state. This does not mean there are no rules, just that they are different.

The way official statements of US foreign policy are framed with respect to Nigeria (and other African states), however, implicitly presumes the government and the governed are bound by mutual obligations and loyalty, and that the government speaks for the Nigerian people. In making such an assumption—that Nigeria, for all its differences, still behaves like a nation-state—American policymakers and diplomats tend to overlook the dysfunctional relationship between the Abuja government and parts, maybe most, of the Nigerian public. The Nigerian government has been described, among other things, as a "vertically integrated criminal organization with the goal of extracting state resources for personal gain" and its activities as "organized crime."[3] Nevertheless, reflecting the international state system with its origins at Westphalia, the American ambassador to Nigeria is the president's personal representative to the Nigerian chief of state. Unless she or he consciously determines to do otherwise, the default is that the ambassador and other diplomats focus on formal state structures rather than traditional, indigenous authorities and other informal power centers. In Nigeria, therefore, the ambassador is engaging with what many or most Nigerians regard as a criminal enterprise, with long-term consequences that are difficult to foresee. Engaging primarily with the chief of state and his supporting structures is not necessarily written in stone, however. In the last years of apartheid South Africa, the US ambassador maintained correct relations with Pretoria, but most of his energy and that of his embassy was devoted to civil society, some of whose leadership would achieve political power after the 1994 "transition to nonracial democracy." Such an approach recognized the facts on the ground at the time but still respected the authority of those officially in charge. In many countries around the world, a good relationship with the official state government is sufficient; not in Nigeria.

Unlike the formation of most federal states, such as Australia, Canada, Germany, and the United States, the precursor to Nigeria—specifically, the Federal Republic of Nigeria—was not a collection of independent territories that joined, or were joined, together. It was a single unit successively divided into subordinate units by a central government—first colonial, then Nigerian—for political expediency. Nigeria's first relationship with a "Western-style" government was with an exploitive British colonial government. But when the British left, little changed for most Nigerians. Departing British officials were replaced by the Nigerian elite, who moved into their vacated houses in the Government Reserved Areas and took the reins of government handed to them by the departing British. When the military took over in 1966, the relationship between the government and the governed also changed little. The massive public corruption during the oil boom in the 1970s made it clear that the primary goal of the indigenous military and civilian elites was personally to profit from Nigeria's natural wealth while providing a minimal level of order and security. Hence, contemporary Nigerian critics maintain that the fundamentally extractive nature of government has not changed significantly since 1914.

STATE BUILDERS: WHITEHALL AND THE MILITARY

British colonial and Nigerian military governments played the leading roles in shaping the dysfunction of the Nigerian state today and its alienation from the Nigerian people. The British colonial authorities designed the state to maintain an "acceptable" level of security by balancing ethnic and regional groups. Divide and conquer was central to British colonial policy in Nigeria and elsewhere, though within a context of British—not indigenous—law and regulation. It was a policy whose goal was to prevent indigenous people from forming common bonds, lest they unite and challenge colonial rule, as happened in Ghana and India.

Reflecting what they regarded as good colonial governance practice, the British imposed six constitutions between 1914, when they combined their disparate possessions into a single entity that they called Nigeria, and 1960, when that amalgamated territory became independent.[4] In the aftermath of two world wars and the erosion of popular European support for colonial rule, they provided for the gradual admission of Nigerians into government. During the same period, Nigerians also won admittance to the civil service. Nevertheless, British officials were slow even to contemplate the possibility of a central, rather than peripheral, indigenous Nigerian role in the colonial government.[5]

The many constitutions were a part of the lip service the British paid to their goal of fostering Nigeria's eventual development into a modern, democratic state. The three most significant before independence were the Richards constitution (1946), the MacPherson constitution (1951), and the Lyttelton constitution (1954), named after the governors-general in office when they were promulgated. The British largely achieved their goal of funding their governance of Nigeria with revenue raised in Nigeria rather than by British taxpayers. But most of this revenue went to pay the salaries and allowances of the tiny number of British civilian and military officials, not for the education, health, or economic development of their colonial subjects. Such initiatives that did exist were largely under the auspices of missionary and church groups and Islamic organizations and brotherhoods.[6]

As superficial as such reforms appeared at the time—that is, the lives of most Nigerians changed little—they nevertheless shaped the government Nigerians would soon inherit. Serious constitutional reform first took place in the context of the end of World War II, in which Britain leaned heavily on its colonies for manpower. For example, Nigerian troops participated on the British side as far away as Burma. The Richards constitution, imposed in 1946, extended participation to Nigerians in a legislative council, though perhaps its most consequential innovation was the principle of federalism, the theory of which has been consistently maintained up to the present. The Richards constitution established three regions, based primarily on ethnicity: the Western Region was predominately Yoruba, the Eastern Region mostly Igbo, and the Northern Region predominately Hausa-Fulani. In all three regions, there were substantial populations from smaller ethnicities that resented and resisted domination by the largest ethnic group. Each region had an assembly, though it was advisory only. Such an ethnically based organization arguably set the stage for the politics, coups, and civil war that immediately followed independence, all of which were colored by ethnicity.

Unlike the Richards constitution and those that preceded it, the subsequent constitution, promulgated by Sir John MacPherson in 1951, involved consultations with Nigerians. Emerging Nigerian leaders, notably Herbert Macaulay, Obafemi Awolowo, and Nnamdi Azikiwe, had been highly critical of the lack of consultation, especially given Nigeria's participation in the two world wars. In the context of a general anticolonial atmosphere, sponsored by the United States and the Soviet Union in the aftermath of World War II, MacPherson initiated three years of consultations that included Nigerians, albeit mostly from the urban and professional elites. Out of such consultations emerged an elite consensus in favor of retaining a federal system. The MacPherson constitution established a national legislature with a president and regional legislatures. It also required that the majority of their members be indigenous Nigerians. This occurred just nine years before Nigeria would become independent.

Following the Westminster system, parliaments at both the national and regional levels were bicameral, with the executive responsible to the majority in the lower house. The majority of national legislators were selected by the legislatures in the three regions, which were in turn directly elected. Suffrage was extended to all taxpayers except in the Northern Region, where women were excluded. The subsequent 1954 Lyttelton constitution increased the authority of regional governments vis-à-vis the central government. Ministers for the first time were given specific responsibilities, unlike under previous constitutions.

The British governments of prime ministers Anthony Eden and Harold Macmillan, having already determined to end colonial rule, convened constitutional conferences in London and in Lagos to prepare the country for independence. British and Nigerian politicians struck a bargain by which two of the regions, the Western and Eastern, would become self-governing in 1957, and the third, the Northern Region, in 1958. Just before independence, the British promulgated an independence constitution by which the country became independent and acquired dominion status within the Commonwealth of Nations. Under the independence constitution, the queen remained head of state and was represented by the governor-general, who would be Nigerian and who could veto legislation. The Privy Council in London, made up of British subjects, remained the ultimate court of appeals.[7] Though minor constitutional ties with the United Kingdom remained, Nigerians take 1960 as the date of independence. Nigeria joined the United Nations and soon adopted the official rhetoric of the nonaligned movement. Even so, prior to the civil war, the Nigerian government was firmly pro-Western in its international relations in the context of the Cold War, as the British had intended.

Regional elections were held in 1957, and federal elections in 1959, but there was no national referendum in conjunction with independence or the constitution. Elite patronage networks organized themselves to contest regional elections. As one of the three major ethnic groups dominated each of the three regions, these elections assumed a strongly ethnic cast; the dominant ethnic group consolidated around a single leader, who inevitably won the election with little reference or outreach to the many other minority ethnic groups. Once political leadership was established in the regions, parties representing the Northern and Eastern Regions formed a parliamentary alliance that provided them with the majority required by the Westminster system to form a government. The Western Region would be in the minority.

NIGERIANS GOVERNING NIGERIANS

Constitutional and other governance arrangements, including elections, were imposed by the British and reflected their Eurocentric experience and assumptions. As such, they were thoroughly "colonial" and lacked roots in the indigenous population. They were, however, embraced by the tiny westernized Nigerian elite that directly benefited from them. For most Nigerians, British-imposed constitutions and other governance arrangements were largely an irrelevant pantomime that ignored ethnic and religious realities, with traditional authority structures with indigenous roots remaining in place, if often modified.

When the British left Nigeria to Nigerians, they had saddled them with a Westminster form of government that, although now run by Nigerians, was so detached from indigenous institutions and realities—especially ethnic competition—that it survived less than six chaotic and violent years. It was then destroyed by a series of military coups that led to a deadly civil war and a generation of military rule.

As its governor-general, the newly formed government selected Nnamdi Azikiwe, an Igbo from the Eastern Region, while Sir Abubakar Tafawa Balewa, a Hausa-Fulani from the Northern Region, became the prime minister. Broadly speaking, the politics of the moment were organized around ethnicity and region. In the words of Ken Saro-Wiwa, the late Nigerian environmental activist, "These men, by their actions, gave the impression that Nigeria consisted of three ethnic groups instead of three hundred."[8] He was referring to the Igbo, Hausa-Fulani, and Yoruba.

Tafawa Balewa and Azikiwe represented the interests of their respective ethnic groups and regions, rather than the interests of all Nigerians. By 1963, relations between the two began to fray, reflecting ethnic suspicion and individual ambition. The Hausa-Fulani Tafawa Balewa was concerned that the Igbo Azikiwe might be able to remove him as prime minister. That was a motivation for declaring Nigeria to be a republic, abolishing the position of the queen as head of state, the governor-general, and the right of appeal to the Privy Council in London. They were replaced by a president—selected by the prime minister—and the Nigerian Supreme Court as the highest court of appeal, respectively. Hence, on October 1, 1963, Nigeria became a fully independent republic, though ties with the United Kingdom remained close.

After independence, the Westminster parliamentary system imposed by the British quickly broke down under the pressure of ethnic rivalry and corruption among competing elites. A junior officer coup, subsequently taken over by General Johnson Aguiyi-Ironsi in 1966, aimed to end alleged northern domination of the federation and restore security, especially in the fractious and violent Western Region. The coup leaders publicly justified their actions as an effort to address corruption. It was followed a few months later by a "revenge coup" by General Yakubu Gowon, a northern Christian from a minor ethnic group with close ties to the Fulani elite. Both coups were bloody, unlike subsequent ones, and reflected ethnic rivalry and hatred. In the first, coup leaders killed the Muslim prime minister, two Muslim governors, and numerous northern military officers. The second resulted in the death of General Aguiyi-Ironsi. The alleged ethnic and religious overtones of the coup sparked a massacre of Christian Igbos in the north. Surviving Igbos then fled in massive numbers back to their ethnic homeland in the south. That was the precipitating event in the secession of Biafra, the name given to the Eastern Region and dominated by the predominately Christian Igbo (though there were numerous other ethnic groups).There followed the civil war from 1967 to 1970, in which perhaps two million died, mostly from disease and starvation, before the federal forces defeated Biafra and reincorporated its territory into the federation.

THE MILITARY STATE

The military era began with the 1966 coup and ended in 1999, a generation later.[9] This period did not enjoy the same stability as colonial rule; there were eleven officially announced, mostly failed, attempts to overthrow the regime, all of which originated within the military. There were seven military chiefs of state, and two aborted democratic civilian governments. Military governance meant rule by a committee made up of army, navy, and air force officers. Though the military chief of state was the most powerful individual, he did not enjoy unlimited power.

The military quickly dismantled the short-lived democratic institutions that had succeeded the colonial government. While it set aside the constitution, the post–civil war military regime nevertheless saw as intrinsic to its credibility the promise to restore civilian, democratic government, without much internal consensus as to what restoration or democracy would mean. They also saw that their international credibility required deference to the principle of constitutional government. After much internal debate within the military and some broader consultation with civilian elites, the Obasanjo military government imposed the 1979 constitution, which established an ostensibly democratic and federal republic. The current constitution, written in 1999, is a slight modification of the 1979 constitution and was also promulgated by the military—again, with no public ratification—prior to the handover of military power to a newly elected civilian government.

During the civil war, the Gowon government established the parameters for military rule, commonly called "military federalism."[10] Under this arrangement, the military retained the federal structure of the state through which it ruled. But military federalism was not true federalism because the states could not raise their own revenue and they had no powers independent of the federal military government.[11] General Gowon (military chief of state 1966–75) established federal control over all revenue, including that from oil and gas, which, at that time, was not yet the predominate source of government revenue. The states were forbidden to raise revenue on their own and were fiscally dependent on the federal military government.[12] In effect, states became the military government's distribution nodes and administrative units. In 1976, the military took over local governments, reorganized them to make them uniform, clarified their subordination to state governors, all of whom were military officers, and then relaunched them in effect as instruments of the central government. Further, military governments governed by decree and were not limited by law. Constitutional Decree no. 1 in 1966 established the principle that military rule was above the law. Later decrees in 1970, 1984, and 1994 further augmented military authority. Military decrees could not be challenged in courts of law, and all executive and legislative functions were vested in the head of state and the regional governors.

The postindependence period had demonstrated that the three regions, each dominated by one of the big ethnic groups, threatened the power of the central state. Accordingly, the Gowon military government abolished the regions and replaced them with states, initially twelve. Subsequently, elite pressure largely driven by competing ethnic identities led to the increase in the number of states from twelve to nineteen during the Murtala (military chief of state 1975–76) and Obasanjo (military chief of state 1976–79) regime and eventually to thirty-six under the military rule of General Ibrahim Babangida (military chief of state 1985–93). The breakup of three large regions into much smaller states in effect augmented the formal power of the federal government. Unlike the regions, the states were too small and too weak to mount a serious challenge to federal authority. But a likely unintended consequence was the increased prominence of ethnicity in politics. Smaller ethnic groups had previously been marginalized by the large ethnic groups that dominated the regions. Now, they dominated some states and held an ethnic balance of power in others, and the new arrangements did little to encourage state-level politicians to reach across the principal ethnic divides. Instead, ever-smaller ethnic groups agitated for their "own" state, a process that continues today.

After the 1975 military coup overthrew Gowon, the Murtala Mohammed and Olusegun Obasanjo regime—which had undertaken the coup because they claimed that Gowon had abandoned the principle of eventual civilian rule—launched a new transition to civilian governance. Their constitution established a presidential system strongly influenced by that of the United States and one that retained the states and the principle of federalism. There was no ratification process involving the Nigerian people or their representatives. Shehu Shagari won the subsequent election held in 1979. Like both previous and subsequent elections, these were strongly characterized by ethnic voting patterns and competitive rigging by the principal candidates. Shagari's civilian administration was marked by corruption, chaos, and exceptional incompetence. In 1983, he was overthrown by General Muhammadu Buhari, who then suspended the 1979 constitution.

Throughout its long years in power, the military justified itself as cleaning up the corrupt, criminal mess made by the civilians and when that process was completed, overseeing a "transition to civilian democracy." The Murtala and Obasanjo military administration, as part of its preparation for the return of civilian government in 1979, established a range of "corrective institutions," including the corrupt practices tribunal and the public complaints commission.[13] Nevertheless, military governments were always more concerned with stamping out actual and potential opposition than corruption, from which many of them personally benefited. As the years went by, successive military regimes became increasingly intolerant of any opposition and unconcerned about the rampant corruption, except to benefit personally from it.

In the late colonial period, under the First Republic, and during the civil war, the independent civil service promoted efficient, noncorrupt government. Arguably, it played a crucial role in the ultimate nationalist victory in the civil war. However, successive military heads of state saw it as a threat to their power. Over time, they emasculated it, lowered entrance requirements, bloated its numbers, and incorporated it into their patronage-clientage networks. The nadir was reached under Sani Abacha, chief of state from 1993 to1998. He presided over the judicial and extrajudicial murder of opposition figures. The hanging of the Ogoni nine, which included environmental activist Ken Saro-Wiwa, drew international media condemnation. Fatal "automobile accidents" involving regime critics became more frequent. Nigeria gradually became an international pariah but lacked the bureaucratic capacity to become a full-blown police state. Instead of outright repression of the press, for example, the military authorities would shut down a newspaper that published something they did not like for two or three days, thereby destroying the profitability for a month while largely avoiding international opprobrium and its consequences.[14] Hence, the media became—and to a certain extent, still is—self-censoring.

With respect to education, incompetence, rather than malice, seemed to be at the root of decline. At independence and continuing under the First Republic, Nigeria had few institutions of higher learning, but they were of world-class quality. The University of Ibadan and the University of Nigeria at Nsukka regularly appeared on international lists of the "best" universities. But, the popular demand for tertiary education was insatiable, and the elitist, British model of university education became unsustainable, especially for weak military governments whipsawed by fluctuating international oil prices. While the military forbade the operation of private universities, it greatly expanded the number of state-run universities, which more or less followed the American model, to curry favor with the public. But successive military governors failed to provide sufficient funding for them. Professors went unpaid, libraries lacked books, and dormitories were overcrowded. The result was a huge increase in enrollment along with a precipitous fall in academic quality from which the system still has not recovered. Moreover, the economy has never been able to absorb the resulting increase of university graduates too often ill-equipped to function in the modern world.

Under the First Republic, primary and secondary education had to a significant extent been the purview of Christian missionaries. In the eastern part of the country, missionaries were associated, rightly or wrongly, with support for Biafra. Accordingly the military abolished missionary schools and transferred their assets to the state. The result was a dramatic fall in quality of secondary education. The poor quality of the nationalized education system helped stymie Nigerian economic development and its sense of national identity left underdeveloped.[15] In health, the military also closed missionary-run hospitals and transferred their assets to the state, which resulted in a similar fall in quality. Nigerian elites now routinely go abroad to South Africa, the United Kingdom, and the United States for medical services, just as they try to enroll their children in foreign universities or private secondary and tertiary institutions, once again permitted after civilian government was restored. Everybody else who must stay home is subject to declining standards. While private health and educational institutions were allowed to return after civilian government returned, access to their services, if better, is still limited to the relatively well-off. Due to travel bans associated with the 2020 coronavirus pandemic, however, many Nigerian elites, particularly those in government, were unable to go abroad for medical help. Yet the unregulated drain of medically trained Nigerians to more developed countries continues unabated.

In support of their own (alleged) incorruptibility, military governments liked to establish ostensibly independent agencies to deal with difficult problems. For example, the Babangida government established by decree the Environmental Protection Agency, which resembled its US counterpart in aspiration. But enforcement of its rulings was weak and compromised by corruption that benefited connected elites. Military governments also liked to appoint nonpolitical commissions of experts to deal with issues such the creation of new states or reform of the civil service. However, the resulting reports, which were often of high quality, usually were suppressed or ignored. In fact, many aspects of the military governments were spectacularly corrupt and outright criminal. Senior and midlevel officers became rich. After the death of Sani Abacha, the last military ruler, the Nigerian government found that he had hidden at least $3 billion in overseas havens.

Personal security deteriorated. The barred windows, razor wire, and ubiquitous guards around private residences of the rich largely date from the era of military rule. In areas of immediate concern to most Nigerians—competent administration, security, service delivery, education, and health care—military government was distinctly harmful. Michael Watts shows how corruption, mismanagement, incapacity, and greed did likely irreparable damage to Nigeria's forests and greater environment, on which many Nigerians directly rely.[16] The military played a major role in the ongoing alienation of many, perhaps most, Nigerians from the state and probably reinforced their loyalty to family, ethnicity, and religion.

For all its faults, the military could justify its continued rule as the self-appointed guarantor of the secular state and a united Nigeria. To that end, the military claimed to—and to some extent, did—promote national unity and downplay ethnic and religious identity. For example, military chiefs of state rarely wore their ethnic dress in public, preferring military uniforms. Military Chief of State Ibrahim Babangida, a Muslim, did not allow himself to be photographed entering or leaving a mosque. Military governments blocked efforts to extend sharia into the criminal domain, as had been permitted under the British. Officers' clubs in predominately Muslim states served alcohol because they were federal facilities not bound by state law. When the Babangida regime decided to join the Organization of the Islamic Conference to strengthen its international voice, there was an uproar from organized Christian groups objecting to the idea that Nigeria was a Muslim state. To mollify Christian opinion, Babangida thereupon recognized diplomatically the State of Israel, considered in Nigeria to be a "Christian" goal. The military government of Yakubu Gowon established the National Youth Service Corps to promote national unity. The program required university graduates to do public service for one year in Nigeria away from home and continues to this day.

Despite their authoritarianism, corruption, and sometimes violent repression, military governments were weaker than they looked. Not only did they lack bureaucratic capacity, the military was as internally divided as the rest of Nigerian society—by ethnic group, religion, and personal ambition—though its spokespersons always denied it. Similar to the rest of Nigerian society, the military was organized into competing and cooperating patronage networks. Successful and unsuccessful coups characterized military rule. But the military always presented itself as preparing for the return of democracy. Hence the palace coup against Gowon, who had backed away from the principle that military rule was temporary. Muhammadu Buhari was also the victim of a palace coup when a military consensus emerged that his methods for fighting corruption were too rough and accordingly were bringing the military into disrepute.

That said, the seeds of civilian rule were nurtured by the military. While he was military chief of state, Ibrahim Babangida imposed on Nigeria a two-party system, with one party "slightly to the left," the other "slightly to the right." Neither party could be ethnically, religiously, or regionally based. They both must be "national" and thereby promote national unity. Traditional rulers were banned from their membership. While Babangida was forced from office in 1993, today's two biggest political parties, the People's Democratic Party and the All Progressives Congress, are successors of the two parties he created by fiat.

THE CIVILIAN STATE

After the failed democratic republics of the 1980s and 1990s and a generation of ineffectual military rule, Nigerian elites, led mostly by army officers, concluded that overt military rule impeded economic development, foreign investment, and their further personal enrichment. Popular disaffection with military rule also was increasing. Reflecting this mood, the military chief of state, Sani Abacha, had been trying to rebrand himself as a civilian presidential candidate in time for yet-to-be-scheduled elections that would mark another transition to civilian government. He died under suspicious circumstances in 1998.[17] With Abacha's death, a shadowy cabal of military and civilian elites decided they could best preserve their position by restoring civilian government.[18] They took the lead in the Provisional Ruling Council (PRC), the military governance committee that Abacha had headed, which became the venue for negotiating the transition. The first involved negotiating an arrangement by which Abacha loyalists within the military came to accept giving up power to the civilians. The second reconciled the military to civilian governance after it had been established.

In the first phase of the transition, the PRC selected General Abdulsalami Abubakar as Abacha's successor.[19] Working with him, former heads of state Yakubu Gowon and Ibrahim Babangida, longtime kingmaker General Theophilus Danjuma, and retired chief of naval staff Admiral Murtala Nyako sidelined Abacha's followers and secured PRC support for a bargain.[20] The most important elements of the bargain included a wave of military promotions for Abacha's allies to help reconcile them to the change from military to civilian rule. The bargain included only the most tepid of anticorruption measures and granted full immunity to participants in the military government for whatever crimes they had committed, including egregious human rights violations. Abubakar and the PRC then proclaimed a constitution without any public input or ratification; it was largely the same as the 1979 constitution and left in place military federalism, which, as has been said, was not true federalism. They scheduled local, state, and presidential elections between 1998 and 1999. The military kingmakers and their business and other elite allies organized themselves in the People's Democratic Party (PDP), the heir to Babangida's "a little to the right" party. They selected former military head of state Olusegun Obasanjo as their presidential candidate. Obasanjo, a born-again Christian Yoruba strongly supported by Pentecostal preachers, was chosen in response to the widespread feeling among the Yoruba that their ethnic group had been cheated out of the presidency in 1993 when the military set aside the victorious candidate, Mashood Abiola.[21] Obasanjo had a good international reputation, and the military likely also saw him, a retired general and former military chief of state, as someone who would protect their interests. The military and its business allies duly installed Obasanjo in the presidency in the rigged 1999 elections that were so bad that former president Jimmy Carter, an election observer, refused to endorse them and abruptly left the country. But for Nigeria's international partners and those Nigerians who wanted the military to return to the barracks, the end result was good enough. Yet again, a form—not the substance—of democratic system of government was imposed by an elite bargain with virtually no popular public input.

The second phase of the transition—reconciling the previous military rulers with their new civilian overlords—had three elements. First, through the PDP and its business allies, the kingmakers established a path for military officers to retire and accumulate wealth through the party and the private sector. In return, they could not participate in politics. Second, there was another round of promotions for those who stayed in the military. With these two understandings in place, the military appeared to be satisfied with relinquishing formal power. Finally, the PDP reaffirmed the principle of "power shift," that the presidency would alternate between the north and the south every eight years. This was necessary to reassure the north, which had dominated military governments, amid the selection of Obasanjo, a Yoruba Christian, as president.

The bargain of 1998–99 set the parameters of prebendal politics in civilian-ruled Nigeria until the elections of 2023, when the arrangements collapsed under pressure for jihadist insurrection in the north and the transformation of civilian culture among Christians by Pentecostalism. While it lasted, the process was entirely driven by the military and their business allies and largely without reference to public opinion. Abubakar, Babangida, Danjuma, and Obasanjo—architects of the settlement of 1998–99—are all still politically active today, twenty years later, though mostly behind the scenes. The personal interests of those who had participated in the military governments were protected, there was no prosecution for crimes committed under Abacha, and the merger of military and business elites was facilitated. Though the civilian government had the form of a democracy, its origins and practice were far from it.

It is no surprise that the Nigerian constitution does not have the popularity and legitimacy enjoyed by the constitution of, say, South Africa, which is associated with the end of apartheid and Nelson Mandela. South Africa's constitution has been the basis for an unbroken stream of credible elections since 1994. It is both a symbol of national unity and a cause of it. Alas, Nigeria has no national icon, and elections since 1999 have been rigged.

THE STATE OF NIGERIA TODAY

Only during the late colonial period and the First Republic was federalism real, with the regions possessing substantial autonomy and the ability to raise revenue. Since the 1966 coup, Nigeria has never been a federal state, in the sense that the states are genuinely independent in certain spheres from the center. The military created a centralized state with only the trappings of federalism, and that arrangement has endured. Similarly, under the Fourth Republic, the principle of the separation of powers nominally exists, with the executive, legislature, and the judiciary coequal. In reality, however, executive power is sweeping, and presidents have regularly ignored the other two branches of government. Presidents have refused to enforce court decisions that they do not like. Similar to the judiciary, the National Assembly remains weak in the face of executive power.

Military governments divided oil and gas revenue according to a formula that strongly favored the federal military government over the states. Offices similarly were distributed. In civilian administrations since 1999, each state had been entitled to a minister and a minister of state. However, following his election as president in 2015, Buhari reduced the cabinet from seventy-two to forty-three. Even so, the cabinet remains large and unwieldy and plays little institutional role.[22] Similarly, ambassadorial posts were distributed among the states, and this arrangement was retained by subsequent civilian governments. On the one hand, in the context of such an arrangement, the personal power of the president has grown since the restoration of civilian government, not least because it directly controls the actual allocation of the oil revenue. Oil became more centralized in the presidency as the state as a whole became weaker. Some presidents, including Olusegun Obasanjo and Muhammadu Buhari, have been their own oil ministers. A president may, on his own authority, exempt any individual or company from payment of taxes, including himself and his enterprises.[23] On the other hand, from an institutional perspective, presidential power is severely limited by a weak bureaucracy with low capacity to carry out executive initiatives. Any president also must manage rival patronage-clientage networks that are too powerful for him to dominate or destroy. Twenty years after the end of military rule, Nigerian chiefs of state still also look over their shoulders at the possibility of another military coup.

Dislike of those governing Nigeria is an old song. For many, perhaps most, Nigerians the state at best is essentially irrelevant to their lives, and at worst, it exploits them. Paying taxes is usually accompanied by a population holding its government accountable. Taxes are a manifestation of a social contract between the government and the governed. Taxes bind together the people and the state. That link is weak in Nigeria. An Afrobarometer poll in 2017 showed that over 40 percent of Nigeria's population would refuse or had refused to pay taxes or government fees when they disapproved of government action. Out of thirty-six African countries surveyed, Nigeria had the highest proportion of such answers.[24] The tax base is generally low. There are nineteen million registered taxpayers, perhaps 25 percent of the working-age population and less than 10 percent of the total population. The process for identifying those Nigerians that should pay taxes often seems erratic and arbitrary. The ratio of tax revenue to gross domestic product is one of the lowest in the world, about 6 percent.[25] But if Nigerians are not paying taxes, they are paying bribes under many circumstances—in effect, an unregulated tax. An analysis of polling data showed that in 2009, about a fifth of respondents had made "side payments" to acquire necessary documents, while 27 percent had paid a bribe during the previous year related to water and sanitation.[26]

The tax revenue raised by the states—which may impose income and other taxes, though not on oil—is, perhaps unsurprisingly, insufficient to cover their budgets. The deficit is usually made up by the federal government, though this too is often insufficient. Even in Lagos, the country's most-developed state economically, the federal contribution was more than a quarter of the state's income for the 2019 budget.[27] In 2015, when oil prices were low, twenty-three of the thirty-six states were unable to pay their civil servants on time because of the decline in payments from the federal government.[28] Altogether, public servants—federal and state—number 870,000. Even when oil prices are not abnormally low, revenue from oil is still insufficient to cover the salaries, allowances, and expenses of politicians and public servants. When government salaries are not paid, civil servants turn to their extended family, their patrons, and corruption, often in the form of extracting bribes.

The Nigerian state depends more on oil than on its citizens to fund its activities, while its citizens often get by with little help from the state. Under these circumstances, it is difficult for the citizenry to hold the state accountable, and the state, controlled by a relatively tiny number of elites, can proceed largely without reference to the general public. The separation, even alienation, of many or most Nigerians from the Nigerian state is fundamental to the ongoing insurrections that plague the country.

GOVERNANCE AND THE GOVERNMENT

After independence, many of the Nigerian elites, though still rooted to traditional mores, nevertheless shared the ultimate goal of the British to create a modern state. By following that path, they would also gain admission to the international system.[29] As a practical matter, new African heads of state and their associated elites had little choice: they and their new states entered a world of European design and definition, and their independence required European legitimization. For example, international organizations upon which independent African states depended, ranging from the United Nations system to the international financial institutions to the organizers of the modern Olympic Games, were of European or American origin and reflected the concerns and preoccupations of their creators. Africa now had borders that were legally inviolable and new rules about how to interact with people on the other side of them.[30] By the twentieth century, if not earlier, there was only one political paradigm universally accepted: the sovereign nation-state.[31] It presumed that the people within a defined country, or state, should have a certain degree of loyalty to it and to each other, and would share some form of identity, even patriotism. At the very least, this iteration of the international system required a central government that commanded the loyalty or the acquiescence of most of the people in its territory—in Africa, as demarcated by European colonial officials—and that the newly independent government maintain a monopoly of force within its borders.[32]

In Nigeria, these attributes were mostly lacking in substance at independence and many remain largely aspirational. Postcolonial elites maintained the form of a modern state without the support of a nation with a commonly accepted history or unifying narrative. Hence, Nigeria's postindependence Westminster parliamentary system lacked roots. It was unable to contain ethnic and religious rivalry, and governance progressively broke down until military coups destroyed it soon after independence. An absence of patriotism and a still-weak sense of shared national identity limit popular loyalty to institutions and underpin the government's political and administrative incapacity, in turn meaning that there have been few brakes on the rapaciousness of Nigeria's cooperating and competing elites.[33] By and large, those who run Nigeria do not see themselves as accountable to the government or the people they ostensibly lead. Evidence of alienation is anecdotal, but it is supported by the testimony of leading Nigerian intellectuals such as Chinua Achebe and Wole Soyinka. But a more recent proxy could be participation in elections, which has declined from a peak of 70 percent in 2003 to a low of 27 percent in 2023. (The extent of violence and intimidation plays an important role in determining voter participation as well, and it varies from place to place.) Instead, they do feel accountable to their families and the patronage networks of which they are a part, not least because they are often the centers of their economic livelihood and because they provide a minimal safety net that in more developed nation-states comes from the state.

The recognition accorded by other sovereign governments to the Nigerian state is stronger than that by many Nigerians. Moreover, international recognition is crucial to the self-regard of Nigeria's competing and cooperating elites. The state, and their control of it, is basic to their interaction with the outside world, ranging from international corporations to the foreign schools and hospitals where they educate their children and receive their health care. As two notable scholars put it: "The legitimacy of a government in the eyes of its citizens must be distinguished from its legitimacy in the eyes of other states; it is international legitimacy that is significant in the juridical attribute of statehood. A government may be legitimate internationally but illegitimate domestically, or vice versa."[34]

Maintaining the trappings of a modern nation-state has become a higher priority for elites than providing health care, education, or security to most Nigerians. There are also practical considerations for elites. For example, they need passports that only the state can provide, while ordinary Nigerians who cannot travel have no such need.

In 2005, the US National Intelligence Council suggested the concept of governed space in African countries resembling islands in a sea of ungoverned spaces, an "archipelago."[35] The term archipelago is associated with Aleksandr Solzhenitsyn. He used it to refer to the network of gulags under Stalin as similar to an archipelago in the "sea" of the Soviet Union.[36] The picture of government authority operating only on islands in a sea of ungoverned spaces fits Nigeria well. The federal government faces constraints in imposing its authority. Nationwide, the police number only about 371,000 in 2021. To meet a benchmark of 1police officer per 450 residents, about 100,000 more officers would be needed. They are poorly trained, poorly paid, and often lack the trust of their communities.[37] There are funding constraints to expanding the police rapidly, and there is a shortage of potential recruits.[38] Security, albeit limited, tends to be provided by the Nigerian army, which has units stationed in every middle belt state and much of the rest of the country. But the army is also stretched thin, often poorly trained and poorly paid. Police and military salaries can be in arrears for weeks or months. In effect, the Nigerian state does not have the ability to monopolize the use of violence or project force. Local communities fall back on vigilantes to provide security.

Ungoverned spaces, hence, are not really ungoverned. In the opening years of the twenty-first century, Nigeria, like many other African states, effectively had two governances. One was the formal state created by the colonial authorities, which was later legitimized by international recognition upon independence. The other was based on institutions and practices that reflected how Nigeria's different religions and ethnicities had organized themselves, how they had been manipulated by the British under indirect rule, and how they have evolved since independence.[39] The latter are often all but invisible to diplomats because they do not look for them, and generally, most foreign policies are too centered on the formal government in the capital to accommodate them.

As has been said, Nigeria describes itself as a federal republic. But in practice if not in theory, the thirty-six Nigerian states have little autonomy. It was the federal military government that created the states; the states did not create the federal government. The Nigerian states lack fiscal independence from the federal government, which meets most of their needs. There is no equivalent to the American state and local police forces. Nigerian states do have specific responsibilities, in education, for example. But because state income is dependent on the federal government, in effect, it is the federal government that determines the scope and direction of education. The fact that each Nigerian state has a governor, a legislature, and usually a university makes them appear more independent than they really are. The Nigerian reality is closer to the French departments than American states or Canadian provinces; they function as administrative units for a central government, albeit one that often lacks the technical and bureaucratic capacity of the highly centralized French government.

Nevertheless, as the central government has weakened under Yar'Adua, Jonathan, and Buhari, the governors of some states have new space in which to assert themselves. As states are increasingly dominated by a single ethnic group, this assertion can assume an ethnic cast, further undermining the independence ideal of Nigeria and a multiethnic democracy. The putative presidential victor in the elections of 2023, Bola Tinubu, established his power base in Lagos state and defied Nigerian presidents. In addition to his advantage as a Yoruba in a Yoruba-dominated state, Tinubu also has the skills to build political alliances outside his orbit. That was crucial to his 2023 presidential victory.

One of the most significant aspects of the 1979 and 1999 constitutions was their institution of Federal Character. Specifically, the conduct of government shall "reflect the federal character of Nigeria and the need to promote national unity and also to command national loyalty."[40] In so doing, the government will ensure "that there shall be no predominance of persons from a few states or from a few ethnic or other sectional groups in that government or in any of its agencies."[41] The constitution stipulated the creation of the Federal Character Commission, which is charged with ensuring that the principle is achieved. This manifested in two important and interrelated ways. First, it reaffirmed the organization of Nigeria into states, most, to varying degrees, controlled by a specific ethnicity and either Christian or Islamic in character. Government jobs were to be more or less equally awarded to people indigenous to all the states.

Second, the principle of Federal Character drove the distribution of Nigeria's oil revenue, which was collected by the federal government. During the civil war, the military chief of state, Yakubu Gowon, established in a 1969 Petroleum Decree that all petroleum revenue would go directly to the federal government. At the same time, he also interdicted states from raising revenue of their own. Federal Character stipulated that federal wealth be distributed equitably to each state by a formula. During the Second Republic, legislators passed the 1981 Petroleum Allocation Act, which allocated 55 percent of oil and gas revenue to the federal government, 32.5 percent to be divided among the states, and 10 percent to local governments.[42] (The remainder was accounted for by a "bonus" to the oil-producing states.) The general principles of this system have been in effect ever since, though with certain amendments and accommodations, particularly for oil-producing states. Recently, for example, 52.68 percent of oil and gas revenue is allocated to the federal government, 26.72 percent to the states, and 20.60 percent to local governments.[43]

In many nation-states, together with strong bureaucracies and institutions, patriotism—or love of country—would help channel these funds to the public good. But in Nigeria, patriotism and the state together have been too undeveloped to serve as a brake on elite behavior. Westernized Nigerians often bemoan the lack of a strong and widespread sense of patriotism, and they see it as a major driver of Nigeria's bad governance and of a society that, despite extraordinary religiosity, too readily exploits the poor to benefit the rich. In Nigeria, the state, rather than a vehicle to protect and support Nigerians, is the means through which elites access hydrocarbon wealth for their own benefit. History is the villain here: Nigerians and Nigerian elites are no better or worse than any other group of people. Rather, British colonialism created a state detached from the people incorporated within it. British rule was racist in its assumptions, authoritarian in its style, and extractive in its intent. The Nigerian elites that succeeded largely followed in their footsteps, substituting ethnicity for racism. They were authoritarian, promoted ethnic identity, and exploited for private benefit the public revenue. Economic policy and practice, under both British colonialists and Nigerian generals, retarded and distorted Nigeria's transformation into a polity worthy of its people's loyalty.

For probably most Nigerians, be they adherents to Christianity, Islam, or traditional religion, citizenship in heaven is more important than on earth. Though the Nigerian state is secular, it has close ties with Christianity and with Islam. In fact, the government provides financial support for pilgrimages to Jerusalem and Mecca. Northern Muslims often see the secular state as created by the British and indigenous Christians and therefore as fundamentally Christian in character.[44] However, Muslims in other parts of the country, especially Yorubaland, accept the secular state and participate in it. For their part, Nigerian Christians tend to downplay conflict between secular and religious authority. However, where there is such conflict, most Christians give precedence to their religious allegiance. Among both Christians and Muslims, the American and French concept of separation of church and state is anathema. And religious loyalty usually supersedes loyalty to the state.

THE "NIGERIA PROJECT"

At the time of independence, the "Nigeria Project" looked to provide for national unity based on democratic values and aspirations rather than ethnicity or religion. But those hopes were soon deferred by coups and a generation of rapacious military rule. Further, given strong ethnic identities, the colonial origin of the Nigerian state, and its shallow democratic roots, it is by no means certain that the goals of the Nigeria Project could have been achieved quickly even under more favorable circumstances. Nevertheless, the Nigeria Project has never altogether disappeared. Interest in the Nigeria Project, sometimes under a different name, appears now to be reviving, especially among the young and Western-educated. Its ideals motivated younger, good-government candidates in the 2019 presidential election and support for the 2023 candidacy of Peter Obi.[45] While in 2019 none of them won a significant number of votes, they contributed an issues-based dimension to the presidential campaign that otherwise largely revolved around personalities and the building of ethnic and regional coalitions. In 2023, however, Peter Obi won more than a quarter of the votes cast. Nigeria's growing candidate pool may indicate that in semi-authoritarian states, repeated elections improve certain aspects of governance without necessarily transitioning a regime any closer to democracy.[46] Exposure to the various debates in the issue-based campaigns shapes political participation and the formation of opinions and fosters a vision for what is best for individual voters and the nation's future. American policymakers would do well to monitor and encourage the revival of interest in the Nigeria Project.

What diplomats see as the politics of the Nigerian state is primarily an elite sport divorced from the concerns of the majority of Nigerians, mostly a matter of how to cut the cake and manage personal rivalries. Political parties and elections thus have an air of unreality about them, even if elections often unleash violence among local ethnic and religious rivals.[47] Despite their shortcomings, participation in elections reflects the aspiration of the Nigerian people for something better than what they have; it implies their recognition of some kind of connection between their personal fate and the Nigerian state.[48]

As we have seen, Nigerians still identify primarily with their family and village, their religion, and their ethnic group, while identification with the formal state is secondary or tertiary.[49] But identification with ethnicity does not preclude the popular expectation that the state will or should provide services. Nigerians, both urban and rural, have an understanding of the functions and the services the state should provide—and that it fails to do so. Hence, the continued widespread disillusionment with the state reflects its failure to meet popular expectations.[50]

When government income soared during the 1970s oil boom, elites captured this revenue and the state for themselves. While the ideals of the Nigeria Project persisted among the few, politics and public life became mostly transactional—a vehicle to accrue wealth through access to oil-based revenue—and centered on individuals seeking maximum benefit for themselves and their families at the expense of their rivals and of Nigerians outside their own charmed circle. Politics became a zero-sum game with winners rotating among the elites, which often had close ties with the military and its regime.

By August 2, 2007, Nigeria had existed longer as an independent state than as an amalgamated colony.[51] So what of the "Nigeria Project," the vision at independence of a multiethnic, democratic state free of corruption and with the heft to give Black Africa a seat at the highest international table? That aspiration is far from having been realized. Personal favors and resources are exchanged for political and other support largely without reference to formal institutions, and public resources are privatized. Urban as well as rural voters expect personal benefits as opposed to public goods from politicians who win office. Hence, under military and civilian government, the impetus of the chief of state has been toward the centralization of resource management at the expense of the rest of government. This reality has undermined fundamentally the principles of federalism and the Nigeria Project.[52]

Chapter 4

Sharing the Cake

The nation was seen as a "cake" that had already been baked. The sharing of the "national cake" was the preoccupation of politicians.

—Ken Saro-Wiwa[1]

In the more developed parts of the country, the modern world seems close at hand. There are innovative technology hubs in Lagos that operate without reference to government at any level.[2] Cell phone use is ubiquitous, and urban roads are choked with traffic. Especially in the Lagos-Ibadan corridor and in Abuja, consumer goods are widely available, and there is a small middle class based on the knowledge economy. Nollywood, the indigenous film industry, is influential all over Africa. There is an array of familiar, formal government institutions including, to take only two examples, the Securities and Exchange Commission and the National Universities Commission. There is an active stock exchange in Lagos. Commercial aviation ties Lagos and Abuja to most parts of the world. Nigeria is represented in nearly every relevant international and regional organization, holding leadership positions in many. Its athletes regularly participate in the Olympics and the World Cup. Over one hundred Nigerian embassies cover the world. For outsiders, Nigeria *looks* like a modern, democratic, and federal state with an influential international presence.

This is largely illusory. Nigeria's heritage of colonialism, coups, a civil war, ethnic and religious conflict, and military rule retarded the development of a Nigerian national identity and of the governing institutions of a modern state dedicated to addressing the needs of its people. The coincidence of authoritarian, military government following a devastating civil war with sudden oil wealth was a disaster. There were not institutions to manage the oil wealth in place, and military rulers encouraged the expansion of prebendalism. A half century after the end of the civil war, the federal government provides few services and therefore matters little for the majority of the population. But for elites, it is, and has been since the end of the civil war in 1970, the primary venue for the sharing-out of public revenue and office and managing their own rivalries, or "sharing the cake," as they say. Through office and patronage networks, they control and use the state. Hence, for elites, the state is essential. As for other Nigerians, however, many turn to informal institutions, ranging from traditional rulers and religious leaders to magic and cults. So, too, do the elites on occasion.

The previous two chapters included three arguments: First, Nigerian national identity is weak. Instead, most Nigerians primarily identify with and are loyal to their family, religion, and ethnic group. Second, the state is largely an agency of exploitation, both a holdover from British colonialism and now the product of corrupt Nigerian elites. More specifically, prebendalism—the entitlement of an officeholder to wealth by virtue of their holding the office, as opposed to their work—defines the behavior of the political system. And third, government control is "archipelagic," made up of mere islands of authority in a sea of spaces in which the writ of the central government does not prevail, just as it was during the colonial period. Sixty years after independence, Nigeria does not fit well into the prevailing paradigm of international relations, in which the fundamental unit of foreign policy is the nation-state. Rather, Nigeria is a prebendal archipelago, with its own rules designed to benefit a narrow elite.

WHO ARE THE ELITES?

A cartel of elites, national in scope, shapes the Nigeria with which the United States pursues bilateral relations and has so often partnered on issues of mutual concern. Effective US diplomacy requires an understanding of them, but also of emerging rivals, especially religious and traditional leaders who are shaping public opinion. There is a useful distinction to be made between the elite cartel that managed the 1998–99 transition to civilian rule and is still active today and the broader category of individuals known as elites. Peter Lewis identifies the ruling elite cartel as made up of certain politicians, high-ranking military officers, a few bureaucrats, traditional rulers, and business tycoons.[3] They are few in number and know each other personally. Ayo Sogunro lays out a useful topography for the broader elite, which overlaps with the cartel.[4] His identification of elites includes: the royal families of Nigeria's myriad ethnic groups; the politicians that succeeded the British after independence and, through their privileged political positions, personally profited from it, the subsequent civil war, and the oil boom; the senior military officers who governed the country for a generation and are probably the largest part of the elite; and finally, business entrepreneurs and top professional people, especially lawyers, accountants, and entertainers. To this list should be added modern religious leaders, especially Pentecostal and evangelical pastors associated with megachurches.

In the aftermath of their rule, the upper ranks of the military largely merged with, or were absorbed by, existing elites. That same process seems to be underway with respect to Pentecostal preachers. They have become a legitimizing force for the elite cartel, especially in the predominately Christian south. They were an important part of the elite base of presidents Obasanjo, Jonathan, and even Tinubu, a Muslim though with a Christian wife.[5] (Christians overwhelmingly supported the failed presidential candidacy of Peter Obi in 2023.)[6]

Given the size of Nigerian extended families, the elites are numerous in absolute terms, though a tiny percentage of the population. If the elites are 1 percent of a population of over 200 million, they would number more than 2 million—multiple times larger than the elites of any other African country. Up to now, most of the elites are directly or indirectly dependent on oil. They are numerous enough to make a splash in the luxury real estate markets of London, New York, Dubai, Johannesburg, and Los Angeles. In one of the poorest countries in the world, not all of the elite are very wealthy, though most are.

Some elites are born, others are made. Many elites acquired their status in the postindependence era, most notably those in the military who worked their way up the ranks to hold senior positions in military governments, positions that they could then exploit for private benefit. During the era of military rule, military leaders would often conduct private business on the side, as would government officials. Upon the transition to civilian rule, one of the measures in the bargain, of course, explicitly sought to provide for private business opportunities in return for the military's acceptance of the new arrangement, hence the many former military leaders in private business. Today, Nigeria's business elites include current and former military and government officials, but also enterprising Nigerians who came from little and "hustled" their way to the top. This includes aspiring politicians who can seek the patronage of a political godfather to make it in politics in exchange for the promise of future access to government money and political control. Entertainers and artists are an even newer category, reflecting the rise of the Nollywood film industry and the growing international popularity of Nigerian music and art. While the elites are predominately male, they do include many women, usually officeholders, businesswomen, entertainers, and daughters of traditional rulers or historic figures.

Boundaries among categories of elites are fluid. A look at the four presidents since the return of civilian government in 1999 is illustrative. Olusegun Obasanjo was born poor but attended Baptist Boys High School in Abeokuta, where he received a modern education. After a short spell teaching school, he entered the army. He then received extensive British military training as he rose through the ranks of the late colonial and early independence army, eventually becoming military chief of state after helping to overthrow the military regime of Gowon. Released from prison in 1998 after the death of the dictator Sani Abacha, who had jailed him on spurious charges of treason, he was all but penniless. But after eight years in the presidency and twelve years as an "elder statesman," one estimate of his net worth is $1.5 billion.[7] While he remains a leader of the national elite cartel, the quasi-hereditary traditional Yoruba elite has never fully accepted him.

Obasanjo's successor as president, Umaru Yar'Adua, was part of the traditional northern elite by birth and through his elder brother, General Shehu Yar'Adua, he too had connections with the military elite; Shehu Yar'Adua had been Obasanjo's deputy when the latter was military chief of state from 1976 to 1979. Umaru Yar'Adua was, in effect, a client of Obasanjo's, and so it was no surprise when, after the National Assembly declined to amend the constitution so Obasanjo could run for a third presidential term, he chose him for the presidency in 2007. Though Yar'Adua had plenty of opportunities, he showed no interest in enriching himself while president.

When Yar'Adua died in office, he was succeeded by Goodluck Jonathan.[8] The new chief of state was born into a family of canoe makers in the Niger Delta. He earned a doctorate in zoology and became an environmental protection officer. After he entered politics in 1998, he became a client of Obasanjo's. With the latter's help, he was elected deputy governor of Bayelsa state in 1999. Obasanjo subsequently engineered his appointment as governor when his predecessor was removed from office quasi-legally. At the start of his political career, Jonathan was not part of an elite.[9] It was office and the wealth it opened to him that made him a part of the national elite cartel, and also of the Ijaw elite. According to an estimate by the Nigerian media in 2014, his net worth was $127 million.[10]

President Muhammadu Buhari self-identifies as Fulani, but he is not accepted as part of the traditional elite, which is primarily hereditary, or by many in that ethnic group. In other words, he is an elite that is Fulani, but he is not a "Fulani elite." Like Obasanjo, who is also not accepted by many of his fellow Yoruba as part of the traditional elite, he made an army career and conducted a successful coup against the civilian government of Shehu Shagari. His tenure as military chief of state was short, lasting fewer than two years before he, in turn, was overthrown by a coup engineered by General Ibrahim Babangida. But his brief term as chief of state guaranteed him a place in the highest elite circles. He ran unsuccessfully for the civilian presidency in 2003, 2007, and 2011. In 2015, he won and was reelected in 2019. He appears to have little interest in accumulating wealth and lives modestly. His official assets declaration in 2015 listed a herd of some two hundred cows, three private houses—one of which is made of mud—and a bank account.[11]

If Buhari lives modestly, many of the elite are very wealthy by international standards, especially those from the military and business. Overseas is the usual venue for conspicuous consumption for Nigerian elites, unlike Gulf oil oligarchs who spend it at home. For example, one of the Nigerian elite kept his yacht in the Caribbean, and more have houses or apartments in Dubai, London, Johannesburg, New York, and Los Angeles. At least four Pentecostal pastors have use of private jets costing up to $30 million each.[12] Nigeria's richest man is Aliko Dangote, worth an estimated $10 billion in early 2020.[13] He built on his father's substantial fortune made in cement and milling. As of September 2019, he is joined by Mike Adenuga with an estimated net worth of $8.7 billion made in banking.[14] Unusual for rich Nigerians, at least up to the 2020 coronavirus pandemic and fall in oil prices, Dangote and Adenuga are some steps removed from oil. The ethnic and religious royals appear less wealthy. They can be politically powerful in the territories where they hold sway, though their power has limits. Sanusi Lamido Sanusi, emir of Kano from 2014 to 2020, for example, publicly criticized the governor of Kano state for corruption. The governor proceeded to remove and replace him. If the acquisition of wealth is easy for elites that have captured the state, hanging on to it may be more difficult. Muslim Hausa-Fulanis and some Yoruba "big men" (Christian as well as Muslim) have multiple wives and many children. Of former president Obasanjo and the former vice president Atiku Abubakar, one Christian, the other Muslim, each has more than twenty, which is not regarded as unusual for men of such stature. Among Muslims, there is equality of inheritance within genders; in other words, sons receive more than daughters, but all sons and all daughters receive the same. There is no system of primogeniture that ensures that great fortunes passed as a package from one generation to another, such as existed in England until 1925. Elaborate estate planning and trust mechanisms are still in their infancy at home, and the wealthiest avail themselves of such services abroad. Further, elite conspicuous consumption and the shortage of a range of investment vehicles means that even great fortunes can start to run out by the second generation. That reality intensifies competition among elites who always need more money for their children, their ever-growing extended families, and their patronage-clientage networks that allow them to keep their privileged positions and exercise influence.

Nigerian elites are not monolithic or well organized, like, say, the eighteenth-century British parliamentary Lords and Commons with shared values and a collective sense of (if often misplaced) responsibility toward the larger society and with ultimate accountability to God. In Nigeria, elites are fiercely competitive in seeking power and money, but they cooperate just

enough to preserve the system—and themselves. Though they are not necessarily more or less self-aware or self-interested than any other ruling group in
any other country at any other time, they do appear to be less public-spirited,
in part because they lack institutions that would encourage working for the
public good and discourage their private gain. These institutions, in turn, are
weak because national identity is weak. Allegiance to the public good too
often is superseded by allegiance to ethnicity, religion, and rival patrons.

Like other ruling elites, they like to think well of themselves, and they do
not perceive the current system and their role in it as maliciously exploiting
their fellow countrymen. Here again is the sense of entitlement described as
prebendalism. For many of them, poverty is the will of God, not the result of
a politico-economic system from which they benefit. Indeed, like their fellow Nigerians, Christian and Muslim, most of the elites have a lively belief
in heaven and hell, of a system of divine rewards and punishments. In this
life, they pride themselves on almsgiving, as the Friday crowds at the front
gates of Muslim "big men" attest. Among the superrich there is even the
beginnings of philanthropy, but it confers no tax benefits, unlike in the United
States.[15] Many Nigerian philanthropists make significant donations to educational and civic institutions abroad rather than in Nigeria, thereby burnishing
their international reputations but also because of the greater certainty that
their contributions will not be seized by a Nigerian government at some point
in the future. For most of them, the current Nigerian political economy is the
reality in which they find themselves at this moment in time, and they are as
insecure about the future as their struggling countrymen, if in a different way.
Most of the time, for them, if there is a villain, it is not the elite individual but
the polity in which they live and over which most of them feel they have little
control. Hence, by and large, they have little personal incentive to change it,
but much to preserve it.

The power and influence of elites is often accessed through certain positions in government. Public officeholders have ready access to oil wealth,
often by means of kickbacks from government contracts, "fees for services
rendered," privileged access to purchase or lease of government-owned oil
blocks, and outright oil theft (called "bunkering" by Nigerians), often by
means of false invoicing and cargo diversion.[16] But though they may rely on
the government to channel their influence, they do not exercise it through
the appendages of the state. Instead, they do so through their patronage and
clientage networks, which involve all types of elites and therefore can span
institutionalized religion, ethnic and religious leaders, and others in the business community. These relationships, especially at the top, are often borne
out of political expediency, not shared political or policy views. Hence, they
are not necessarily forever and can be broken by either party. For example,
two of the three presidential successors to Obasanjo have been his clients,

Yar'Adua and Jonathan. On the one hand, after a year in office, Yar'Adua managed to establish his independence from Obasanjo and largely excluded him from governance. On the other hand, Obasanjo broke with Jonathan during the last two years of the latter's presidency, largely because of the president's incompetence. Though the federal government is weak, the president is strong because of his control over government revenue. Hence, he is the center of the system.

HOW NIGERIANS ORGANIZE

Elites, then, operate in two primary spheres. Peter Ekeh describes this situation as one of "two publics." There is the civic public, associated with the Western institutions of government and politics introduced during colonial times, and the traditional public, which relates to the precolonial polities and identities. As was already discussed, Western conceptions of government and citizenship, such as democracy, an independent judiciary, and the government bureaucracy, were imposed by the British and in some ways are still treated as foreign. These institutions and the people that run them wield government power but with little moral authority.[17] Institutions associated with traditional leaders and ethnic organizations command loyalty in part because they are imbued with a moral authority that is based on history, culture, and religion. If it is no sin to steal from the federal government, it is unacceptable to steal from a traditional ruler, from the family, or from one's patron or client. Within such parameters, most Nigerians are as honest as anyone else.

Stealing from the government is largely acceptable because the government offers Nigerians nothing. Instead, the extended family and Christian, Muslim, and ethnic structures provide what safety net there is. Christian churches and Muslim brotherhoods provide services to their respective flocks ranging from medical care to education to charity. As with other aspects of Nigerian society, they are organized around patronage-clientage networks. Bishops, preachers, emirs, imams, and mallams directly intervene in secular politics, instructing their respective flocks to vote for particular candidates. Among Christian denominations, boundaries are fluid. Traditionally, the Yoruba have been Anglican while the Igbos have been predominately Roman Catholic. However, the explosive growth of Pentecostalism has made distinctions among denominations of European origin increasingly irrelevant, and many Christians move easily from one "brand" to another. Among Muslims, especially in the north, brotherhoods are closely aligned with traditional emirate structures. However, the emergence of Salafist radical forms of Sunni Islam and the arrival of Shia Islam are unsettling the brotherhoods and the emirate system as a whole. Boko Haram, as will be discussed in chapter 5, is an all-out assault on traditional Nigerian Islam, targeting establishment leaders where it can.

Elites usually operate within patronage-clientage networks of people and organizations defined by ethnicity, religion, government position, business interests, or some combination thereof. These run the gamut from respectable professional and cultural organizations such as the Nigeria Bar Association and the Nigeria Medical Association to vigilante bands that promote specifically ethnic interests to criminal thugs. Especially in the south, a potent mixture of magic and fear is centered at shrines and oracles, often of precolonial origin. While they are anathema to Muslim and Christian religious leaders, they hold strong sway among parts of the population.

Federal Character is the primary organizing principle of national politics. It seeks to ensure the distribution of government office—and all the power, prestige, and money that comes from it—throughout the country. Put simply, it institutionalizes patronage in the political system.[18] But the states are increasingly captured by a specific ethnic group. The operation of Federal Character accentuates the country's ethnic and regional differences among elites and sharpens ethnic competition. The formula for the distribution of oil revenue, a major dimension of Federal Character, is a continuous irritant. Elites in the oil-producing states on the one hand have a strong sense of grievance that they benefit inadequately from the oil that is produced on their land and in their waters. That grievance is shared by the general population in the Niger Delta. On the other hand, elites in other parts of Nigeria accuse those in the Delta of profligacy and misuse of the extra dividend they receive as oil-producing states.

In the Delta, traditional elites have been weaker and more diffuse than elsewhere since the colonial period. There was no equivalent to the emirs in the north or the Yoruba kings, despite British efforts to create "warrant chiefs" through whom they could rule indirectly. In many places in the oil patch, environmental degradation has long since destroyed the small-scale fishing and farming by which most local people earned their living. Organized militants with some popular support challenge traditional elites, such as they are, whom they disdain as having sold out to the federal government and the oil companies. Militants feed off a popular, profound sense of grievance over the "unfair" allocation of oil wealth. Though the population is almost entirely Christian, precolonial religion and religious practices remain strong, with oracles and shrines providing one alternative to the secular state.

The traditional system of intra-elite bargaining appears to be strongest in Yorubaland and the southwest. Traditional religion continues to be an important part of Yoruba identity, supported by traditional Yoruba institutions and cultural practices, even though the "imported" religions of Christianity and Islam each claim half of the Yoruba population. A traditional ruler, the ooni of Ife, is an important focus of Yoruba unity, including those now living elsewhere in West Africa and in Brazil. However, the explosive growth of Lagos, Ibadan, Abeokuta, and numerous small cities poses a challenge to the power of traditional elites.

In the north, Fulani elites are still largely organized according to the precolonial emirate hierarchies. Perhaps because Fulani traditional rulers retain so much power and are more salient than other traditional rulers, the federal and state governments intervene more frequently than in other regions in their affairs. For example, the dictator Sani Abacha deposed one emir of Kano and replaced him with another. In 2019, the governor of Kano moved to divide the single Kano emirate into five, thereby dramatically diminishing the power of the then emir, Sanusi, with the tacit—if not more—approval of President Buhari. As we have seen, the governor later dethroned the emir because of the latter's outspoken criticism of gubernatorial corruption.

Elites dominate Yoruba, Hausa-Fulani, and Igbo "cultural associations" through which they wield considerable political power outside formal government institutions. The Yorubas have Afenifere, which regularly takes political positions designed to increase Yoruba influence. Yoruba leaders can field a powerful militia, the Oodua's People's Congress (OPC). Its initial purpose was to counter the Hausa-Fulani that have pushed into Yoruba areas, sparking clashes over land and water along ethnic lines. In 2006, in a court affidavit, the Nigerian government accused the OPC of having been complicit in the killing of up to ten thousand people since 1999. Around the same time, the Bakassi Boys, an Igbo vigilante group, was accused of involvement in one thousand executions.[19] The Arewa Consultative Forum is ostensibly a Hausa-Fulani cultural organization. It, too, has significant political influence and has links with the Arewa People's Congress, a militant organization. In the south and southeast, among the Igbos, current militias are focused on revival of the independent state of Biafra, especially Ohaneze Ndigbo. The better-known Movement for the Actualization of the Sovereign State of Biafra (MASSOB) and the Indigenous People of Biafra (IPOB) are political groups rather than militias. Egbesu, an ethnic Ijaw militia, focuses on their alleged political and economic grievances, though they also have a criminal element.[20] Ethnic militias, often self-appointed, vary in their degree of centralization and discipline depending on circumstance.

Where the state cannot provide security, communities organize militias and vigilante groups to carry out the functions that otherwise would be assumed by the military and police. They respond to local security issues, such as cattle rustling and other criminality, and some have protected their community against the depredations of both Boko Haram and the security services. In January 2020, it was estimated that local vigilante groups had been created in roughly two-thirds of Nigerian states, and many are explicitly or implicitly ethnically denominated. Ebonyi and Lagos states, for example, have neighborhood watch groups that primarily provide information to the official police force. The six states of Yorubaland, in response to rising criminality, primarily kidnapping, set up Amotekun, a regional operation that was meant to support the federal police in their effort to, among other things, curb kidnapping.[21] In many northern states, the Hisbah enforces compliance with sharia. Some local Hisbah organizations are supported politically and financially by the state government, while others are volunteer-led and do not involve the state.[22] Though these groups can differ greatly, they are all, in one way or another, responding to the same fundamental problem: the inability of the state to provide security.

Perhaps the most well known of such groups is in Borno state, where the Civilian Joint Task Force (CJTF) assists the military in its fight against Boko Haram. It helps gather information, polices communities, and even participates in combat operations. Local hunters, men and women who know the area well, can also assist the military in tracking down Boko Haram operatives, and some are absorbed by the CJTF for particular operations.[23] Organized in response to Boko Haram in 2013 and currently numbering about thirty thousand volunteers, the CJTF functions in many ways like a militia.[24] It has some formal links to the regular security services, which it is supposed to assist and supplement.[25] A small percentage of its operatives even receive wages from the Nigerian government. But community reliance on vigilante groups can be problematic. Some, including the CJTF, illegally recruit child soldiers, defined under Nigerian law as being under eighteen years of age. As are members of the Nigerian security services, they are accused of many other human rights abuses, including score-settling in local feuds. Still, local militias are a reality of insecurity. Nigerians protect themselves where their government cannot.

JUJU AND SHARIA: SEEKING LAW AND ORDER

Under the British and continuing up to the present time, there has always been alternative, extralegal governance to that of colonial Lagos or postindependence Abuja. These alternatives are based on precolonial practices and involve religion, magic, and other aspects of the spirit world. For outsiders, shrines are shrouded in mystery, with occasional, hysterical media reportage that hints at human sacrifice and cannibalism.[26] But a large number of Nigerians, including elites, turn to them for justice, to resolve disputes, and even foretell the future, not least because they conclude they cannot get such services from the federal or state governments that are based on Western law and procedure.[27] In the southeast, oracles and shrines controlled by priests devoted to local gods continue to be deeply involved in the administration of justice according to prevailing social norms and without reference to the secular state. Shrine cults are so powerful at the grassroots that state and federal governments, be they colonial, military, or civilian, have not been able to suppress them. Their judgments and sanctions are respected and accepted by local communities. Oracles are closely associated with traditional, pantheistic religion. Nominally Christian, Muslim, or secular persons will resort to them, especially for oath-swearing and to determine whether a witness is telling the truth. Political figures regularly exploit shrines and oracles to advance their personal agendas. However, it would be wrong to infer cynicism on their part. They make use of the supernatural centered on oracles and at shrines to advance their highly materialist agendas while nevertheless firmly believing in the spirit world. For example, Chinwoke Mbadinuju, the Anambra state governor from 1999 to 2003, required his cabinet to swear their loyalty to him at a local shrine.[28] The overall magical system is called "Juju."

At its most fundamental level, Juju is a form of magic. Magic, in turn, is a human effort to subdue the gods and forces of nature normally beyond human control. For many Nigerians, the gods, ancestors, and spirits are near at hand, sometimes literally so; many Nigerians routinely bury close relatives in or adjacent to their houses, and they regularly consult their spirits. Juju is sometimes dismissed as folkloric or a reaffirmation of ethnic identity. Many Americans—estimates are 12 to 25 percent—including former first lady Nancy Reagan, consult with the supernatural, especially through astrology.[29] Yet for its adherents, and they are legion in Nigeria, Juju is a much larger part of their lives than astrology or other forms of the occult are typically among Americans.

Belief in truth-telling Jujus is widespread and influences popular media. The Nollywood film industry regularly produces videos about crime and misconduct in which the villains are brought down by gods invoked by the righteous through Juju. However, Nollywood videos will also show wrongdoers accessing Juju for evil purposes.[30] The premise of Nollywood and its audiences is that Juju is an objective reality that exists alongside—and is not inferior to—that which is based on modern science. Most markets in Nigeria have stalls where Juju apparatus is sold.

Like any supernatural belief system, Juju is often exploited to advance criminal or quasi-criminal agendas. For example, traffickers in Edo state, in the country's south, will promise a woman a job in Europe and will lend her the necessary fare. Prior to her departure from Nigeria, a trafficker will make the woman swear a Juju oath that promises to visit destruction on her family should she not pay back her debt. Once the trafficked woman arrives in Europe, there is no job and she faces a massive debt; to pay it off, she will be forced to turn to sex work. Bound by the Juju oath, should she somehow escape or fail to pay, Nigerian traffickers and pimps based in Europe will contact their colleagues in Nigeria and order them to exact revenge, such as setting the girl's family home afire.[31]

Juju's flourishing, especially in the oil patch, reflects a collision between the traditional world of gods, spirits, and demons and the modern, secular world with its pollution of the natural environment and its political and social marginalization of people living in the Delta. Militant fighters invoke charms that will protect them from bullets and wear amulets linking them to a particular deity. The role of Juju in kidnapping of foreigners is almost completely ignored by outside negotiators seeking their release. Indeed, most negotiators have no idea how to access Juju and its priests. As one Africanist has noted, "Houston oil men and Washington bureaucrats struggle to understand how the world price of oil can be affected by the antics of Niger Delta warlords sporting juju amulets as well as AK-47s."[32] More generally, the persistence of Juju is also a reflection of the weakness of the Nigerian secular state and its inability—thus far—to meet the needs of most Nigerians. Moreover, Juju also contributes to state weakness by positing a more powerful and more attractive pole of popular loyalty than the Nigerian state.

Sharia—a highly sophisticated system of law based on the Koran and ancient Islamic texts found in the Hadith and the Sunna—is, like Juju, a kind of answer to the weak state. Among Muslims, it is an important alternative to secular law. Sharia is a living, legal tradition that has evolved over time. Judges, called qadis, administer a system of justice that has extensive protections for the rights of the accused but can also exact extreme punishments.[33] Some Nigerian qadis dismiss sharia's horrific punishments, such as stoning and amputation, as non-Islamic imports from Saudi Arabia.[34] Such punishments are rarely, if ever, carried out in Nigeria. During the colonial period, the British recognized sharia in the predominately Muslim parts of Nigeria. Though it never applied to British subjects or to Christians, in cases involving families that include both Muslims and Christians, it can in effect be applied to the Christian party. In the run-up to independence, sharia was banned from the criminal domain as part of a British-sponsored effort to reconcile the north and the south with the goal of moving the country quickly toward independence.

But sharia courts are popular and justice is quick. Without the requirement for expensive lawyers they are conducted in the local language, usually Hausa, and not in English, which many plaintiffs do not speak. Accordingly, in 1999, with the end of military rule and with it, the government's repression of salient religious identity, most of the northern states moved to restore sharia to the criminal domain. Sharia fundamentally contradicts the secular nature of the Nigerian state, but Obasanjo at the time allowed it to go forward, in part to appease northern sentiment, in part, because he likely was not strong enough politically to oppose it. It was met with controversy and viewed with suspicion by Nigeria's Christian population, which often sees the growing popularity of sharia courts as evidence of an effort to "Islamicize" the entire country. Among non-elites, the belief was widespread that the restoration of sharia would end the exploitation of the poor. The failure, presided over by Nigeria's traditional Islamic establishment, gave life to antiestablishment forces, more radical and sometimes violent, that are part of the origin of Boko Haram.[35]

SHARING THE CAKE: HOW NIGERIA STAYS TOGETHER

As fractious as Nigeria is—with its competing elites and variegated systems of formal and informal local governance—it stays together thanks to the reliance of national patronage networks on the state. The state is the means by which elites access government revenue, historically derived primarily from oil, often referred to as the "national cake." They access it both for themselves personally and to fund their patronage networks and any political ambitions they or their clients may have. But the state is kept institutionally weak so that it does not challenge elite interests. Under indirect rule, elites shared power with each other as subordinates to the British, and, subsequent to independence, with military rule, many of whom they co-opted. By now the system they have created has absorbed potential rivals, be they upstart politicians or entrepreneurs. They have "captured" the state, which in turn has "captured" profits from oil and gas. Nigeria's elite-dominated political system has become even more predatory on the majority non-elite Nigerians.[36]

The 1999 elite bargain that led to the transition from military to civilian rule included the principle of "power shift," ensuring that power rotated between a Christian from the south and a Muslim from the north every eight years. It also confirmed Federal Character, the principle that high office and revenue were apportioned among the states by a politically determined formula. Hence, the 1999 bargain was an effort to share political power and access to oil wealth. Ensuring that elites from all regions and ethnic groups share the cake inoculated the country against an ethnically and regionally based civil war, such as had happened during the civil war of 1967–70. Subsequently, President Yar'Adua extended the principle of sharing the cake to Delta militants in his "amnesty," whereby their leaders were, in effect, transformed into a prebendal elite through the receipt of "amnesty payments."[37]

Before the cake is to be cut, it must be baked. That task has fallen to the Nigerian National Petroleum Corporation (NNPC), the state-owned monopoly that historically has overseen, in one way or another, the generation of all revenue from oil and gas.[38] The Nigerian state owns all oil and natural gas within Nigeria's territory, including its territorial waters. However, almost all of Nigeria's oil is produced through joint ventures or production-sharing contracts between NNPC and the big Western producers and a growing number of independents, often Nigerian-owned.[39] The oil companies are responsible for most of the costs of production and share the revenues above a determined threshold with the Nigerian government. ExxonMobil, the largest producer, is American owned. Shell, once the largest oil company operating in Nigeria, is Anglo-Dutch, though a large percentage of its shareholders is American. Other large producers are Chevron (American), Statoil (Norwegian), and Petrobras (Brazilian). Many American companies also have prominent positions in the oil services industry. While Chinese companies have expressed interest in a Nigeria presence, thus far they have been largely unsuccessful. That may change; President Buhari expressed interest in swapping oil blocks for Chinese construction of infrastructure in Nigeria.

After it subtracts the costs of production, has paid its foreign partners, usually in oil, and has sold its crude on the international markets, the NNPC is meant to send the remaining US dollars, in which oil sales are denominated, to the federal government's Federation Account. The web of revenue streams, shell companies, and subsidiaries that make up the NNPC is complicated to a fault. How the NNPC is funded and structured at present make it rife with opportunities to steal oil revenues before they ever make it to the Federation Account.[40] The Petroleum Industries Bill (PIB), in the works for years, is designed to reform the oil industry. It has recently been signed into law; the challenge will be its implementation.

In 2013, as governor of the Central Bank of Nigeria during Goodluck Jonathan's presidency and before becoming emir of Kano, Sanusi released a three-hundred-page report stating, among other things, that he could not account for $20 billion of NNPC revenue. His claims were dismissed by most members of the administration, including Diezani Alison-Madueke, Jonathan's oil minister at the time, and Jonathan fired him.[41] A subsequent investigation largely exonerating NNPC and government officials lacked credibility. In 2017, Alison-Madueke became the center of corruption allegations relating to her time as minister. According to allegations from the US Department of Justice in 2017, she used her influence to steer no-bid oil contracts to Atlantic Energy, a Nigerian energy company co-owned by Kolawole Aluko, and Seven Energy, which he cofounded in 2004. In exchange, the owners of the company funded her "lavish lifestyle," conspiring to, among other things, "purchase millions of dollars in real estate in and around London for Alison-Madueke and her family members."[42] At issue was the fact that Atlantic Energy and Seven Energy did not have the technical capacity to fulfill their contracts; soon after receiving them, the two companies subcontracted production to other firms. Aluko was just one of "the minister's men," which refers to young oil traders who received lucrative contracts from the NNPC.[43]

Such corruption is costly. From 1970 to 2008, Nigeria lost $217.7 billion in cumulative illicit financial flows, defined as "cross-border transfers of funds that are illegally earned, transferred utilized." In other words, ill-gotten wealth was transferred out of Nigeria. Of this $217.7 billion, 60 percent involved commercial activities, specifically, multinational corporations hiding their wealth by evading taxes, skirting payment of customs duties and levies, and mis-invoicing imports and exports. Further, between 2004 and 2013, Nigeria lost $17.8 billion each year in potential revenue.[44] Mis-invoicing alone cost Nigeria $46.5 billion between 1996 and 2014.[45] In 2014, the $2.2 billion lost to mis-invoicing represented 15 percent of the country's total trade and 4 percent of that year's government revenue.[46] According to Raymond Baker, the founding president of Global Financial Integrity, "the practice of trade mis-invoicing has become normalized in many categories of international trade."[47]

Once the NNPC revenue that survives the complicated machinery of corruption reaches the Federation Account, it is divided among federal, state, and local governments, with a "bonus" paid to the oil-producing states in the Niger Delta. A formula, painstakingly derived through a political process in the National Assembly, determines how much money goes to each level of government. The revenue that goes to the federal government and its expenditure is relatively transparent. However, the revenue intended for state and local governments is disbursed to state governors. They, in turn, are responsible for its distribution to the state and local governments. That process is not transparent. In theory, state legislatures should hold governors accountable. As a practical matter, they rarely do as they are often part of the governor's patronage network.

PRESIDENTIAL ELECTIONS

Winning elected office at virtually any level provides access to the cake, including government contracts and influence. As Elnathan John puts it:

> The Nigerian God loves elections and politics. When you have bribed people to get Party nomination, used thugs to steal and stuff ballot boxes, intimidated people into either sitting at home or voting for you, lied about everything from your assets to your age, and you eventually, (through God's grace) win the election, you must begin by declaring that your success is the will of the almighty and living God and that the other candidate should accept this will of God.[48]

Competition for office and related dealmaking takes place within the two major political parties, the All Progressives Congress (APC) and the People's Democratic Party (PDP). While neither reflects or addresses the issues that have bedeviled politics in the past, especially ethnicity and religion, competition is nevertheless fierce and deadly. Still, the APC and PDP are better understood as two parts of a single party than two distinct parties. In this way, Obasanjo and his civilian successors in effect have a one-party system, with the PDP and the APC functioning as its two wings. In terms of policy, the two are indistinguishable from each other. Both are instruments of the elites, and politicians and candidates and voters move easily from one to the other depending on their self-interest. Neither party is democratic in reality, though they both feature primaries that are the venue for elite manipulation and competition. The run-up to primaries is often the occasion for violence as rivals seek to eliminate their opponents.

Elections are organized by the Independent National Electoral Commission (INEC). There is a chairman, appointed by the president, and a commissioner in each state, whose appointment is usually strongly influenced by the governor. Many chairmen have been little more than appendages to the presidency, but Attahiru Jega, who presided over the 2015 elections, was widely known for his independence and his integrity. That being said, INEC's ability to do its job is limited by the fact that it usually is starved for funds, making it particularly dependent on international donors and politically weak. Its lack of resources contrasts sharply with the lengths that aspirants to political office will go to get their piece of the cake.

While competition is fierce, and official administration of elections anemic, the system still has rules. Hammered out during the contentious negotiations leading up to the transition to civilian government, chief among them is "power shift." Since the colonial period, a dilemma of governance has been how to reconcile the north to its incorporation into the federation. Part of the dilemma was that by the mid-twentieth century, the south was so much more developed economically, and notably richer, that the north feared its dominance. As has already been noted, the north was unenthusiastic about independence, which meant substituting (from its perspective) close-at-hand Lagos for faraway London and the end of indirect rule, by which the northern elite had maintained its power. During the postindependence period, and during the long years of military rule, the north dominated governance, not least because the military was heavily officered from the north, and Buhari, Babangida, Murtala Mohammed, Abacha, and Abubakar were all Muslims from the north and middle belt.[49] The end of military rule and the coming of civilian administration meant that, inevitably, there would be a power shift in favor of the south. Further, Yorubaland—which includes Lagos and the heart of the modern economy—deeply resented the military's annulment of the elections of 1993 in which a Yoruba, Mashood Abiola, had won the presidency in credible elections. The elite cartel that orchestrated the transition recognized the need for addressing Yoruba grievances and reconciling the north to civilian rule. Hence, the cartel searched for a way that Yorubaland in the south would supply the first civilian president but would not forever dominate the federation.

The elite cartel, charged with bringing the country to civilian, democratic rule, settled on Olusegun Obasanjo, a Yoruba, as the next president. At the same time, the cartel secured the formal acceptance by the PDP of the principle of "power shift." That is, every eight years (two presidential terms) the PDP candidate would alternate between the north (Muslim) and the south (Christian). A corollary in practice was that if the presidential candidate were Christian, the vice presidential candidate would be Muslim, and vice versa. Accordingly, the Christian Obasanjo was president for eight years. To recapitulate, at the end of his second term, he tried but failed to set aside "power shift" by amending the constitution so that he could run for a third term. The elite cartel was sufficiently united to block him. He then handpicked as PDP presidential candidate a northerner, Umaru Yar'Adua, a Muslim and the brother of his deputy when he had been military chief of state. Obasanjo also engineered the selection of a southern Christian, Goodluck Jonathan, as the vice presidential candidate. The opposition presidential candidate was the northern Muslim, Muhammadu Buhari; his vice presidential running mate was a southern Christian. The elites then saw to it that Yar'Adua and Jonathan were rigged into office in the elections of 2007.

After a long illness, Yar'Adua died in 2010. Jonathan became president. The understanding, strongest in the north, was that Jonathan would step aside in 2011 after finishing Yar'Adua's term and the PDP presidential candidate again would be a northern Muslim; the north's turn would then run until 2015. However, well lubricated with money, Jonathan won the PDP nomination and was rigged into the presidency in the 2011 elections. He appeared to have successfully set aside the principle of "power shift." However, his victory was followed by violent rioting in the north, with an estimated eight hundred killed in Kaduna alone. The rioting morphed into what appears to have been a religious pogrom, in some places against Muslims, in other places against Christians. Subsequently, the elite cartel and the broader northern political and business establishment appeared to turn away from Jonathan. His presidency was characterized by eroding security associated with Boko Haram and economic hardship resulting from low international oil prices.

Jonathan ran again in 2015. His victory would have meant that a southern Christian would have occupied the presidency from 2010 to 2019 and for a total of seventeen years of the Fourth Republic's twenty years by then, thereby compromising the principle of "power shift." He secured the PDP nomination, but significant numbers of PDP "big men" left the party and joined the All Progressives Congress (APC), the party of opposition candidate Muhammadu Buhari. Supported, often quietly, by the principal personalities that had negotiated the transition in 1998–99, the opposition won the presidency at the ballot box for the first time in Nigeria's history.

The restoration of "power shift" was confirmed by the elections of 2019. It was still the north's turn, so both the PDP and the APC fielded northern, Muslim candidates, incumbent president Buhari for the APC and Obasanjo's former vice president, Atiku Abubakar for the PDP. Both also had southern, Christian running mates. But the elections were problematic. Turnout was low, only about 35 percent of registered voters; there appeared to be widespread vote buying; and the security services, under the authority of the president, were widely accused of voter suppression. Results, once collected, were collated at centers after dark and with little scrutiny, feeding suspicion that final tallies would be manipulated. Indeed, the elections resembled those of 1999, 2003, and 2007.

Despite the apparent survival of power shift in 2019, it may have been dealt a mortal blow by the elections of 2023. After eight years of the presidency of Buhari, a northern Muslim, it was the southern Christian turn. But, two Muslim "big men," Bola Tinubu and former vice president Abubakar Atiku, successfully manipulated the machinery of both parties and secured their presidential nominations, Tinubu of the APC, Aiku of the PDP. So, both mainstream parties ran Muslim presidential candidates, though Tinubu is a Yoruba from Lagos. A candidate of a minor party, Peter Obi, a southern Christian, won about a quarter of the vote. It remains to be seen, but the "duopoly" by which the presidency rotated between north and south, Christian and Muslim, every eight years appears to have ended.

In the aftermath of 2015, many international observers thought that Nigeria had turned the corner and was embracing a democratic culture. A. Carl LeVan, in a study published before the 2019 elections, concluded that the electorate in 2015 had responded at least in part to issues rather than traditional "big man" politics, that there was genuinely independent voter behavior.[50] Based on a study of media, he concluded that the APC had campaigned on the basis of bread-and-butter issues while the PDP campaigned on security. In a period of economic recession, a significant number of voters went for the APC. LeVan ultimately concedes, however, that religion and ethnicity still factored heavily into voter choice. In other words, religion and ethnicity were still the best predictors of how voters voted in 2015. In 2023, Peter Obi was in effect the "Christian" candidate

The conventional wisdom, then as now, is that the elections of 2015 marked a significant step forward in Nigeria's governance with Jonathan conceding to Buhari without riots or lawsuits. However, especially in light of the shortcomings of the 2019 presidential elections, the 2015 elections appear to have been a reversion to the 1999 elite bargain, including the principle of "power shift," which Jonathan had violated by running in 2011. But if the elections of 2019 reaffirmed the consensus surrounding power shift, the elections of 2023 would indicate that it has imploded, under the pressures of economic misery, COVID-19, and the general collapse of security nationwide.

THE 2003 GUBERNATORIAL ELECTIONS IN ANAMBRA STATE

The Anambra state gubernatorial election of 2003 has become the poster child for the intense competition for elected office. Those elections illustrated the clash of patronage and clientage networks, the use of traditional institutions including shrines, the role of "godfathers," and the influence of money.[51] In Nigeria, a godfather is said to be the person who is able to determine which potential candidate a party nominates for office and then to ensure that his candidate is elected. Once elected, the successful candidate repays his godfather for his support under terms dictated by the latter. As a former governor says, "Money flows up and down . . . these honorable members [of the Oyo state assembly] during the election period, they want the patronage of the puppeteer. Afterward, money flows in the opposite direction—back from the puppet to the puppeteer."[52] Hence, the purpose of an officeholder is to advance the private interests of the godfather, which usually means providing access to public money for his private use. The relationship between the godfather and the officeholder is largely transactional; both stand to gain financially at the expense of a state entity, whether federal, state, or local. Money, not policy, is what ties them together.

In the 2003 Anambra gubernatorial elections, the incumbent governor, Chinwoke Mbadinuju, was a member of the ruling party, the PDP, and was therefore more or less guaranteed his party's endorsement for reelection. In the PDP party primary, he won all but seven of the almost two hundred delegate votes. When Mbadinuju had been first elected governor in 1999, it was with the help of his political godfather, Chief Emeka Offor, who was a close friend of Vice President Atiku Abubakar. He has been described as "one of the twenty wealthiest Igbos." According to Nigerian media, the source of his wealth was oil and gas and government contracts.[53] Mbadinuju was said to have guaranteed ten million naira a month in state revenue to Offor in exchange for his election in 2003. Fulfilling that obligation may be why he had trouble paying state government salaries, which routinely were in arrears.

Shortly after receiving the 2003 nomination, the party big men forced Mbadinuju out of the race, most likely because he fell out with Chief Offor.

With his departure, new primaries were held within the PDP. Chief Chris Uba, close to President Obasanjo, somehow met Chris Ngige, a medical doctor and a former civil servant with modest political ambitions. Uba then played godfather to Chris Ngige, who won over 70 percent of the PDP primary votes.[54] Chief Uba then oversaw the successful rigging of the gubernatorial election in favor of Ngige.

To secure the chief's support, Ngige agreed that Uba would have control of "all government contract awards and appointments in Ngige's cabinet." Ngige also promised to "exercise manifest absolute loyalty to the person of Chief Chris Uba as my mentor, benefactor and sponsor."[55] The agreement was ratified at the Okija shrine in Anambra state, implying to all parties that to break the oath could result in supernatural consequences, even death. (Members of the state assembly that Uba sponsored also swore shrine oaths.) Uba also required Ngige to sign a letter of resignation that he would hold, presumably should there be a falling-out.[56]

And there was indeed a falling-out. According to media sources, Ngige refused Uba's demand for three billion naira for his installation as governor. Ngige also refused to release 860 million naira to Uba for work for Anambra state that Uba's companies had not completed. After their falling-out, Chief Uba, with dozens of state politicians loyal to and dependent on him, had Ngige arrested by the inspector general of the Anambra state police, and he presented the pre-signed resignation letter to the state assembly, many of whose members were already clients of Uba. The deputy governor was then sworn in as governor. However, Ngige was able to contact Vice President Abubakar, who ordered him released and reinstated, and eventually the PDP expelled many of the perpetrators of the episode, including Chief Uba, from the party. The PDP in Anambra was coming apart.[57]

President Obasanjo then intervened, characterizing the episode as a "family affair" to be resolved within the party. He appointed a reconciliation committee, headed by the then senate president and a former governor. They hammered together the "Owerri Accords." Under this agreement, Ngige agreed that Uba was entitled to "influence" a certain number of his appointments as his benefactor. Ngige was restored to the governorship. By his sponsorship and acceptance of the Owerri accords, Obasanjo signaled that Uba's expectation of access to Anambra state resources in exchange for his support for Ngige was reasonable.[58]

As the 2003 Anambra elections show, political godfathers used communal and religious identity, together with cash, to mobilize supporters and get their clients on the party ticket and into office. Securing party nomination for an office, from the lowest to the highest, is too often characterized by use of thugs. Gangs such as the Area Boys in Lagos or the Yandaba gangs in Kano or the antecedents of Boko Haram in Maiduguri provide the muscle for candidate brawling. But despite the sometimes chaotic and violent competition for these lucratively remunerative positions, there is the understanding that this is all part of the game.

ACCESSING THE CAKE

The atmosphere in elections is winner-take-all, and the take is much. The Socio-Economic Rights and Accountability Project (SERAP), a Nigerian good-governance watchdog, reviewed state laws governing benefits that governors were entitled to once out of office. Among other things, the ex-governor of Akwa Ibom state receives a yearly pension of 200 million naira (about $550,000 in 2019), a new utility vehicle every four years, an aide, a cook, chauffeurs, and security guards, free medical care anywhere in the world, and a five-bedroom house in Abuja. This is in addition to the privileged access a government official would have to state contracts when in office, itself a further avenue toward their personal enrichment and that of those in their network.[59] In the National Assembly, the number of committees has increased by more than half since 2011. Committee chairs often receive a pay bump, and so creating new committees is understood to be another way to reward loyalists with chairmanships and deputy chairmanships.[60] A riddle that makes the rounds in the Niger Delta city of Port Harcourt is "Why does Abuja, which has no water, have so many bridges [highway overpasses], but the Delta has too much water and no bridges? Answer: Abuja controls the contracts."[61]

Within that context, widespread election rigging is common. Rather than being centrally directed at the national level, local elites appear to determine where and when rigging is necessary. While rigging can be exceedingly sloppy, it is no less effective.[62] In the Second and Third Republics, rigging was characterized by ballots failing to arrive at selected polling places, the destruction of ballots, and the use of violence and intimidation to suppress turnout, often by ad hoc groups of thugs. In the 2019 elections, the government deployed the military nationwide to ensure "peaceful elections," even though it is illegal for the military to be near voting stations. In effect, soldiers intimidated and impeded voters, particularly in those areas where Buhari's then challenger, Atiku Abubakar, had the most support. Elsewhere, vote buying has become common. According to anecdotal evidence, a vote cost about $35 in some parts of Lagos state. Finally, as in the past, vote tallies are collated at night, often out of the sight of election observers, and totals can be "adjusted." According to former president Obasanjo, "With all due respect, if Jesus Christ could come to the world and be the chairman of [the

Independent National Electoral Commission], any election he would conduct will be disputed."[63]

As elections have become more important to the international reputation of the Nigerian government and the elites that control it, so too have election observation teams. The largest number are fielded by Nigerian civil society. The Situation Room, led by human rights activist Clement Nwankwo, is an umbrella organization of civic groups that observed the 2019 elections all over the country. There are also numerous international observers, including teams from the United States, the European Union, the Commonwealth, and the African Union. Because of security and other concerns, what they actually observe is limited. However, their presence often provides a shield for domestic observers from security service intimidation. In presidential elections, the losing candidate invariably appeals to the courts to have the results set aside because of voting and counting irregularities. There is a hierarchy of judicial procedures, culminating in the Supreme Court. However, the judiciary at its upper reaches is controlled by any incumbent presidency, and no presidential election results have ever been set aside.

In the 2019 national elections, Obi Ezekwesili, Donald Duke, and Kingsley Moghalu were presidential candidates of minor parties. They addressed serious policy issues, seeking to make elections about policy rather than personality. All three were well educated. All three had lived for significant periods in the United States, and all three were outside the purview of traditional Nigerian politics based on patronage-clientage networks. Though they tried, they were never able to unite behind a single "good government" candidate and none resonated with the electorate. Peter Obi, in 2023, shared some similarities with Ezekwesili, Duke, and Moghalu. He was much younger than Tinubu and Atiku, well educated, and an advocate for "good governance." But his electoral appeal was based on his Christian religion.

HOW TO THINK ABOUT CORRUPTION

Nigerian public life is corrupt from both a Nigerian and American perspective. But while Nigerians also denounce corruption, and a candidate's anti-corruption platform is always popular, individual Nigerians also want a slice of the corruption cake for themselves. "The citizenry are simultaneously victims, accomplices, and active participants in their own corrupt downfall," wrote historian Max Siollun.[64] Corruption extends throughout the warp and the woof of Nigerian life. Recall that Yoruba chieftain and founding father Obafemi Awolowo's supporters applauded his personal corruption as a manifestation of their own political power vis-à-vis other ethnic groups. The expectation of his fellow tribespeople was that he would share what he stole.

Failure of a patron to share generously with his clients results in popular censure. In his own book, however, Awolowo called corruption the "greatest defect of the Native Court system."[65] Corruption is the essential lubricant for these patron/client networks, high or low. In a very poor country with most government salaries so low and so often in arrears, survival would be all but impossible without bribes. Participation in corruption is a requirement for any individual who needs a government service, no matter how small.

Stephen Ellis observes that there is a difference in understanding between the developed world and Africa about the appropriate behavior of government. In Nigeria, Ellis argues, activities often classified as corruption are actually the product of three factors: first, patron-client relations; second, the application of technocratic and academic approaches and models of foreign origin that do not fit Nigeria's reality; and, third, the history of the government's exploitive exercise of power. Ellis summarizes: "In short, corruption in Nigeria is a shorthand term for a complex situation in which the reality of governance differs from the legal framework that formally constrains the operations of government. It is precisely in this gap that political power is generated and vast fortunes are to be made."[66]

Corruption in Nigeria, then, is largely a social and political way of operating, rather than purely criminal. Has corruption become so structural and elite exploitation of everybody else so pervasive that the Nigerian state is essentially a criminal enterprise? The answer is not straightforward. Within the local context, illegal behavior is normalized to the point that it is no longer viewed as corruption. There are, however, understood limits to corruption. Small payments "for the boys" to a policeman at a checkpoint is relatively acceptable, if a nuisance.[67] Looting the state of millions of dollars of oil revenue and moving it offshore, as former petroleum minister Diezani Alison-Madueke stands accused of, is not. A "big man" is expected to share the profits of his corruption with this clients and other dependents. Should he not do so, he risks losing his clients. Clients are also expected to share upward any windfalls, however, meager. Should they not, they risk losing their patrons.

NIGERIA'S GLUE IS LOSING ITS STICK

The country's cooperating and competing elites have succeeded in preserving the state, for themselves and for their clients. From the end of the civil war in 1970 to the outbreak of an insurrection in the oil patch in 2005, a modicum of security was maintained, though criminal violence greatly increased even within its relative stability.[68] A federal government that commands international recognition remains important to the ruling elites, but it must be kept weak so as not to interfere with elite activities and interests. A weak government manages access to oil wealth, the NNPC "bakes the cake," and the elites cut it to their advantage largely without opposition from outside their charmed circle. Despite the concentration of oil production in the southeastern part of the country, the fundamental principle of distribution, enshrined in Federal Character, is that oil revenue is to be shared throughout the country and not remain solely in the oil-producing region. Hence, elites outside the oil patch have access to oil revenue only because they are part of the Nigerian state, a powerful incentive to keep the country together.

But the future of this oil-centric model of governance is far from certain. In early 2020, on the heels of a price war between Saudi Arabia and Russia and made worse by the global coronavirus pandemic and subsequent drop in world economic activity, the oil price plunged. The price of oil eventually stabilized. But it is hard to see oil prices ever again achieving their former levels; as recently as 2011, oil sold on the international market for over $110 a barrel, and Nigeria, as well as many other African governments, was flush with cash. Such volatility, even if prices do return to previous highs, will likely push countries away from oil. Many in the West are proposing low-carbon postpandemic stimulus packages, which will contribute to keeping oil prices low. In Nigeria, leaders must therefore confront how they fund their political system. Predation is likely to increase until oil prices stabilize or a new source of easy money is found.

Prebendal Nigeria is far from stable. The current population explosion, rapid urbanization, and the stresses of climate change are posing new challenges to elite-dominated governance and introducing a new element of unpredictability. Abroad, Nigeria is scaling back its diplomatic presence: in 2019 the foreign minister announced that the Nigerian embassies in Sri Lanka, Serbia, Ukraine, and the Czech Republic would be shuttered because of lack of funds, likely a blow to the pride of the "Giant of Africa." By some estimates, the 2019 budget allocated funding for only 30 percent of Nigeria's diplomatic missions.[69] In 2023, the Tinubu administration's response to the wave of coups in Francophone Africa has been largely feckless. As the political economy is breaking down, with insurrections in the northeast and the oil patch and conflict in the middle belt, the elite system that has dominated Nigeria since the end of the civil war is stressed. Insurrections and ethnic strife are also strongly colored by criminality, ranging from cattle rustling to kidnapping for profit. The organization of the population into villages in which headmen knew who was coming and going is disappearing. Similarly the religious structures that sustained society are challenged, by the Pentecostals among the Christians and by Salafist radicals and the Shia among the Muslims. For most Nigerians, the system is not working.

Chapter 5

The Elections of 2023

A democracy is more than a form of government; it is primarily a mode of associated living, of conjoint communicated experience.

—John Dewey

The previous chapter argued that Nigeria's political system—a bargain among elites—is inherently fragile. To recapitulate, under its terms, never defined but widely understood, elites compete for access to oil and gas revenue, the fountain of power and wealth, but usually cooperate across ethnic and religious divisions to preserve the system from which they benefit. On occasion, they selectively inflame at local levels these divisions for personal benefit. Violence is endemic in politics, though there are rules: "big men" do not kill other "big men," but their retainers are fair game. The elites operate with an unchallenged expectation of appropriating state-owned oil revenue and public office for their private use—a prebendal approach to governance.

The context is weak government. Bureaucratic and administrative machinery is underdeveloped and has made a totalitarian system all but impossible, even during the days of military rule. Rather than blanketing the country, the government's authority resembles an archipelago of islands in a sea of ungoverned spaces. Official violence tends to be episodic rather than part of a coherent pattern of repression. Where the state is absent or especially weak, nonstate actors, such as religious movements and institutions, traditional ethnic polities, militant organizations, or combinations of all three, take its place. The formal institutions of government, seemingly familiar to those in developed countries, serve primarily as a way to distribute government revenue to elites and to provide access to lucrative government salaries and contracts. While the system works for those who control it—the elites—it does not for most Nigerians. While this fragile system has persisted and evolved, it is breaking down.

As a sign of the times, the Arewa Research and Development Project, the Sir Ahmadu Bello Memorial Foundation, the Savannah Centre for Diplomacy, Democracy, and Development, and the Committee of Northern Youth Associations jointly organized a security conference in Kaduna in November 2018. The organizations represented the northern Nigerian establishment, mostly Fulani by ethnicity and Muslim in religion. These organizations have been a venue for elite cooperation and a link between the secular state and traditional emirate society and governance in the north. Present at the conference were retired army generals, inspectors general of police, academics, and security technocrats. The gist of the presentations was that Nigeria was drifting into anarchy because of the federal government's failure to address its security challenges. A convener of the conference, Usman Bugaje, directly tied kidnapping, armed robbery, and banditry across the country to Abuja's failure to address general insecurity.[1]

Sounding many of the same themes, former president and retired general Olusegun Obasanjo published an "open letter" to President Buhari in July 2019. He said, inter alia:

> I am very much worried and afraid that we are on the precipice and dangerously reaching a tipping point where it may no longer be possible to hold danger at bay. . . . When people are desperate and feel that they cannot have confidence in the ability of government to provide security for their lives and properties, they will take recourse to anything and everything than can guarantee their security individually and collectively.[2]

Such comments are indicative that the system by which the elites traditionally have been able to exercise power is being challenged by accelerating levels of violence that, in turn, reflect environmental degradation, the demographic explosion, and rapid urbanization that all contribute to poverty and misery. These factors, discussed in chapter 6, are at the root of the unsettling of a political system that was, until about a decade ago, sufficient to maintain a modicum of order and security.

The more immediate and obvious challenges to the system are decentralized insurrections and often unrelated, inchoate episodes of criminal violence. In the northeast, Boko Haram has split into factions, apparently murderous rivals but with the shared goal of the destruction of the Nigerian state. In the northwest, banditry threatens the lives and livelihoods of farmers and herders, while similar violence—with the addition of an often bloody ethnic and religious dimension—plagues the middle belt. In the Delta, though militants continue to receive amnesty payoffs in exchange for peace, they threaten violence and vandalism against the oil industry. In the east, a grassroots Biafran independence movement that largely lacks the support of the Igbo elites is reviving, though it remains largely peaceful. Finally, where it was once possible to traverse much of the country by road, kidnapping and banditry now threaten Nigerians, rich and poor, nearly everywhere.[3] These security challenges, and Abuja's poor response to them, should sound a cautionary note for Americans and other friends of Nigeria.

The elites and their system have endured up to now because of the fundamental lack of unity among peoples divided by ethnicity and religion, and subject to growing impoverishment. To distort Benjamin Franklin's aphorism, they hang separately rather than hang together.[4] Elites, like their colonial predecessors, have benefited from a divide-and-conquer strategy. How sustainable this strategy will be in the future is questionable. High levels of violence are a sign of elite fragmentation. Yet Nigeria and its political economy has proved to be resilient since independence in 1960, surviving a bloody civil war, a boom-and-bust economy, a generation of military rule, and an incomplete transition to a civilian democracy.

THE ELECTIONS OF 2023

On February 25, 2023, Nigerians went to the polls for the seventh time since the restoration of civilian rule in 1999. The elections highlighted the dysfunctionality of the political system, the breakdown of consensus among the elites, and religious and demographic pressures against the backdrop of the pervasive poverty of most Nigerians. The elections also highlighted the policy dilemmas that Nigerian political developments pose for US policymakers, as coups proliferate across West Africa and anti-Western jihadism directly challenges democratic values. The challenge for Americans is to build and sustain a bilateral relationship based on shared interests and ideals, encouraging necessary reforms while recognizing that their leverage and influence is limited.

In 2023, all three leading presidential candidates were pillars of the dysfunctional Nigerian political establishment. Bola Tinubu, born in 1952, for many years the political boss of Lagos state and very rich, was soon declared the 2023 victor by the Independent National Electoral Commission (INEC). Atiku Abubakar, born in 1946, Obasanjo's vice president and rival, multiple times a presidential candidate and rich from the oil services industry, was the runner-up. Peter Obi, born in 1961, came in third. He is younger than the other two, not as rich—but rich enough—and a former governor of Anambra state. According to the Independent National Electoral Commission, Tinubu polled 8.8 million votes (36.6 percent), Atiku 6.9 million (29.1 percent), and Obi 6.1 million (25.4 percent).[5]

Voter participation in 2023 was at an all-time low of 27 percent of those who had taken the considerable trouble to first register to vote and then collect their Permanent Voter Cards (PVC), required if they were to cast a ballot. Observers reported numerous irregularities in the polling, and the results contradicted preelectoral polling that had indicated an Obi victory. Subsequent to the INEC announcement of Tinubu's victory, Atiku and Obi sued in the courts seeking to overturn the results of the election. Such suits have been filed by presidential losers in every one of Nigeria's presidential elections since the restoration of civilian rule in 1999. Just as now, all have cited, inter alia, polling irregularities and pervasive violence. In the past, suits have dragged on for years, but the results of a presidential election have never been overturned, though gubernatorial results have been. Notably, Obi successfully challenged the gubernatorial election results in Anambra state in 2006 and became governor. Nevertheless, there appears little sense of urgency among the political class for a final judicial ruling on the elections. Atiku appears to be spending most of his time out of the country in Dubai. Obi's supporters are quiet, and he appears to be positioning himself as the "Christian" candidate of the future.

Tinubu was the candidate of the All Progressives Congress (APC). The party was a lineal descendant of that established by the Babangida military regime to be "a little to the left"; Atiku was the candidate of the People's Democratic Party (PDP), which is "a little to the right," also with its origins in the days of military rule. Every president since 1999 has come from one of the antecedents of these two parties, which are largely indistinguishable from each other, have little or no policy content, and serve primarily as machines for winning elections and the mechanism by which the elites divvy up among themselves public offices and the wealth that derives from them. Absent policies or principles associated with either party, ambitious politicians freely switch from one to the other and to minor parties as they calculate their self-interest.

Under Nigeria's tradition of presidential "alternation" enshrined in elite practice but not in law, every eight years the presidency rotated between south and north, Christian and Muslim. An alternation corollary was that when the presidential candidate was a northern Muslim, the vice presidential candidate would be a southern Christian, and vice versa. Following the eight years of the northern, Muslim Buhari presidency, in 2023 under the principle of alternation it should have been the turn of the southern Christians for the presidency.

But Tinubu and Atiku are both Muslims. Atiku chose as his vice presidential running mate medical doctor Ifeanyi Okowa, a Christian Igbo-speaking ex-governor of the Delta, a southern state. Tinubu fielded Kashim Shettima, a northern Muslim and former governor of Borno state, resulting in a Muslim/

Muslim ticket. The two major political parties' nomination of Muslim presidential candidates when it was the turn of the Christians would seem to have put paid to the religious alternation arrangements that had promoted whatever shred of political stability that had existed since the restoration of civil government in 1999. The 2023 nomination of Muslim presidential candidates by both of the major political parties should have been a political earthquake—and it was, among some Christians, especially Pentecostals, who had had privileged access to the presidency ever since the restoration of civilian rule.[6]

However, there were significant nuances that lessened the drama. There was a precedent for a Muslim/Muslim ticket: M. K. O. Abiola, like Tinubu a Yoruba Muslim, won the presidential elections with a Muslim running mate in 1993. Those elections are still regarded as the most credible in Nigeria's history. Abiola never served as president because of a military coup that ultimately brought General Sani Abacha to power and later died under suspicious circumstances. But Abiola is still favorably remembered as the only victorious presidential candidate to win the relatively freest and fairest of Nigeria's elections.

Tinubu is a Yoruba from the south and has only one wife, a Christian Pentecostal pastor. Many northern Muslims see those of the Islamic faith that are Yoruba as somehow not as orthodox as they should be. Tinubu's running mate, Kashim Shettima, is from Borno state in the far northeast where Boko Haram and successor jihadist movements are active. As a Yoruba Muslim, Tinubu appears to have concluded that he, a southerner, could win the northern parts of the country only with a northern, traditional Muslim vice presidential running mate. While there is a significant Christian minority in the north, conventional wisdom holds that a northern Christian candidate for high office is unacceptable to the Muslim majority and local Muslim elites.

Northerner Atiku's running mate was from Delta state. So, both tickets bowed toward the principle of regional, if not religious, alternation. Atiku is a Hausa-speaking Fulani from the north with multiple wives. He is said to have required the conversion of two of them from Christianity to Islam. Atiku more than Tinubu fits the traditional profile of a northern, Muslim presidential candidate as envisioned by alternation. By contrast, Tinubu with his Pentecostal wife and Yoruba ethnicity was more problematic from a traditional northern Muslim perspective. In fact, in the 2023 elections Atiku swept the most conservative, predominately Muslim states in the north—not Tinubu.

Tinubu and Atiku had won the presidential nominations of their respective parties through a typical Nigerian process reflecting the patronage organization of society and politics in which money and violence play a major role. They are conventional politicians. Yet most Nigerians appear to think the country is moving the wrong way and support political change. The victories of Tinubu and Atiku looked backward, not forward, and set the stage for the candidacy of Peter Obi, who could be presented as a relatively new face and a Christian to boot. In 2023, for the first time a nominee from outside the two major parties contested for the presidency and won a significant number of votes.

Obi is also an Igbo, and no Igbo has been president since the 1967–70 civil war, a continuing source of resentment among the third-largest ethnic group in Nigeria. Nevertheless, he was Atiku's chief rival for the PDP nomination in 2023, and in 2019, he had been the vice presidential running mate in Atiku's failed bid for the presidency. In 2023, under alternation, Obi's supporters believed it was his turn for the PDP nomination. When Atiku outmaneuvered and outspent Obi and secured the PDP presidential nomination, Obi left the party and aligned himself with the small, almost fringe Labour Party. He easily secured Labour's presidential nomination.

Charismatic, Western-educated, and media-savvy, to those Nigerians with a foot or more in the modern world Obi was a breath of fresh air as well as being the only major Christian candidate. He rapidly became a media sensation, not only in Nigeria but also among Africa watchers in the United Kingdom and the United States. Obi's youthful followers, heavily concentrated in Lagos, the center of Nigeria's modern economy, called themselves "the Obidient" and their hero soon acquired the attributes of a rock star. Obi, a Roman Catholic, successfully cultivated Pentecostal preachers and their enormous congregations.

Obi's appeal was a matter of style and hope for the future, not specific policies, and, unlike the candidates of the two major parties, he was not perceived as geriatric. Youthful obsession with Obi reflected in social media was taken up by much of the southern, Christian media and, in turn, by such Western media centered in New York and London that paid attention to Africa. Western media attention then stimulated further the Nigerian media's fascination with Obi. As Ebenezer Obadare has shown, a Lagos–New York–London echo chamber operated, with Western observers especially overestimating the political power of urban-based youth and seeing Obi's presidential victory as inevitable. Obi seemed to be the good news out of Africa that Americans and Europeans are always looking for and rarely find. Nevertheless, Tinubu apparently won the most votes.[7] But the widespread belief among "modern" Nigerians that Obi had won likely has sapped their confidence in democracy.

What happened?[8] Obi did win more than a quarter of the votes cast and thereby ended, if for the time being, the automatic domination of Nigerian presidential politics by the two political parties initially created by Nigeria's military rulers. He carried all the states dominated by the Igbos and won the votes of Christians in such religiously mixed areas as Lagos and Abuja. (Each of the three leading candidates won ten states and easily met the voter distribution requirements of the Nigerian constitution.) However, unlike the PDP and the APC, the Labour Party lacked a nationwide campaign organization. Obi had almost no campaign presence or support in the northern, predominately Muslim half of the country, where a probable majority of the country's population lives. In contrast, Tinubu and Atiku benefited from their patronage networks throughout the country. Outside Lagos, Abuja, and a few other urban centers, Nigerians vote the way their patrons tell them to, and those "big men" were in the pockets of Tinubu and Atiku—except in some of those states where the big men were Christian or Igbo.

A surprise was Obi's victory in Nigeria's Big Apple, Lagos. One of the largest urban agglomerations in the world, Lagos is in Yorubaland. The Yoruba Tinubu has dominated its politics and patronage networks for a generation. Yet he lost to an Igbo outsider. But by 2023 Lagos had become multiethnic, and Lagosians will often say that the Yoruba have become a minority, even that they are outnumbered by Igbos seeking the economic opportunities it provides. Further, Lagos is the center of Nigeria's youth culture and fueled by social media to which Obi appealed so strongly and that is largely absent elsewhere. There may have been less interference in the polling than elsewhere. Hence, Tinubu lost at home but won enough elsewhere to be declared the winner by INEC.

Contrary to INEC, Tinubu only *may* have won the most votes nationwide; it is by no means certain. The number of Nigerians that went through the time-consuming process to register to vote was high, 93,469,008. Of them, 87,209,007 collected their Permanent Voter Cards (PVC), which made them eligible to cast ballots in the 2023 elections. Yet INEC reported that only 25,286,616 ballots were cast.[9] How to account for the huge difference between voters registered, voters who picked up their PVCs, and the number of ballots actually cast?

The answer appears multifaceted. The elections took place during a period of significant economic dislocation resulting from the Buhari government's decision to swap out old naira notes for new ones within a restricted time period just before the elections.[10] But the Central Bank failed to print anywhere near enough of the new notes. The result was empty ATM machines and a cash shortage in an overwhelmingly cash and barter informal economy that impacted all aspects of life in the run-up to the elections. Many Nigerians could not travel, across town or across the country. That surely reduced the ballots cast.[11]

As in past elections, those of 2023 took place in a general atmosphere of violence nationwide. How much is all but impossible to quantify, given the underreporting of crime even in normal times. But kidnapping is ubiquitous nationwide, jihadist violence continues in the north, and ethnic and land-use quarrels explode into violence, especially in the middle of the country (i.e., the middle belt). Against this generalized backdrop, election-related violence in Nigeria appears to be highly decentralized and reflects local rivalries and other often parish-pump factors. It may frequently have overlapped with ethnic, land-use, religious, and other quarrels. It does not appear to have been coordinated from the headquarters of political parties or candidates. But violence can and does prevent voters from casting their ballots on election day. Perhaps of greater significance is that even rumors or reports of violence discourage potential voters with voter cards from setting out for the polls.

On election day, there were numerous technical failures in the voting process. Polls opened late. Technologies intended to prevent fraud too often failed. The posting of the results at polling places too often did not take place. It is hard to avoid the conclusion that disorganized voter suppression played a role in the small turnout, as even the cautious and circumspect American embassy finally acknowledged. On March 21, 2023, the US embassy publicly stated: "The United States is deeply troubled by the disturbing acts of violent voter intimidation and suppression that took place during those polls in Lagos, Kano, and other states. Members of the U.S. diplomatic mission observed the elections in Lagos and elsewhere and witnessed some of these incidents first-hand."[12]

Hard to quantify but real, in 2023 there was a general malaise in Nigeria about voting and "democracy" writ large. Tinubu emerged as president with less than 10 percent of those registered to vote. For many Nigerians, Tinubu's victory was not credible. Indeed, Atiku would have been the more likely winner if all of the ballots cast had been counted because his support was more broad-based. Absent the Obi candidacy, he would have certainly won. But because of the media hype, many of Obi's media-savvy followers were convinced that Tinubu had stolen the election from their candidate.

Reflecting this malaise, there was remarkably little public reaction to the election results in Nigeria. There were no riots or even significant public demonstrations. It is true that Atiku and Obi called for calm, but such appeals in the past have had little impact if the public were exercised. And in 2023, the public appeared apathetic.

DOMESTIC ISSUES

Superficially, Tinubu has been more successful at home than abroad. Unlike his predecessor Buhari, he moved quickly to appoint a cabinet. He appointed forty-five ministers, compared with forty-three in Buhari's cabinet during his second term. (During his first term, it took months for Buhari to assemble a cabinet.) Under the Nigerian constitution, each of the thirty-six states must be represented in the cabinet. Such a large number is unwieldy, and Tinubu, like his predecessors, is governing through a kitchen cabinet, the membership of which is not yet fixed.

Already, however, Tinubu has undertaken certain economic initiatives that have been praised by the international financial and business community. Notably, he has ended many of the exchange rate restrictions and a subsidy on domestic consumption of petroleum, which was a major drain on the government budget. (Nigeria has almost no capacity to refine oil; it exports oil to be refined abroad and then imports back the refined product to be sold domestically significantly under market rate.) Ending the exchange rate restrictions reduces the periodic shortages of foreign exchange and the economic distortions caused by a currency black market. But ending the restrictions also resulted in a drop in the value of the national currency to record lows and accelerated inflation.[13] His ending of the fuel subsidy may prove to be problematic. Many Nigerians have viewed cheap gasoline and kerosene (used for cooking) as their only benefit from the country's oil wealth.

In Tinubu's first few months in office, the country has been increasingly roiled by popular discontent with economic policy. Much more important, however, has been the general breakdown in public security.

COUPS

In 2020–2023, there was a wave of military coups across West Africa, six successful and two attempted: Mali, Chad, Sudan, Guinea, Burkina Faso, Niger, and, more distant, Gabon. While all of the coups were antidemocratic, the degree of popular support for the coup makers has varied. But it is clear that there is a democratic recessional underway, the result of poor governance, enduring poverty, and unresponsive elites. The coups have taken place in Francophone Africa; but the borders between Nigeria and its northern neighbors, especially Niger, cut across enduring ethnic identities. It is likely, especially in the north, that coups among its neighbors have undermined confidence in democracy in Nigeria as well.

In all of them, with the exception of Gabon, jihadist movements are active and constitute a direct threat to Nigeria. With the exception of Chad, Sudan, and Gabon, these countries were part of the Economic Community of West African States (ECOWAS), once dominated by Nigeria, which sold them oil at below market rate, subsidized ECOWAS operations, provided the organization with the largest number of its personnel, and hosted its headquarters in Abuja. As recently as the 1999–2007 administration of Olusegun Obasanjo, Nigeria had taken the lead in opposing and reversing coups through ECOWAS and the African Union. However, such has been the decline of

Nigeria that the administration of Bola Tinubu has been ineffectual in rolling back the coup wave.

Nigeria was ruled by military governments from 1965 to 1999 with only a short interregnum. With the restoration of civilian government in 1999, elite Nigerians are fond of saying that the era of coups is over. Obasanjo, himself a successful coup maker, was aware of the possibility of a threat against his own government when he became nominally a civilian head of state in 1999. Accordingly, he took steps to reduce the power of Nigerian military forces as a prophylactic against coups, and he strongly opposed coups elsewhere in West Africa, concerned about the spillover potential on Nigeria's own internal stability. It remains to be seen what the impact on the Nigerian military will be of the current coup wave, and Tinubu's inability to counter it. Tinubu's Nigeria is more unstable than Obasanjo's was. The issue will be whether Nigerian military officers, likely at the colonel level, are tempted to mount a coup of their own.

Especially in the immediate aftermath of the 2023 coup in Niger, Tinubu sought to rally the African Union and the Economic Community of West African States (the regional security organization) to end the coup and restore the elected civilian government. He cut off electricity and even threatened military intervention. But there was little stomach for it among neighboring states, and opinion in Nigeria opposed it. In the north, especially, elite Nigerian opinion saw the boundary between Niger and Nigeria as a colonial construct that, in effect, divided the same Hausa-Fulani people. From that perspective, there was no stomach for brother-against-brother warfare. Electricity was quickly restored, and talk of military intervention largely disappeared.

Chapter 6

Falling Apart

We can no longer say with certainty that we have a nation.

—Professor Oko Anya (quoted by former president Olusegun Obasanjo)[1]

Below elite political maneuverings, there are forces beyond politics that are shaping Nigeria's future. Nigeria's political leadership is weak and self-serving. These forces are largely beyond the capacity of any government to address. Nevertheless, the failure of the political system to credibly address these issues undermines popular confidence in governance. It also undermines confidence in democracy.

THE POPULATION EXPLOSION

Official statistics are of poor quality. There has never been a census throughout the country that commanded credibility. In the zero-sum game of Nigerian ethnic and religious politics, census figures are distorted and politicized following the notion that bigger is always better. Hence, population statistics should be taken as indicative, not definitive. The most recent census, conducted in 2006, concluded that Nigeria's population was 140 million, but there was credible evidence of severe undercounting in the southern and eastern parts of the country by a federal government at that time dominated by the Yoruba and Fulani. As of now, the general consensus is that the population is north of 200 million.[2] At independence in 1960, the population was estimated to be 45 million, smaller than that of the United Kingdom's 52.4 million at the time. Nigeria's population has since more than quadrupled while the UK's has increased about 20 percent. According to the World Bank, in 1960, Nigeria shared a similar fertility rate with Kenya, India, and Indonesia. But since then, Nigeria's has decreased only slightly, while the others' have more than halved.[3] Like the fertility rate, Nigeria's population growth rate has varied little since independence, remaining at about 2.5 percent annually.

Within the federal government there has long been recognition that the population is growing too fast. In 1988, the then military government established a population policy designed to reduce the fertility rate and curtail early marriages. It was soon abandoned. In 2004, the civilian administration of Olusegun Obasanjo launched a National Policy on Population for Sustainable Development, in part with funding from USAID. It included a roadmap for reducing the rate of population growth. However, a federal government assessment report in 2015 concluded that the population policy had failed. It noted that between 2005 and 2015, the population had grown by some fifty million and the fertility rate had declined only marginally. The assessment identified the causes of failure as "a weak enabling environment, characterized by pervasive cultural/religious practices, gender norms, and poverty." Under "gender norms" the report noted the preference for male children and that a high number of children fathered was a status symbol. The assessment also cited lack of government political will and the slow release of funding for the program. These realities made global family planning methods ineffective.[4] The assessment indicates that the population boom is not ending anytime soon.

A growing population is not necessarily a bad thing. Proponents of the "demographic dividend" contend that growth in the proportion of the population that is in its productive years, between late adolescence and late middle age, may result in high levels of economic growth because the proportion of the population that is dependent—children and the elderly—declines. But Nigeria has not managed this boom well. In addition to being one of the world's youngest, Nigeria's fast-growing population is one of the shortest-lived and poorest. Out of about 230 polities, it ranks 210 in median age, 211 in life expectancy, and 166 in per capita income.[5] It has the highest absolute number of poor people in the world, with estimates of the rate of poverty ranging from 44 percent to 61 percent.[6] The poverty rate is growing, and in 2010, nine out of ten Nigerians felt that they were getting poorer.[7] The median age in 2018 was eighteen years, slightly younger than at independence, when Nigeria had a median age of nineteen years. Life expectancy in Nigeria increased from thirty-seven years in 1960 to fifty-four years in 2017, mostly reflecting a decline in infant and child mortality. But it is still one of the lowest in the world.[8] Hence, Nigerians continue to have many children, die young, and have low incomes.

GROWING CITIES

As Nigeria's population grows, security concerns, rural poverty, and hopes for greater economic opportunity are driving people to cities. In the decade between 2007 and 2017, the proportion of Nigerians living in cities grew from 41 percent to about 50 percent of the population.[9] According to UN data, at independence in 1960, Lagos had an estimated population of 763,000; today it is about thirteen million. Together with Lagos state, which is sometimes used interchangeably with Lagos city as they are a single metropolitan area, the population reaches twenty-one million.[10] In 2019, there were seven Nigerian cities with a population of one million or more. There were also eighty with a population ranging between 100,000 and one million, and 248 with a population in the 10,000–100,000 range.[11] Such urbanization is unplanned, chaotic, and almost entirely lacks the necessary investment in infrastructure, such as water, roads, schools, and housing. In bringing diverse people together, urbanization can ameliorate ethnic conflict, such as in Lagos, or exacerbate it, such as in cities in the Niger Delta.

The realities of life in Nigerian cities is far from what those who migrate there hope for. The ever-expanding population has placed stress on already-inefficient local government agencies. In June 2019, the head of the federal mortgage bank of Nigeria estimated a shortage of twenty-two million housing units across the country.[12] Of those living in cities, an estimate is that about 80 percent live in slums.[13] Rather than being regulated or improved, over the past decades, some informal settlements in Abuja, Lagos, Kano, Zaria, and Port Harcourt have been targeted for official demolition to release land for development.

According to the World Health Organization, 122 million Nigerians lack access to basic sanitation. The streets and waterways of Nigerian cities are often choked with litter. Every year, Nigerian cities produce an estimated 25 million tons of municipal solid waste, the vast majority of which is commonly dumped untreated.[14] Access to piped water on premises actually decreased in Nigerian urban areas, from 32 percent in 1990 to around 3 percent in 2015. (In part, this also reflects the dramatic growth in urban population.) This decline is driven by the increase in slums but also poor government management. Many urban households must purchase water from private vendors at inflated prices or rely on unsafe sources of drinking water, such as unregulated boreholes.[15] According to a World Bank report on African cities, they "feel crowded precisely because they are not dense with economic activity, infrastructure, or housing and commercial structures."[16]

But despite poor living conditions, life persists. The informal economy provides employment that is rarely captured by statistics. In Lagos, there are few beggars; everyone has a hustle. Vendors working the city's ubiquitous traffic jams ("go slows") sell everything from mops and buckets to Juju materials to the complete works of Shakespeare. Others provide services, such as washing the feet of market ladies several times a day. Unlike the south, the north has many more beggars, at least in part driven by the Islamic tradition of almsgiving. But, like the south, the hustle is there, too.

Particularly in the Muslim north, as the population urbanizes, elites lose some of their power. In much of what they do, traditional rulers rely on rural-based support and face-to-face contact. In seeking justice, access to emirs (or other traditional rulers) was quick and easy; a plaintiff could show up at the emir's court and be heard the same day. Complaints would feed into the traditional ruler's view of his community, which he then transmitted up his chain of traditional authority, for example, to the sultan of Sokoto or the shehu of Borno. Urbanization breaks that essential face-to-face link as villagers flood cities.[17] This reduces a ruler's ability to surveil his ostensible subjects. Village headmen cannot account to the emir or other traditional ruler for those that have gone to the cities. Traditional rulers across the country have developed only incompletely equivalent means of control among those packed into informal settlements.

Other traditional means of social mobilization are also breaking down. Trade unions, once an organizer and shaper of urban opinion, have declined as manufacturing has atrophied; they remain important now primarily in the petrochemical industry, which is concentrated in the south. An urbanized population largely outside traditional authority structures is more susceptible to antiestablishment radical Muslim influences, cults, bandits, or militant groups. Boko Haram started in Borno state's largest city and capital, Maiduguri, not in the rural areas it now often dominates. Before it emerged, the traditional religious authority had already fractured under the pressure of population growth, rapid urbanization, and growing poverty. The same could be said of other northern cities.

Even with urbanization, Nigerians remain closely linked to their native village through family ties, patronage-clientage networks, and sentiment. Villages in southern Nigeria will often sport an enormous house built by a local "big man" who visits once a year. But if asked, he will say he lives in the village, not in Lagos or Port Harcourt where he makes his money and spends most of his time. Villages may also serve as a lifeline for urban dwellers that have fallen on hard times. When England urbanized in the late eighteenth and early nineteenth centuries, most of those who moved from rural villages to towns or cities traveled only a few miles. That pattern may also hold for Nigeria. For Nigerians, it remains usual to go home to the village for family and life events, and especially to die. Hence, morgues are smaller in Lagos than in, say, Abidjan. Villages may also be where urban Nigerians go when they are hungry. If so, the social and political break associated with urbanization in other parts of the developing world may be less drastic in Nigeria, and institutional patterns of authority may persist, helping to hold together an otherwise fractured polity. Still, many who go to Lagos often travel far, and a journey to their home village for religious holidays, such as Christmas and Eid, could take days.

ENVIRONMENTAL CHANGE

Attributing specific phenomena to climate change is difficult and sometimes controversial, even if Nigerian opinion leaders agree that it profoundly impacts the environment. The Sahara has expanded 10 percent since 1920—including a southward creep toward Nigeria.[18] Over 60 percent of Nigeria's total land is subject to water shortages every year.[19] Sea levels around the world are expected to rise more than thirty inches by the end of the century.[20] Rising sea levels in the Gulf of Guinea have advanced over one hundred feet of land in some areas in a single year—perhaps the fastest rate in the world—threatening tens of millions of people who live in cities at sea level, such as Lagos and Port Harcourt.[21]

Erratic patterns of rainfall have resulted in river flooding in some areas, while in others there has been too little rain to sustain traditional agriculture. For example, in August 2019, the Norwegian Refugee Council (NRC) in an urgent plea for funding reported that torrential rain had destroyed much of an internally displaced persons camp in inland Adamawa state. The NRC country director said:

> Displaced people are living in sub-human conditions across the region. There are no sanitation or draining facilities in most camps. People are going to the toilet in open spaces because there are no facilities for them to use and now that the camps are filled with stagnant flood water, water-borne diseases like cholera quickly spread.[22]

Despite its reliance on oil exports, agriculture still plays a vital role in Nigeria's economy. It accounts for nearly 70 percent of jobs and 26 percent of GDP. Crop production accounts for nearly 90 percent of agriculture's share of GDP, while the remainder comprises fishing, livestock, and forestry. However, there is still room for the agricultural sector to grow. According to the UN's Food and Agriculture Organization (FAO) in 2016, Nigeria is only cultivating 40 percent of its 70.8 million hectares of arable land.[23] The job sector's heavy reliance on agriculture can magnify the impact of natural disasters on the economy as a whole.

But many of Nigeria's problems are exacerbated by bad elite decision-making. For example, the apparent increase in livestock to meet the demands of an expanding population has resulted in overgrazing that promotes land erosion and makes the consequences of drought more severe. Plowing more land, and in general subsistence farming practices themselves, are often the consequence of underinvestment in agriculture and the depletion of groundwater. Overgrazing and overcultivation lead to the desertification of an estimated 351,000 hectares of land each year.[24] Urbanization and overdevelopment have destroyed wetlands. The disappearance of those wetlands has exacerbated periods of drought, which in turn promotes periodic and intense floods when the soil cannot absorb rainwater. Annual flooding poses a major threat by its spreading disease in crowded areas and destroying billions of dollars' worth of property. This, in turn, can lead to significant loss of human life, particularly for those in slums, shelters, and displaced persons camps.[25]

In the Delta, it is estimated that 1.5 million tons of oil have spilled during the first fifty years of oil production, equating to about one *Exxon Valdez* oil spill's worth of oil every year. In many cases the oil and gas infrastructure is old and breaks down, leading to leaks. More recently, there has been deliberate sabotage by militants, inevitably leading to oil spills, or local residents puncture pipelines to steal oil for cooking or refining and sale. These residents may be operating on their own initiative, or they may be directed and funded by certain elites. The oil pollutes rivers, destroying the local fishing industry, while the heavy industrial footprint has led to the destruction of mangroves and other forests and coastal erosion.[26] The ubiquitous practice of gas flaring has long been illegal, but the government does not have the capacity or perhaps the political will to enforce the law.[27] An estimated eight billion cubic feet of gas is flared annually according to satellite data, making Nigeria the seventh-largest source of flared gas in the world and one of Africa's largest contributors to global warming.[28] Further, industry gas flaring can lead to local acid rain, which in turn damages soil and agriculture. Criticism is ubiquitous of the big oil companies and their partner, the federal government, for failure to prevent and cleanup oil spills and address gas flaring.

Responsibility for the environment is divided. For example, the federal government is responsible for water resource management; state governments for water delivery in urban areas; and local governments for water in rural areas. As a practical matter, responsibility for sewage is unclear. Nigeria has a plethora of laws intended to prevent environmental degradation. However, enforcement is weak. Michael Watts sums it up:

> Central to this story is not the absence of environmental laws as such—Nigeria has instituted a broad-ranging set of legislation since the establishment of the Federal Environmental Protection Agency by Decree 58 in 1988—but

rather weak (and often nonexistent) enforcement, monitoring, and oversight, a compromised judiciary, and corrupt governance practices designed to benefit Nigeria's elite cartel (sometimes in cahoots with foreign capital operating in the resource sector).[29]

Nigeria is a very poor country in which the wealth is concentrated in few hands that are able to avoid the worst of environmental degradation. Environmental cleanup is not high on the elites' list of priorities, even if it should be. While climate change should not be ignored, poor governance is probably more to blame for the degradation of the environment.

SECURITY CRISES

Since the return of ostensibly civilian government in 1999, there have been two principal venues for ongoing insurrection against the Nigerian state: the northeast, with the Salafist Boko Haram, and the south and southeast, with the Movement for the Emancipation of the Niger Delta (MEND), subsequently the Niger Delta Avengers, and the separate, largely unrelated revived agitation for Biafran independence. Unlike Boko Haram and Delta militant activities, revived Igbo interest in Biafra is not violent nor is it an insurrection at this stage, but it has the potential to become so, especially if the security services overreact to what is still a peaceful movement. While not centrally led or necessarily politically driven, violence in the middle belt is also a response to weak and absent government, and it has escalated in the face of government inaction. The explosive growth of population, rapid urbanization, degradation of the environment, and growing poverty did not directly cause the Boko Haram insurrection, conflict in the middle belt over land use, or unrest in the Delta. But they set the table for all three.

BOKO HARAM

There is underway, essentially, a civil war in northeast Nigeria between the national security services and the traditional Islamic establishment on the one hand and Boko Haram on the other.[30] In some sense, Boko Haram is a millenarian religious movement, but it is also an insurrection against traditional elites. The group's official name has been Jama'at Ahl al-Sunnah li-l-Da'awah wa al-Jihad (JAS), which means "People Committed to the Prophet's Teachings for Propagation and Jihad" when translated from Arabic. But as the movement has fragmented, other names have been used. The term Boko Haram, still in common use, is a moniker applied somewhat derisively by local people that roughly means "Western education is forbidden," reflecting one of the group's most infamous tenets.[31] It is also an instrument of revenge involving local grievances, and it has a self-serving, criminal element, but also one apparently bent on establishing a truly Islamic polity. Boko Haram will continue to be a drain on the energy and treasury of Abuja for the foreseeable future. The threat it poses, therefore, is both military and political. The grievances underlying Boko Haram are widely shared (even if their methods are not) among Muslims in northern Nigeria, and they are deeply rooted in history.

From 2011 to 2023, the conflict has killed an estimated 35,000 to 50,000 people, including Boko Haram fighters, Nigerian soldiers, and civilians (see figure 6.1), and resulted in up to two million internally displaced persons.[32] Within the region affected, agricultural production has fallen steeply, driving up the price of food. In 2018, it was estimated that around 3.8 million people would face "critical food insecurity" and around 7.7 million would need "life-saving humanitarian assistance."[33] By 2017, it was estimated that Boko Haram had destroyed 1,400 schools and killed 2,300 teachers. Boko Haram militants make use of child soldiers; it impresses some, others appear to join willingly. The Civilian Joint Task Force (CJTF), the vigilante group

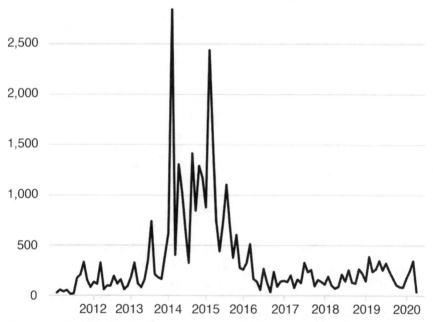

Figure 6.1. Deaths of Boko Haram members, members of the security services, and civilians per month related to the Boko Haram conflict, including Cameroon, Chad, and Niger. *Source:* Nigeria Security Tracker, created by Asch Harwood.

that supports and assists the security services, has also enlisted child soldiers, though it is against Nigerian law.[34] In 2014 and 2015, the conflict was at its most deadly (see figure 6.1) and occupied territory roughly the size of Belgium. With the significant assistance of South African mercenaries and the CJTF, the Nigerian and Chadian militaries dislodged the group from much of this territory and drove them back into the bush, where they have survived.

In 2016, Boko Haram split into two—subsequently three—main factions, one of which is affiliated with the Islamic State, the other led by the infamous Abubakar Shekau. (In 2021, Shekau was killed in a fight with a rival faction.) Among observers, there is little consensus as to each faction's relationship with the other, with the Islamic State, or with al-Qaeda in the Islamic Maghreb (AQIM).There exists scant information on the internal structure and leadership of Boko Haram. While there may be a supreme council, or *shura*, its membership is unknown, and even evidence of its existence is not definitive. Nor is much known about the depth of popular support Boko Haram enjoys, though there are indications that it is not insignificant. A 2014 survey by the Pew Research Center finds that about one Nigerian Muslim in five was favorably inclined toward the Islamic State.[35] In 2015, another Pew survey indicated that around 12 percent of Nigerians of all religions were favorably disposed toward Boko Haram, but that number had fallen to just 1 percent by the next year.[36] Still, even just a couple percent of the population would translate into millions of Boko Haram sympathizers. Hence, it is likely that the movement can still draw on a reservoir of support or acquiescence.

With its highly diffuse, religious, even millenarian dimensions, Boko Haram aims to create a polity through violence and rage but without a political program or even much of a structure. In this way, Boko Haram (and its sympathizers) might constitute a new type of revolution in Nigeria. Intensely parochial, it defies conventional analysis based on the precedents of the 1789 French, 1917 Russian, or even the 1979 Iranian revolutions. It also lacks democratic aspirations and so does not fit with the Arab Spring. Nor does it fit with the internationalist agendas of al-Qaeda, the Islamic State, or other jihadist frameworks, though it shares the same Islamic rhetoric, that of Salafism through a peculiar Wahhabist lens. This approach to Islam is rejected by most devout Muslims, including those in Nigeria. Finally, unlike many jihadist terror groups outside the Middle East, Boko Haram does not appear to be operationally directed by the Islamic State or AQIM.

BOKO HARAM'S ORIGINS

Establishment Islam in northern Nigeria is part of the Sunni tradition. It has long had a mystical dimension, called Sufism, which includes a cult of the saints and some elements of African traditional religion. Its powerful brotherhoods have a spiritual and a political dimension.[37] It is broadly tolerant of Christians, if not of "pagans," but it is jealous of its historical predominance. The Islamic establishment accepted British rule and still largely supports the secular Nigerian state, actively participates in its governance, and benefits from its distribution of oil revenue. Though not necessarily anti-American, elite northern Nigerians tend to have closer ties with the conservative monarchies of Saudi Arabia and the Persian Gulf. Those with a Western orientation tend to look to the United Kingdom rather than the United States.

Since the end of the civil war in 1970, Islam in northern Nigeria and the broader Sahel region of West Africa has become more and more influenced by Salafism, or more specifically, a variety of Salafism called Wahhabism, the dominant form of Islam in Saudi Arabia. Salafism, and by extension, Wahhabism, refers to a literalist, strict, puritanical approach to Islam. In principle, its adherents take the words of the Koran and other ancient texts literally, without regard to historical context. Hence, if a woman was caught committing adultery in the seventh century, she was stoned to death, and some Salafists will argue she should be today. Some Salafists regard violence against those they deem enemies, expressed by them as jihad, as a legitimate and necessary expression of Islam. Others retreat inwardly, avoiding contact with secular life, as did some antecedents of Boko Haram. Saudi missionaries and Saudi money helped strengthen that approach to Islam by funding mosques and Islamic schools in the Salafist tradition. Those thereby influenced in Nigeria and West Africa rejected the alleged "accretions" to Islam from African traditional religions that Sufism would tolerate, such as the veneration of local saints. In 2012, for example, jihadist fighters destroyed the ancient tombs of such saints in Timbuktu, Mali, which were part of a UNESCO World Heritage Site. Over the past generation, establishment Islam in Nigeria has been challenged by the influence of Wahhabism and, to a lesser extent, the Shia tradition sponsored by Iran.

Though Boko Haram is heavily influenced by Salafist theological thinking from abroad, it has deep roots in Nigerian Islamic protest movements.[38] In northern Nigeria, popular protest against the established order and state corruption has taken the form of radical Islamic renewal since precolonial times. Dan Fodio's reformist jihad established the Sokoto Caliphate in 1806 by destroying ostensibly Muslim emirates that he regarded as heterodox, corrupt, and exploitive of the poor. Boko Haram uses rhetoric similar to that of Dan Fodio, perhaps in a deliberate echo.[39] In 1978, Sheik Gumi founded Izala, a Salafist movement that also sought to purge African elements from Nigerian Islam. That same year, Shia preacher Ibrahim Zakzaky founded the Islamic Movement of Nigeria. Both are active today.[40] In the same decade Mohammed Marwa, a charismatic preacher known as the Maitatsine, began a movement of the same name.[41] Persistent clashes between his followers, or Yan Tatsine, and police in the late 1970s prompted military involvement. By the time of Maitatsine's death in 1980, an estimated five thousand people had been killed. Boko Haram appeared two decades later, and it is likely that some of the Yan Tatsine drifted into it.

Dan Fodio's jihad, Izala, and Boko Haram are part of the Sunni tradition; the Islamic Movement of Nigeria is Shia; while Maitatsine, broadly Sunni, had more heterodox elements than Izala or Boko Haram. These contemporary movements had in common a charismatic leader and advocated justice for the poor, though the leadership was often from the Islamic elite. They were hostile to Western, secular civilization, rejected modern science though not modern technology and, while highly patriarchal, sometimes provided more scope for women than traditional northern Nigerian society. For example, there is anecdotal evidence that Boko Haram allows women to fight and use modern weapons.[42] In some cases, it appears that women may choose to be suicide bombers. Boko Haram rejected Western education as fundamentally un-Islamic. Not only were they hostile to the secular Nigerian state, by and large they did not recognize or use national symbols, such as the flag or the national anthem, seeing them as promoting state-worship, itself a form of idolatry. They rejected the traditional Islamic establishment that participates in the Nigerian secular state. They started as nonviolent movements, but with the exception of Zakzaky they have embraced violence as a legitimate part of jihad, usually in response to official security service attacks.

In 1999, freed from the constraints of a generation of rule by military government, some Nigerians in the north renewed the periodic protests against what they saw as misgovernment, corruption, and exploitation of the poor by Nigeria's elite. Influenced by Salafist ways of thinking, they chose to withdraw from the world so they would have little contact with the government. In some places, communities as large as five thousand people set up self-sufficient habitats where they could live according to their religious dictates. Most were nonviolent, however extreme they might have been in their thought and religious interpretations. It was also during this period that nine of the twelve Muslim states in the north adopted sharia in the criminal domain.[43] Hence, Boko Haram did not drop out of the sky when it first attracted media attention in 2009. Rather, it should be seen as part of a long-standing tradition of protest that uses an Islamic vocabulary and advocates for justice for the poor even if its theological formulations owe much to Saudi Arabia and its rhetoric to the Islamic State.

THE BEGINNING WITH MOHAMMED YUSUF

In 2002, the charismatic preacher Mohammed Yusuf established a large community at the Railway Quarter mosque in Borno state's capital city of Maiduguri.[44] Yusuf was born in Yobe state and was probably part of the Kanuri ethnic group, and Kanuri appears to have been his first language, though he knew Arabic, Hausa, and at least some English. His education was at Koranic schools in Niger and Chad, and he apparently studied at the University of Medina in Saudi Arabia. Like other such teachers, his support came from the grassroots, but his followers also included some young men from the northern Nigerian Islamic establishment. He preached that Western civilization and the secular state were absolute evil, and that Muslims should withdraw from contact with the secular world. No compromise with Western secularism was possible. It has been suggested that the American invasion of Afghanistan and Iraq promoted his radicalization.[45] Such communities as the Railway Quarter Mosque that he founded in Maiduguri were not unusual in Nigeria following the return to civilian rule.

Early in 2009, some Boko Haram members confronted the police under murky circumstances in Maiduguri. A fight ensued and several police officers were killed. The reaction was a police and military crackdown on the section of Maiduguri where Yusuf and his community lived. Yusuf was captured by the military and turned over to the police, who murdered him. He was (probably) thirty-nine years old. The event was captured in real time by an Al Jazeera video that went viral on Nigerian social media. Army and police also murdered several members of his family, killed up to eight hundred of his followers, burned down his compound and those of his family members, and destroyed the Railway Quarter Mosque.[46] The group then largely disappeared from view, at least to those in Abuja and the West.

BOKO HARAM UNDER ABUBAKAR SHEKAU

Following Yusuf's murder, Boko Haram went underground under the leadership of one of his deputies, Abubakar Shekau. During that period Boko Haram may have received a small amount of financial assistance and training from al-Qaeda elements in the ungoverned spaces of the Sahara desert, beyond the reach of any government.[47] In 2011, Boko Haram reappeared, with several dramatic jailbreaks that freed some of its fighters imprisoned in 2009. It staged an attack on national police headquarters and a large UN office in Abuja in 2012, attempted to murder the shehu of Borno, and succeeded in killing the emir of Gwoza. This was part of an escalating, violent campaign against the secular state and its Islamic allies. In 2014, it attracted worldwide attention when it kidnapped 276 schoolgirls gathered together at a state school to take their final examinations. There was international and domestic uproar over the Jonathan administration's seemingly lethargic response.

Shekau became the "face" of Boko Haram because of his brutal internet videos.[48] He was particularly associated with killing "apostates," whom he defined broadly as those Muslims who did not subscribe to his particular theology and who do not accept his leadership.[49] The Shekau faction claimed that those Muslims have "sold out" to the secular state by participating in it. With an eye toward the upcoming 2015 national elections, President Jonathan put together an alliance with Chad, Niger, Cameroon, and Benin to counter Boko Haram. In March 2015, the Nigerian army, supported by Chadian troops and South African–led mercenaries, drove Boko Haram out of the territory it had occupied. Nevertheless, the movement has never been definitively defeated. It regroups, morphs, changes tactics, and continues the struggle up to the present.

THE ISLAMIC STATE AND BOKO HARAM

In 2015, Shekau swore allegiance to the Islamic State and the shrinking territory he controlled officially became Wilayat Gharb Ifriqiya, or the Islamic State in West Africa (ISWA).[50] The gesture appears to have had little operational significance. The following year, however, the Islamic State announced a new leader of its "West African province," Abu Musab al-Barnawi, who is understood to be the son of Mohammed Yusuf. The Islamic State leadership apparently was concerned that Shekau was killing too many Muslims who diverged from his views and it objected to his attacks using suicide bombers on "soft" targets such as markets or bus stations. Sometime in 2016, such differences led Boko Haram to split into multiple factions. One, ISWA, was led at that time by Abu Musab al-Barnawi with the endorsement of the Islamic State, another by Shekau, referred to interchangeably as Boko Haram or JAS. In 2018, the Islamic State apparently changed the leadership of ISWA again, this time to Umar al-Barnawi, implying at least a degree of oversight. (The name "al-Barnawi" means "from Borno" rather than being a family name; the two al-Barnawi are not apparently related.) As part of the second leadership change, Abu Musab al-Barnawi was likely killed, as were other influential leaders allied with him. As we have seen, Shekau was killed in 2021.[51]

The significance of Boko Haram's split into factions or Shekau's death can be overread. The movement has long been decentralized with little apparent organizational structure. Assassinations or murders within the leaderships have been common. Between the two best-known factions, ISW and JAS, far more deadly overall is JAS, especially toward civilians. From 2016 to 2019, violence involving JAS killed over three thousand civilians, while that of ISWA killed almost two hundred. Put another way, JAS has killed seventeen times more civilians than ISWA in this time. But attacks by both factions have led to the deaths of about a thousand soldiers each. ISWA focuses on the security services, killing about six soldiers for every civilian, while JAS has killed about three civilians for each soldier.[52] These statistics are congruent with reporting on the ground, which holds that ISWA has been relatively careful to respect and protect the civilian population, and it appears to have deliberately been building popular support. There are reports that it does not indiscriminately kill civilians, does not forcibly marry girls, and does not interfere with farming. In fact, both factions may even support the local economy. The Nigerian military, conversely, closes certain markets because they have become venues where Boko Haram trades, apparently involving the larger community. Taking advantage of the resulting hardship, representatives of ISWA have reportedly then come to preach and to offer certain financial services.[53] It appears that ISWA is trying to make clear that its enemy is the state, not the people.

WHAT IS BOKO HARAM'S FUTURE?

Boko Haram factions now appear to be embedded in northeastern Nigerian society. Their end goals are the same: destruction of the Nigerian secular state, the creation of an Islamic state governed according to sharia, and the purging of northern Nigeria of all Western and secular influences. Though with much overlap, the two factions have different areas of operations. ISWA is active in northern Borno and along the border with Niger; JAS operates across the middle of Borno and farther south along the border with Cameroon.[54] Both factions attack military bases, though JAS still seems to target and kill civilians. Where it operates, reports indicate that ISWA is able to control much larger swaths of territory after dark than during the day. In the territory it occupies on a more-or-less permanent basis, it was putting into place governing structures and collecting taxes, and it has operated sharia courts. The extent to which this may be true of JAS as well is less clear.

Recall that though at first appearance Boko Haram seems not unlike other jihadist terrorist organizations—and there are similarities—it has a specifically Nigerian flavor. Its terrorism feeds off Nigeria's corrupt political economy, exploitation of the poor, and security service abuses. Boko Haram's rhetorical focus on providing for the poor highlights that it is, among other things, an insurrection of the poor against the rich within a specifically Islamic context and in the long-standing tradition of revolt against bad governance in what is now northern Nigeria. But neither faction has published a concrete plan for economic development or poverty alleviation.

While most of its victims have been Muslim, Boko Haram kills Christians where it can, especially in the middle belt, where Christians are more numerous than in Borno, Yobe, and Adamawa, its primary areas of operation. Many of the soldiers, police, and government officials it kills are from elsewhere in Nigeria and are Christian. But Boko Haram appears to kill them primarily because of their government affiliation rather than their religion. In predominately and traditionally Christian states, notably Plateau, Boko Haram represents itself as a shield for Muslims. In this way, the middle belt may become a future area of operation amid the ethnically and religiously charged violence there, as discussed below.

Boko Haram operatives captured by the Nigerian security services pose a challenge to Abuja. What should be done with them? There are small-scale programs, some funded by the European Union, some modeled on similar programs in Saudi Arabia and the Gulf, that seek to "deradicalize" former Boko Haram members. Nigerian, European, and American NGOs provide counseling, job training, and apprenticeships through Nigerian government programs, Operation Safe Corridor being the best known. A significant number of combatants are children and up to two thousand, mostly boys, have been detained on suspicion of their sympathy with Boko Haram. In this setting, children are generally treated as adults by the military.[55] The success rate of deradicalization programs is difficult to assess. There is also anecdotal evidence of local communities refusing to accept back those who participated in Boko Haram, even when it was against their will, and other accounts of women rescued that have fled back to Boko Haram.

It is difficult to see how Boko Haram will end. Unlike other insurrections, when it occupied significant amounts of territory under Shekau it did not move to create an alternative government. The ISWA faction, however, does seem to be establishing here and there an administration that collects taxes and provides services in the small territories it now occupies. In the past, millenarian religious movements in northern Nigeria have burned themselves out only to subsequently revive later in a different form and with different leaders. Shekau's killing of Muslims may still turn the population against his faction. The Nigerian government's response has been almost entirely military and characterized by numerous human rights abuses against noncombatants. It regularly claims to have all but destroyed Boko Haram, so much so that the credibility of its spokesmen is badly compromised. Up to now, it has not overtly pursued a political settlement, though it is hard to imagine what would be possible. In its public statements, Boko Haram has steadfastly refused to negotiate with Abuja, even though some negotiations do take place. The International Committee of the Red Cross and the Swiss government, for example, secured the release of some of the Chibok schoolgirls. There is also anecdotal evidence of negotiation at the local level.[56] Nevertheless, negotiations continue to be fraught. For example, Mamman Nur, a popular disciple of Yusuf, was apparently killed because he attempted to negotiate with government figures.

MILITANCY IN THE NIGER DELTA

Unlike Boko Haram, far away in a poor part of the country, insurrection in the Niger Delta directly threatens the national cake. The Delta is "like a keg of gunpowder under Nigeria. If the Delta explodes, Nigeria goes with it."[57] Though states in the oil patch, in return for the oil they produce, receive a larger allocation of revenue from the government than the formula would usually dictate, the area has long been characterized by poor governance, militant activity, and environmental disasters. In some communities, governance is an ad hoc mixture of traditional rulers; conventional local, state, and federal authority; and the oil companies, which have often been called upon to provide education and health services that are normally the purview of state and local governments. Magic and cults on many occasions play an important role as well. This is arguably true of many areas of Nigeria, but the Delta's poverty and poor governance it is more politically significant than elsewhere because, since the 1970s, the region has produced much of Nigeria's wealth.

The Niger Delta, strictly speaking, comprises just three states—Bayelsa, Delta, and Rivers.[58] It is located in the south-south geopolitical zone of the country, which also includes Akwa-Ibom, Cross River, and Edo. This larger region is often referred to informally as the Delta.[59] The largest ethnic groups are the Ijaw, which is the fourth largest in the country, and the Itsekiri, though there are about forty other ethnic groups making a total population of around thirty million in the three core states, an area about the size of South Carolina or Portugal. These core states comprise one of the most densely populated regions of the country. For centuries, the Delta has been the venue of sometimes, but not always, exploitive trade, first in slaves, later in palm oil, and now in oil.

"THE OIL PATCH"

While providing the Nigerian government with hundreds of billions of dollars over time, the oil industry has done little for the people of the Delta. Much of the Delta is an environmental wasteland. Pollution related to the oil industry has led to the destruction of the farming and fishing industries, resulting in high levels of unemployment and deep levels of poverty, even if other parts of Nigeria, such as the north, are still poorer. While much of the oil industry's pollution results from its own negligence and poor state regulation, a significant amount is the result of oil theft and sabotage by militants.

Commercial oil production began in the 1950s after about fifty years of exploration, led by British firms. The British and subsequently the military governments established that the Nigerian state owns all oil and natural gas within Nigeria's territory, including its territorial waters. By 1963, it became clear that Nigeria's reserves were of global significance, and by the 1970s the Nigerian state was utterly dependent on oil for its revenue. In 1972, two years after the end of the civil war, oil provided almost five times as much state revenue as all other sources combined. These were boom times: in 1975, the Nigerian government placed cement orders greater than the exporting capacity of Europe and the USSR combined. The estimated $2 billion price tag was a quarter of Nigeria's oil revenue.[60]

In the Niger Delta, there is pervasive and long-standing popular distrust of the federal government, of the traditional rulers first installed by the British, and of the oil companies. During the civil war, Port Harcourt, with Nigeria's sole oil refinery, was included in the breakaway republic's territory, as were many oil wells. This forced international oil companies to choose between an independent Biafra and the Nigerian government, and all chose the federal government. Since then, Delta residents see the federal government as in cahoots with the international oil companies. It does not help that Abuja can, and does, displace local communities for the benefit of oil companies.

Under these circumstances, conflict is endemic. Low-level insurrections, sabotage, and oil theft in the Delta can cut the country's oil and gas production in half. Communities rebel against the international oil companies and the federal government over land rights and compensation for environmental damage. There is conflict at every level over the possession of land slated for the construction of oil facilities. Though most of the oil patch population is Christian and religious conflict is rare, there are still significant ethnic rivalries in the region that can turn bloody.[61]

LOCAL PUSHBACK

In the 1990s, radical Delta groups emerged during the brutally repressive Abacha government. One of them, the Movement for the Salvation of the Ogoni People (MOSOP), was founded by Ken Saro-Wiwa. The Ogoni were a minority ethnic group in the Delta, and their homeland, Ogoniland, had been the site of oil drilling since the 1950s. Saro-Wiwa called international attention to the plight of those living in the Delta and the environmental degradation caused by the oil industry. Following multiple arrests, Saro-Wiwa was executed after a sham trial orchestrated by the Abacha government, along with eight other MOSOP leaders. They became known as the Ogoni Nine and are widely regarded as martyrs. MOSOP remains active today.

As with the antecedents of Boko Haram, politicians after the restoration of civilian governance in 1999 recruited Delta militant groups to serve as political muscle during state elections. Dropped from the payroll when the elections were over, militants often turned to oil theft. The Movement for the Emancipation of the Niger Delta (MEND), apparently founded in 2004, launched a rebellion in 2005. MEND is the most well-known and largest Delta militant organization and the primary one behind the uprising. But it is highly decentralized, attracts temporary partners, and there are other major groups. The militants attacked with impunity throughout the coastal region, including the outskirts of Lagos. They successfully attacked offshore oil platforms sixty miles out to sea. MEND carried out kidnappings of local and expatriate officials and oil company personnel. Oil production dropped to 800,000 barrels per day (bpd), far below its estimated capacity of up to three million bpd.[62] Government revenue dropped precipitously. The militants and criminals, with their access to sophisticated weapons smuggled from abroad or looted from police and military installations, often outgunned the Nigerian military and police.[63]

The insurgency resulted in a fall of oil production in Nigeria by approximately 25 percent from 2005 to 2009.[64] The NNPC reported over 2,000 incidences of pipeline vandalism in each year from 2005 to 2008, with over 3,500 in 2006.[65] In December 2009, President Umaru Yar'Adua put in place an amnesty for Delta militias to end the insurrection. Elements included disarmament, retraining of insurgents to make them employable, and payoffs of the militia leaders—often by means of government contracts. Former insurgents did participate in training programs, though they did not necessarily get jobs when they finished and it is unlikely that there was much genuine disarmament. The militia leaders did very well by this arrangement, with some moving to the luxurious Abuja Hilton, far from the Delta. Since then, the region has been relatively quiet. However, the Nigeria Security Tracker shows a steady increase in incidents since 2011.[66] There is no political process or political will in the rest of the country to address the long-standing grievances of Delta residents. Critics of the Yar'Adua amnesty, which was continued by the Jonathan and Buhari administrations, see it as merely a temporary ceasefire resulting from the Nigerian government's payment of a modern form of Danegeld to militia leaders or warlords, who can resume their attacks at any time. It remains to be seen if the Tinubu administration will follow the same course.

NO END IN SIGHT

Any Nigerian government will likely have its hands tied with respect to Delta militants: continue to pay them off, with scarce government revenue, or risk a new insurrection that could threaten the oil industry and with it a significant chunk of government revenue. Of course, the dramatic fall in oil prices in 2020 weakened the hand of militants temporarily, but it also calls into question whether the federal government will be able to continue the amnesty payments going forward. On the other hand, by 2023, oil prices had recovered. In any event, meeting the demands of the militants is likely to have consequences that will reverberate well beyond the Delta. Already in northern Nigeria, those who participated in the Civilian Joint Task Force on the government side against Boko Haram are agitating for similar arrangements.[67] After all, they argue, they were on the side of the government while the Delta militants were fighting against it.

The Delta militants and Boko Haram differ in their ideologies, goals, and trajectories. Nevertheless, there are themes common to both. For one, they are active in regions where there has long been a sense of alienation from the relatively wealthy islands of Lagos-Ibadan and Abuja. This alienation is fed partly by the government's inept political responses to their regional challenges. Both (as well as the revival of Biafra, discussed below) are movements of the poor against the rich, among much else. Though each are at war with local traditional rulers and institutions that participate in the elite bargain, the Delta militants appear amenable to being bought off by these rulers and institutions. Boko Haram, conversely, seems much more content trying to destroy the system. It targets the establishment—and even the insufficiently antiestablishment—Muslim leaders of northern Nigeria, among them sultans, emirs, imams, and mallams. For their part, Delta militants sometimes humiliate traditional rulers, especially those who were established by the British and hence have shallow roots in the local culture.

THE NEO-BIAFRA MOVEMENT

The neo-Biafra movement in Nigeria ostensibly comprises the Movement for the Actualization of the Sovereign State of Biafra (MASSOB) and the Independent People of Biafra (IPOB), though they are not necessarily allies, and often butt heads. Broadly speaking, both draw on the perceived injustices associated with the civil war and the discrimination toward Igbos ever since. Today, the Igbo dominate five states—Abia, Anambra, Ebonyi, Enugu, and Imo—and number around thirty million. Physical damage in the former Biafra was repaired quickly after the fighting stopped in 1970, and Nigeria's booming oil-based economy benefited many Igbos. With the war over, they once again flooded out of the now former Biafra to all over Nigeria.

At the heart of the 1967–70 civil war was the place of the Igbo ethnic group within Nigeria. For many Igbos, this remains unresolved today. Active, energetic, often the proprietors of small enterprises, Igbos are frequently viewed by other Nigerians as arrogant and obsessed with money. In an anti-Semitic and anti-Igbo slur, they are often called "the Jews of Africa." There has not been an Igbo chief of state since the war, and Igbos regularly complain, not always credibly, that they are discriminated against by other ethnic groups in all endeavors. The Igbo accuse the security services of being especially heavy-handed in the former Biafran territories. Many point to the fundamental problem being the unified Nigerian state. Sir Arthur Richards, the governor-general of Nigeria in 1948, aptly observed: "It is only the accident of British suzerainty which has made Nigeria one country. . . . They do not speak the same language and they have highly divergent customs and ways of life and they represent different stages of culture."[68] Biafran secessionists would agree.

Biafra is an issue on which the traditional Nigerian leadership is neuralgic. Nigeria's current leadership remains in many ways a product of the civil war. Generals Buhari, Danjuma, Babangida, and Obasanjo were all combatants on the national side. At a political level, successive Nigerian presidential administrations have been heavy-handed with Biafra advocates. The security services often overreact, sliding into human rights violations.

LEADERS OF BIAFRA

The principal Biafran secessionist organization, MASSOB, was founded in 1999 by Ralph Uwazuruike and is still led by him. He is old enough to remember the civil war. He says he is fascinated by Mahatma Gandhi and Martin Luther King Jr. and the effectiveness of their nonviolent resistance. He graduated from Punjab University and the law school of Bombay University, both in India. In 2005, he reintroduced the Biafran currency to circulation, he said at the request of the Biafran diaspora with whom he maintains close ties. At one point it was trading at par with the naira. He was outspoken in his condemnation of "Fulani" allegedly killing Igbos in northern Nigeria. As MASSOB gradually became popular, he was arrested numerous times on a variety of charges, and in 2005, for treason. Though never tried, his bail hearings lasted over two years.

Nnamdi Kanu, leader of the IPOB, holds British as well as Nigerian citizenship. Born in Nigeria in 1967—and therefore, unlike Uwazuruike, not old enough to remember the civil war—he moved to London, where he studied political economics at what is now London Metropolitan University. He founded the IPOB in 2012, building on the success of his London-based radio station, Radio Biafra, which he founded in 2009. He also has an active X account, which sometimes traffics in conspiracy theories. He says that IPOB is nonviolent, but he can come close to calling for violence. For example, at the 2015 World Igbo Congress in Los Angeles, he told his audience made up largely of Nigerian expatriates that "we need guns and we need bullets."[69] Subsequently he said Igbos need weapons and ammunition to protect themselves from attacks by Fulani herdsmen.

There were protests following his October 2015 arrest in the states that were once part of Biafra and subsequently in Abuja. He was held for eighteen months without trial, despite various court orders that he be released. Eventually released on bail, his house was raided by the security services in 2017. He then disappeared. Some of his supporters believed that security services had murdered him, others that he was being held on a Nigerian naval vessel. Various parts of the Nigerian government insisted that it did not know where he was. A year later, he turned up in Israel, announcing his presence in a broadcast on a pirate radio station, and that he was a convert to the Jewish faith. Once back in the public sphere, in 2019, Kanu conducted North American rallies for an independent Biafra in Toronto, Los Angeles, Houston, Chicago, and New York, all cities with Igbo communities. The IPOB claimed the rallies were a success: "Biafrans living in the United States of America and Canada have proven through his visit and town hall meetings that our people are fully determined, united and committed to the pursuit of Biafra independence as undisputedly championed by IPOB."[70] Subsequently, he was rearrested and escaped, ultimately to Kenya. There, he was extradited to Nigeria, and as of 2023, he remains in jail.

BIAFRAN POLITICS TODAY

The position of the two neo-Biafra groups are reflected in their public statements. IPOB spokesman Emma Powerful talks about the threat posed by the "Fulani caliphate." He calls Igbo political figures who criticize Kanu as "Hausa-Fulani errand boys." He claims that among the so-called Igbo errand boys there is "an ongoing battle as to who will emerge the anointed son of the Fulani caliphate."[71] Fear of northern, Muslim domination of Nigeria is a long-standing theme in Igboland and other parts of the south. Some current Biafra supporters continue to characterize the 1967–70 Nigerian civil war as a struggle between Christians and Muslims, in which the latter were victorious because of the "betrayal" of Yorubaland (western Nigeria) that allied with the Muslims of the north to destroy Biafra. The fact that the former president, Muhammadu Buhari, is a Fulani Muslim encourages this way of thinking. (Reaction to Bola Tinubu is ambiguous; he is a Muslim but a Yoruba, not a Fulani, and has a Christian wife.) If fear of Fulani domination is one of Emma Powerful's themes, another is bad governance. He states, "Our leader, Mazi Nnamdi Kanu before his abduction by Nigerian Army has brought an end to the era of cash and carry politics of subservience to Hausa Fulani to the detriment of Biafra."[72] MASSOB spokesman Uchenna Madu also raises the northern specter, if perhaps with more subtlety than Emma Powerful: "This artificial entity called Nigeria will never be united or exist as one nation as long as these [*sic*] established mentality of a section of the country seeing themselves as the lords of Nigeria."[73] He accused the Buhari administration of turning a blind eye toward the crimes of Fulani herdsmen. Broadly speaking, Kanu and Uwazuruike, and IPOB and MASSOB, have the same goals: an independent Biafra, but IPOB appears to be the more dynamic. Both Kanu and Uwazuruikeregularly denounce violence against Igbo and Christians by the "Fulanis," but Kanu appears to get more media attention.

MASSOB and IPOB both appear to draw their strength from some in the diaspora rather than at home. Yet, most of the diaspora in the United Kingdom and the United States does not currently promote the independence of Biafra. Diaspora Igbos are different from the various IrishAmerican groups that provided assistance to the Irish Republican Army (IRA) and its different iterations in Northern Ireland. Igbo diaspora movements in the United States appear to be primarily concerned with the preservation of their cultural heritage and with providing assistance of various kinds to their old home. It is easy to overestimate the neo-Biafra movement's importance, in part because the movement's leaders use social media effectively. Though it is not as dangerous to Abuja as Boko Haram, Delta militants, or violence in the middle belt, the large demonstrations that occur when Uwazuruike and Kanu have been arrested indicate that they can marshal real support. The treatment of Kanu, specifically his long detention despite court orders, is reminiscent of the ham-handed treatment by the federal government of other such leaders, including those of the Ogboni, Boko Haram, and the Islamic Movement of Nigeria. Mishandling by the Abuja government could inflame opinion with the potential of making a revived Biafra a mass movement, which for now it is not. There is the potential that the federal government will drive some Igbos toward violence by closing off avenues of peaceful protest. To address the roots of separatism, the government would need to acknowledge the concerns and grievances of the Igbos through dialogue as opposed to the use of arrests. Otherwise, agitation for an independent Biafra is unlikely to go away.

The current movement for Biafra is less than what it was during the civil war—then an elite movement that established and administered a territorial state and was willing to go to war to defend it. Today, it is a state of mind and administers no territory. The state of Biafra was in many ways a creation of the Igbo elites; Ojukwu, its military chief of state, was the son of one of the richest men in late colonial Nigeria. Now, the Igbo elites that control the formal institutions of government in the region oppose secession, as has been made clear by the southern governors. It appears that the current revival of pro-Biafra sentiment receives much of its support from the powerless Igbo poor and marginalized, and some of the diaspora.

CONFLICT IN THE MIDDLE BELT

The middle belt stretches across Nigeria from east to west. It is a geopolitical zone with imprecise boundaries. States usually placed in the middle belt are Benue, Plateau, Taraba, Niger, Kogi, Nasarawa, and the Federal Capital Territory of Abuja. However, parts of Kaduna, Kebbi, Bauchi, Gombe, Yobe, and Borno also are often included. The population of these states may number thirty-five million, or between 15 and 20 percent of the population of Nigeria. The middle belt marks the transition from the dry, predominately pasture lands in the north to well-watered farmland in the south. It is unusually ethnically diverse, with no one group predominating. It is also the borderland between the predominately Muslim north and the predominately Christian south. Historically, Fulani of the Sokoto Caliphate would prey on the smaller animist ethnic groups primarily engaged in farming to their south for the slave trade, but it is also true that farming and herding communities have a history of living peacefully and even symbiotically together.

Much of the north—save for the northeast—of what is now Nigeria has been dominated by Fulani Muslims for hundreds of years. Fulani emirs associated with Sokoto pushed south into what is now the middle belt to convert and incorporate the smaller tribes. Fulani conquest also fed the trans-Saharan slave trade. Recall that, at the time the British conquered the Sokoto Empire in 1902, the latter was the world's largest slave state. Hence, in many cases, when the small tribes abandoned their traditional religion, they embraced Christianity rather than the Islam of the slave-catching Fulani. In turn, these ethnic and religious differences also coincided with different uses of land, as the Muslim Fulani are historically semi-nomadic herdsmen, while smaller tribes, notably the Berom and the Tiv, are predominately Christian settled farmers.

After the restoration of civilian rule, elites often exploited the overlapping conflicts in the middle belt—as they have elsewhere—to enhance their power and advance their personal agendas.[74] In particular, they have exploited the concept of "indigeneity," the quasi-legal principle that persons whose origins are in a particular place have greater rights than "settlers," those who have come from elsewhere, even if "settlers" had come generations ago. The Fulani, then, tend to be the "settlers" in this situation. In many cases, northern groups were moved south into the middle belt to act there as political officials in the colonial government or as laborers in certain industries. This legacy has real legal and political consequences. In Benue, in 2017, legislation provided different criteria for indigenes and settlers to establish ranches. In Jos, a city in the mostly Christian Plateau state, ethnic Hausa Muslims had been brought in to mine tin during the colonial period. The locals were largely Christian Berom farmers and therefore stuck to the countryside, while Jos became increasingly Hausa and Muslim. Initially, these groups appeared to live in harmony. But with increasing urbanization, farmers have been moving to the city. Unscrupulous politicians then hired gangs of thugs to incite violence between the Muslim Hausa "settlers" and the Christian Berom "indigenes" to score political victories.[75] Such violence was at a high in 2008 and 2009.[76] As is so often the case—with, for example, Boko Haram—politicians either end their sponsorship of such groups or just lose control of them.

LAND, WATER, AND RELIGION

Resource scarcity, population growth, and environmental degradation are at the heart of violence in the middle belt. One credible source estimates that between 1975 and 2013 the land available for grazing had decreased by 38 percent.[77] Herders in search of pasture and water are pushed farther south. Population growth and rapid urbanization is also putting stress on traditional grazing routes and pastures, resulting in more frequent conflict between herders and members of sedentary communities. Disputes over who has a right to the land can sometimes lead to violence and reprisals. With population growth, economic incentives for each group are changing. According to Amnesty International, "increasingly, the Fulani herders are taking to farming crops as a means of livelihood, while members of farming communities also now own cattle," threatening the traditional system of coexistence, cooperation, and conflict resolution.[78]

Generally speaking, varying combinations of competition for ever-scarcer resources, such as land and water, criminal banditry fueled by the proliferation of small arms, and ethnic and religious conflicts, often stoked for political advantage, can explain much of the violence occurring in Nigeria's middle belt. In turn, these factors are in some ways driven, in other ways exacerbated, by a population boom, urbanization, the decrease in arable land due to desertification, and changes to the agricultural industry. But the weight to give each of these factors is difficult to know and is different from incident to incident across the region. What is clear, however, is that "conflict in the middle belt" is deadly and destructive, at times resulting in more monthly casualties than the Boko Haram conflict. And unlike the conflict with Boko Haram, which occurs in a predominately Muslim part of the country, the middle belt is where the two religions meet. Thus, it is vulnerable to popular fears of a "Muslim takeover," which are fanned in the Christian south by social media and driven in part by the fact that President Buhari is himself a Fulani Muslim. According to his critics, his administration did little to address the crisis and was biased toward the Fulani.

Over the past generation, both Islam and Christianity in the middle belt have become more militant. Nine northern states have adopted Islamic law, sharia, in the criminal domain. While it is supposed to apply only to Muslims, it affects Christians as well, especially in families of mixed religion, on issues of marriage, divorce, and inheritance. The Wahhabist form of Islam has also spread rapidly. On the one hand, it is hostile to religious pluralism. On the other hand, the Nigerian media is dominated by southern Christians, and it tends to demonize the Fulani. Western media reports on the middle belt are often taken directly from the Nigerian media. Hence, in political circles in Washington, it is the Fulani that are often held responsible for middle belt violence. But religion and ethnicity cannot account for all such violence. In 2019, the state of Zamfara was one of the most violent, but it is in the north and almost entirely Muslim.

WHO'S WHO?

Villages routinely ascribe attacks to the "other," whether that be someone of a different religion, ethnicity, or someone who uses land differently (i.e., herders or farmers) rather than simply identifying the attackers as bandits or cattle rustlers, which in at least some cases they are. By contrast, federal and state government spokesmen are quick to blame "bandits" or "terrorists" for attacks, minimizing the ethnic or religious dimension. The categories are fluid, and many times attackers bear various combinations of labels that can make it difficult to definitively identify them. When, for example, are fighters merely criminals intent on cattle rustling and when are they protecting their own communities from attack? How fighters are perceived depends on their community and that of their victims. Muslim and Christian spokesmen routinely claim that victims come disproportionately from their particular community. Solid evidence is lacking, but a working hypothesis might be whichever religious group has the largest numbers in a particular geographical area will provide the most victims.

Many Christians believe that their religion is under Muslim assault in the middle belt. This is also true of pastors based in Lagos or other parts of the country far from the middle belt. They are susceptible to rumor and exaggeration of undeniable Muslim attacks on their fellow Christians, which they too uncritically claim are driven by the religion of the victim. Rather than organized or centrally directed, most of the middle belt violence appears to be populist, often spontaneous, and sometimes with overt criminal motivation— especially cattle rustling. Still, many Western commentators characterize "the Fulani" as a terrorist group.[79] Rumors that "the Fulani" are centrally directed to move south, attack locals, and occupy land are widespread in Nigeria. People may point to the fact that militants are well armed as evidence, but an NGO working in the middle belt for more than a decade has seen no credible evidence of such coordination.[80]

Among many Muslims, not just Boko Haram, there is the parallel belief that Islam is under attack by the secular world. And they see that attack as abetted by Christianity, which they often identify with the modern, secular world. Muslim leaders are often ill at ease with the movement of Christians from other parts of Nigeria into areas that have been traditionally Islamic. Those Christians usually have a strong ethnic identification and when they settle in predominately Islamic areas, they often resist interchange with Muslims. Muslims, in turn, will try to segregate Christians into specific ghettos, called Sabon Gari, the strangers' quarter. There is often little social mixing between the two communities, and unlike in Lagos and elsewhere in Nigeria, intermarriage is rare. There is lively interfaith dialogue between Christians and Muslims, but it tends to be at the top of the social pyramid, at universities, and involving the most senior of traditional rulers such as the sultan of Sokoto, the Roman Catholic cardinal, and the Anglican primate. Participants in that dialogue have been less successful in incorporating "the street" into the national conversation.

Though much of the violence may involve the use of "traditional" weapons—spears, knives, and machetes—that are readily available in even the poorest villages, West Africa and Nigeria are home to weapons left over from civil wars in Liberia, Ivory Coast, and Sierra Leone. More recently, significant numbers of weapons have also probably come from the aftermath of the Libyan civil war. Other sources include Nigeria's domestic arms manufacturing industry and homemade firearms and ammunition. One estimate is that 17 percent of rural gun holders and 10 percent of Nigerian city dwellers possess at least homemade weapons.[81] The recent surge in and deadliness of banditry, such as cattle rustling, is facilitated by the fact that the region is awash with small arms.[82] According to an analysis of data from the Council on Foreign Relations' Nigeria Security Tracker, the vast majority of violence in the middle belt involved at least one gun.[83] The bottom line is that weapons are many, cheap, and easily stolen.

GOVERNMENT AND LOCAL RESPONSES

In 2018, there were an estimated two thousand violent deaths from "farmer-herder conflicts," exceeding those from the war between the security services and Boko Haram, and that pattern has continued.[84] In some areas, ethnic cleansing—the radical separation of populations on religious and ethnic lines—is far advanced. Jos, for example, the capital of Plateau state, once was characterized by neighborhoods of mixed ethnicity. No more. There is anecdotal evidence that if a person of a particular ethnicity/religion finds himself in the "wrong" neighborhood, he risks death. In Benue alone, the State Emergency Management Agency reported that farmer-herder conflict has led to 480,000 internally displaced persons.[85] Altogether, these are forces beyond the ability of elites to control through their traditional bargaining and dealmaking. Many local elites decamp for the comparative safety of Abuja where they can continue to enjoy access to oil revenue.

The causes of specific conflicts are diffuse and local. "Farmers" and "herders" have no single representative, though the Miyetti Allah Cattle Breeders Association of Nigeria purports to advocate on the herders' behalf, and many in the south ascribe to it control over the attacks on Christians. The mostly Christian farmers from smaller ethnic groups are ostensibly represented by the All Farmers Association of Nigeria (AFAN). It is not clear what level of influence or even relevance, especially in the case of banditry, these organizations have. Successful initiatives incorporate early-warning systems along with joint Christian-Muslim interventions, usually led by small teams. They seek to mobilize local leaders against violence. Especially where the intervention is granular, involving a single, small village or neighborhood, there has been considerable, verifiable success. One of the more robust organizations doing this is Search for Common Ground, which helps organize the Forum on Farmer and Herder Relations in Nigeria (FFARN), a research collaboration between academics, government agencies, and practitioners that seeks to better inform policy. The group also organized numerous, small-scale peace dialogues to bring together relevant stakeholders, such as representatives of the communities involved, representatives of state and local governments, the police, and religious leaders, among others.[86] There are also Nigerian-led organizations, like the Pastor and the Imam, which is representative of cross-religious dialogue at a high level.

The federal and state governments have made proposals, such as providing space for ranches or creating designated corridors for pastoralists to travel through. One such proposal is the establishment of "Ruga settlements," an initiative of the Buhari administration to restructure the cattle industry. It proposed the resettlement of pastoralist Fulani and their cattle at fixed locations. As a condition for their settlement, the government would provide these settlements with schools, hospitals, roads, veterinary clinics, and markets. In addition, the government promised to establish manufacturing capabilities that would allow the pastoralists to process the meat and other animal products they raise.[87] Criticism of the Ruga settlements is that the federal government did not sufficiently consult with state and local authorities, though some states voluntarily signed up for the program. Still, none have been fully implemented, and it remains to be seen whether the Fulani pastoralists will participate, and if they do, whether the administration will make available sufficient funding for resettlement to work. It appears that these are more focused on managing the situation politically rather than addressing the causes of the conflict. Proposals tend to approach the cattle industry from an economic perspective, with little attention paid to the cultural basis for the herders' way of life. They do not address the practical consequences of the huge increase in both the human and the cattle population, nor the persistence of drought over larger and larger areas. Criminality, especially cattle rustling, is a driver of violence. At times, it overlaps with intercommunal conflict. Concrete proposals to address rising criminality are rare.

In the short term, however, addressing the escalating violence in the middle belt is the greatest need. Police presence throughout the region—indeed, throughout the entire country—is weak. The writ of the federal and state governments does not run across large areas of the middle belt. In the past, traditional authorities—emirs, chiefs, and kings—often enforced the peace. However, under the pressure of the demographic boom of people and cattle, a decline in available land and water, and the knock-on effect of Boko Haram, the authority of traditional rulers has weakened. Though middle belt violence undermines the credibility of the Nigerian political economy throughout the country, the conflicts remain local and multifaceted.

FALLING APART

Central to Nigeria's survival as a state has been the cooperation of otherwise competing elites. Their reasons for cooperation—access to and distribution of government revenue—has not changed, but their ability to exert power and influence is being tested. Population growth, environmental degradation, and urbanization result in a young, urban population increasingly without opportunities. Following decades of ineffectual governance, Boko Haram and ISWA are challenging elite control of state authority in the northeast, offering an alternative vision and at times overwhelming the security services. In the Delta, militants hold the country's oil industry hostage, extorting the government for amnesty payments, though Delta militant activity has not led to significant benefits for most of its people. The revival of Biafra appears so far to be relatively minor and largely peaceful, though the fear is a bungled government response to peaceful protesters could radicalize them. In the middle belt, a confluence of environmental degradation, a growing population, and ethnic and religious differences set the table for hundreds of intensely local and otherwise separate conflicts, which together can be as deadly as Boko Haram. These three concurrent security crises pose a greater threat to Nigeria now than in the past. However, this is far from the first time Nigeria has faced serious challenges. The civil war was the greatest crisis the state has had to overcome, and it did so remarkably more effectively than many thought it could. Ever since, Nigeria has persisted, surviving massive corruption, military coups, three aborted attempts at democracy, and now numerous insurgencies. However, the elites who in the past kept the country together are losing their grip, and democratic institutions remain weak. It is not for nothing that the title of my first book is *Nigeria: Dancing on the Brink*.

Chapter 7

International Relations and a Prebendal Archipelago

Nigerian officials are proud, hypersensitive, and prickly. Diplomatic and other dealings with them will present challenges, and Nigerians will be slow to accept the US as a friend, even if Washington is fairly forthcoming in matters of economic and military assistance.

—US National Intelligence Estimate, November 2, 1970[1]

Previous chapters described how Nigeria does not fit the model of a conventional nation-state. Nevertheless, for most of its postindependence history, Nigeria has looked the part to outsiders. It has been an active participant on the regional, African, and world stages. It pursued conventional diplomatic goals related to its security, expanding its influences and promoting economic development using conventional diplomatic methods in bilateral and multilateral settings, such as the UN and its specialized agencies, the World Trade Organization, or the Organization of African Unity (OAU) and later the African Union (AU). Moreover, with the restoration of nominally civilian government in 1999, Nigeria increasingly played the role of regional hegemon. With the largest military in West Africa, it often dominated the reinvigorated Economic Community of West African States (ECOWAS) and the AU and was the most active African state in the UN. Abuja promoted and sometimes imposed a modicum of order in its region, working to end the civil wars in Ivory Coast, Sierra Leone, and Liberia, leading the search for the peaceful resolution of disputes—between itself and Cameroon over the Bakassi Peninsula, and between Sudan and South Sudan over the latter's independence—and ushering in the end of West Africa's coup culture.

But the previous chapters also detailed how internal crises, beginning in 2005 with the Niger Delta insurrection, are threatening the means by which Nigeria has functioned since the end of the civil war. Trouble at home has provoked a recessional from the world stage. Without Nigeria to provide regional ballast, instability has spread rapidly throughout the West African region, with Islamist-linked insurrections in Mali, Burkina Faso, and Niger. There has been a wave of military coups from the Red Sea to the Atlantic. In 2023, France announced its military withdrawal from the region, joined by its European Union partners. The democratic recessional and internal turmoil, exacerbated by the dramatic fall in world oil prices and the arrival of the coronavirus, made conducting diplomatic relations with Nigeria more challenging. The partnership between Washington and Abuja that characterized the presidencies of George W. Bush and Olusegun Obasanjo largely atrophied.

PREBENDALISM AND FEDERAL
CHARACTER IN FOREIGN POLICY

Since independence, under military and civilian governments, there has been a foreign ministry, a diplomatic service, a diplomatic academy, and, eventually, a large network of embassies and other diplomatic establishments around the world. In conducting foreign relations, Nigerian diplomats used standard diplomatic language and followed the usual diplomatic protocols. They sent and received diplomatic notes, made demarches to their host governments, and the foreign ministry granted *agrément* to those whom foreign governments proposed to send as ambassadors. Embassies and consulates offer consular services to their citizens abroad, insofar as limited financial resources allow. But matters of policy are reserved for the president. Active engagement with the African Union, the United Nations, and selected bilateral partners, even if mostly about matters of protocol and procedure, nevertheless provided presidents and other elites with a larger stage for their personal ambitions.

The prebendal nature of Nigerian politics is pivotal to diplomatic appointments, and it partly explains the length of time it takes to fill vacancies. The Ministry of External Affairs is responsible for some two hundred diplomatic missions around the world and operates a diplomatic training academy in Lagos. But Nigerian diplomats are often part of patronage networks that are obscure to diplomats from other countries, and lines of authority among Nigerian diplomats may be fluid. As with other ministries, External Affairs is chronically underfunded, and diplomats often go for long periods with their salaries and allowances in arrears, reinforcing their dependence on patrons. Yet, Nigeria's professional diplomats tend to identify with the Nigerian state to a much greater extent than their fellow citizens, and they are less governed by ethnic and religious identities. Well educated, Nigerian diplomats are usually Western-oriented in their outlook, if often personally critical of whatever Washington administration is in office at the time, and for many, English is their first language. Two foreign ministers have been women, Ngozi Okonjo-Iweala and Joy Ogwu, both notable for their competency, and both had spent long periods of time living in the United States.

As in other developing countries, Nigeria's political masters and elite cartel underuse their diplomatic service, and Nigerian foreign ministers, with the exception of Okonjo-Iweala and Ogwu, are rarely memorable. Reflecting a pervasive suspicion of diplomatic expertise as well as ethnic and religious rivalries and jealousies, Nigerian political leaders too often turn to American or British lobbying firms rather than their own diplomats to manage their relations with the United States and other countries. Such reliance on the private sector is also found in other African states. This is as true of minor logistics as of high policy. Instead of asking the Nigerian embassy to schedule an appointment for a visiting mid- or high-level Nigerian official through the Department of State, the request may be made through a private lobbying firm without reference to the Nigerian embassy. The possibility of a presidential meeting might be broached through an American lobbyist rather than by the Nigerian ambassador, who might even be unaware of the initiative. Hence, Nigerian diplomats overseas often have less influence with their own government than do foreign lobbyists. A frequent exception is Nigeria's permanent representative to the UN, who has often had a distinguished career in public service. Nigeria sees its presence at the UN as vital to its international standing and successive presidents have taken care to appoint personnel of high quality to its New York mission. The UN post is the exception that proves the rule: when it comes to Nigerian foreign relations, the personal is usually more important than the institutional.

While Nigerian ministerial and diplomatic appointments may confer little actual authority and influence, they are nevertheless subject to Federal Character. Appointments must be balanced among the elites and their patronage networks of the thirty-six states, but also between the two dominant religions and among the major ethnicities. Ambassadors are subject to Nigerian senate confirmation, though such confirmation is not linked to a specific post. The post to which the president assigns an already senate-confirmed ambassador is subject to in-house horse-trading informed by the need for Federal Character balance. The three most prestigious ambassadorships are London, Washington, and the UN headquarters in New York. Principles of balance apply to these three as a subgroup, as well as to the larger universe of diplomatic appointments. Hence, making diplomatic appointments is highly complex, and filling vacancies can take a long time.

The trajectory of Nigerian foreign policy is similar to that of other African countries. After independence, Nigeria officially was nonaligned in the Cold War, though much of the time its tilt was toward the West. Its primary diplomatic focus has been on Africa, and it was fervent in its opposition to colonialism in Africa, especially apartheid South Africa, Rhodesia, and the Portuguese empire. Nigeria proudly considered itself to be a "frontline" state in the struggle against apartheid, and Nigerians will often take undue credit for apartheid's demise. Many Nigerians view with suspicion France's former close involvement with its former colonies. As in other newly independent states, Nigeria's foreign policy professionals strongly advocate for multilateralism.

This weak institutional structure with only the façade of a nation-state obscures the reality that Nigeria's foreign policy is largely personal to the president. Hence, the Nigerian presidency often emphasizes head-of-state diplomacy, especially presidential contacts and visits. Olusegun Obasanjo was the first African chief of state to call on President George W. Bush at the White House after the terrorist attacks of September 11, 2001. He thereafter actively pursued a personal relationship with the American president, which was reciprocated. President George W. Bush visited Nigeria in 2003, primarily to endorse the country's democratic trajectory. His visit was considered a great success from the perspective of President Obasanjo because it symbolized American approval of his consolidation of civilian political power just four years after the end of military rule. First Lady Laura Bush and her daughter Barbara made a follow-up visit in 2006. With its focus on literacy, a widespread Nigerian preoccupation, the visit was enthusiastically received by Nigerians in all walks of life. By contrast, President Obama declined to visit Nigeria, thereby underscoring to the Jonathan administration American concern about security service human rights abuses in the context of the Boko Haram insurgency and rigged elections.

As president, Obasanjo traveled incessantly, mostly in Africa, to meet with foreign heads of state. He led efforts to resolve African conflicts in Sierra Leone, Ivory Coast, and Liberia, and worked personally toward peace in Darfur and between Sudan and South Sudan. Obasanjo's power was uniquely personal, rather than bureaucratic or institutional. In resolving a territorial dispute with Cameroon over the Bakassi Peninsula, he and Cameroonian president Paul Biya personally negotiated Nigeria's withdrawal from disputed territory. In this tradition, after his election in 2015, President Buhari visited the chiefs of state of Niger, Chad, Cameroon, and Benin to organize a Multinational Joint Task Force (MNJTF) to counter Boko Haram.

Nigeria is usually most active in multilateral affairs. It helped found the Organization of African Unity (OAU) and later the African Union (AU). It is the linchpin of ECOWAS, hosts its headquarters, and accounts for about 40 percent of its member contributions.[2] After some hesitation, in 2019 it signed the African Continental Free Trade Area (CFTA) agreement, which would unite 1.3 billion Africans into a $3.4 trillion economic area encompassing all African countries.[3] Should it be implemented, the agreement could be a major step toward improving intra-African trade by eliminating tariffs on 90 percent of goods. It would be the largest free-trade area in the world since the creation of the World Trade Organization.

Nigeria is also an active participant in the Commonwealth, and the Nigerian Igbo politician and diplomat Emeka Anyaoku was its secretary-general for a decade. When it was its turn, Nigeria hosted with pomp and circumstance the Commonwealth Heads of Government Meeting in 2003 and the Commonwealth Games in 2014. With multilateralism so important, the United Nations is a major venue for Nigerian diplomacy and is actively working to assume a permanent African seat on a reformed UN Security Council. In this effort, and in other multilateral fora, its primary African rival is South Africa. The emphasis on multilateralism by Nigeria and shared by most African states reflects their relative weakness in the postcolonial international system: they have more voice in multilateral fora where they often coordinate more closely than in bilateral situations in which their interlocutors are more powerful.

Particularly at the UN General Assembly (UNGA), Nigeria will generally vote with other members of the African Union, which means there is usually a bias toward Palestine and against Israel, despite the generally good bilateral relationship between Abuja and Jerusalem. In 1975, Nigeria voted for a UNGA resolution that Zionism was a form of racism. But, in 1992, Nigeria also voted for the US-sponsored resolution for its repeal.[4] Successive Nigerian governments have regarded Israel as a "Christian" issue. As already mentioned, in 1986 the Babangida administration balanced Nigeria joining the Organization of the Islamic Conference (now the Organization for Islamic Cooperation) with the establishment of diplomatic relations with Israel. In a polity that attempts to balance Christians and Muslims, a pro-Israel vote can be the result of Nigerian domestic as well as foreign policy considerations, much as Israel-related foreign policy decisions in the United States have unusually large domestic political considerations.

Typically, the Nigerian delegation to a multilateral international meeting is large compared to others; Nigerians perceive its size as an indication of their country's importance, and, equally, members of a delegation see their participation as an affirmation of their own personal high status. It also reflects a pernicious mutual lack of trust among rival patronage networks that send representatives to keep an eye on their rivals. Nigerian delegates are testy about maintaining their own—and Nigeria's—self-regard. They are quick to take offense at what they regard as lectures by foreigners or being patronized. Even their foreign friends find Nigerians hard to work with in international settings.

Nevertheless, from the perspective of the UN, the AU, ECOWAS, the European Union (EU), and the United States, Nigerian state activism in multilateral fora was almost entirely positive and has promoted regional stability. In Darfur, for example, Washington recognized the need for peacekeepers but there was little or no public support for sending American soldiers. Nigeria stepped in. In some ways, Nigeria's peacekeeping role was probably more valuable to Washington than its oil. The oil market is fungible, and the world supply of oil and natural gas has been growing, not least in the United States. But American domestic support for peacekeeping missions was finite, and there has long been a consensus against US military forces serving as peacekeepers. Nigerian peacekeepers have been active in the Congo, Liberia, Sierra Leone, and in Darfur. Peacekeeping raised the prestige of the Nigerian state and the elites associated with it. For many individual Nigerians, participation in UN and AU peacekeeping missions was personally profitable, with opportunities to acquire consumer and other goods that they would resell upon their return to Nigeria, while the Nigerian treasury also profited from UN payments for peacekeepers.

But as Nigeria's challenges have mounted, particularly after 2005, Abuja has drastically reduced its peacekeeping commitments. With respect to UN missions, after providing a high of 5,800 peacekeeping personnel (police, military observers, and troops) in 2011, Nigeria provided about 4,500 in 2014, and just 290 by mid-2019.[5] Still, Nigeria remained diplomatically active in West Africa, particularly through ECOWAS. For example, following the December 1, 2016, presidential election in the Gambia, President Yahya Jammeh, who lost, set off a constitutional crisis by refusing to step down. Nigeria helped institute a naval blockade of the Gambia and a patrol of its airspace while an ECOWAS force, including a contingent from Nigeria, marched toward the Gambian border by land. Subsequently, Jammeh agreed to go into exile.[6] Though a small lift for Nigeria—it was estimated the Gambia had just 1,200 soldiers in its military—it reaffirmed Abuja's commitment to ending military dictatorships, supporting elections, and peaceful transfers of power in West Africa. However, by 2023 and in the face of the African coup wave, Nigerian activism had become almost entirely rhetorical. Racked by security crises at home and with a military that had been hollowed out, President Tinubu failed to rally effective opposition to military coups in Ethiopia, Sudan, Niger, Mali, Burkina Faso, Guinea, and Gabon. In the years after the restoration of ostensibly civilian governance in 1999, a cornerstone of Nigeria's Africa policy had been opposition to military coups, and it enjoyed significant success in rolling back dictatorship in Liberia and Sierra Leone. But, by 2023, that policy was in tatters, and Nigerian pretense to be the "hegemon" of West Africa was hollow.

THE US-NIGERIAN RELATIONSHIP

A review of the US-Nigerian relationship shows little US effort to take into account Nigeria's prebendalism and, in turn, craft a country strategy that fits. Instead, Nigeria's principle diplomatic partners, including the United States, relate to Abuja as though it were the capital of a conventional nation-state. The lack of understanding and consideration of how Nigeria works accounts, in part, for the "uneasy friendship," the result of unmet expectations that characterize the official relationship between Washington and other capitals and Abuja.[7] This is particularly true in the post-2005 breakdown of West Africa's political economy.[8]

A review of the US-Nigeria bilateral relationship underscores the importance of security questions and, to a lesser extent, Washington's efforts to promote better governance. There is little bilateral dialogue regarding climate change to which Nigeria is a contributor through gas flaring. Nigeria has no policy to address the mass migration that is related to the youth bulge and changing demographics, and in both Washington and Abuja, there is little effort to understand the uniquely indigenous roots of jihadist radicalism. Instead, there are exchanges over arms sales initiated by the Nigerians and largely unrealistic American calls for better elections and more effective Nigerian moves to end corruption. On both sides, there is ignorance or misunderstanding about how the other works.

Though the United States maintained a consulate in Lagos and offices at various times in Enugu, Ibadan, and Kaduna during British colonial rule, it had no formal diplomatic relations with Nigeria's colonial government. Such offices were primarily for public outreach and to provide services to American citizens. Despite inchoate American opposition to colonialism in principle, Washington was largely uninterested in irritating London, Paris, Lisbon, and Pretoria on African issues. After all, during World War II, the United Kingdom and France, by far the largest colonial powers in Africa, were close allies, as was pre-apartheid but racially segregated South Africa.[9] The minimal diplomatic business that involved Nigeria was carried out with British officials in London and Washington. Hence, prior to Nigerian independence, Nigeria was a minor element in the much larger Anglo-American relationship.

Besides, European colonial rule in Africa was congruent with widespread American white supremacist views during the twilight era of legal segregation. During the Second World War, President Franklin D. Roosevelt spoke out against colonialism on one occasion, taking Prime Minister Winston Churchill to task about conditions in British-ruled Sierra Leone during a stopover on his way to the wartime Cairo conference.[10] In 1948, President

Harry S. Truman racially integrated the US military, furthering the legal erosion of white supremacy in post–World War II America. He welcomed the
dissolution of Britain's Indian Empire and the end of the British mandate in
Palestine. But America's anticolonial focus, such as it was, tended to be on
the British in India, the Dutch in Indonesia, and the French in Vietnam, rather
than the European tropical empires in Africa or South Africa. A distinct US
policy toward Nigeria, and much of sub-Saharan Africa for that matter, really
only emerged after 1960 when most African states became independent.

The first serious challenge to the United States and its bilateral relationship with Nigeria was the civil (or Biafra) war. The episode shows how
Washington and Lagos (then the capital of Nigeria) talked past each other
and were mutually ignorant of the domestic drivers of their respective policies. Throughout the civil war, official US policy was to support the unity of
Nigeria, which meant opposition to the secession of Biafra. In public, however, Washington's support for the nationalists was muted, perhaps reflecting
inherent caution about African issues within the Johnson and Nixon administrations. US policy was largely parallel to that of the United Kingdom and the
Soviet Union. France, then in the aftermath of the Algerian war, and apartheid
South Africa, which resented Nigeria's anti-apartheid activism, were sympathetic to Biafra. The major oil companies lay low but generally supported the
nationalists. Nevertheless, there were persistent fears in Lagos of clandestine
oil company support for Biafra.

With millions starving in Biafra, American supporters called on their congressional representatives to push for humanitarian aid. From July 1, 1968,
to February 10, 1969, the Department of State answered more than 550 congressional inquiries relating to the civil war, at that time an unusually large
number for an African issue. Most were favorable to Biafra.[11] The American
media also favored Biafra and made wide use of a picture of a starving Igbo
child, which the Biafran propaganda agency produced to great effect.[12] On
college campuses, Biafra was yoked to the anti–Vietnam War protests, wom-
en's liberation, and the civil rights movement. The general, if not necessarily
informed, view in the United States was that if Biafra were defeated, the
Igbos would be subject to genocide, as they had been in northern Nigeria in
1966. Though the US government's formal opposition to secession was genuine, it was not obvious at the time to outsiders; from a Nigerian perspective,
most American sentiment favored Biafra.

US official documents calendared in the *Foreign Relations of the United
States* series (*FRUS*) show that the official understanding of Nigerian developments was limited. It also shows a degree of policy incoherence during the
civil war within both the administrations of Johnson (1963–69) and Nixon
(1969–74), reflecting emotion, sentiment, and failure to apply on-the-ground
information. As an example of the latter, the Central Intelligence Agency in a

memorandum dated August 5, 1969, stated that "the minority tribesmen now in control of the federal government are not bent on genocide against the Ibos, and the top leaders, like General Gowon, will probably take great pains to prevent the massacre of Ibos if the federal forces ever do overrun the Biafran enclave."[13] This assessment proved correct. However, six months later, in February 1970, Alexander Haig, then the president's deputy assistant for national security affairs, expressed his surprise in a memorandum to Henry Kissinger (then national security advisor) that after winning the war, Gowon's soldiers had not committed an Igbo genocide.[14] He either had no knowledge of the CIA assessment or little confidence in it.

But the intelligence community made mistakes, demonstrating significant bias toward Biafra and against the Federal Military Government that, in part, reflected the shortcoming of reporting and analysis from the US embassy in Lagos. This resulted in the underestimation of Yakubu Gowon, the head of the Federal Military Government, and an overestimation of Emeka Ojukwu, the leader of Biafra. A postscript to the annual US policy assessment of 1967 noted that Americans viewed the war as a struggle between two mismatched individuals. The report stated, "We like romantic leaders, and Ojukwu has panache, quick intelligence and an actor's voice and fluency." The contrast with Gowon—"troubled by the enormity of his task, painfully earnest and slow to react, hesitant and repetitive in speech"—was stark.[15] Hence Washington had at best an incomplete understanding of the civil war. For its part, the Lagos government displayed little understanding of the multiple drivers of the American responses to the war, and particularly the distinction between activists and media organizations and actual US government policy.

Washington also made specific missteps from the perspective of Lagos. Former US ambassador to Nigeria Elbert Matthews identified four actions taken by the State Department during the war that were irritants to US-Nigerian relations: the refusal to sell a certain type of ammunition that the Federal Military Government wanted; resistance to terminating the USAID and Peace Corps projects in Biafra; a US public statement opposing the Nigerian military government's request for arms; and a statement condemning the Soviet supply of arms to the Federal Military Government.[16] Washington's position on these issues reflected world power concerns beyond Nigeria. Three relate directly to arms sales, a contentious issue in the US bilateral relationship even now. Soviet arms sale to Lagos raised the specter of the growing influence of Moscow in Africa during an intense period in the Cold War. With respect to USAID and Peace Corps activities, Washington was loath to surrender to host governments a veto over their activities. Yet these issues would not seem important enough to frost the bilateral relationship and did indeed reflect the differing perspectives of a regional power and a global one. A deeper

understanding of what made the nationalists tick might have resulted in better diplomatic management, but, ultimately, US policy during the civil war
was sound. What was lacking was an effective public diplomacy strategy to
explain it to Nigerians and to concerned Americans.

The decisions taken by Washington cited by Ambassador Matthews did
not necessarily imply a policy shift in favor of Biafra. But those in the
Lagos-based government took it that way. Combined with the pro-Biafra
drumbeat from American media, NGOs, and churches, many Nigerian
nationalists were convinced that Washington favored Biafra. For example,
returned Peace Corps volunteers were prominent in the American Committee
to Keep Biafra Alive, the most important American organization to emerge
during the civil war, which pushed Washington toward supporting greater
humanitarian relief for Biafra.[17] Though returned Peace Corps volunteers
were not American government officials, that nuance may have been lost on
many Nigerians.

In a sense, Washington's Biafra policy resulted in the worst of both possible worlds. It officially supported the nationalists, thereby sacrificing any
possible leverage it might have had with the Biafrans. But it received little
or no credit for supporting the unity of Nigeria from the nationalists. Today,
some Nigerians have a sinister interpretation of American policy because of
US actions during the civil war.

Nigeria's post–civil war military governments were not especially repressive, save that of Sani Abacha. Accordingly, the bilateral relationship with
the United States was usually mutually cordial, and American ambassadors
had personal access to military chiefs of state, but it was otherwise not well
developed. There were areas of political cooperation, notably narcotics inter-
diction. These were years of oil boom and bust. The energy in the bilateral
relationship tended to be around economics rather than politics. Friction
tended to be over multilateral issues, such as the US position on the civil war
in Angola or Nigerian perception of American foot-dragging on apartheid
South Africa, but it was contained. Though the relationship deteriorated significantly during the darkest days of military rule—the Abacha dictatorship—
full diplomatic relations were maintained, including the regular exchange of
ambassadors. It is now understood that the military era saw an exponential
expansion of official corruption involving chiefs of state and their military
subordinates. One estimate is that Abacha alone stole $2–4 billion in public
money.[18] But, at the time, US policymakers appeared to be largely unaware
of the way corruption was transforming the state.

The 1999–2007 administration of Olusegun Obasanjo marked a transition, albeit incomplete at the time, from military to democratic, civilian
government. The bilateral relationship became closer than it had been
with Nigeria's military governments. The George W. Bush administration

applauded Obasanjo's diplomatic activism in strengthening African institutions such as the African Union and the Economic Community of West African States but also his deep involvement in UN and AU peacekeeping. During those years, the United States imported up to one million barrels of Nigerian oil a day, about half of the country's production. Obasanjo made it clear that should Middle East sources of oil be inhibited, Nigeria would do what it could to increase production. Consultation and cooperation on African security issues dominated the relationship. In addition to Nigeria's positive role in multilateral peacekeeping, Obasanjo's gesture of solidarity following the attacks of September 11, and his subsequent support of the US-led Global War on Terror, positively colored the relationship. President Bush, for his part, greatly expanded US medical assistance to Nigeria through his President's Emergency Plan for AIDS Relief (PEPFAR). He remains widely popular among Nigerians. But since the high-water mark of the Bush-Obasanjo friendship, the United States no longer imports significant amounts of Nigerian oil, and Abuja has reduced its diplomatic activism as it responds to Boko Haram and other internal conflicts. While the relationship is less close than it was under presidents Bush and Obasanjo, Nigeria nevertheless remains potentially an important partner to the United States.

The most significant shift in the US security relationship with Nigeria—and likely many other countries—occurred in the aftermath of the September 11, 2001, terror attacks on the United States. At the time, American policymakers had become concerned about the potential for jihadist extremists in the Sahel and looked to partner with Nigeria, not least because it is the most populous country in Africa. The fragility of West African states raised the possibility that ungoverned spaces in the Sahara and the Sahel could provide shelter for extremists, as the ungoverned spaces in Afghanistan did for al-Qaeda. Hence, the United States has been directly involved in the security of the Sahel since 2002, when the George W. Bush administration established the Pan-Sahel Initiative (PSI), followed by the Trans-Saharan Counterterrorism Partnership (TSCTP) in 2005. They included US training of local security forces so that the latter could better respond to terrorist threats. In 2007, President Bush established the Unified Africa Command (AFRICOM), one of now ten US combatant commands. It became active in 2008, expanding the military's security capacity in Africa and adding an important humanitarian dimension. For example, AFRICOM provided significant assistance to West African countries responding to the 2014–16 Ebola outbreak, and it is involved in ongoing antipiracy efforts in the Gulf of Guinea.

However, at the time of AFRICOM's rollout, there was Nigerian suspicion that the new command somehow represented a challenge to Nigeria, which was then still secure in its position as the hegemon of West Africa. The abrupt and insensitive rollout of the command further soured hope of a productive relationship, and Nigeria did not cooperate with AFRICOM. Abuja worked against the establishment of AFRICOM's headquarters on the African continent and its headquarters have remained in Stuttgart, Germany.

There is no permanent US military presence in Nigeria beyond the offices of the Defense Attaché and Office of Defense Cooperation, offices that also exist in other US embassies across the continent. In addition, American Special Operations forces, always small, are deployed from time to time in Nigeria, Niger, Somalia, Libya, Mali, Chad, and Mauritania, usually for training host-government military personnel to counter insurgencies.[19] A US drone base in Niger was involved in the Sahel with countering jihadist terrorism and transnational criminal activity. There has also been an increase in less-permanent unarmed drone bases and facilities to support them, notably in Niger and Cameroon at those countries' invitation. (In the aftermath of recent coups, it remains to be seen whether US military training will continue.)

In 2018, the Department of Defense announced a shift in strategy from countering terrorism to great power confrontation. It looked toward reducing American military personnel in Africa by half.[20] Amid looming threats of a troop drawdown, President Trump had nevertheless pledged $60 million to support the G5 Sahel Force, a French-assisted, multilateral military force established by five Sahelian countries under assault from jihadist movements.[21] French withdrawal from West Africa announced in 2023 in the face of anti-French coups makes it questionable whether the Force will survive. Though in 2019, America's military presence in Africa was greater than it had ever been, in absolute terms, it was quite small. The largest concentration of US military personnel on the continent is in East Africa, at Camp Lemonier, whose focus is the Red Sea.

AMERICA AND BOKO HARAM

Since 2014, Boko Haram has defined the bilateral security relationship, but there has seemingly been little American attention or resources focused on the diverse and local drivers of Nigerian terrorism. Nor has there been close coordination between Washington and other capitals on Boko Haram even though its brutality repelled policymakers and media around the world. Overall, there has been little outside involvement in the war between Abuja and the movement, though Canada, the United Kingdom, and the United States have offered assistance. Only gradually did Abuja move to increase coordination and cooperation with other African states also suffering from the Boko Haram onslaught. But, as of 2023, it remains unclear how such cooperation will survive as there are now military dictatorships in Chad, Niger, Mali, and Burkina Faso that to varying degrees are hostile to France and its Western allies.

Western attention reached a fever pitch when Boko Haram kidnapped over two hundred girls from a school in Chibok, Nigeria, in 2014. First Lady Michelle Obama, along with many other prominent figures, joined the #BringBackOurGirls campaign on social media, and the United States offered support in locating the girls. But, Nigeria's slow and inept response to Boko Haram, which, at its height in 2014–15 occupied territory the size of Maryland, complicated relations with London, Ottawa, and Washington. The government's approach included the wholesale rounding up of men and boys following any particular Boko Haram incident. Conditions inside military holding facilities such as the Giwa Barracks were unspeakable and were well documented by the Western media.[22] Indeed the brutality of the government response appears to have been an important dimension of Boko Haram recruitment.

Spurred by the kidnapping of the Chibok girls, US congressional interest peaked in 2014 and 2015. In a bipartisan effort, the House of Representative passed three resolutions and the Senate passed one, all four condemning the various acts perpetrated by Boko Haram. The resolutions noted the Obama administration's offer, and Goodluck Jonathan's acceptance, of military personnel, law enforcement officials, and other experts to aid in the search for the Chibok girls. The Obama administration also placed a $7 million bounty on Shekau's head, $2 million more than the bounty for Mullah Omar, the leader of the Afghan Taliban.

Despite the clear willingness of the United States, the United Kingdom, and other Western states to support Nigeria, actual on-the-ground cooperation with Nigerian military units proved difficult. There was suspicion on all sides. While American, British, and Nigerian military personnel identified where Boko Haram was holding some of the girls, the commanders of the forces concluded that were they to assault the holding camp, the hostages would likely be killed. Subsequent diplomatic efforts carried out by the International Committee of the Red Cross (ICRC) and the Swiss government secured the release of about half of the Chibok schoolgirls. As of 2024, an estimated 90 remain in captivity.[23]

During the Obama administration, the security relationship with the United States frayed as human rights concerns mounted. Nigerians and Americans often talked past each other when discussing the treatment of actual or suspected Boko Haram members. Especially in southern Nigeria, Boko Haram fighters were often viewed as "vermin" to whom human rights did not apply. Many Nigerians see their murder and roundups as justified.[24] Western human rights NGOs, on the other hand, were appalled at the lack of legal process and the conditions in which individuals charged with no crime were kept. They argued that Nigeria, a democracy, should be held to a higher standard than a terrorist movement. Such concerns over human rights led to further controversies over the sale of arms and provision of military training to Nigeria.

The consistent view of the Abuja government has been that Boko Haram is yet another chapter in a global jihad and an explicit threat to the West, including the United States. Proponents of this viewpoint rely on evidence of the group's international terror contacts. Among the evidence cited are reports of the training of Boko Haram militants abroad in Libya, documents found at Osama bin Laden's house in Abbottabad, Pakistan, showing contacts between Boko Haram and al-Qaeda, and Shekau's 2015 declaration of allegiance to the Islamic State, followed by the emergence of the Islamic State in West Africa (ISWA). However, while there has certainly been contact between Boko Haram and global jihadist movements, and while they share a theological outlook that is reflected in similar rhetoric, there is less evidence of tactical or strategic coordination. Boko Haram *looks and sounds* like a province of the Islamic State, but Shekau's declaration of allegiance appears to have had little practical consequence. Especially in its early days, al-Qaeda and other jihadist groups probably provided small numbers of Boko Haram operatives with training, but it does not appear to have been transformative.

Rather than seeing Boko Haram as part of a global jihad, the other, more credible view is that Boko Haram is primarily a local antigovernment group that has evolved into a radical Islamist movement. While it looks like other transnational terror groups and uses similar tactics and rhetoric, it still has both feet planted firmly in Nigeria and the Lake Chad Basin, from which it draws its recruits. Aside from the 2014 bombing in Abuja of a UN building, the targets of Boko Haram have been local. Boko Haram is highly flexible and it is certainly possible that factions of it could draw closer to international jihadist movements in the future, especially if it feels under siege. For now, however, Boko Haram does not directly threaten American security.

The framing of the debate could change this, and for the worse. If Boko Haram is, indeed, an integral part of the global jihad, the argument for US intervention is strengthened. If Boko Haram is, in essence, a local revolt, the argument for greater US involvement fades. However, these arguments are not mutually exclusive. Boko Haram and its various factions could have local goals while still cooperating where it could with global jihadis and using their rhetoric. US policymakers lack a more granular analysis of Boko Haram, in part because they are too dependent on unreliable official Nigerian sources, which tend to argue that Boko Haram is, indeed, an integral part of the global jihad.

The US policy debate on Boko Haram and jihadist groups in Nigeria and the Sahel is reminiscent of the earlier policy debate involving Iraq and the alleged desire of Iraqis for American intervention. US policymakers simply assumed Iraqis would embrace Western-style democracy when offered.

Hence, there was the famous assertion by Vice President Dick Cheney that the United States would "be greeted as liberators."[25] This debate was based on a misreading of Iraq's political, religious, and social realities. In Nigeria, there is the potential for a similar misreading. Especially among many Muslims, there is dislike and distrust of democracy; some view it as fundamentally non-Islamic and deeply distrust the United States.

WEAPONS, TRAINING, AND SECURITY ASSISTANCE

In the US-Nigerian security relationship, the advanced Western democracy and the prebendal archipelago have largely talked past each other. American military cooperation with Nigeria includes training programs, officer exchanges, and tactical assistance—such as airlifts and reconnaissance. But what Abuja really wants is advanced military technology from the United States. Nigerian motives appear mixed: some see the solution to Nigeria's security dilemmas as essentially the greater use of technology; for others, however, it is a matter of "toys for the boys," a means of satisfying the security services, especially the army. The history of US arms sales to Nigeria has long been fraught. A telling example: in the 1970s, the United States sold three C-130 military transport aircraft to the Nigerian Air Force. The air force used the planes to move Nigerian peacekeepers to hot spots but failed to maintain the planes properly. One crashed and another was cannibalized for parts, leaving only one operational. Subsequently, because of the lack of Nigerian Air Force capacity that the three C-130s had been intended to address, the United States provided airlifts at the request of the Nigerian government to transport Nigerian soldiers and their equipment to their peacekeeping theater of operations. However, some within the Nigerian defense establishment resented that the United States did not sell or otherwise replace Nigeria's own lift capacity. The Americans expected the Nigerians to properly maintain the C-130s; the Nigerians expected the Americans to sell the necessary replacement aircraft. Both parties were irritated.

The legal limits on the sale of military equipment and provision of training to militaries involved in human rights abuses are thorny issues in the relationship. The Leahy Amendment attached to a 1997 foreign aid bill and sponsored by Senator Patrick J. Leahy (D-VT) prohibits the training or equipping of foreign units that commit "gross human rights violations." The amendment was revised in 2013 to require the suspension of aid to an entire unit even if only a few of its members were implicated in human rights violations.[26] The vetting of units is the responsibility of the Department of State. Under most circumstances, the initial investigations are conducted by the US embassy in the relevant country. In Nigeria, the process can take months, not least because of a shortage of embassy and State Department resources, itself the result of a generation of underfunding on the US side.

During the Obama administration, the Goodluck Jonathan presidency wished to acquire Cobra attack helicopters for use against Boko Haram. The US administration denied the sale on the basis that the Nigerian Air Force was not doing enough to minimize civilian casualties in its war against Boko Haram. In 2014, the Nigerian Air Force had mistakenly strafed a residential area, killing hundreds of people. The Nigerian authorities held no one accountable.[27] Moreover, in January 2017, the Nigerian Air Force killed more than a hundred civilians in an accidental air strike targeting Boko Haram in Borno state (the Nigerian Air Force accepted responsibility for this episode).[28] In response to the Cobra decision, the Nigerian ambassador to Washington charged that the United States shared responsibility for the Boko Haram carnage because of its refusal to sell to Nigeria the military equipment it needed. President Buhari echoed the same point in a 2015 public presentation during his first visit to Washington following his inauguration, setting American policymakers' teeth on edge.

Some of the Cobra issues were at play when Nigeria sought to purchase Super Tucano aircraft, a turboprop designed for counterinsurgency, though the outcome was different. President Buhari said that the aircraft would be used only for reconnaissance. Nevertheless, the *New York Times* editorial board opposed the US sale of military aircraft to Nigeria in 2016 during the Obama administration. It argued that President Buhari had not done enough to respond to charges that the Nigerian army and air force had committed war crimes in its fight against Boko Haram. The newspaper also asserted that "Nigeria's government cannot be entrusted with the versatile new warplanes, which can be used for ground attacks as well as reconnaissance."[29]

The Obama administration eventually approved the sale but then suspended it amid concerns that misuse of the aircraft could result in significant civilian casualties, which would turn the local population against the government and also the United States. Washington policymakers recalled that the misuse by Afghani and Iraqi forces of highly sophisticated aircraft had led to civilian deaths, alienating the local population. Nevertheless, in 2018, the Trump administration authorized the sale.[30] Similar to the episode with the C-130s, questions remain about the Nigerian military's ability to keep up these planes once they have been delivered. But the largest question is whether they will improve Nigeria's ability to fight Boko Haram or whether they will lead to the deaths of more civilians.

While of less political salience than arms sales, the United States has long provided limited training and other assistance to the Nigerian military. US training of Nigerian military personnel, while relatively consistent in extent over the past two decades, remains small.[31] From 2000 to 2018, the United

States spent $7.2 million on International Military Education and Training (IMET) in Nigeria. This program aimed to promote leadership within the ranks of the Nigerian military by equipping participants with the skills required to operate specific weapons and fulfill the duties of their specialized positions.[32] For example, twelve US army soldiers trained two hundred Nigerian soldiers at the lieutenant level in ground combat tactics and leadership skills for seven weeks in 2018. The training took place at the invitation of the Nigerian government at the Nigeria Army Infantry School.[33]

Have two decades of IMET improved Nigeria's armed forces' effectiveness and respect for human rights? Nigerian recipients of US military training are usually enthusiastic about it while it is actually underway, but they are frequently transferred or leave the service within a short period after its conclusion. Elsewhere in West Africa, there is concern that US military training has encouraged a culture of military coups, and many Nigerian civilians are suspicious of it, just as many are suspicious of their own government. For example, they cite Amadou Sanogo, the military officer who led the 2012 coup that overthrew the government of Amadou Touré in Mali. Sanogo had participated in IMET training programs in Georgia, Virginia, and Texas. China and South Asia now train more Nigerian military, reducing the relative importance of US military training, and, anecdotally, both Nigerian and American military officers say that they have less contact with their opposite numbers than in the past.

If US-Nigerian security cooperation is generally fraught, combating piracy is the exception. The Gulf of Guinea is now the world's most dangerous maritime environment with respect to piracy; it is estimated that armed robbery at sea, oil theft, and piracy may cost Nigeria $1.5 billion per month. Successive Washington administrations have long seen maritime security in the Gulf of Guinea as an American strategic interest, and bilateral cooperation is good. AFRICOM conducts regular exercises in the Gulf of Guinea, including ship visits to Nigerian ports. In addition, the United States trains and equips the militaries in the Gulf of Guinea littoral and conducts joint exercises with them designed to enhance African maritime capacity.[34]

There is a relationship between piracy and oil theft in the Gulf of Guinea and Delta unrest. Delta militants, politicians, and oil-industry personnel have long participated in criminal syndicates involved with oil theft and, likely, narcotics, human, and other trafficking. Residents of the Delta tend to acquiesce to such activity because of their collective sense of grievance over the degradation of the environment by the oil industry, depriving them of their traditional livelihoods based on fishing and farming. Delta unrest does not currently play a major role in the bilateral relationship, but US oil companies are deeply involved in Nigeria's oil production. Renewed attacks on oil infrastructure could lead to their calls for more US military assistance to the Nigerian security services.

DEVELOPMENT, ELECTIONS, AND HEALTH

Though the security relationship has dominated US-Nigerian relations, especially at the highest levels, the non-security relationship is significant. Reference has been made to PEPFAR and a US program to combat malaria. There is also significant US financial and programmatic support for girl-child education administered through USAID. Other programs are designed to facilitate and encourage public-private commercial partnerships. Each administration since President Clinton has put forward a signature Africa policy focused on economic development, and Nigeria has been a beneficiary.

In the early 1960s, the US official view, shared throughout the developed world, was that a foreign assistance bureaucracy could bring about major change in Africa, a view not so far removed from some colonial thinking. But today, American official thinking is that African nations bear the major responsibility for creating an environment that attracts private investors.[35] President Bill Clinton's African Growth and Opportunity Act (AGOA) reflected this approach. Approved by Congress in May 2000, AGOA gave most African exports duty-free entry to the United States. It was designed to encourage Americans to invest in African enterprises that would export what they made to the United States. With bipartisan support in 2015, Congress extended it to 2025. However, especially among some Republicans in Congress, in 2024 there is opposition to renewal.

President George W. Bush established the Millennium Challenge Corporation in 2004, which engages external experts to rate African countries with respect to the environment for private business, political freedom, and overall stability. Countries with high ratings receive larger amounts of aid to finance major infrastructure projects. Though Nigeria is an early adopter of the Millennium Challenge goals as official policy, meeting them is a work in progress.[36] President Barack Obama established Power Africa in 2013, a program coordinated by the US Agency for International Development (USAID) that helps African countries create conditions to attract private investment in power generation. He also established Feed the Future in the same year, which brings modern agricultural technology and practices to the African farmer. The goal is to end the need for African nations to spend export earnings to import food. The program was developed by the US Department of State and is largely coordinated by USAID.[37] Nigeria participates in both. President Trump launched "Prosper Africa," a private-sector-led growth initiative. It is supported primarily by the Development Finance Corporation. At present, the United States is usually one of the largest of Nigeria's bilateral donors, averaging over $450 million per year.[38] US assistance to Nigeria enjoyed bipartisan support in the US Congress and has been congruent with long-standing American values. Some programs, notably PEPFAR, simply cannot be terminated: were that to happen, patients would die. That would be unacceptable to the American public. PEPFAR is worth doing for its own sake, but it provides Washington with little or no political leverage over Abuja because it is too small given the size of Nigeria. In part for that reason, by 2023 there was significant Republican congressional opposition to continuing to fund PEPFAR at its current levels.

For casual observers of Nigeria, elections would appear to receive the most Western attention. Every four years, Western media is awash in editorials and analysis; elected officials make public statements supporting democracy; and many former elected officials participate in observer missions. Americans view elections as intrinsic to democracy and voting as a fundamental human right. That democracy characterized by free and fair elections promotes prosperity and stability is a largely uncontested American assumption; hence, support for Nigerian elections is a fundamental American goal in Nigeria. This support largely takes the form of funding for election monitoring groups as well the provision of technical and material support to election commissions. Certain USAID-funded programs are designed to strengthen Nigeria's Independent National Electoral Commission (INEC), to encourage the development of political parties, and to promote issues-based political debate. Washington, however, has traditionally been unwilling to spend more than a pittance on such initiatives, dolling out $250–350 million a year in all of West Africa.[39] Even so, elections do not a democracy make.[40] "Democracy, after all, is less about elections than about impartial institutions."[41] This last point was especially clear in Malawi's May 2019 election. After being declared "well-managed, inclusive, [and] transparent" by the European Union observer mission, Malawi's highest court overturned the elections in February 2020, ruling that Peter Mutharika, the election's winner, was "not duly elected."[42] America's fixation on the forms of democracy, especially the mechanics of national elections, is sometimes misplaced, particularly in Nigeria.

In 2015, the president and the secretary of state were personally engaged in seeking credible elections in Nigeria. But this approach misunderstands the role of elections by presuming that Nigeria is, and therefore behaves like, a conventional nation-state. The approach is the result of a failure to recognize how little faith Nigerians have in the state, how weak their sense of national identity is, and how limited they are in their ability to vote as they wish, even in those instances where the voting and counting is credible. As chapter 4 discussed, results of elections are largely determined by bargains struck among

elites. Instead of being the center of the democratic process, elections are a
competition among elites for access to the cake, and a pageant that reaffirms
their dominance. In Nigeria, where leaders have a prebendal relationship
with a state characterized by limited government authority, support for the
rule of law, governance, and assistance to the judiciary might better promote
a democratic trajectory.

FIGHTING CORRUPTION

Just as US election support should be framed by understanding how politics
works in Nigeria, the official American response to corruption should consider the political culture of the prebendal state. The population loathes its
effects but also wants to benefit from it, not just to enrich themselves but,
in many cases, simply to get by. Petty corruption—at police checkpoints,
for example—can be seen as a redistribution technique that benefits the
very poor at the expense of the somewhat less poor. Nevertheless, there is
something of a consensus about "excessive" corruption, that is, the wholesale
looting of enormous amounts of public money, often in the millions of dollars
per episode, and then laundering it abroad. The "poster child" for excessive
corruption is Sani Abacha's looting the state of an estimated $2–4 billion
during his time as military chief of state. Successive Nigerian governments
have sought to recover those funds from abroad, with the cooperation of
Switzerland, the United Kingdom, and the United States.

When it comes to this form of "unacceptable" Nigerian corruption, the US
courts have been the primary venue for official American involvement. In
1970, the Bank Secrecy Act was the first US legislation that aimed to detect
and prevent money laundering.[43] Two court cases were pivotal to US moves
against foreign corruption and illicit financial flows.[44] They established that
wire transfers and foreign money exchanges into New York were a "transaction" of business. This provided the basis to force all banks—foreign and
domestic—to respond to civil litigation involving possible illicit funds. Most
notably, using these court decisions, funds from Sani Abacha—long after his
death—continue to be seized in the United States from accounts belonging
to his family and associates. In 2019, funds totaling $267 million hidden in
offshore accounts were seized on the island of Jersey (UK) with the help of
the United States government.[45] But much of this sort of cooperation requires
Nigerian initiative that is often not forthcoming because of the prebendal and
neopatrimonial relationships that rely on perpetuating the status quo. Further,
the US government resources devoted to law enforcement involving Nigeria
are anemic and interagency coordination is poor. Hence, the Nigerian media,

reflecting a popular view, accuses the United States of foot-dragging on looted Nigerian funds in US financial institutions.

Congressional interest in Nigeria has often revolved around corruption, and several senators and members of Congress have introduced legislation that would have addressed it, always defining it in American terms. Until recently, proposed anticorruption resolutions have failed to gather enough support to pass. In 2019, the House of Representatives passed the Kleptocracy Asset Recovery Rewards Act to help identify stolen assets linked to foreign government corruption and money hidden in financial institutions in the United States and abroad. The act referenced the over $480 million in corrupt funds belonging to former Nigerian dictator Sani Abacha that were seized by the Department of Justice in 2014.

On occasion, the United States revokes visas of individual Nigerians tied to various forms of corruption. At the time of the 2019 national elections, the United States and the United Kingdom announced that they would be revoking the visas of Nigerians who tried to impede or pervert the election process. They renewed that announcement during the run-up to the elections of 2023. Though they followed through on their threat, because of US privacy laws, there is no "name and shame" follow-up with respect to those whose visas have been revoked. Visa revocation is a cumbersome, slow process that eats up precious resources at the Department of State, which may lead to some reluctance to pursue it. In fact, compared to the number of Nigerian officials seemingly deserving visa revocation, the United States has revoked only a small number.

Viewing corruption through a primarily criminal lens overlooks its role as the glue that holds contemporary Nigeria together. More important, then, is understanding the role played by corruption in the Nigerian prebendal state. Corruption is a mélange of culture and politics and crime that runs through every level of political, business, and even personal relationships. According to Matthew Page, US diplomats face a basic dilemma when it comes to Nigerian corruption: they are charged with building a relationship with powerful individuals who operate within a corrupt system; the bilateral relationship is multifaceted and more than corruption; hence the temptation to turn a blind eye.[46] It goes without saying that corruption is "bad," but in its present form it plays a major role in holding the elites—and the country—together.

TIME TO CHANGE

It is striking that the issues that animated the US-Nigerian bilateral relationship have been and are currently conventional, mostly having to do with security and, to a lesser extent, Washington's efforts to promote better governance and health. The dialogue lacks sufficient consideration of the effects of climate change, environmental degradation, mass migration (Nigeria has no population policy), and the uniquely indigenous roots of jihadist radicalism. Instead, there are exchanges over arms sales initiated by the Nigerians and largely toothless American calls for better elections and more effective Nigerian moves to end corruption. On both sides, there has been ignorance or misunderstanding about how the other worked.

Nevertheless, US conduct of its relations with Nigeria has worked well enough for most of the postindependence period. There was, in effect, a bargain. Nigeria provided much-needed peacekeepers, rhetorically supported democracy and presidential term limits—both pillars of America policy in West Africa—and in general, Nigeria supported US initiatives in the UN. But, more recently, Nigeria has faced serious challenges at home and its international influence has declined. Now, with security threats in the Sahel, the consequences of climate change clear to see, an African population boom and a resulting youth bulge generating mass migration, a new American approach to managing the bilateral relationship is required. The pretense of treating Nigeria like a nation-state—something that it is not—will no longer do.

Following the 9/11 al-Qaeda attacks in New York and Washington, a Manichean US Global War on Terror distorted Washington's view of the world. The results were wars in Iraq and Afghanistan. To some, at least, the next front in the war on terror is Nigeria and the broader Sahel. Of course, there are important differences among Afghanistan, Iraq, and Nigeria, but all three have in common multiple ethnic groups and faiths, criminally inflected governments controlled by self-interested cabals, and weak national identities. With a Manichean or simplistic outlook on terrorism, Washington administrations have tended to focus on military solutions rather than diplomacy and development in Afghanistan and Iraq. As with those wars, Nigeria's struggle with Boko Haram is essentially a civil war. In the aftermath of the failures in Afghanistan and Iraq, conventional US military engagement, with inevitable US casualties, is foreclosed for the time being. A new approach, with a greater emphasis on diplomacy and soft power, is needed. In the world of massive environmental change, mass migration, and security threats by non-state actors, Washington's engagement must move significantly beyond its official Nigerian interlocutors, who in the disarray at home and in the region are becoming ever weaker and more irrelevant to the people they are meant to govern. Washington's focus in Nigeria has been at the margins, and so its influence has been marginal. While this is unlikely to change dramatically, with the right kind of engagement, Washington can efficiently nudge Nigeria toward a democratic trajectory based on the rule of law, the vision of the independence-era Nigeria Project.

Chapter 8

A New Approach

Much of Africa's future support for democracy will depend on the outcome of events in Nigeria.

—Princeton Lyman[1]

The international system up to now has been based primarily on nation-states, but Nigeria is not one. While Nigeria's external appearance and its conduct of foreign relations certainly looks familiar, it does not reflect its reality. It is a prebendal archipelago, with a weak national identity, a government with archipelagic authority, and myriad security, economic, and demographic challenges. Many countries in the postcolonial world share similar characteristics, so Nigeria's example can be broadly instructive. Going forward, Washington should keep the often-dysfunctional relationship between Abuja and Nigerians front and center, and recognize, but not accommodate, the country's quasi-criminal governance. Diplomatic interchange should refocus away from the presidency and foreign ministry, emphasizing contact with the Nigerian grassroots by building a dialogue with nonofficial authority figures, such as religious and traditional leaders, and states and localities. Washington should support those Nigerians working to build effective organs of government, democratic institutions, and the rule of law. And it should reflect the ideals of the Nigeria Project. In doing so, the United States should not be hesitant to use the powerful tools at its disposal. Progress should be measured over decades, not by the US electoral calendar. Nigeria's leadership is important, but nevertheless the United States can sacrifice some immediate political goodwill for more lasting and positive change.

For a few years after the restoration of civilian rule, Nigeria was the hegemon of West Africa, ensuring a degree of regional stability, opposing military coups, and sponsoring a general democratic trajectory.[2] Now, however, it can no longer fill that role. Domestic insurrections, the consequences of climate change, an exploding population, and a weak and unresponsive government

have oriented its political and military resources internally. Nigeria's recessional has contributed to general regional instability. In 2020, the temporary
collapse of international oil prices destabilized the financial underpinnings of
the ruling cartel just as the coronavirus pandemic began spreading in Nigeria.
Oil prices have recovered, but the industry is characterized by boom and bust
and they could decline again. As a prebendal archipelago, Nigeria does not
have a strong sense of national identity and patriotism upon which to draw
in difficult times, nor does it have a strong government that can manage such
crises, at home and abroad. Captured by a self-serving elite cartel with little
concern for the increasingly impoverished people it ostensibly governs, the
federal government's power is ebbing toward the states, religious leaders, and
precolonial institutions dominated by traditional rulers. Building a productive
relationship with Nigeria will be challenging but nevertheless essential given
the country's large and growing population and potential economic heft. It
is not hyperbole to say that as goes Nigeria, so goes the region, even the
continent.

WHAT'S AT STAKE

Africa and Nigeria specifically have not usually been a major focus for US
administrations, with the notable exception of George W. Bush's. Europe, the
Middle East, Asia, and even Latin America have historically more directly
affected American interests. But the current American inattention to Africa
will be unsustainable in the future. Africa's population is already more than
twice as large as that of all of North America, with 1.2 billion Africans
compared to 579 million North Americans in 2019. The UN's "medium scenario" projects Africa's population to grow to 2.5 billion by 2050. Half of the
continent's population lives in cities, many of which lack the infrastructure
or capacity to support the growing urban population, which is expected to
account for over two-thirds of all Africans by 2050.[3] On the one hand, all of
those people raise the potential for expanded markets for exporters and new
opportunities for investors. But on the other hand, if that growth is not accompanied by economic development, requisite infrastructure growth, and effective government, Nigeria and other African countries could face a Malthusian
demographic crisis with unregulated population flight from hunger, violence,
and the myriad consequences of climate change. Already Africans are the
largest component in the flow of migrants to Europe.[4] The huge increase in
the population could further degrade the environment, with consequences
such as growing food insecurity from overfarming, the destruction of rain
and mangrove forests and their concomitant environmental impacts, and

emergence and spread of new diseases as expanding human settlements encroach on hitherto untouched environments.

In the past, security issues of concern to the United States involving Russia, China, the Middle East, and South Asia rarely involved the continent. Now, they often have an African dimension. Islamic State and al-Qaeda militant groups have an African presence of varying capacity and reach. Against the backdrop of the Trump and Biden administrations' attention to great power competition, China's political and economic influence has grown dramatically and Russia's expanding presence, though small, is causing unease in Western capitals. Civil wars and insurrections may drive foreign humanitarian and sometimes security intervention by foreign powers. The US military presence in sub-Saharan Africa quietly increased from 936 bootsontheground in 2005, to about 7,200 in 2019.[5] However, it remains to be seen if it will continue in Niger following the antidemocratic coup.

Especially in the context of the wave of coups in West Africa, the United States and other democratic states have an overriding interest in the democratic trajectory of Nigeria. Instead of disengagement, more and better diplomacy is required. Nigeria's official leaders, for their part, will insist on continued engagement, and they will do their best to co-opt friendly partners in a way that promotes the interests of the prebendal elites for which the state exists. Washington should take care that it is not Abuja alone that frames the bilateral relationship. Still, in an uncertain political environment, the watchwords for the stewards of American policy, and that of Nigeria's other international friends, should be Hippocrates's famous dictum: "First, do no harm."

Nigeria requires a more decentralized American diplomacy that reflects the country's increasingly decentralized power structure. Currently, the US diplomatic establishment in Nigeria is limited to an embassy in Abuja and a consulate general in Lagos. Chronically underresourced and understaffed, the embassy and consulate general will be challenged to expand their contacts with increasingly influential governors, religious leaders, entrepreneurs, and traditional rulers that Nigeria's governance trajectory mandates. But it must. Adding further complications, such an effort will occur in the context of the widespread deterioration of security in Nigeria, which poses increased risk for diplomats, media, and businesspeople. For diplomats, personal risk is part of the job. Eight US ambassadors worldwide have been killed in the line of duty since 1950.[6] The American public appears to be increasingly risk averse with respect to official activity abroad. Especially in the aftermath of the 2012 Benghazi killing of the American ambassador to Libya and its unscrupulous politicization for partisan political advantage in the US Congress, the death of diplomats is unlikely to go away as a focus of political attack on the White House. That genie is out of the bottle. At least in part reflecting the popular and congressional mood, the Bureau of Diplomatic

Security has become increasingly powerful within the Department of State. It is risk adverse and will try to block diplomatic travel that it regards as too dangerous, a judgment call the others might not share. Deaths of diplomatic personnel, when they do occur, are now subject to a State Department Accountability Review Board, which may hold an ambassador or other senior embassy officer responsible. While Accountability Review Board procedures are under congressional review, American diplomats travel less in Nigeria now than a decade ago. Most of Nigeria's other Western, democratic partners face similar constraints.

With respect to policy, the Nigeria recessional means that Washington no longer has a strong West African partner on issues of mutual concern. Nigeria's absence places a premium on Washington consulting and coordinating with traditional allies and partners that often have deeper concerns about West African developments than Americans do, including France, China, India, Turkey, and the Gulf states. There has already been some coordination. For example, the French organized a partnership with Mauretania, Mali, Burkina Faso, Chad, and Niger, the G-5 Sahel. But whether it will survive the wave of military coups, often with an anti-French cast, remains to be seen. For the time being, the United States provides significant funding and political support. In the Lake Chad Basin, the United States provides assistance to Chad, Niger, and Cameroon, and dialogue with Nigeria. The European Union has established a 4.6 billion euro Trust Fund for Africa (EUTF) with twenty-four African countries in the Sahel and Lake Chad, the Horn of Africa, and North Africa, three hot-spot regions. A development strategy, it seeks to mitigate the root causes of migration from Africa to Europe by addressing unemployment and forced displacement. Despite the monitoring and evaluation challenges posed in implementing the EUTF, Washington should give serious attention to participating financially and politically.

China, the Gulf States, Saudi Arabia, and Turkey are also active in the Sahel and Nigeria. As elsewhere in Africa, China is involved with infrastructure construction and oil. In previous administrations, there has been a formal Washington dialogue with Beijing on Africa that paid dividends in Sudan. Washington should enhance its dialogue with the Gulf States, Saudi Arabia, and Turkey, especially on issues of jihadist radicalism in Nigeria and the Sahel. Washington should also strengthen its dialogue with the Economic Community of West African States (ECOWAS) and the African Union (AU) whenever there is an opportunity to do so. There are US ambassadors accredited to each, but, up to now, they have been underused. Iran is also active in the region. Washington should encourage allies with Iranian ties—notably the United Kingdom and France—to pursue a dialogue with Tehran on Africa.

WHERE IS NIGERIA GOING?

It remains to be seen whether Nigeria can continue to function as it has in the recent past or whether it will chart a new path forward. At present, the outlook appears dark. But Nigerians are celebrated for their resilience, for their solutions to seemingly intractable problems by workarounds. They rely on their extended family and networks for their day-to-day survival. Religion gives Nigerians hope and purpose and accounts for their celebrated cheerfulness. In addition to the family, religious and ethnically based institutions also provide something of a safety net.

Given current challenges, what are Nigeria's possible futures? In other words, given the demographic, economic, environmental, and security challenges faced by Nigeria, how might its politics respond? The breakup of Nigeria into three or four independent states over the next decade is widely mooted among the "chattering classes" of Lagos and Abuja. At its most positive, the breakup of Nigeria would be by agreement among political elites; as Azikiwe once said shortly after independence, "It is better that we disintegrate in peace and not in pieces."[7] Such a cheerful outcome seems unlikely. Oil production is centered in the Niger Delta. Without the Nigerian state, elites from other parts of the country presumably would be unable to share in oil wealth. Hence, as they did in 1967, they are likely to unite to prevent the breakup of the country. Moreover, in the event the country did fragment— orderly or not—there would probably be massive internal migration as the various ethnic groups consolidated themselves in their traditional homelands, either willingly or because they were pushed out of their adopted homes. In all likelihood, this process would be accompanied by ethnic and religious strife, raising the specter of the bloodshed and violence that accompanied the partition of India and Pakistan in 1947–48 or Yugoslavia in the 1980s. Hence, a reversal of "the mistake of 1914," the British amalgamation of northern and southern Nigeria, is unlikely. For good or ill, Nigeria will stay together. But that doesn't mean it will necessarily continue in its current form.

Continuation of the prebendal state as federal authority slowly erodes— effectively the status quo—is Nigeria's most likely future, especially if oil prices remain erratic and if the country's leadership remains geriatric. (President Tinubu was born in 1952.) A federal government with less money would gradually lose the ability to project power. State governors would move to fill the resulting vacuum. Forced to respond more independently to various economic, environmental, and security crises, they may try to raise a larger portion of their own revenue. The effectiveness of the federal security services, underfunded and undertrained, is likely to continue to decline, and state governors could come to rely more on vigilante forces that could become, in effect, a state's militia. This is already happening across the country.[8] The Lagos-Ibadan corridor, the most developed region, would likely continue to pull ahead of the rest of the country, with closer ties to the other countries bordering the Gulf of Guinea rather than to the rest of Nigeria.

But a significant escalation in any one of Nigeria's myriad security crises could upend the status quo. Already in some parts of the country, government authority has broken down with little to replace it. In parts of the middle belt, the struggle over water and land with ethnic and religious rivalry has rendered some—though not all—territory beyond the reach of government authority. Warlords may emerge, promising protection against bandits in return for loyalty, while the security services remain untrusted and underfunded. In the northeast, Boko Haram and its offshoots have been attempting to replace the secular state and its institutions with an Islamic state based, however loosely, on some version of Islamic law. Boko Haram already exercises a shadowy authority over certain rural areas where the federal and state governments cannot exercise control. The Nigerian military has withdrawn in some places to fortified supercamps. With the military isolating itself, Boko Haram may be able to expand the territory it controls. But, based on its 2011 to 2015 trajectory, Boko Haram is unlikely to extend its operations beyond the northeast. It remains to be seen whether the Boko Haram factions move closer together or seek to destroy each other. Such grim scenarios leave unscathed the Lagos-Ibadan corridor and the oil patch. Abuja, however, has been a Boko Haram target in the past and could be again.

Is there a realistic prospect for violent revolution, such as occurred in France starting in 1789, Russia in 1917, or Iran in 1979? Nigerian elites appear to have little to fear and are flexible enough to incorporate the newly rich, the powerful, and the lucky. The country is too fragmented for a nationwide revolutionary movement and has no history of one that transcended its ethnic, class, and religious divisions. It lacks the cultural unity of France before Robespierre, Russia before Lenin, or Iran before Khomeini. Nor have there been Nigerian independence figures of their stature. Local insurgencies are endemic, but they pose no nationwide threat to the system.

CIVIC ACTIVISM

What about a peaceful sociopolitical protest movement like the Arab Spring of the early 2010s, or Sudan in 2019? The paradox is that, even though Nigeria is less economically developed than the countries of the Arab Spring, it conducts regular elections and has respected term limits. Elections and term limits may inoculate somewhat the cartel against nationwide protest movements by providing the illusion of choice. Moreover, civic organizations in

Nigeria are currently not strong enough to overcome the entrenched interests of the prebendal state. Levels of civic awareness, education, and literacy in Nigeria are much lower than they were in those countries affected by the Arab Spring. There is little evidence that an Arab Spring would have popular support beyond the Western-educated and urbanized—those who voted for Peter Obi for president in 2023. The cartel that benefits from the current system, even if divided among themselves, would likely unite enough to block such a movement—as it did with Obi's 2023 candidacy. Indeed, no movement for peaceful reform has ever been able to unite Nigeria's competing ethnic and religious groups. The closest were the demonstrations and strikes in 2012 against the Jonathan administration's efforts to end the fuel subsidy. It collapsed in a few days when the government compromised somewhat—and bought off a number of labor leaders.

The best-known example of Nigerian civic activism in the United States and Europe is the #BringBackOurGirls campaign, led by future presidential candidate Oby Ezekwesili. It made expert use of social media, garnering the attention and support of international celebrities, including Michelle Obama. Though it probably helped energize the Jonathan administration, about ninety of the Chibok schoolgirls were still in captivity as of 2024, demonstrating the limits of what civic groups can accomplish. (Since Chibok hundreds of other girls have been kidnapped in separate operations that have had little publicity in the Western media or among Nigerian civil society.) In a different area, international pressure generated by Nigerian groups has contributed to the release of Nigerian journalists subject to apparent arbitrary arrest. Their cases were brought to international attention by civil organizations. Nevertheless, the scope of civil society remains limited, as is the Western-educated, urban basis of its support. Civil activists currently lack the strength to bring about fundamental change.

FEDERALISM

The prospect for the implementation of true federalism by the elite is another topic of conversation among urban, westernized reformers in Nigeria. There is close to a consensus that the implementation of true federalism could transform the state for the better. Up to now, however, true, managed federalism—the devolution of power from the center to the states, rather than the slow ebb of power to the states and other subnational authorities as the center weakens—has lacked a champion. Atiku Abubakar, the presidential candidate of the People's Democratic Party in 2019 and 2023, advocated for more power and autonomy given to the states, including the ability for them to create state police forces.[9] In some cases, this would have entailed regularizing the informal vigilante groups, ranging from neighborhood watches to full-blown militias, that almost thirty states have felt compelled to create. But he was defeated by incumbent president Muhammadu Buhari in 2019 and by Bola Tinubu in 2023. Nevertheless, it is possible that a transformational figure might emerge in Nigeria with sufficient support from the political class. In Ethiopia, for example, Abiy Ahmed became head of state and instituted reforms that most observers thought unlikely or impossible.[10] But, absent such a transformational leader, it is difficult to see the cartel that has long since captured the state agreeing to risk their privileged positions.

Implementation of true federalism would be difficult because it would require a change in the way revenue is collected and allocated. Since the days of military rule, the federal government has collected the oil revenue and then distributed it to the states. Dependent on the central government for revenue, the states had little power. However, as in the case of Lagos, where states can raise significant amounts of revenue without reference to the federal government, a degree of independence becomes possible. The Lagos state government has seized the initiative on infrastructure. In terms of security, states have already felt it necessary to turn inward for support, organizing or allowing units to supplement and support the national police, such as the CJTF in Borno, the Hisbah in the north, and Amotekun in Yorubaland, among others. But Nigeria has entered unchartered waters in this regard.

Surely Nigeria's advocates for reform are right: a Nigeria that stays together and moves toward the implementation of federalism in a democratic trajectory would provide the best future for its citizens. Nevertheless, and despite the uncertainty caused by the fall in oil prices, it is the status quo that is likely to persist given the country's fragmentation and the lock the cartel has on the state. The federal government will likely continue to shed authority and power, with the resultant vacuums filled by state governments and a variety of subnational bodies that could include the ethnically based, such as the Yoruba Afenifere, traditional rulers, or terrorist movements such as Boko Haram. There is little evidence, though much wishful thinking, that ethnic and religious differences will decline, at least so long as politicians continue to fuel ethnic and religious tensions for political advantage, and poverty is likely to remain the lot of tens of millions Nigerians.

THE NIGERIA PROJECT

With the status quo as the necessary starting point, the question then becomes how Nigeria can avoid the worst-case scenarios and start moving toward a future where it can deliver services and security to its people. Nigerians have already provided themselves an answer.

The Nigeria Project is associated with an independence-era vision of a democratic, multiethnic country and with the three founding fathers of Nigeria, Obafemi Awolowo, Nnamdi Azikiwe, and the sardauna of Sokoto. The Project has always been an aspiration rather than a concrete political program. Its lodestars were democracy and national unity. As Nigeria was an artificial creation of the British, the Project was an answer to the problem of how to create national unity where there had been none. Nigeria's unity would not be founded on shared language, religion, or culture but rather on shared ideals. Its unity would have to be created in a different way from that of, say, Italy or Germany, which were seen as "organic," founded on shared history, language, and culture. The concept was also embraced by the British architects of Nigerian independence, who wanted the country to remain united, partly because it would be big enough to serve as a barrier to Soviet influence in West Africa. The founding fathers, too, supported a big Nigeria as a means of advancing Africa's influence on the world stage. In the early days, the Project was not directly connected to federalism, but over the years the two became associated as a means of achieving genuine democracy by managing Nigeria's size and diversity. This vision is widespread among the Nigerian diaspora living in the United States, the United Kingdom, and Canada. It is often articulated by those in the diaspora who return home, and the various good-government candidates that run for office, such as Oby Ezekwesili, Kingsley Moghalu, and Donald Duke.

For many of Nigeria's reformers and their foreign friends the goal is to strengthen the independence and capacity of government institutions and develop a culture of the rule of law. Civic space would expand, enabling the media and civil society to operate freely and call attention to citizen needs and government misconduct. Elections would continue on schedule and their conduct would improve, with less rigging, less violence, and more credible results. Substantive policy discussions would be at the center of campaigning. The judiciary would grow its competence and independence, ruling against the government when appropriate, and have its decisions respected. The government would end or contain the various security crises afflicting ordinary Nigerians through the effective use of military force, community policing, and political settlements. Such developments would improve governance and keep democracy on the table, awaiting new leaders, new expectations of government, and ultimately staving off violent alternative futures.

But how can a sometimes unscrupulous political class come to accept these ideals, or, at the very least, allow space for those who do? Part of the answer may be that the Nigerian political class cares what the governments and business communities of the United Kingdom, the United States, Canada, and the European Union think and say, at least up to a point. Public statements by senior American, British, and European political figures can catch the attention even of the elite cabal at the top of Nigerian politics. Supporting the development of civic space, though a multidecade endeavor, would take only modest US resources and would ultimately help Nigerian civil society become more effective. That said, American engagement with Nigeria is likely to be less sustained than that of the United Kingdom and the European Union. On the one hand, with its growing self-sufficiency in oil, Washington finds Nigeria less strategically important than it was a decade ago. On the other hand, in the aftermath of Brexit, British interest in the Nigerian market is growing, and Nigeria is already one of the largest markets for French champagne. Following massive migration to Europe from the Middle East and Africa, and with the specter of more to come, the importance of Nigeria and its neighborhood to the EU is growing. The ability of Nigeria's foreign friends to shape events is limited. Nevertheless, the Nigerian political class can be influenced from the outside.

By seeing Nigeria as it is, US policy can be more effective. Americans are ahistorical, even with respect to their own history, often overlooking the past as the creator of the present. Yet more obviously than elsewhere, contemporary Nigeria is a product of its history of colonialism, military rule, poor leadership, and incomplete modernization. To counter the slide toward authoritarianism and strengthen democracy in an era of regional disarray, US policy should remain much as it has been since Nigeria became independent. Washington should support the unity of Nigeria, even if it is loose, even chaotic. The alternative, a breakup of Nigeria into ethnically denominated polities, would be a humanitarian disaster, almost certainly involving the United States in ways difficult to foresee.

US FOREIGN POLICY MAKING

In the American system, the White House has the lead in making foreign policy and its implementation. It delegates this function primarily to the US State Department, though also involved is the US Agency for International Development (USAID), the Defense Department, the Commerce Department, and the Agriculture Department, all of which have a substantial overseas presence. A host of other US domestic agencies also have an important role, not least the Treasury Department and the Centers for Disease Control and Prevention. The National Security Council, a part of the White House, coordinates differing views among federal agencies and prepares options for presidential decisions.

Foreign relations are not the exclusive purview of the executive in the United States, as it is in Nigeria. The US Congress plays a central role. The House of Representatives appropriates the funding for the conduct of international relations; the senate confirms high-level diplomatic appointments; both hold hearings on policy. Congress can draw on executive branch expertise, but it also has the Congressional Research Service, its own public policy research institute. Unsurprisingly, the number of members of Congress engaged with Africa or Nigeria at any particular time is very small. Just two or three senators will typically be present for the confirmation hearing for an American ambassador to an African country. A handful of members of Congress may have close ties to Nigerian evangelical and Pentecostal churches, predisposing them to view conflicts in the middle belt and elsewhere from a Nigerian, Pentecostal perspective often hostile to Muslims. Others may have influential Nigerian diaspora communities, which can both drive attention and color the perspective. The private sector, including the media, business, churches, and other nongovernmental organizations, may influence both the administration and Congress on US foreign policy issues as it did with South Africa under apartheid and Sudan during the Darfur genocide.

The American official bilateral relationship with Nigeria, and with most other countries, is built brick by brick through specific engagement on interests of mutual concern. Washington policymakers take the lead, while the embassy in Abuja acts as the means of communication with the Nigerian federal government. On security issues, the US policy lead rests with the State and Defense departments. USAID and CDC take the lead on cooperation with respect to health issues such as HIV/AIDS through the President's Emergency Plan for AIDS Relief (PEPFAR), and US assistance for Nigeria's political, social, and economic development. Treasury and Commerce usually have the lead on trade and investment, though State can also be heavily involved. Within the US foreign policy establishment, there can be considerable overlap and disagreement on Nigerian issues. For example, State and Treasury disagreed in 2005 on the issue of Paris Club debt relief for Nigeria; the former supported it as a "democracy dividend" for the postmilitary Obasanjo government and the latter opposed it because of the precedent it would set. On Paris Club debt relief, the NSC and subsequently President Bush adopted State's position.

On the ground in Nigeria, American engagement and policy formulation comes together at the embassy in Abuja and the Consulate General in Lagos. The embassy contributes, through cables and visits, to policy deliberations in Washington, where the final decisions are made. Under the ambassador's leadership, the American embassy is the chief in-country tool for managing the bilateral relationship and protecting US interests. The embassy also coordinates with US agencies on the management of a range of Nigerian requests, such as assistance with criminal activities, most notably money laundering through US financial markets. The embassy adjudicates Nigerian requests for visas to travel to the United States and provides a host of services for

Americans temporarily or permanently resident in Nigeria. The ambassador leads a country team made up of representatives of all the federal agencies operating in Nigeria. Its operation is a reflection of the interagency process led by the National Security Council in Washington. Day-to-day diplomatic activity tends to orient a bilateral relationship toward Abuja, Nigeria's capital, rather than toward the broader Nigerian political class, including those outside of government office and the capital.

Underlying the implementation of any US foreign policy in any region of the world is the across-the-board erosion of US diplomatic capacity and expertise dating at least from the end of the Cold War and accelerating under the Trump administration.[11] The American and Nigerian recessionals both contribute to instability in their respective spheres.[12] Since the end of the Cold War, the State Department and USAID have been progressively hollowed out, and the United States Information Agency (USIA) has been abolished. Between 1985 and 2000, the State Department and broader foreign affairs budget was cut by 50 percent in real terms. The cuts were justified as the "Cold War dividend." More recently, there has also been serious loss of expertise—during the Trump administration, three of the State Department's five career ambassadors left. Perhaps more serious has been the decline in career ministers (the next highest diplomatic rank) from thirty-three to nineteen as of November 2017.[13] (There has been some rebuilding by the Biden administration.) The positions of career ambassador and career minister represent the longest-serving and most distinguished US diplomats, and provide an essential link from State's professional bureaucracy and career Foreign Service officers to an administration's political appointees. A strong relationship between political and career employees is at the core of a functioning, coherent, and consistent foreign policy. Periodic hiring freezes also reduced the number of junior diplomats available to do the routine work of any embassy.

Established by President Dwight Eisenhower during the Cold War, USIA was perhaps the primary reservoir of American soft-power expertise and public diplomacy. It was quixotically shut down in 1999, largely at the insistence of Senator Jesse Helms (R-NC), though ostensibly for budgetary reasons and to promote efficiency in the conduct of post–Cold War international relations.[14] Though its functions were partially moved to the State Department, much of USIA's soft-diplomacy expertise dissipated; a large number of veteran public affairs officers elected to retire. Those that did not were assigned to State Department regional bureaus that often had little interest in public diplomacy. In addition, expenditure for public diplomacy declined.[15] As former deputy secretary of state William Burns writes, "At first lulled by the experience of post–Cold War dominance and then shocked by 9/11, we gradually devalued diplomatic tools. All too often, we over relied on

American hard power to achieve policy aims and ambitions."[16] (Ambassador Burns was made the director of the Central Intelligence Agency by President Biden in 2021.)

THE NIGERIAN CONTEXT

Nigeria's prebendal political system—one based on corruption, private gain, and personal relationships—is the context in which the United States must operate. It is the context in which friends of Nigeria must support it as it responds to Boko Haram, the Delta insurgency, middle belt conflicts, and in which Nigeria will face its "black swans," such as the coronavirus and the periodic collapse of oil prices. The explosion of Nigeria's population is likely to lead to a massive exodus, already underway. Those with even a modicum of Western education are likely to seek out the United States and Europe. In a time of Western anxiety about migration, such an issue will require the most careful management. The consequences of climate change and environmental degradation—drought, flooding, desertification, habitat loss—will render more land uninhabitable, water undrinkable, and air unbreathable, pushing people to seek, and compete for, greener pastures. If, as seems likely, responding to the climate crisis becomes an official foreign policy preoccupation of the United States and others, Nigeria will likely become a focal point.

The reality of Nigeria's fragmented development and political power structure requires a different diplomatic footprint. In the Lagos-Ibadan corridor, Nigerians see something of a modern state emerging, with a social contract between the Lagos state government and Lagos residents, which includes the accountability of the former to the latter, who pay taxes. In the northeast, an as-of-yet undefined Islamic polity may emerge out of the Islamic revival and Abuja's struggle with Boko Haram. Another alternative appears to be chaos—demonstrated by the current crime wave that affects the entire country and the geographic expanse where the government's writ does not run. The accelerating decentralization of political power in Nigeria suggests that US engagement, too, should include state, local, and traditional centers of power. Abuja is likely to view with suspicion closer US ties with the states, which it will feel it cannot control, but such concerns should not derail a new approach; instead, efforts should be made to allay these suspicions through yet-to-be cultivated relationships and spearheaded by a US ambassador with a strong relationship to Aso Villa.

A DIFFERENT KIND OF DIPLOMACY

Real Nigerian domestic political power—as opposed to its *form*—exists increasingly outside of Abuja. The apparent decline in the powers of federal officials and politicians places a premium on building relationships outside the capital with informal leaders of civil society, traditional rulers, and religious figures. At the State and Defense departments, there tends to be insufficient emphasis given to the role played by such nonofficial leaders and subnational groups. They operate within structures of power and rely on subnational loyalties parallel to the state, often defined by clan, ethnicity, or religion. In many ways, they may drive and resolve conflict without reference to the federal government, and very often they can play a positive role. Not taking into account such subnational distribution of power can set policy up for failure.

It is worth recalling some American foreign policy missteps grounded in similar misunderstandings. In Vietnam, clouded by aversion to Communism, the United States saw Ho Chi Minh as a puppet of Communist China. This despite Ho's and "the Vietnamese people's deep distrust of China," the latter a perennial invader and occupier of the former.[17] Further, Vietnam's Chinese minority controlled roughly 80 percent of South Vietnam's industry and 90 percent of non-European private capital. In effect, most US development assistance went to the Chinese minority.[18] As Thomas Friedman writes, the United States failed "to understand that the core political drama of Vietnam was an indigenous nationalist struggle against colonial rule—not the embrace of global communism, the interpretation we imposed on it."[19]

In Iraq, as discussed previously, the United States did not sufficiently account for the reality that the country was held together not by identity or history, but by a brutal dictator enforcing colonial British borders and keeping three fractious regions together through force. "When we came to Iraq, we didn't understand the complexity—what it meant for a society to live under a brutal dictatorship, with ethnic and sectarian divisions. . . . [We] made a lot of mistakes. We were like a blind man, trying to do the right thing but breaking a lot of things,"[20] recalled H. R. McMaster, who commanded the 3rd Armored Cavalry Regiment in Iraq in 2005. McMaster, who would later become President Trump's national security advisor, went to great lengths to ensure that he and his soldiers understood local customs and the various tribal and religious divisions present in the northern Iraqi city of Tal Afar, where he was at one point stationed. His work clearing insurgents from Tal Afar is considered one of the bright spot of US strategy in Iraq. As General John Allen, a commander of US forces in Iraq, would later acknowledge, "Tribal society makes up the tectonic plates in Iraq on which everything rests." Former US Secretary of State Condoleezza Rice acknowledged that "we didn't probably understand fully the role of tribes."[21] These examples are indicative of what the United States sometimes misses when decisionmakers apply a nation-state framework to societies they do not understand and are preoccupied by ideologies that may be irrelevant.

Instead of a large embassy in Abuja and a consulate in Lagos, a more effective platform for American diplomacy would be to reduce the size of the embassy and supplement it with the establishment of regional offices. These centers might be named for Martin Luther King Jr., a well-known hero in Nigeria. Even in a time of straitened diplomatic resources, these centers would represent a redeployment of resources, not a significant addition to them. Staffing would be modest, and their focus would be on public diplomacy—telling America's story and connecting more deeply with the Nigerian communities in which they are based. America's story has the capacity to inspire; we should tell it better. Building such relationships is not merely a "nice" thing to do; it can provide invaluable information and perspective to diplomats and Washington policymakers on otherwise overlooked or misunderstood issues and regions. The more diplomats can connect with Nigerians and gain an understanding and appreciation of their diversity, the more both sides can benefit.

Initially these King Centers could be established in Enugu, the heart of Igboland and the old Biafra; Kano, the largest city in the Muslim north; and in Ibadan, the site of Nigeria's oldest university and in the center of Yorubaland. They could collectively be staffed by a total of six American diplomats redeployed from Abuja and Lagos and a relatively small number of locally engaged staff. In some respects, the operation of the three King Centers would recall the more than four hundred Confucius Institutes and Centers established by the Chinese government around the world, which teach Chinese culture and language—with a large one already operating in Lagos. (However, unlike Confucius Centers, King Centers would not be engaged in language training.) Security is a legitimate concern, but risk is a fact of effective diplomacy. The goal should be to minimize the risk, not to eliminate it altogether by hunkering down in a fortress embassy.

A broader diplomatic presence in Nigeria would benefit from greater involvement of the often-underutilized Foreign Commercial Service and the Foreign Agricultural Service—sisters of the State Department's Foreign Service and also under the ambassador's chief-of-mission authority. They could provide important points of entry for American diplomacy outside the capital, just as the US Agency for International Development (USAID) and the Centers for Disease Control (CDC) already do.

In addition, there are numerous interchanges that only marginally involve the two governments yet do much to build and strengthen the bilateral relationship. The United States should lobby for the return of the Peace Corps, which ended its presence during the civil war and its aftermath and for which Nigeria has since refused reentry.[22] This is regrettable, as the Peace Corps embodies the American ideals that are central to soft diplomacy. A less-well-known example, though one worth replicating, is the YES program of the Iowa Resource for International Service, which arranges for predominately Muslim high school students from northern Nigeria to spend a year in an Iowa public high school living with a host family.[23] That program transforms for the better the way its Muslim participants see the role of Islam in the United States.

Many Nigerians have a mindset different from that of Western secularism, and religious leaders are politically and socially important, more so than in the United States. They could be an important means of getting out the American message, but, at a minimum, they can also be an antidote to freely circulating gossip and hearsay that is often hostile to the United States. Small American gestures can pay big dividends. For example, while I was ambassador, the Library of Congress restored, catalogued, and digitized ancient Islamic manuscripts in northern Nigeria, but left them in the hands of their owners, thereby helping correct the stereotype that the United States is Islamophobic. The American embassy on several occasions has invited a local imam to lead its annual commemoration of the September 11, 2001, terrorist attacks, underscoring President George W. Bush's point that the attack was about terrorism, not Islam. USAID provided $43.6 million in funding to an American NGO to launch a four-year program establishing eight Nonformal Learning Centers in two northern, predominately Muslim states. Through coordination with Nigerian government officials and local mallams, the target was the most vulnerable of children, including orphans, with an emphasis on education and health, and the program included peace-building messages drawn from the Koran. There are numerous other examples of small-scale partnerships among the US government, American and Nigerian NGOs, local officials, and community leaders. Such programs at once support a vulnerable portion of the population, build relationships between the United States and local officials, and likely provide a better understanding of the situation on the ground for those US officials involved. Americans can find partners, but it must look for them. To do that, they must go beyond Abuja and Lagos.

The relationship is a two-way street on multiple levels. Nigeria is now a major exporter of Christian clergy, and growing numbers of Americans are being pastored by Nigerians. Hospital emergency rooms all over the United States are staffed with Nigerian-origin personnel. Hence, the spiritual and physical health of some Americans is in fact in Nigerian hands, and those numbers are likely to grow. The Nigerian cultural efflorescence is intensifying, even as the political and security problems at home escalate. The *New*

York Times chronicles Nigerian influence on contemporary American fashion, drama, music, and cuisine. Novelists of Nigerian origin are among the most celebrated in the United States. If the United States as a world power and the largest economy can shape aspects of Nigeria's future, Nigerians are shaping the American present. The bilateral relationship is more than the official relationship between Washington and Abuja.

Nigerian distrust of Washington dating back to the Nigerian civil war continues to distort relations. Mutual interest in defeating Boko Haram and combating terrorism is complicated by the Nigerian military's poor human rights record and general ineffectiveness, as well as Boko Haram's popular roots. Delivery of aid and economic programs geared toward development must contend with a corrupt political system. So, too, does greater private-sector engagement. Political cooperation, such as in the UN, must take into account Nigerian diplomats' place in a corrupt system essentially divorced from the needs of much of the population. But it is crucial that the relationship grow and deepen; Nigeria will remain an important and necessary security partner, with great potential for increased cooperation.

DEFEATING BOKO HARAM

Boko Haram is guilty of unspeakable crimes, and its rhetoric is hostile to the United States. Nevertheless, Washington should not be drawn into what is, in effect, a civil war between a prebendal state that is alienated from many of its own people and an insurgency that is predominately local in character, though whose rhetoric is similar to other jihadist groups. Whatever Boko Haram's links to the Islamic State and al-Qaeda in the Islamic Maghreb (AQIM), they more likely reflect opportunism than a deeper relationship. Policymakers and diplomats should continue to monitor carefully the Boko Haram insurgency, with the failed wars in Vietnam, Iraq, and Afghanistan serving as salutary reminders of what incomplete and distorted information about insurgencies can yield. Even though the Boko Haram conflict pits a friendly state against an intrinsically hostile, anti-Western movement, its factions, at least for the time being, pose no security threat to the United States. Further, the United States must walk a fine line. According to former assistant secretary of state for Africa Herman J. Cohen, "it must adopt and advocate for strategies that address the underlying reasons Africans may become radicalized—without further contributing to their radicalization."[24]

The reduction of US diplomatic capability argues for expanding counterterrorism cooperation with the countries of the Lake Chad Basin affected by Boko Haram, as well as countries in the Sahel facing other jihadist threats.

In the Lake Chad Basin, these include Niger, Cameroon, Chad, and Benin, organized with Nigeria into the Multinational Joint Task Force (MNJTF). However, military coups in Niger and Chad complicate coordination and cooperation. France, a close ally of the United States, has been deeply involved with the Francophone states in the Lake Chad Basin and the Sahel. French withdrawal from the region following coups with a strongly anti-French twist is a setback with respect to the struggle against Boko Haram and other jihadist groups operating in the region.[25]

The war between Boko Haram and the Nigerian state has been a humanitarian disaster. There are over two million internally displaced people in northeast Nigeria and across the border in Niger and Cameroon.[26] The northeast remains insecure, inhibiting reconstruction efforts, but the magnitude of reconstruction required, once it is possible, is so great as to be beyond the capacity of Nigeria alone. Nothing short of an international reconstruction effort is necessary. With France and the Lake Chad Basin states, Washington should push Abuja to allow unfettered access by humanitarian organizations to the Lake Chad Basin and proactively offer multilateral assistance to remedy the immediate humanitarian consequences of Boko Haram. In preparation for humanitarian relief, it is necessary to establish and strengthen contacts with traditional rulers and religious leaders in the northeast.

Since President Obasanjo's call on President Bush in Washington after the attacks of September 11, 2001, Nigeria has cooperated with US counterterrorism in terms of public rhetoric and its diplomacy, especially in the African regional context. Maintaining US sanctions on Boko Haram and its leaders has little to no practical consequence, but it underscores the principle of American opposition to terrorism and support for the Nigerian government. It should be seen as an aspect of a public affairs strategy about solidarity in the face of terrorism, reflecting Obasanjo's call on Bush.

MITIGATING INTERCOMMUNAL CONFLICT

Conflict in the middle belt is ostensibly over land and water use, but its participants often differ in ethnicity, language, and religion. US experts from the Foreign Agricultural Service or US Geological Survey, as well as USAID, could be of assistance to local parties. Some NGOs, Nigerian and American, have proved effective at the local level in reducing conflict by providing fora for effective communication among those involved in the conflict. As it already does, the American embassy should support and facilitate the work of NGOs pursuing peace and reconciliation in the region. Many members of the National Assembly are largely silent in public about these conflicts; in their interactions with them during the course of official visits, American diplomats and visitors should question how they would propose to address violence in the middle belt.

The conflict has led to calls from some Christian churches in Nigeria for the United States to intervene in what they characterize as religiously motivated attacks against Christians. These calls are also taken up by some American clergy, especially from the Pentecostal and evangelical churches, and sometimes regurgitated in the American news media. Further, in parts of the middle belt, federal and state governments have all but imposed a media blackout. This encourages rumors, the flowering of fake news, and are undemocratic in spirit.

With respect to the Niger Delta, militant activity is driven by a sense of grievance over the degradation of the environment by the oil industry, a sense that the revenue from oil and natural gas are not distributed equitably, and the pursuit of personal profits by certain elites. The intensely local nature of Delta grievances makes the conflict hard to monitor, but it is imperative that it is. Even though the United States no longer imports oil from Nigeria, and even though the collapse of oil prices may have thrown into flux Nigeria's petroleum industry, oil is, at least for now, the single largest source of Nigerian government revenue. In the past, during upsurges in kidnapping, the United States has made experts in kidnapping available to the Nigerian authorities. It should continue to do so, and should also offer American expertise on a host of environmental issues, such as forest and water management. After all, there is a strong environmental aspect to both the insurgency in the Delta and middle belt violence, one that is often overlooked amid ethnic and religious tensions.

SUPPORTING MORE ACCOUNTABLE
SECURITY SERVICES

These are challenging times for the security dimension of the bilateral relationship. As the constitution permits, the Nigerian military services have recently been deployed to as many as thirty-five of the thirty-six states to try to maintain order, though they are not trained in domestic policing. The government uses the military services because the police, a national gendarmerie controlled by the federal government, is institutionally weaker. Yet, the army appears to be overstretched and underfunded, in part because Nigeria spends only about .5 percent of its budget on the military despite mounting security crises nationwide. Further, the military service chain of command is fractured. With the service chiefs appealing directly to the president over the head of the minister of defense, service rivalries are largely unchecked.[27]

The Nigerian military currently has a deplorable human rights record. The curricula at the American war colleges has an important human rights dimension, as well as centering on the proper relationship between the military and civilian populations. Washington could expand the number of training opportunities for Nigerian military personnel, especially at the US Army, Navy, and Air Force war colleges and at the National Defense University. Skeptics might argue that such training is unlikely to be transformative, but the cost is low, it might contribute to a desirable change in Nigerian military culture, and US students will gain new perspectives and contacts from the interchange.

US law essentially bars assistance to foreign police forces without a cumbersome waiver process. As a result, less than 2 percent of US security service funding to sub-Saharan Africa goes to police forces.[28] But police in Nigeria, whose work is often done by the military, could benefit enormously from US training and expertise, which would have a strong human rights component. Congress should revise the 1975 law banning the training of foreign police, which was initially drafted in response to brutality by American-trained police in El Salvador in the 1960s and 1970s. Changing the law could take time, given congressional suspicion of the police and their ongoing involvement in human rights abuses. In the meantime, the United States can financially support British programs aimed at training police forces. They have been successful, but are generally small.

In chapter 4 of Nigeria's constitution, which outlines the fundamental rights of Nigerians, articles 38, 39, and 40 guarantee freedom of religion, expression, the press, and of assembly.[29] Despite such guarantees, these freedoms are routinely violated by the security services. The government's response to demonstrations by Biafra independence movements are harsh, and it resorts to the imprisonment of demonstration leaders without charge for long periods.[30] The gerontocracy that governs Nigeria has enduring memories of the carnage of the civil war, and so responds disproportionately. Further, the processions of the Islamic Movement of Nigeria, a Shia religious organization, are often met with deadly force, most notably in 2015, when the military killed perhaps 350 members and buried them in mass graves. While they are accused of plotting the overthrow of the Nigerian government, recalling the Iranian revolution in 1979, the Shia in Nigeria have remained largely peaceful.[31] Nigerian journalists that document human rights violations, official corruption, or otherwise criticize government have been detained and their news offices raided and occupied.[32] In its exchanges with the Nigerian government, US officials and diplomats should make it clear that the frequent and indiscriminate use of force is counterproductive and damages Nigeria's international reputation.

GOVERNANCE AND THE RULE OF LAW

An important aspect of security sector reform is support for the rule of law and the ability of Nigerian institutions to enforce it. But the Nigerian judiciary is notoriously sclerotic and severely underresourced. Notably, Nigerian justice is often delayed and therefore denied. Part of the issue is that the court system is operated almost entirely by hand. The US provision of word processing and other office technologies along with constant electrical power in courtrooms, for example, could speed up the judicial process. The State Department in Washington and the embassy in Abuja should also facilitate greater contact and exchanges between Nigerian and American bar associations.

Improving cooperation against financial crime is a potential growth area in the US-Nigeria relationship. However, at base, this is a legal process that can take years, as it has with the Abacha money. Given the ubiquity of corruption in the upper reaches of the Nigerian government, lack of Nigerian political will may be a brake. So while the potential is great, US administrations should be aware of the limitations in tackling corruption in partnership with a criminally inflected political system.

The focus on elections by successive Washington administrations is misplaced. Foreign election observers often fail to see what is going on. Their time in-country is short, and their leadership, often political celebrities on tight schedules, encourages early judgment. As is sometimes said, "Only amateurs steal elections on Election Day."[33] Nevertheless, the United States should continue to provide funding for US election observers because their presence provides Nigerian NGOs with some cover from security service violence. Regular elections, even when rigged, play a role in building a democratic culture over time. Election observation missions should be understood for what they are: a temporary stopgap until domestic institutions can do the job themselves. The focus, then, should be on the development of real political parties; strong, speedy, and independent election appeals processes; voter registration and education; and independent media, among other things. Success should be measured beyond a single election cycle.

A NEW APPROACH

What will a successful US-Nigerian relationship look like? Washington and Abuja would cooperate more closely on regional issues. Closer ties with state governments and more extensive dialogue with religious and traditional leaders should frame US efforts to encourage popular democracy, better governance, and the rule of law. Washington should guard against a security relationship that while beneficial to the elites erodes ties with most Nigerians who are not part of the elite cartel. With respect to security, Washington must promote a relationship that can improve and support the Nigerian security services while speaking out about their human rights abuses, recognizing that such abuses generate crises. Goodwill may have to be sacrificed for longer-lasting change.

The United States should pick its battles. Effective American diplomacy requires Washington to identify where it can make a meaningful difference and tread lightly where it cannot. In general, initiatives involving human sexuality and family planning are fraught and should be treated with caution. There are also other issues where American domestic political realities constrain what Washington can do in Nigeria. For example, it is unrealistic to think that there could be a massive uptick in the dollar amount of US health and development assistance. There is little constituency for it in Congress, and Nigerians would object to the auditing and other requirements when US public money is disbursed. US arms sale policy and restrictions are also a perennial irritant to the bilateral relationship. Especially on the most divisive issues, Washington should be prepared to make its position clear, even if it risks the anger of Nigerian officials. Americans would expect no less from their diplomats. Nevertheless, policymakers should be under no illusion as to the ease of changing Nigeria's strongly held official positions without strong and widespread domestic calls for change. The art will be to prevent disagreement on those issues from spilling over into other arenas where cooperation would be mutually beneficial.

However a Washington administration defines American interests, successfully pursuing them requires an understanding of the motivations and realities behind Nigeria's foreign and domestic policies. For Americans, they are not obvious. Nigeria is an entity of a special type. It is a state whose authority is archipelagic and whose relationship with its people is prebendal. These realities require a departure from the business-as-usual, nation-state framework of international relations.

Nevertheless, Nigeria's challenges are not altogether unique. In 1992, William J. Burns, who would later become the US ambassador to Russia and director of the Central Intelligence Agency, observed:

> From the disintegrated Soviet empire to the Balkans, to much of Africa and the Middle East, what is happening is that traditional elites who have either excluded significant national or ethnic groups from power or failed to deliver political and economic goods are under attack. . . . The consequences of this political proliferation, and that crisis of legitimacy at its core, are uncertain ones for the U.S.[34]

American diplomats and policymakers must avoid the complacency of assuming all states are alike, or even similar, in how they work and what motivates their rulers. American involvement in Nigeria's challenges requires skilled diplomatic management that takes into account the country's distinct political economy. Collectively, Boko Haram, Delta militias, middle belt violence, the collapse of oil prices, the coronavirus, and the potential revival of Biafra pose a major threat to Nigeria. The challenges of managing the bilateral relationship productively will require Washington to think about Nigeria in a new way.

Conclusion

Thinking Differently

*[A] country so maddening, so inventive, so soul-affirming and so
soul-destroying it defies attempts to capture it.*

—David Pilling[1]

Nigeria deserves a rethink. So, too, do other postcolonial countries. They all
deserve more than the application of a European framework that is likely
to encourage a misunderstanding of how they work. Nigeria is a prebendal
archipelago. It lacks a unifying historical narrative, has an artificial identity
imposed by the British Empire, and copes with a weak and corrupt government while its elites are fundamentally satisfied with the status quo. Its citizens are largely alienated from these elites and a formal state that provides
few services and little security, but they are astonishingly resilient, solving
seemingly intractable problems by ingenious workarounds. The same should
be said of Pakistan, Iraq, and a host of other postcolonial states. Religion
gives Nigerians hope and purpose and accounts for their celebrated cheerfulness. Nevertheless, they are at present too divided by ethnicity and religion to
bring about transformational change. Fraught relationships between government and society and the inability of government to project power beyond
its archipelago are at the root of the violence and insurrection that now dog
Abuja and the capitals of other postcolonial states.

Since the end of the civil war in 1970, the competing and cooperating elites
prevented the breakup of Nigeria along ethnic lines and managed the 1998–
99 transition from military to civilian governance. Put bluntly, they prevented
another civil war while preserving their privileged positions. But the stability
of this arrangement is now being challenged by Boko Haram, bandits in the
middle belt, militants in the Delta, and a nationwide crime wave. The rise of
nonstate actors challenging government authority is not unique to Nigeria. As
observers in *Foreign Affairs* argued, "Ethnic groups, warlords, youth gangs,
terrorists, militias, insurgents, and transnational criminal organizations—all

are redefining power across the globe."[2] Driving these challenges in Nigeria and elsewhere is rapid population growth, urbanization, degradation of the environment and poverty.

It is unlikely that Nigeria can continue to function much as it has in the recent past, and at present, the outlook is dark. The most likely scenario for Nigeria is that it will continue to function as a prebendal archipelago, but with an ever-weaker central government, ever-stronger subnational institutions (such as states), and the persistence, even resurgence, of traditional authorities and religious leaders. However, even if history has not been kind, Nigeria has been blessed by the absence of foreign intervention by neighboring predatory states, unlike Iraq or the Democratic Republic of the Congo. Hence, the state, weak though it is, has not been pushed to the point of collapse by predatory powers. Instead, its challenges are internal.

Nigeria teaches four lessons about sovereign states and subnational polities that diverge from the more conventional models. The first is that history matters, especially as remembered by religions and ethnic groups. Nigeria's history severely limits how and how fast it might evolve. Like that of much of Africa, the Middle East, and South Asia, Nigeria's history is characterized by colonialism, military rule, and incomplete modernization, which in turn leads to unresolved tensions among the nations, tribes, clans, and communities that make it up. Nevertheless, Nigeria's current challenges were not inevitable, and more recently they have been exacerbated by poor political leadership.

To engage effectively with Nigeria—and with any state—requires a grasp of its past. Nigeria's history has produced not a nation-state, but something different, what this book calls a prebendal archipelago. Indeed, Nigeria's second lesson is that the application of the conventional thinking that all states are effectively nation-states will not do. The Western idea of a nation-state presupposes a kind of relationship between the government and the governed that is often absent in postcolonial, multiethnic countries dominated by rapacious elites. These largely unconsidered assumptions, uncritically applied by American political leaders to Afghanistan, Iraq, and Vietnam, have contributed to America's foreign policy failures. In all three countries, there was neither an unquenched thirst for Western-style democracy and capitalism, nor, contrary to expectations, were US soldiers universally welcomed as liberators. More important were the lingering historical grievances based on ethnicity and religion that American leaders failed to understand. Better engagement beyond the capital might have exposed such fallacious assumptions.

Third, Western governments should engage differently with postcolonial, multiethnic states such as Nigeria. The international environment created by climate change, a population explosion, and rapid urbanization will require increased engagement with weak states. Nigeria shows that a diplomatic focus on capitals is no longer good enough. Instead, a more decentralized approach that reaches subnational political, religious, and ethnic leaders is increasingly necessary to build a productive partnership. In many countries, security service human rights abuses are widespread and underlying drivers of conflict are left unresolved by the self-serving elites that have captured the government. In these countries, the traditional emphasis on military relationships is increasingly counterproductive.

Finally, for outsiders engaged with Nigeria and countries like it, a bit of humility and self-reflection is in order. Too much criticism is based on the expectation that Nigeria and other developing countries ought to act more like conventional, modern nation-states. The limitations imposed by history are ignored. In this regard, American officials, policymakers, and politicians should watch their rhetoric. "Tone certainly matters," wrote former deputy secretary of state William Burns. "I have yet to meet the foreign leadership or society that responds well to being lectured to or patronized by Americans."[3] Americans often forget how long it took the United States to achieve its present, still imperfect form, enduring a civil war and the chronic mistreatment of racial and ethnic minorities. In 1956, William Faulkner (1897–1962), one of the greatest of American literary figures, said in the context of unresolved racial issues, "If I have to choose between the United States government and Mississippi, then I'll choose Mississippi." Faulkner went on to say, "If it came to fighting, I would fight for Mississippi against the United States."[4] Is Faulkner's choice of loyalty so very different from the sentiments of an Igbo separatist?

As I said in the preface, much of what this book argues is based on my personal experience with Nigeria primarily as a US diplomat and a senior fellow at the Council on Foreign Relations. But I have relied heavily on the work of Nigerian scholars and thinkers. If the picture I paint is dark, it is so painted by Nigerians. Obafemi Awolowo understood the sheer arbitrariness of Nigeria's existence when he famously called it a "mere geographical expression."[5] Ken Saro-Wiwa, the human rights activist killed by the brutal regime of Sani Abacha, understood well the prebendal nature of the elite cartel that took the reins of leadership from the British upon independence: "Ruling Nigeria became, for them, not nation-building but the control of federal power and therefore the resources of the nation."[6] Celebrated Nigerian writers Chimamanda Ngozi Adichie, Chinua Achebe, and Wole Soyinka describe in detail the country's political and social dysfunction. And the writer Elnathan John uses satire to expose the unaccountable elites driven by self-interest. Oby Ezekwesili, the former Nigerian minister of education in the Obasanjo government, bewails that Nigeria is usually at the bottom of international indices of well-being. The former governor of Cross Rivers state Donald Duke laments—and has chronicled—election rigging.[7] Prior to his enthronement as emir of Kano, the governor of the Central Bank went public with the massive corruption infecting the oil industry. (The emir was subsequently removed from office by the governor of Kano.) The oft-maligned media courageously, and sometimes at great personal risk, profiles the daily injustices and indignities suffered by Nigerians. These are Nigeria's better angels. Nigeria's friends should heed them.

Notes

PREFACE TO THE REVISED EDITION

1. United Nations Department of Economic and Social Affairs, "World Population Prospects 2019," United Nations, 2019, https://population.un.org/wpp/Publications/Files/WPP2019_Highlights.pdf.

2. Marabouts are Muslim holy men largely outside the traditional Islamic establishment. Highly influential among Nigerian governing-class Muslims, marabouts often come from West African countries closer to the Sahara.

3. Ebenezer Obadare explores the religion of enchantment and its influence on the public in his *Pentecostal Republic: Religion and the Struggle for State Power in Nigeria* (London: Zed Books, 2018).

4. Chinua Achebe, *The Trouble with Nigeria* (Enugu, Nigeria: Fourth Dimension, 2005).

5. A recent example: Wale Adebanwi and Ebenezer Obadare, eds., *Democracy and Prebendalism in Nigeria: Critical Interpretations* (New York: Palgrave Macmillan, 2013). The editors have assembled ten essays on prebendalism, with a foreword by Larry Diamond and an epilogue by Richard Joseph.

6. The pioneering work on prebendalism is Richard Joseph, *Democracy and Prebendal Politics in Nigeria: The Rise and Fall of the Second Republic* (Cambridge: Cambridge University Press, 1987).

7. Neopatrimonialism, as defined by Christopher Clapham, is a "form of organization in which relationships of a broadly patrimonial type pervade a political and administrative system which is formally constructed on rational-legal lines." Christopher Clapham, *Third World Politics: An Introduction* (London: Routledge, 1985), 48.

8. Under the leadership of the ambassador, the political counselor heads the embassy section engaged with the host government on bilateral and multilateral political issues.

9. The state I missed was Borno, far from Lagos and then quiet. Two decades later, it became the heart of the Boko Haram insurrection.

10. Richard Sklar calls this reality "double majesty," the "coexistence of two self-subsistent realms of government." See his "The African Frontier for Political

Science," in *Africa and the Disciplines*, ed. Robert H. Bates, V. Y. Mudimber, and Jean O'Barr (Chicago: University of Chicago Press, 1993), 86.

INTRODUCTION

1. Carlin Romano, "African Novel of the Century," *Philadelphia Inquirer*, March 28, 2008, http://www.inquirer.com/philly/entertainment/20080327_African_novel_of _the_century.html.

2. Phillip Connor, "International Migration from Sub-Saharan Africa Has Grown Dramatically since 2010," Pew Research Center, https://www.pewresearch.org /fact-tank/2018/02/28/international-migration-from-sub-saharan-africa-has-grown -dramatically-since-2010.

3. Varieties in the number of ethnic groups reflects, at least in part, differences in definition of what constitutes a separate ethnic group. By some estimates, there are about 350 distinct ethnic groups.

4. Sharkdam Wapmuk, Oluwatooni Akinkuotu, and Vincent Ibonye, "The Nigerian Diaspora and National Development: Contributions, Challenges, and Lessons from Other Countries," *Kritika Kultura*, no. 23 (August 2014): 292–342, https://journals .ateneo.edu/ojs/index.php/kk/article/view/1898/1900. Nobody really knows the size of the Nigerian diaspora. One estimate is seventeen million, which is equivalent to about 8 percent of the population.

5. This is an accepted, and descriptive enough, myth, but figures are hard to come by. The last census was in 2006 and fraught with controversy. Murtala Mohammed, when he was military chief of state in 1976, decreed that the two religions were equal in size, and Nigerians have accepted his determination ever since.

6. Dalia Fahmy, "Americans Are Far More Religious Than Adults in Other Wealthy Nations," Pew Research Center, July 2018, https://www.pewresearch.org/fact-tank /2018/07/31/americans-are-far-more-religious-than-adults-in-other-wealthy-nations.

7. Some Nigerians object to analysis based on the north/south, Muslim/Christian dichotomy, citing the large religious and ethnic minorities living all over the country. Yet the reality is that there is a fundamental difference between the north and the south of the country based on religion and ethnicity: the north is, indeed, predomi- nately Muslim, while the south is predominately Christian. Those two cultures are dominant in their respective parts of the country.

8. "Oil Production," Nigerian National Petroleum Corporation, http://www .nnpcgroup.com/nnpcbusiness/upstreamventures/oilproduction.aspx. In 2012, Nige- ria was ranked twelfth in terms of total oil production and the tenth in terms of crude oil production. See "Total Petroleum and Other Liquids Production—2018," US Energy Information Administration, https://www.eia.gov/countries/country-data.cfm ?fips=NI&trk=m#pet.

9. The former finance minister and foreign minister of Nigeria, Ngozi Okonjo-Iweala, along with many others, has expressed her concern over Nigeria's dependency on oil. John Campbell, "Nigeria Is Oil Dependent, Not Oil Rich," *Africa in Transition* (blog),

Council on Foreign Relations, February 13, 2019, https://www.cfr.org/blog/nigeria
-oil-dependent-not-oil-rich.

10. "2014 Oil and Gas Industry Audit Report," Nigeria Extractive Industries
Transparency Initiative, December 23, 2016, http://www.eiti.org/sites/default/files/
documents/neiti-oil-gas-report-2014-full-report-301216.pdf.

11. Odunayo Eweniyi, "ICT Face-Off: Lagos, Kenya or South Africa. Which Is the
ICT Capital of Africa?," *TechCabal*, May 12, 2014, accessed June 24, 2019, http://
www.techcabal.com/2014/05/12/ict-face-off-lagos-vs-kenya-vs-south-africa.

12. In 2016. See "Electricity in Nigeria: Powerless," *Economist*, March 2, 2016,
https://www.economist.com/middle-east-and-africa/2016/03/03/powerless. Though
Nigeria produces little electricity, according to the Oak Ridge National Laboratory,
in 2014, Nigeria ranked 40 out of 220 in CO_2 emissions from fossil-fuel burning,
cement production, and gas flaring. It ranked 180 out of 220 in emissions per capita.
See https://cdiac.ess-dive.lbl.gov/trends/emis/top2014.cap and https://cdiac.ess-dive
.lbl.gov/trends/emis/top2014.tot

13. Ngozi Okonjo-Iweala, *Reforming the Unreformable: Lessons from Nigeria*
(Cambridge, MA: MIT Press, 2012), 43.

14. "Nigerian Mobile Report 2018," *Jumia*, 2018, http://www.jumia.com.ng/
mobile-report.

15. Jeffrey A. Frankel, "The Natural Resource Curse: A Survey of Diagnoses and
Some Prescriptions," HKS Faculty Research Working Paper Series RWP12–014,
John F. Kennedy School of Government, Harvard University, https://dash.harvard.edu
/bitstream/handle/1/8694932/rwp12-014_frankel.pdf?sequence=1.

16. Homi Kharas, Kristofer Hamel, and Martin Hofer, "The Start of a New Poverty
Narrative," *Future Development* (blog), Brookings Institution, June 19, 2018, http://
www.brookings.edu/blog/future-development/2018/06/19/the-start-of-a-new-poverty
-narrative.

17. Peter Opatewa, "From Excess Crude to Extinct Crude: Which Way Nigeria?,"
Guardian (Nigeria), July 22, 2015, https://guardian.ng/features/from-excess-crude-to
-extinct-crude-which-way-nigeria-1.

18. Matt Timms, "Nigeria Urgently Needs to Tackle Corruption and Theft in Its
Oil Industry," *World Finance*, July 21, 2016, accessed June 24, 2019, http://www
.worldfinance.com/markets/nigeria-urgently-needs-to-tackle-corruption-and-theft-in
-its-oil-industry. Nigerian statistics are indicative at best, not definitive.

19. Among others, Stephen Ellis develops this theme at length with extensive docu-
mentation. See his *This Present Darkness: A History of Nigerian Organized Crime*
(New York: Oxford University Press, 2016).

20. Goran Hyden, *African Politics in Comparative Perspective* (Cambridge: Cambridge University Press, 2005), 7.

21. Olufunmbi Elemo, "Fiscal Federalism, Subnational Politics, and State Creation
in Contemporary Nigeria," in *The Oxford Handbook of Nigerian Politics*, ed. A. Carl
LeVan and Patrick Ukata (New York: Oxford University Press, 2018), 189–206.

22. The concept of islands of government authority—an archipelago—in a sea of
ungoverned spaces was developed by the US National Intelligence Council in 2005 as
a way of thinking about governance in much of sub-Saharan Africa. The is presented

in "Mapping Sub-Saharan Africa's Future," National Intelligence Council, CR 2005-02 March 2005. The NIC is composed of scholars assembled by the US government to consider various issues. However, its publications are not official US policy.

CHAPTER 1

1. Peter Ekeh, "Colonialism and the Two Publics in Africa," *Comparative Studies in Society and History* 17, no. 1 (January 1975): 97.

2. Alan Cousins, "Governing Africa: The Imperial Mind in British Colonies, 1938–1947, in Light of Indian Experience," *Social Scientist* 27, no. 7/8 (1999): 162.

3. John Flint, "Planned Decolonization and Its Failure in British Africa," *African Affairs* 82, no. 328 (1983): 411.

4. Emmanuel C. Eze, "Hume, Race, and Human Nature," *Journal of the History of Ideas* 61, no. 4 (2000): 691, doi:10.2307/3654076.

5. H. R. Trevor-Roper, *The Rise of Christian Europe* (New York: Harcourt, Brace & World, 1965), 871.

6. Arthur de Gobineau (1816–82) came from the French nobility. He passionately hated the French Revolution and all aspects of social equality. His book, *Essay on the Inequality of the Human Races*, was 1,400 pages in length. He was strongly critical of the United States because of the "mongrelization" of its population, a trope believed by Adolf Hitler. (His editor deleted the anti-American material from the US edition.) Originally published in French, an English translation was published in the United States in 1856. Arthur de Gobineau, H. Hotz, and Josiah Clark Nott, *The Moral and Intellectual Diversity of Races* (Philadelphia: J. B. Lippincott, 2012).

7. Stephen Ellis, *This Present Darkness: A History of Nigerian Organized Crime* (New York: Oxford University Press, 2016), 32.

8. In seventeenth-century Virginia, there was similar ambivalence about enslaving Christians and a reluctance to convert newly arrived African slaves to Christianity. Only in the latter part of the century was consensus reached that Black Africans could be both Christian and enslaved.

9. John McCauley, *The Logic of Ethnic and Religious Conflict in Africa* (Cambridge: Cambridge University Press, 2017), 156.

10. McCauley, *The Logic of Ethnic and Religious Conflict in Africa*, 156. "Fulani" is a problematic term. It properly refers to a migratory people that speak Fulfulde and raise cattle. However, in southern Nigeria it is often used to refer to Muslims from the north that seek to impose Islam on the entire country. From the early nineteenth century on, Fulfulde-speakers have intermarried with other ethnic groups in the north that are not necessarily migratory but speak Hausa. The result is an amalgamated ethnic group, the Hausa-Fulani, the largest in the country. Today, Fulfulde is spoken only by those Fulani who are still migratory.

11. See Philip D. Curtin, *The Atlantic Slave Trade: A Census* (Madison: University of Wisconsin Press, 1972).

12. See Humphrey J. Foster, *Slavery in the History of Muslim Black Africa* (New York: New York University Press, 2001).

13. On the organization of the transatlantic slave trade and conditions on slave ships, see Marcus Rediker, *The Slave Ship: A Human History* (New York: Penguin, 2007). See also Curtin, *The Atlantic Slave Trade*. On the trans-Saharan trade, the literature is less extensive. See McCauley, *Logic*, and Foster, *Slavery*.

14. "The Transatlantic Slave Trade," Harvard Divinity School, accessed June 19, 2019, http://www.rlp.hds.harvard.edu/faq/transatlantic-slave-trade-nigeria.

15. Hilaire Belloc, *The Modern Traveller* (London: E. Arnold, 1898).

16. Cannibalism was a staple of the British yellow press. But Flora Shaw, later Lady Lugard, also wrote about it in the *Times*, then a highly influential newspaper widely read among the British political class. For example, see "Cannibal Rising in Southern Nigeria," *Times* (London), January 11, 1906, 5, accessed November 1, 2019, The Times Digital Archives, http://www.tinyurl.gale.com/tinyurl/C7AHG3.

17. Oil palms are not indigenous to West Africa. The British introduced their cultivation from South Asia.

18. For this little-known dimension to great power rivalry, see Mostafa Minawi, *The Ottoman Scramble for Africa: Empire and Diplomacy in the Sahara and the Hijaz* (Stanford, CA: Stanford University Press, 2016).

19. Ellis, *This Present Darkness*, 8.

20. Femi Fani-Kayode, "Lord Lugard's Magic and Flora Shaw's Spell," *Premium Times*, September 8, 2015, http://www.opinion.premiumtimesng.com/2015/09/08/lord-lugards-magic-and-flora-shaws-spell-by-femi-fani-kayode.

21. Sanya Osha, "Birth of the Ogoni Protest Movement," *Journal of Asian and African Studies* 41, no. 1/2 (2006): 22.

22. Ellis, *This Present Darkness*, 9.

23. Ellis, *This Present Darkness*, 43.

24. Margery Perham quoted in Felia Allum and Stan Gilmour, *Routledge Handbook of Transnational Organized Crime* (London: Routledge, 2015), 133.

25. The literature on modernization is huge, and there is a lively debate on, among other aspects, its epistemology. Among many others, see Lynn M. Thomas, "Modernity's Failings, Political Claims and Intermediate Concepts," *American Historical Review* 116, no. 3 (2011): 727–40, http://jstor.org/stable/23308225; Yahia Mahmoud, "Modernism in Africa," in *The Routledge Encyclopedia of Modernism* (London: Routledge, 2016); Dean C. Tipps, "Modernization Theory and the Comparative Study of Societies: A Critical Perspective," *Studies in Society and History* 15, no. 2 (March 1973): 199–226, http://jstor.org/stable/178351.

26. David Motadel, "Islam and the European Empires," *Historical Journal* 55, no. 3 (2012): 831–56, http://jstor.org/stable/23263276.

27. Ellis, *This Present Darkness*, 8.

28. Lamin Sanneh, *Translating the Message: The Missionary Impact on Culture* (Maryknoll, NY: Orbis Books, 1989).

29. Godwin Onu (2001) referenced in McCauley, *The Logic of Ethnic and Religious Conflict in Africa*.

30. Moses Ochonu, *Colonialism by Proxy: Hausa Imperial Agents and Middle Belt Consciousness in Nigeria* (Bloomington: Indiana University Press, 2014).

31. Samuel O. Okafor, "Review: The Warrant Chiefs: Indirect Rule in Southeastern Nigeria, 1891–1929," *Journal of Modern African Studies* 11, no. 3 (1973): 487–89, http://jstor.org/stable/159621. See also Adiele Afigbo, "The Warrant Chiefs: Indirect Rule in Southeastern Nigeria, 1891–1929," *School of Oriental and African Studies* 36, no. 3 (1973): 725–27.

32. On British suspicion of westernized elites and desire to preserve traditional structures, see Flint, "Planned Decolonization and Its Failure in British Africa," 94; Robert Pearce, "The Colonial Office and Planned Decolonization in Africa," *African Affairs*, 83, no. 330 (1984): 77.

33. Ellis, *This Present Darkness*, 75.

34. Thomas S. Gale, "Segregation in British West Africa (La Ségrégation en Afrique Occidentale Britannique)," *Cahiers D'Études Africaines* 20, no. 80 (1980): 495–507, http://jstor.org/stable/4391717.

35. Gale, "Segregation in British West Africa (La Ségrégation en Afrique Occidentale Britannique)."

36. Sir Bernard Bourdillion, *Memorandum on the Future Development of Nigeria* (confidential, Government Printer, Lagos, 1939, 4, cited in Ellis, *This Present Darkness*, 43.

37. Toyin Falola and Matthew M. Heaton, *A History of Nigeria* (Cambridge: Cambridge University Press, 2008), 136, 146, 148.

38. On the evolution of British thinking about Nigerian governance see, inter alia, Alan Cousins, "The Imperial Mind in British Colonies, 1938–1947, in the Light of Indian Experience," *Social Scientist* 27, no. 7/8 (1999): 140–67; Robert Pearce, "The Colonial Office and Planned Decolonization in Africa," *African Affairs* 83, no. 330 (1984): 77–93; Flint, "Planned Decolonization and Its Failure in British Africa," 389–411.

39. Senghor and Houphouët-Boigny were both French-educated Roman Catholics; Senghor had a French, white wife.

40. One way to measure these ties is through current trade statistics. For the United Kingdom, trade with its former colonies accounts for about 2 percent of its total trade. For France, trade with its former colonies accounts for about 3.5 percent of its total trade. Additionally, the total trade of former British colonies is about 3.5 times larger than the total trade of former French colonies; meaning, the proportion of trade between France and its former colonies is much more significant. Based on an analysis of "United Kingdom | Export to All Country | 2016 | WITS | Data," *World Integrated Trade Solution*, The World Bank, http://www.wits.worldbank.org/CountryProfile/en/Country/GBR/Year/2016/TradeFlow/Export; Keith Head et al., "The Erosion of Colonial Trade Linkages after Independence," *Journal of International Economics* 81, no. 1 (2010): 1–14, doi:10.1016/j.jinteco.2010.01.002.

41. Whether formally banned by law or not varied from possession to possession. But throughout the British Empire, interracial marriage was condemned in strong terms.

42. The closest British equivalent to Senghor might be India's Prime Minister Jawaharlal Nehru, who was close to the upper reaches of the British establishment.

But for the British, India was vastly more important than Africa, and the rules regarding race were somewhat different.

43. The French used colonial troops in the Rhineland because of the shortage of other troops by the end of World War I.

44. Sir Martin Ewans, HM High Commissioner to Nigeria, April 1988, Dispatch to the Foreign Office, printed in Matthew Parris and Andrew Bryson, *Parting Shots* (London: Viking, 2010), 352.

45. Derek Leebaert, *Grand Improvisation: America Confronts the British Superpower, 1945–1957* (New York: Farrar, Straus and Giroux, 2016), 213–14, 499.

46. Gale, "Segregation in British West Africa," 495–507.

47. James S. Coleman, *Nigeria* (Berkeley: University of California Press, 1963), 50; Barclays Bank, *Nigeria* (Dominion, Colonial and Overseas, 1966), 50.

48. Isobel Coleman and Terra Lawson-Remer, eds., *Pathways to Freedom* (New York: Council on Foreign Relations, June 2013), 216.

49. Coleman, *Nigeria*, 46.

50. Ellis, *This Present Darkness*, 62.

51. John Hare, *Last Man In: The End of Empire in Northern Nigeria* (Kent, UK: Neville & Harding, 2013), 7.

52. Purwarno Purwarno and Andang Suhendi, "Colonialism as a Redeeming Evil in Chinua Achebe's 'Things Fall Apart,'" September 2017, http://www.researchgate.net /publication/324950118_Colonialism_as_a_Redeeming_Evil_in_Chinua_Achebe's _Things_Fall_Apart.

53. Hare, *Last Man In*, 4.

54. Coleman, *Nigeria*, 52.

55. In Nigeria, as in England, college normally refers to a secondary school.

56. See Jan Lahmeyer, *Nigeria: Population Growth of the Whole Country*, http: //www.populstat.info/Africa/nigeriac.htm for university education, and Coleman, *Nigeria*, 141, for secondary school.

57. By comparison, the British Empire in India lasted from 1667 to 1948, and in Virginia from 1607 to 1776. Of course there were British forts on the Nigerian coast dating from the eighteenth century, and the Lagos colony dated from 1861.

58. John Campbell et al., *Pathways to Freedom* (New York: Council on Foreign Relations, June 2013), 202.

59. John Campbell, *Nigeria: Dancing on the Brink*, 2nd ed. (Lanham, MD: Rowman & Littlefield, 2013), 6.

60. On the role of religion in British rule, see Olufemi Vaughan, *Religion and the Making of Nigeria* (Durham, NC: Duke University Press, 2016).

61. Joseph C. McKenna, "Elements of a Nigerian Peace," *Foreign Affairs* 47, no. 4 (1969): 668–80, https://www.foreignaffairs.com/articles/nigeria/1969-07-01/ elements-nigerian-peace.

62. McCauley, *The Logic of Ethnic and Religious Conflict in Africa*, 165.

63. McCauley, *The Logic of Ethnic and Religious Conflict in Africa*, 164–67.

64. McCauley, *The Logic of Ethnic and Religious Conflict in Africa*, 154.

65. John Campbell, "What's in a Name? For the Nigerian Civil War, Everything," *Africa in Transition* (blog), Council on Foreign Relations, October 18, 2017, https://www.cfr.org/blog/whats-name-nigerian-civil-war-everything.

66. The term commonly refers to military rule; military officers regularly rode horses.

67. A. Carl LeVan, *Contemporary Nigerian Politics: Competition in a Time of Transition and Terror* (Cambridge: Cambridge University Press, 2019), 63–65.

68. Ellis, *This Present Darkness*, 145.

CHAPTER 2

1. Saleh Ibrahim Bature, "Nigeria on a Knife's-Edge," *Sahara Reporters*, December 2, 2011, http://www.saharareporters.com/2011/12/02/nigeria-knife%E2%80%99s%E2%80%93edge.

2. Quoted by Tunji Olaopa, the permanent secretary of the Federal Ministry of Communication Technology, in "The Zik-Awo-Sardauna Legacy," *Daily Trust* (Abuja), May, 8, 2015, http://www.dailytrust.com.ng/the-zik-awo-sardauna-legacy.html.

3. Mathias Adamu Abuh, "Nigeria Has Receded, Emefiele Declares," *Guardian*, May 16, 2019, http://www.guardian.ng/news/nigeria-has-receded-emefiele-declares.

4. Yomi Kazeem, "Nigeria's Ongoing Middle-Class Brain Drain Is Costing It Two Generations in One Swoop," *Quartz Africa*, May 25, 2019, accessed June 24, 2019, http://www.qz.com/africa/1615518/nigerias-middle-class-keep-emigrating-to-canada-australia.

5. The ages on Tinubu and Atiku are disputed. Both are likely between seventy-five and eighty years of age.

6. Quote from Chinua Achebe, *The Trouble with Nigeria* (London: Heinemann, 1987), 1.

7. This idea, that, rather than differences in character, it is differences in institutions that helped determine a country's trajectory, was expounded at length in Daron Acemoglu and James A. Robinson, *Why Nations Fail: The Origins of Power, Prosperity, and Poverty* (New York: Currency, 2012). See especially chapters 1 and 2.

8. For example, Benedict Anderson, a leading scholar, sees a nation as an "imagined political community . . . both inherently limited and sovereign," with geographical boundaries, "beyond which lie other nations." He identifies specific political, linguistic, and technological developments in Europe to explain the birth and evolution of the idea of a nation. See Benedict Anderson, *Imagined Communities: Reflections on the Origin and Spread of Nationalism* (London: Verso, 2016), 6–7. Peter Alter sees nationalism as "both an ideology and a political movement which hold the nation and sovereign nation-state to be crucial indwelling values, and which manages to mobilize the politics of a people." On the other hand, Peter Sahlins argues that "national identity is a socially constructed and continuous process of defining 'friend' and 'enemy,'" that national identity does not depend on linguistic or cultural differentiation, "but on the subjective experience of difference." For Alter and Sahlins, see

Lloyd Kramer, "Historical Narratives and the Meaning of Nationalism," *Journal of the History of Ideas* 58, no. 3 (1997): 525–45, doi:10.2307/3653913, 525–26. Strobe Talbott, a former deputy secretary of state, appears sympathetic to the idea that nations and nationalism are modern phenomena, without premodern roots, with practical purposes, including building mass support for elite goals. See Strobe Talbott, *The Great Experiment: The Story of Ancient Empires, Modern States, and the Quest for a Global Nation* (New York: Simon & Schuster, 2009), 23–25.

9. Anderson, *Imagined Communities*, 6–7.

10. Robert H. Jackson and Carl G. Rosberg, "Why Africa's Weak States Persist: The Empirical and the Juridical in Statehood," *World Politics* 35, no. 1 (October 1982): 1–24, http://doi.org/ 10.2307/2010277.

11. Jill Lepore, *This America: The Case for the Nation* (New York: Liveright, 2019), 26–33. In a piece for *Foreign Affairs*, Lepore quotes historian David Armitage to identify a "state-nation, which arises when the state is formed before the development of any sense of national consciousness. The United States might be seen as a, perhaps the only, spectacular example of the latter." Jill Lepore, "A New Americanism," *Foreign Affairs* (March/April 2019), https://www.foreignaffairs.com/articles/united-states/2019-02-05/new-americanism.

12. Lepore, *This America*, 33.

13. See Stephen Ellis, *This Present Darkness: A History of Nigerian Organized Crime* (New York: Oxford University Press, 2016), 61–68 and 114–17, for some examples of major politicians subordinating the national interest to ethnic, regional, and personal interest in the First and Second Republics.

14. Afrobarometer data suggest that people living in former British colonies identify with the state 10 percent less than people living in other former colonies. Instead, they prefer to identify with other subnational groups. See Amanda Lea Robinson, "National versus Ethnic Identity in Africa: State, Group, and Individual Level Correlates of National Identifications," Afrobarometer, Working Paper no. 122 (September 2009): 19, http://www.afrobarometer.org/sites/default/files/publications/Working%20paper/AfropaperNo112.pdf.

15. The phrase was first used in a parliamentary debate in New Zealand in 1868.

16. Epstein was writing explicitly about Uganda, but her observation is appropriate to Nigeria. Helen C. Epstein, "Can Bobi Wine Unite Uganda and Bring Down a Dictator," *Nation*, August 30, 2018, http://www.thenation.com/article/can-bobi-wine-unite-uganda-and-bring-down-a-dictator.

17. The idea that one-third of Americans favored independence, one-third opposed, and one-third were indifferent when the war started is commonly attributed to Benjamin Franklin. If by the end of the War of the American Revolution nearly everybody favored independence from King George III, they did not necessarily think of themselves as Americans.

18. The British-Ijebu War of 1892, the Benin Expedition of 1897, and the Anglo-Aro War (1901–2) involved bloody, indigenous movements against British domination. But they were ethnic and local in character, never morphing into a larger movement for independence. See Rotimi Ajayi, "The Anticolonial Struggle in Nigeria," in *The Oxford Handbook of Nigerian Politics*, ed. A. Carl LeVan and Patrick

Ukata (New York: Oxford University Press, 2018), 89–102. There were also periodic riots and other protests, also local in character. The British easily suppressed them all.

19. F. K Donnelly, "A Possible Source for Nathan Hale's Dying Words," *William and Mary Quarterly* 42, no. 3 (January 1, 1985): 394–96, doi:10.2307/1918934. JSTOR 1918934.

20. Robinson, "National versus Ethnic Identity in Africa," 19.

21. The data is from the World Bank for 2017. For Ethiopia, Africa's second-largest country by population, it is 4.1; for Congo (DRC) it is 6; for India, it is 2.3; for the United States, 1.8. "Fertility Rate, Total (Births per Woman)," World Bank, http://www.data.worldbank.org/indicator/SP.DYN.TFRT.IN?locations=NG.

22. "The Future of World Religions: Population Growth Projections, 2010–2050," Pew Research Center, April 2, 2015, http://www.assets.pewresearch.org/wp-content/uploads/sites/11/2015/03/PF_15.04.02_ProjectionsFullReport.pdf.

23. For example, former vice president Atiku Abubakar has twenty-three children; large numbers of children are also found among non-Muslims: former president Olusegun Obasanjo, a born-again Baptist, has about twenty-two.

24. "Nigeria Population 2019," http://www.worldpopulationreview.com/countries /nigeria-population.

25. Goran Hyden, *African Politics in Comparative Perspective* (Cambridge: Cambridge University Press, 2012), 74.

26. Quoted by Ebenezer Obadare, *Pentecostal Republic: Religion and the Struggle for State Power in Nigeria* (London: Zed Books, 2018), 13.

27. Obadare, *Pentecostal Republic*, 10–11.

28. Salem Village, Massachusetts, was the venue for the 1692 witchcraft trials in which nineteen accused were judicially murdered.

29. "Internet Users Hit 115.9 Million in March—NCC," *Premium Times Nigeria*, May 20, 2019, accessed June 24, 2019, http://www.premiumtimesng.com/news/more -news/330709-internet-users-hit-115-9-million-in-march-ncc.html.

30. Bim Adewunmi, "Nigeria: The Happiest Place on Earth," *Guardian*, January 2011, http://www.theguardian.com/global/2011/jan/04/nigerians-top-optimism -poll; "Gallup International's 41st Annual Global End of Year Survey," Gallup International, http://www.gallup-international.bg/en/Publications/2017/407-Gallup -International%E2%80%99s-41-Annual-Global-End-of-Year-Survey-Economically -More-Difficult-Year-To-Come.

31. I am grateful to Jacob Olupona of the Harvard Divinity School for this insight.

32. John McCauley, *The Logic of Ethnic and Religious Conflict in Africa* (Cambridge: Cambridge University Press, 2017), 156.

33. Inemesit Udodiong, "How VP Became a Born-Again Christian," *Pulse*, May 17, 2018, http://www.pulse.ng/communities/religion/yemi-osinbajo-how-vp-became -a-born-again-christian/byhjm0h.

34. Ebenezer Obadare develops clerical political influence in his book *Pentecostal Republic*.

35. Private conversation with a Church of Nigeria bishop in May 2019. On political Catholicism, see Iheanyi M. Enwerem, *Crossing the Rubicon: A Socio-Political Analysis of Political Catholicism in Nigeria* (Ibadan, Nigeria: Book Builders, 2010).

36. Anderson, *Imagined Communities*, 42.

37. For a discussion on ethnic and religious identification, see McCauley, *The Logic of Ethnic and Religious Conflict in Africa*.

38. The Hausa and the Fulani are sometimes listed as separate ethnic groups; however the two have largely merged, primarily through intermarriage.

39. Robinson, "National versus Ethnic Identity in Africa," 19, 24.

40. These population figures are from the CIA's *World Factbook*. Population estimates for Nigeria vary considerably. The *Factbook* estimates Nigeria's total population was 203.5 million in 2018. *The World Factbook*, Central Intelligence Agency, 2019, http://www.cia.gov/library/publications/the-world-factbook/geos/ni.html.The 2006 official census, discredited by many, concluded that the country's population was 140 million.

41. Robinson, "National versus Ethnic Identity in Africa," 19.

42. On the identification of "nation" with ethnic groups, see Chukwuemeka Onwubu, "Ethnic Identity, Political Integration, and National Development: The Igbo Diaspora in Nigeria," *Journal of Modern African Studies* 13, no. 3 (September 1975): 399–413.

43. David B. Abernethy, quoted in Peter Ekeh, "Colonialism and the Two Publics in Africa: A Theoretical Statement," *Comparative Studies in Society and History* 17, no. 1 (January 1975): 105.

44. T. Hodgkin, quoted in Ekeh, "Colonialism and the Two Publics in Africa," 105.

45. Nigerians never speak of the divine origins of the Nigerian state. For them, Nigeria was formed by the British, not by God.

46. From about 1550 to 1860, the vast majority of African slaves went to the Caribbean and South America. Only 4 percent went to North America. Brazil alone received around 4.8 million African slaves. In 2011, the *Guardian* estimated that Brazil was in fact that second-largest "African" country in the world, behind Nigeria and just ahead of Ethiopia. See Tom Phillips, "Brazil Census Shows African-Brazilians in the Majority for the First Time," *Guardian*, November 17, 2011, http://www.theguardian.com/world/2011/nov/17/brazil-census-african-brazilians-majority?CMP=share_btn_tw; and Andrew Kahn and Jamelle Bouie, "The Atlantic Slave Trade in Two Minutes," *Slate*, June 25, 2015, http://www.slate.com/articles/life/the_history_of_american_slavery/2015/06/animated_interactive_of_the_history_of_the_atlantic_slave_trade.html.

47. William F. S. Miles and David A. Rochefort, "Nationalism versus Ethnic Identity in Sub-Saharan Africa," *American Political Science Review* 85, no. 2 (June 1991): 393–403.

48. "Afrobarometer Round 7 Survey of Nigeria: Summary of Results," *Afrobarometer*, May 2017. See question 2B.

49. David M. Eberhard, Gary F. Simons, and Charles D. Fennig, eds., "What Is the Most Spoken Language?," *Ethnologue: Languages of the World*, 2019, http://www.ethnologue.com/guides/most-spoken-languages.

50. Anderson, *Imagined Communities*, 42–46.

51. Monica Mark, "Nigeria's Love of Pidgin dey Scatter My Brain yet Ginger My Swagger," *Guardian*, September 24, 2012, http://www.theguardian.com/

world/2012/sep/24/nigeria-pidgin-scatter-brain-swagger; and Malaka Gharib, "Why Prince Charles Said 'God Don Butta My Bread!' in Nigeria," NPR, November 20, 2018, http://www.npr.org/sections/goatsandsoda/2018/11/20/668604714/why-prince -charles-said-god-don-butta-my-bread-in-nigeria.

52. According to Pew's Global Attitudes survey for spring 2017, when asked "How important is religion in your life?" 94 percent of respondents in Nigeria responded "very important," while 4 percent responded "somewhat important." Jacob Pushter, Janell Fetterolf, and Christine Tamir, "How People around the World View Religion's Role in Their Countries," Pew Research Center, April 22, 2019, http://www .pewresearch.org/global/2019/04/22/how-people-around-the-world-view-religions -role-in-their-countries.

53. Jacob Olupona, *Beyond Primitivism: Indigenous Religious Traditions and Modernity* (New York: Routledge, 2004), 14.

54. Jill Salmons, "Mammy Wata," *African Arts* 10, no. 3 (1977): 8–87, doi:10.2307/3335295.

55. The British and French divided among themselves the German colony of Kamerun after World War I. The British portion functioned as a part of Nigeria, though its legal status was ambiguous.

56. Queen Elizabeth II made Ahmadu Bello a knight of the British Empire in 1959 when he headed Nigeria's largest political party. Sardauna is a traditional title in the court of the sultan of Sokoto.

57. For Azikiwe's religion, see Patrick J. Furlong, "Azikiwe and the National Church of Nigeria and the Cameroons: A Case Study of the Political Use of Religion in African Nationalism," *African Affairs* 91, no. 364 (July 1992): 433–52.

58. Bature, "Nigeria on a Knife's-Edge."

59. Ray Ekpu, "Geographical Expression: So What?," *Guardian*, August 15, 2017, http://www.guardian.ng/opinion/geographical-expression-so-what; and Bature, "Nigeria on a Knife's Edge."

60. "Nigeria: Toward Disintegration?," *Time*, August 12, 1996, http://www.content .time.com/time/magazine/article/0,9171,842599,00.html.

61. Wole Soyinka, *Of Africa* (New Haven, CT: Yale University Press, 2012), 10.

62. For example, the UN Development Program (UNDP) ranks Ghana at 140 out of the 189 countries and places it in the "medium development" category. It ranks Nigeria at 157, in the "low development" category. *UNDP Human Development Index 2018 Statistical Update* (New York: United Nations Development Program, 2018), 24, http://www.hdr.undp.org/sites/default/files/2018_human_development_statistical _update.pdf.

63. Robinson, "National versus Ethnic Identity in Africa," 13.

64. Ghana, first to achieve independence in sub-Saharan Africa, set the standard pattern of developing nationalist movements as a means of nation-building. The singular dominant nationalist model spread across most French-speaking nations and later to Tanganyika, Malawi, and Zambia.

65. Kwasi Konafu and Clifford C. Campbell, *The Ghana Reader: History, Culture, Politics* (Durham, NC: Duke University Press, 2016), 1.

66. "(1959) Nnamdi Azikiwe Honors Kwame Nkrumah on His Visit to Eastern Nigeria," *Black Past*, September 2, 2009, http://www.blackpast.org/major_speeches /1959-nnamdi-azikiwe-honors-kwame-nkrumah-his-visit-eastern-nigeria.

67. Women won the right to vote and to stand for elections only in 1954. "Africa," *Women Suffrage and Beyond*, http://www.womensuffrage.org/?page_id=203.

68. Catherine of Braganza had no children. The London street slur against her was: "Three things to be seen. Bombay, Tangier, and a barren queen." Charles II fathered fifteen children by numerous mistresses.

69. In fact, Gandhi's protest against colonial rule began in South Africa as a lawyer in 1906 with the Satyagraha campaign advocating for the rights of Indians against discriminatory laws and leading the 1913 Natal Indian Strike against the ill-treatment of Indians in the British gold mines.

70. Mainland Tanzania was originally a German colony, called German East Africa, which also included present-day Rwanda and Burundi. Following the 1919 Paris Peace Conference, Britain was granted mainland Tanzania, called Tanganyika, as a League of Nations mandate, and Belgium ultimately received Rwanda and Burundi as a mandate. Tanganyika became independent in 1961 and merged with Zanzibar in 1964 to become Tanzania.

71. Karsten Legère, "JK Nyerere of Tanzania and the Empowerment of Swahili," in *"Along the Routes to Power": Explorations of Empowerment through Language*, ed. Martin Pütz, Joshua A. Fishman, and JoAnne Neff-van Aertselaer (Berlin: Mouton de Gruyter, 2006), 379.

72. Jan Blommaert, "Language Policy and National Identity," in *An Introduction to Language Policy: Theory and Method*, ed. Thomas Ricento (Malden, MA: Blackwell, 2006), 248.

73. Lyndon Harries, "Language Policy in Tanzania," *Africa: Journal of the International African Institute* 39, no. 3 (July 1969): 275, http://www.jstor.org/stable /1157997.

74. Deboah Fahy Bryceson et al., "Tanzania," in *Encyclopedia Britannica*, accessed January 1, 2019, https://www.britannica.com/place/Tanzania#ref1036097.

75. Nic Cheeseman, *Democracy in Africa* (New York: Cambridge University Press, 2015), 206.

76. The Swiss, however, do not extend this mutual recognition to the wave of asylum seekers from the Middle East and Africa.

77. See Charles Blattberg and Jon Tattrie, "Canadian Identity," in *The Canadian Encyclopedia*, updated February 29, 2016, http://www.thecanadianencyclopedia.ca/ en/article/canadian-identity.

78. Adele Oltman, "The Hidden History of Slavery in New York," *Nation*, November 7, 2005, http://www.thenation.com/article/hidden-history-slavery-new-york; and Ira Berlin and Leslie Harris, *Slavery in New York* (New York: The New Press, 2005).

79. Douglas Southall Freeman, *R. E. Lee: A Biography* (New York: Charles Scribner's Sons, 1934), 633.

80. Total deaths resulting from the Civil War are estimates. See Guy Gugliotta, "New Estimate Raises Civil War Death Toll," *New York Times*, April 3, 2012, D1.

81. Quoted in Isaiah Negedu and Augustine Atabor, "Nationalism in Nigeria: A Case for Patriotic Citizenship," *American International Journal of Contemporary Research* 5, no. 3 (June 2015): 74–79.

CHAPTER 3

1. Stephen Ellis, *This Present Darkness: A History of Nigerian Organized Crime* (New York: Oxford University Press, 2016), 219.

2. For example, on the one hand Ernest Gellner writes, "The 'state' is that institution or set of institutions specifically concerned with the enforcement of order (whatever else they may also be concerned with). The state exists where specialized order-enforcing agencies, such as police forces and courts, have separated out from the rest of social life. They *are* the state," from *Nations and Nationalism* (Ithaca, NY: Cornell University Press, 1983). For Max Weber, on the other hand, "The modern state is a compulsory association which organizes domination. It has been successful in seeking to monopolize the legitimate use of physical force as a means of domination within a territory." From H. H. Gerth and C. Wright Mills, trans. and ed., *From Max Weber: Essays in Sociology* (New York: Oxford University Press, 1946), 77–128. "By the concept of state, Weber went a step further by suggesting that it refers to a set of political institutions that is capable of enforcing its rules and regulations, and thus exercises a monopoly of legitimate force over a territory." Goran Hyden, *African Politics in Comparative Perspective* (Cambridge: Cambridge University Press, 2007), 66. There are many other definitions.

3. For the first, Sarah Chayes initially used this phrase to describe Afghanistan after years of working in the country for an NGO and also as an advisor to the US military. Later in her policy career, she found that this described not only Afghanistan, but to a greater and lesser extent, Uzbekistan, Nigeria, Egypt, Tunisia, and the sixteenth-century Catholic Church. See Sarah Chayes, *Thieves of State: Why Corruption Threatens Global Security* (New York: W. W. Norton, 2015), 62 and appendices. For the second quotation, see Ellis, *This Present Darkness*, 4.

4. The 1914 Lugard constitution provided for a thirty-six-seat council, of which seven would be held by Nigerians. The Nigerians that held those seven seats were all traditional rulers, including the oba of Lagos, the sultan of Sokoto, and the ooni of Ife. The council was advisory only to the British governor-general. The 1922 Clifford constitution, promulgated after World War I and in light of Nigerian participation in that struggle, replaced the advisory council with a legislative council of forty-six, ten of whom were Nigerians. Of the ten, the governor-general appointed six, while three were elected from Lagos and one from Calabar. However, a very high income requirement of one hundred pounds sterling per annum to vote prevented nearly all Nigerians from voting for these four seats. Nevertheless, the Clifford constitution established the principle that Nigerians were admitted to the franchise. The legislative council could legislate on all issues in the south but only on money and the budget in the north. The governor-general was supreme. He legislated on all other issues in the north and had a veto on all legislation that the council could not override. So, while

the Nigerian component to the legislative council was small, it reflected the votes of a minuscule percentage of Nigerians, and it only had authority over the south, which was subject to a British veto, it was nonetheless the first instance in Britain's tropical African empire to provide for any indigenous participation in elections.

5. Ellis, *This Present Darkness*, 43.

6. Lamin Sanneh, *Translating the Message: The Missionary Impact on Culture* (Maryknoll, NY: Orbis Books, 1989); Frederick D. Patterson, "Education in Nigeria," *Journal of Negro Education* 24, no. 2 (1955): 96–97, doi:10.2307/2293472.

7. Joseph O. Ashgabat, "The Legislatures in the First and Second Republics," in *The Oxford Handbook of Nigerian Politics*, ed. A. Carl LeVan and Patrick Ukata (New York: Oxford University Press, 2018), 208.

8. Ken Saro-Wiwa, *On a Darkling Plane: An Account of the Nigerian Civil War* (Port Harcourt, Nigeria: Saros International, 1989), 21.

9. Obasanjo's tenure as president, 1999–2007, was ostensibly civilian. However, it was military in style and behavior and his administration's personnel was only partially civilian. A former military chief of state himself, he was picked by the military to head the post-1999 ostensibly civilian government, and they rigged him into office in the 1999 elections. From 1979 to 1983, there was an elected, civilian government headed by Shehu Shagari; his government was overthrown by a military coup carried out by General Muhammadu Buhari, himself deposed by General Ibrahim Babangida in a coup less than two years later. Since 2015, Buhari has been the civilian chief of state.

10. The term was developed by Jonah Isawa Elaigwu in *The Politics of Federalism in Nigeria* (London: Adonis & Abbey, 2007).

11. Rotimi Suberu, *Federalism and Ethnic Conflict in Nigeria* (Washington, DC: United States Institute of Peace, 2001), 19–20.

12. Suberu, *Federalism and Ethnic Conflict in Nigeria*, 19–20.

13. Eghosa Osaghae, "The Long Shadow of Nigeria's Military Epochs," in *The Oxford Handbook of Nigerian Politics*, ed. A. Carl LeVan and Patrick Ukata (New York: Oxford University Press, 2018), 180.

14. Author's personal observation in Lagos in 1988.

15. Amanda Lea Robinson, "National versus Ethnic Identity in Africa: State, Group, and Individual Level Correlates of National Identifications," Afrobarometer, Working Paper no. 112 (September 2009): 6–7, http://afrobarometer.org/sites/default/files/publications/Working%20paper/AfropaperNo112.pdf.

16. Michael J. Watts, "Ecologies of Rule," in *The Oxford Handbook of Nigerian Politics*, ed. A. Carl LeVan and Patrick Ukata (New York: Oxford University Press, 2018), 135–46.

17. Officially, he died of a heart attack. The story repeated on the street, however, is that he died from an overdose of Viagra while cavorting with three Indian prostitutes procured by a Lebanese businessman. Other stories retain the prostitutes but substitute strychnine for Viagra. See John Campbell, *Nigeria: Dancing on the Brink*, 2nd ed. (Lanham, MD: Rowman & Littlefield, 2016), 230. However, a meticulous review of the evidence by Max Siollun establishes that Abacha and his rival, Moshood

Abiola, did, indeed, die of heart attacks. See Max Siollun, *Nigeria's Soldiers of Fortune* (London: Hurst, 2019), 161–75.

18. A clear and insightful discussion of the transition is provided by A. Carl LeVan, *Contemporary Nigerian Politics: Competition in a Time of Transition and Terror* (Cambridge: Cambridge University Press, 2019). See especially chapter 2.

19. General Abdulsalami Abubakar was born in 1942 in northern Nigeria. An army general, he was chief of defense staff under Abacha. He is Muslim.

20. Yakubu Gowon was born in 1934. An army general, he was military chief of state from 1966 to 1975. He is Christian and from a minority ethnic group in the middle belt. Ibrahim Babangida was born in 1943. An army general, he was the military chief of state from 1985 to 1993. He is a Muslim and from a minority tribe in the middle belt. Theophilus Danjuma, a Christian, was born in 1938. A general, he was chief of defense staff and minister of defense in a number of military governments. Frequently described as a billionaire and a "kingmaker," he was never himself a military chief of state. Murtala Nyako was born in 1943 in northern Nigeria. An admiral in the navy, chief of naval staff, he is now an agricultural entrepreneur. He is Muslim.

21. Mashood Abiola, a rich Yoruba Muslim businessman, had won the most votes but was pushed aside by the military, which did not trust him. Abacha had him jailed. He died in jail in 1998 during the transition. He was likely murdered.

22. By comparison, the United States cabinet is usually around twenty.

23. Ayo Sogunro, "Don't Just Vote. Mobilise. (Aka Why Elections Won't Change Nigeria)," African Arguments, January 29, 2019, http://www.africanarguments.org .2019/01/29/nigeria-vote-mobilise-elections-won-chanage.

24. Thomas Isbell, "Tax Compliance: Africans Affirm Civic Duty but Lack Trust in Tax Department," Afrobarometer, December 2017, 8, https://afrobarometer.org/sites/ default/files/publications/Policy%20papers/ab_r6_policypaperno43_tax_compliance _in_africa-afrobarometer.pdf; "Afrobarometer Round 7: Summary of Results: Survey in Nigeria 2017," Afrobarometer, Compiled by Practical Sampling International, http://afrobarometer.org/sites/default/files/publications/Summary%20of%20results/ nig_r7_sor_28032018_eng.pdf, 16.

25. Ana Monteiro and David Malingha Doya, "Nigeria Tax Base Surges, yet 1 in 4 Working-Age People Registered," Bloomberg, May 2018, http://www.bloomberg .com/news/articles/2018-05-10/nigeria-tax-base-surges-yet-1-in-4-work-age-people -registered. A 5 percent tax is payable on earned income starting at N30,000 ($83), rising to 25 percent on N160,000 ($444) or higher. The top marginal tax rate for individuals is 25 percent. For comparison, in South Africa it is 45 percent, and in the United States it is 37 percent.

26. Michael Bratton, "Citizen Perceptions of Local Government Responsiveness in Sub-Saharan Africa," Afrobarometer, Working Paper no. 119 (May 2010): 6. Also cited in Olufunmbi Elemo, "Fiscal Federalism, Subnational Politics, and State Creation in Contemporary Nigeria," in *The Oxford Handbook of Nigerian Politics*, ed. A. Carl LeVan and Patrick Ukata (New York: Oxford University Press, 2019), 194.

27. According to the 2019 Lagos State Budget, https://yourbudgit.com/wp-content /uploads/2019/11/Lagos-State-Budget-2019-Budget.pdf.

28. Yemisi Adegoke, "Nigeria Has a Culture of Not Paying Workers and It's Not about to Change Anytime Soon," *Quartz Africa*, June 6, 2019, accessed June 24, 2019, http://www.qz.com/africa/663626/nigeria-has-a-culture-of-not-paying-workers-and-its-not-about-to-change-anytime-soon.

29. Robert H. Jackson and Carl G. Rosberg, "Why Africa's Weak States Persist: The Empirical and the Juridical in Statehood," *World Politics* 35, no. 1 (October 1982): 17–18, http://www.doi.org/10.2307/2010277.

30. Jackson and Rosberg, "Why Africa's Weak States Persist," 17–18, http://www.doi.org/10.2307/2010277.

31. Yuval Noah Harari, *21 Lessons for the 21st Century* (New York: Speigel & Grau, 2018), 100–1.

32. For Max Weber's famous definition of statehood, see Jackson and Rosberg, "Why Africa's Weak States Persist," 2, http://www.doi.org/10.2307/2010277; and Gellner, *Nations and Nationalism*, 4–7.

33. For comparison, the South African Revenue Service (SARS) was the pride of South Africa's postapartheid new government. Tax collections increased year after year. Contrast this with apartheid-era taxes, which, together with bills of all sorts, were avoided and ignored by the mass of the population. During the profligacy of the Jacob Zuma administration (2009–17), however, scandals and corruption drastically reduced people's faith in government and, by extension, tax collection. See John Campbell, "Zuma's Corruption Stalls Popular Trust in South African Taxation," June 13, 2018, *Africa in Transition* (blog), Council on Foreign Relations, http://www.cfr.org/blog/zumas-corruption-stalls-popular-trust-south-african-taxation.

34. Jackson and Rosberg, "Why Africa's Weak States Persist," 7.

35. The concept of governed spaces in Africa being "islands" in a "sea" of ungoverned spaces is presented in "Mapping Sub-Saharan Africa's Future," National Intelligence Council, CR 2005-02, March 2005, http://www.dni.gov/files/documents/africa_future_2005.pdf.

36. Aleksandr Solzhenitsyn, *The Gulag Archipelago* (New York: Harper & Row, 1974).

37. Despite journal and media claims that this is a UN benchmark, the Office of Internal Oversight Services of the United Nations asserts that this ratio is not supported by historical documents. Rather, it is a consensus on the optimal number of police personnel dating to the United States' policing in Germany in 1945, where there was one American policemen for every 450 German civilians. United Nations, General Assembly, Report of the Office of Internal Oversights Services on the comprehensive audit of the United Nations Interim Administration Mission in Kosovo mandate implementation, A/62/807 (April 18, 2008), available from http://www.africacheck.org/wp-content/uploads/2017/01/N0831055.pdf. According to Owen, "Anecdotes abound in which police leak information, tell suspects who has informed on them, tip off thieves about where rich pickings are to be found, rent out weapons to armed robbers, take off their uniforms and commit robberies, hire themselves out as assassins, and so forth. Sometimes these are rumours and apocryphal urban myths and at others, attributable incidents. The everyday effect of these concerns is to make most members of the public extremely wary of communicating information to the police."

Oliver Owen, "The Nigeria Police Force: An Institutional Ethnography," PhD diss., St. Cross College, Oxford, October 2012, https://ora.ox.ac.uk/objects/uuid:e824783a -8ba0-4d96-8519-0ee2b2090fc8, 113.

38. Funding constraints could be overcome with a restructuring of state spending priorities, however there appears little elite political will to do so.

39. Peter Ekeh, "Colonialism and the Two Publics in Africa: A Theoretical Statement," *Comparative Studies in Society and History* 17, no. 1 (1975): 91–112; Ellis, *This Present Darkness*, 194.

40. Kayode Asaju and Tony Egberi, "Federal Character and National Integration in Nigeria: The Need for Discretion and Interface," *Review of History and Political Science* 3, no. 1 (2015), doi:10.15640/rhps.v3n1a12.

41. Section 153(1), Constitution of the Federal Republic of Nigeria, Act No. 24, 1999.

42. "Tax and Legal Framework," Nigeria Extractive Industries Transparency Initiative, http://www.eiti.org/es/implementing_country/32#revenue-allocation.

43. "Tax and Legal Framework," Nigeria Extractive Industries Transparency Initiative, http://www.eiti.org/es/implementing_country/32#revenue-allocation.

44. This is a change. During the late colonial period and through the epoch of military rule, the military officer corps was perceived as largely Muslim. However, Obasanjo and Jonathan made many high-level Christian appointments to the military. By 2019, in the north, the military is now perceived as being "secular" or "Christian."

45. The three most prominent were Obi Ezekwesili, Kingsley Moghalu, and Donald Duke.

46. Yonatan L. Morse, "Presidential Power and Democratization by Elections in Africa," *Democratization* 25, no. 4 (2018): 710.

47. Especially after the 2011 presidential elections, violence was intense between the two major religions and among certain ethnic groups in the north, notwithstanding foreign accolades (not least by US observers and commentators) as to the credibility of that election process. On the other hand, the presidential elections of 2019, in which the two rival candidates were both Muslim Hausa-Fulanis, were not followed by an outbreak of violence.

48. Thomas Isbell and Oluwole Ojewale, "Nigerians Support Elections and Multiparty Competition but Mistrust Electoral Commission," Afrobarometer, Dispatch no. 275 (February 2019), http://www.afrobarometer.org/sites/default/files/publications /D%C3%A9p%C3%AAches/ab_r7_dispatchno275_nigerian_views_on_elections .pdf.

49. M. A. O. Aluko and O. A. Ajani, "Ethnic Nationalism and the Nigerian Democratic Experience in the Fourth Republic," *African Research Review* 3, no. 1 (2009): 483–99. Afrobarometer polling data confirms this.

50. See especially Chinua Achebe, *There Was a Country* (New York: Penguin, 2012); and "Afrobarometer Round 7: Summary of Results: Survey in Nigeria 2017," Afrobarometer, Compiled by Practical Sampling International, http://www .afrobarometer.org/sites/default/files/publications/Summary%20of%20results/nig_r7 _sor_28032018_eng.pdf. See question 43A-K, which asks respondents: "How much do you trust each of the following, or haven't you heard enough about them to say?"

The survey asks this question thirteen times regarding different organs and levels of government, and regarding authority figures, from the president, to the legislature at the national and state levels, to the police and the judiciary. The percentage of respondents that answers "not at all" or "just a little" (distrust) is over 50 percent for every group, save for when asked about religious leaders (36 percent) and the Nigerian army (41 percent).

51. There are, of course, various dates that one could take as the beginning and end of British rule. The dates used here are the amalgamation on January 1, 1914, and the declaration of independence, though as a dominion of the Crown, on October 1, 1960, what Nigerians consider Independence Day.

52. Elemo, "Fiscal Federalism, Subnational Politics, and State Creation in Contemporary Nigeria," 189.

CHAPTER 4

1. Ken Saro-Wiwa, *On a Darkling Plane: An Account of the Nigerian Civil War* (Port Harcourt, Nigeria: Saros International, 1989), 21.

2. Davo Olopade, *The Bright Continent: Breaking Rules and Making Change in Modern Africa* (Boston: Mariner Books/Houghton Mifflin Harcourt, 2015), 104–5.

3. Peter Lewis, "Boundaries and Bargains: Managing Nigeria's Fractious Society," in *On the Fault Line: Managing Tensions and Divisions within Societies*, ed. Jeffrey Herbst, Terence McNamee, and Greg Mills (London: Profile Press, 2012), 29.

4. Ayo Sogunro, "Don't Just Vote. Mobilise. (Aka Why Elections Won't Change Nigeria)," *African Arguments*, January 29, 2019, http://www.africanarguments.org /2019/01/29/nigeria-vote-mobilise-elections-won-chanage.

5. Ebenezer Obadare, *Pentecostal Republic: Religion and State Power in Nigeria* (London: Zed Books, 2018), 7, 123–40.

6. For a thorough discussion of the growing political power of Pentecostal preachers, see Obadare, *Pentecostal Republic*, and his *Pastoral Power, Clerical State: Pentecostalism, Gender, and Sexuality in Nigeria* (Notre Dame, IN: Notre Dame University Press, 2022).

7. Chuka Udeze, "Olusegun Obasanjo—Biography, Children, Net Worth, House, Age," *BuzzNigeria*, June 22, 2018, accessed June 24, 2019, http://www.buzznigeria .com/olusegun-obasanjo-biography. His predecessor, Sani Abacha, had a net worth in the billions in US dollars. Mfonobong Nsoho, "Who Were Africa's Richest Dictators?," *Forbes*, November 8, 2011, http://www.forbes.com/sites/mfonobongnsehe /2011/11/08/who-were-africas-richest-dictators/#69208a401708.

8. In November 2009, Yar'Adua fell ill and left Nigeria to receive treatment in Saudi Arabia for an illness, reportedly pericarditis. His absence created a power vacuum within the Nigerian government. As what was thought to be a short-term solution to the void in power, Oluwarotimi Odunayo Akeredolu, president of the Nigerian Bar Association (NBA), appointed Vice President Goodluck Jonathan as acting president during Yar'Adua's absence. The Supreme Court of Nigeria later upheld this decision, and the senate officially transferred the powers of the presidency

to Goodluck Jonathan on February 10, 2010, until Yar'Adua returned to full health. However, Yar'Adua died from his ailment and Goodluck Jonathan remained in power.

9. He became president upon the death of Umaru Yar'Adua. He was elected president in his own right in 2011.

10. Vivian Falae, "Is Goodluck Jonathan Net Worth Revealed?," *Legit*, 2014, http://www.legit.ng/1140009-is-goodluck-jonathan-net-worth-revealed.html.

11. "Nigeria's President Muhammadu Buhari Declares Assets," BBC News, September 4, 2015, http://www.bbc.com/news/world-africa-34150508; John Ameh, "Buhari, Osinbajo Get Asset Declaration Forms 24hrs to Deadline," *Punch Newspapers*, May 28, 2019, http://www.punchng.com/buhari-osinbajo-get-asset-declaration-forms-24hrs-to-deadline.

12. "Apostle Suleiman Acquires First Private Jet—Like Oyedepo, Ortsejafor, Adeboye," *Sahara Reporters*, April 23, 2019, http://www.saharareporters.com/2019/04/23/apostle-suleiman-acquires-first-private-jet-%E2%80%94-oyedepo-oritsejafor-adeboye; Nsehe, Mfonobong, "Wealthy Nigerians, Pastors Spend $225 Million on Private Jets," *Forbes*, April 25, 2019, accessed June 20, 2019, http://www.forbes.com/sites/mfonobongnsehe/2011/05/17/wealthy-nigerians-pastors-spend-225-million-on-private-jets/#3f5d73503b44; John Campbell, "Preaching, Power, and Private Jets in Nigeria," *Africa in Transition* (blog), Council on Foreign Relations, April 25, 2019, http://www.cfr.org/blog/preaching-power-and-private-jets-nigeria.

13. "Aliko Dangote," *Forbes*, accessed June 20, 2019, http://www.forbes.com/profile/aliko-dangote/#7cd2b75922fc. Neither of these fortunes was initially based on oil. Dangote's core interests were cement and milling. His fortune fluctuates: since 2010, it has ranged from $2.1 billion to $25 billion.

14. "Mike Adenuga," *Forbes*, accessed September 11, 2019, http://www.forbes.com/profile/mike-adenuga/#137cb45c55e3.

15. Among those who have funded big foundations are Atiku Abubakar, T. Y. Danjuma, Aliko Dangote ("Africa's richest man"), Mike Adenuga ("Africa's second richest man"), and Tony Elumelu.

16. For a meticulous breakdown of how the Nigerian National Petroleum Corporation (NNPC) functions, see Aaron Sayne, Alexandra Gillies, and Christina Katsouris, "Inside NNPC Oil Sales: A Case for Reform in Nigeria," Natural Resource Governance Institute, August 2015, http://www.resourcegovernance.org/sites/default/files/NRGI_InsideNNPCOilSales_CompleteReport.pdf.

17. Peter Ekeh, "Colonialism and the Two Publics in Africa: A Theoretical Statement," *Comparative Studies in Society and History* 17, no. 1 (January 1975): 92–93. Ekeh refers to the traditional public as "primordial."

18. See chapter 3.

19. "Yoruba Militia 'Killed 10,000,'" News24 (Archives), March 9, 2006, news24.com/Africa/News/Yoruba-militia-killed-10-000-20060308.

20. See chapter 4, "New Year Crackdown in Yangoa and Kaiama," in *Nigeria: Crackdown in the Niger Delta* 11, no. 2(A) (New York: Human Rights Watch, 1999), accessed June 20, 2019, http://www.hrw.org/sites/default/files/reports/Nigeria0599.pdf.

21. Olawunmi Ojo, "Operation Amotekun: Metaphor for FG's Indecisiveness on Insecurity," *Guardian* (Nigeria), January 18, 2020. https://guardian.ng/saturday -magazine/operation-amotekun-metaphor-for-fgs-indecisiveness-on-insecurity.

22. See "The Case of Hisbah: Policy Brief No. 2," in *Sharia Implementation in Northern Nigeria over 15 Years* (Kano, Nigeria: October 2016), based on a study conducted by the Nigeria Stability and Reconciliation Programme, funded by the British Council, https://www.qeh.ox.ac.uk/sites/www.odid.ox.ac.uk/files/Sharia%20 -%20POLICY%20BRIEF%20TWO%20Final%20Version.pdf.

23. For a story on Aisha, "the huntress," see Rosie Collyer, "Meet Aisha, a Former Antelope Hunter Who Now Tracks Boko Haram," *Guardian*, February 8, 2017, http:// www.theguardian.com/world/2017/feb/08/antelope-hunter-boko-haram-nigeria; Max Siollun, "Nigeria's Election Is Shattering Political Taboos," *Foreign Policy*, February 13, 2019, https://foreignpolicy.com/2019/02/13/nigerias-election-is-shattering -political-taboos-buhari-atiku-restructuring-federalism-oil-wealth.

24. Audu Bulama Bukarti, "Nigeria's Child Veterans Are Still Living a Nightmare," *Foreign Policy*, August 15, 2019, http://foreignpolicy.com/2019/08/15/children-boko -haram-nigeria-borno-cjtf.

25. Joshua Odeyemi, "Nigeria: FG May Integrate Civilian JTF into Military, Policy—Buhari," *AllAfrica*, May 16, 2016, http://www.allafrica.com/stories /201605161141.html.

26. For examples of hysterical media, see Stephen Ellis, "The Okija Shrine," *Journal of African History* 49, no. 3 (2008): 445–66; for examples of human sacrifice and cannibalism, see J. Adele Bamgbose, "The Place of Deities in African Political Systems, Essence," *Interdisciplinary Journal of Philosophy* 2 (2005): 231–42.

27. There is extensive literature. The foundation is Ekeh, "Colonialism and Two Publics in Africa," 91–112.

28. Stephen Ellis, *This Present Darkness: A History of Nigerian Organized Crime* (New York: Oxford University Press, 2016), 201–2.

29. Linda Rodriduez McRobbie, "How Are Horoscopes Still a Thing?," *Smithsonian Magazine*, January 5, 2016, https://www.smithsonianmag.com/history/how-are -horoscopes-still-thing-180957701.

30. Ellis, *This Present Darkness*, 209–10.

31. Arwa Damon, "The Sex Trafficking Trail from Nigeria to Europe," CNN, March 21, 2018, http://www.cnn.com/2017/12/04/africa/nigeria-benin-city-sex -trafficking/index.html.

32. Ellis, *This Present Darkness*, 195.

33. In Nigeria, they are called "cadis."

34. Author's conversation with northern qadis in 2007.

35. For a discussion of the relationship between the failure of sharia and the rise of Boko Haram, see Jacob Zenn, *Unmasking Boko Haram: Exploring Global Jihad in Nigeria* (Boulder, CO: Lynne Rienner, 2020), 9.

36. In other words, Nigerian elites have shown "a willingness to act dishonestly in return for money or personal gain," which typically involved bribery and embezzlement (the misappropriation of state funds for personal use). "Corrupt | Definition of

Corrupt in English by Lexico Dictionaries," *Lexico Dictionaries*, accessed June 24, 2019, http://en.oxforddictionaries.com/definition/corrupt.

37. This is the insight of Terry Pflaumer, former political counselor at the American embassy in Abuja.

38. Still underexploited, Nigeria's reserves of natural gas may exceed those of oil.

39. "Nigeria," U.S. Energy Information Administration, October 16, 2012, http://www.eia.gov/beta/international/?fips=NI. Other tax and legal frameworks include service contracts, marginal field concessions, and sole risk contracts. See Alexander Malden, "Nigeria's Oil and Gas Revenues: Insights from New Company Disclosures," Natural Resource Governance Institute, December 2017, http://www.resourcegovernance.org/sites/default/files/documents/nigeria-oil-revenue.pdf.

40. Sayne, Gillies, and Katsouris, "Inside NNPC Oil Sales."

41. Tim Cocks, "Special Report: Anatomy of Nigeria's $20 Billion 'Leak,'" Reuters, February 6, 2015, accessed June 20, 2019, http://www.reuters.com/article/us-nigeria-election-banker-specialreport/special-report-anatomy-of-nigerias-20-billion-leak-idUSKBN0LA0X820150206.

42. "Diezani Alison-Madueke," *Asset Recovery Watch*, August 29, 2018, http://star.worldbank.org/corruption-cases/printpdf/20499; "Department of Justice Seeks to Recover over $100 Million Obtained from Corruption in the Nigerian Oil Industry," United States Department of Justice, April 13, 2018, http://www.justice.gov/opa/pr/department-justice-seeks-recover-over-100-million-obtained-corruption-nigerian-oil-industry.

43. Will Fitzgibbon, "The Panama Papers: Secret Documents Expose Nigerian Oil Mogul's Offshore Hideaways," International Consortium of Investigative Journalists, July 25, 2016, https://www.icij.org/investigations/panama-papers/20160725-nigeria-oil-mogul.

44. Festus Okoromadu, "Nigeria: Oil Sector Tops U.S. $218 Billion Illicit Financial Flows from Nigeria," *AllAfrica*, February 28, 2019, http://www.allafrica.com/stories/201902280015.html. From 1970 to 2008, African nations lost $850 billion in illicit financial flows—50 to 60 billion yearly. Nigeria's illicit flows account of 30 percent of that total.

45. Mis-invoicing involves the falsification of trade numbers, creating a gap between the values of goods exported and the number reported by the receiving trade nation. By manipulating the invoice numbers, money can quickly be transferred across international borders. These unaccounted gaps in trade numbers, the result of underinvoicing and overinvoicing, represent stolen goods or the siphoning of cash. Okoromadu, "Nigeria: Oil Sector Tops U.S. $218 Billion Illicit Financial Flows from Nigeria."

46. Tom Cardamone, "Global Financial Integrity Releases New Study on Trade Misinvoicing in Nigeria," Global Financial Integrity, October 31, 2018, http://www.gfintegrity.org/press-release/global-financial-integrity-releases-new-study-on-trade-misinvoicing-in-nigeria.

47. Quoted in Cardamone, "Global Financial Integrity Releases New Study on Trade Misinvoicing in Nigeria."

48. Elnathan John, *Be(coming) Nigerian: A Guide* (Abuja, Nigeria: Cassava Republic Press, 2019), 11. John is a lawyer, a journalist, and an award-winning novelist. His best-known novel is *Born on a Tuesday*.

49. Of Nigerian chiefs of state from 1965 to 1999, only Ironsi, Gowon, and Obasanjo were Christians. Gowon was from the north, but from a small Christian ethnic group. He had particularly close ties with the northern Islamic establishment.

50. A. Carl LeVan, *Contemporary Nigerian Politics: Competition in a Time of Transition and Terror* (Cambridge: Cambridge University Press, 2019), especially chapters 3 and 4.

51. Leena Hoffmann, "Fairy Godfathers and Magical Elections: Understanding the 2003 Electoral Crisis in Anambra State, Nigeria," *Journal of Modern African Studies* 48, no. 2 (2010): 285–310, http://www.jstor.org/stable/40864718.

52. "Criminal Politics: Violence, 'Godfathers' and Corruption in Nigeria," *Human Rights Watch Report* 10, no. 16(A) (2007), http://www.hrw.org/report/2007/10/11/criminal-politics/violence-godfathers-and-corruption-nigeria.

53. Elizabeth Soriola, "Top 20 Richest Igbo Men and Women," *Legit News*, October 2, 2018, http://www.legit.ng/1193784-top-20-richest-igbo-men-women.html.

54. Chief Uba's brother was Obasanjo's special advisor and married to his wife's sister.

55. "Criminal Politics: Violence, 'Godfathers' and Corruption in Nigeria."

56. The text of the agreement is printed as an annex to "Criminal Politics: Violence, 'Godfathers' and Corruption in Nigeria."

57. Ngige's restoration to office was accomplished through court rulings.

58. Hoffmann, "Fairy Godfathers and Magical Elections."

59. "SERAP Urges Orji Kalu, Goje, Okorocha, Others to 'Stop Collecting Pensions,'" SERAP, June 30, 2019, http://www.serap-nigeria.org/serap-urges-orji-kalu -goje-okorocha-others-to-stop-collecting-pensions.ngo. For comparison, California governor Jerry Brown, who retired in January 2019, receives an annual pension of $120,000 a year, based on length of service in a variety of state positions and his age, which was eighty when he retired. "Former Gov. Jerry Brown Gets $120,000-a-Year Pension in Retirement," *Mercury News*, January 29, 2019, http://www.mercurynews .com/2019/01/28/jerry-brown-gets-120000-in-retirement.

60. Nasir Ayitogo, "Analysis: The Making of Gbjabiamila's House Committees; Why Jibrin, Others Lost Out," *Premium Times* (Nigeria), August 6, 2019, http://www.premiumtimesng.com/news/headlines/345025-analysis-the-making-of -gbajabiamilas-house-committees-why-jibrin-others-lost-out.html.

61. Author's numerous conversations in Lagos in May 2018.

62. For example, according to Hoffmann: "In Anambra the results of one National Assembly race in which a candidate was declared the winner with 14,405 votes were suddenly cancelled and four days later new official results reported an increase in voter turnout by approximately 150%. This boost benefited the previously losing candidate who saw his vote count soar from 13,076 to 67,857, while the original winner's votes mysteriously shrunk to just 5,065." Hoffmann, "Fairy Godfathers and Magical Elections," 297.

63. Ben Shemang, "Jesus Could Not Conduct Free Elections in Nigeria, Says Obasanjo," Radio France Internationale, May 5, 2010, http://en.rfi.fr/africa/20100505 -jesus-could-not-conduct-free-elections-nigeria-says-obasanjo.

64. See chapter 10, "The Love of Money," in *Soldiers of Fortune: A History of Nigeria (1983–1993)*, by Max Siollun.

65. Obafemi Awolowo, *The Path to Nigerian Freedom* (London: Faber and Faber, 1947), 97, quoted in Ellis, *This Present Darkness*, 19.

66. Ellis, *This Present Darkness*, 207.

67. Amina Yuguda, "Why Nigeria Wants to Remove Police Roadblocks," BBC World News, September 26, 2017, http://www.bbc.com/news/world-africa-41403334.

68. Since 2006, the country has faced insurrections in the Delta and the northeast and endemic violence in the middle belt.

69. John Campbell, "Strapped for Cash, Nigeria Plans to Close Some Embassies," *Africa in Transition* (blog), Council on Foreign Relations, March 29, 2019, http://www.cfr.org/blog/strapped-cash-nigeria-plans-close-some-embassies; Sunday Isuewa and Ahuraka Isah, "Nigeria Set to Close Down 80 Missions," *AllAfrica*, Leadership (Abuja), April 3, 2019, http://www.allafrica.com/stories/201904040076.html.

CHAPTER 5

1. Jerrywright Ukwu, "Nigeria Is Drifting into Anarchy—Northern Leaders Warn," *Legit*, July 17, 2019, accessed July 18, 2019, http://www.legit.ng/1246603-northern -leaders-raise-alarm-nigeria-drifting-anarchy.html.

2. "Obasanjo Writes Buhari, Says Nigeria Reaching a Tipping Point," *Punch Newspapers*, July 15, 2019, accessed July 18, 2019.

3. John Campbell, "High-Profile Attack on Maersk Manager Rattles Lagos Establishment," *Africa in Transition* (blog), Council on Foreign Relations, December 13, 2019, https://www.cfr.org/blog/high-profile-attack-maersk-manager-rattles-lagos -establishment.

4. "We must all hang together or most assuredly we will hang separately," Benjamin Franklin's observation at the signing of the Declaration of Independence in 1776. See Theodore P. Savas and J. David Dameron, *A Guide to the Battles of the American Revolution* (New York: Savas Beatie, 2013).

5. As reported by *Africa Confidential*, vol. 64, no. 5, March 2, 2023. INEC is the public agency charged with conducting elections. It is the agency that announces official results of elections.

6. See Ebenezer Obadare, *Pentecostal Republic* (London: Zed Books, 2018).

7. Ebenezer Obadare, "The Lagos–New York–London Echo Chamber," March 7, 2023, https://www.cfr.org/blog/lagos-new-york-london-echo-chamber; Ebenezer Obadare, "Peter Obi and a Dream Deferred," March 22, 2023, https://www.cfr.org/ blog/peter-obi-and-dream-deferred.

8. *Africa Confidential* has published a useful map that shows the states carried by the three presidential candidates: vol. 64, no. 5, March 3, 2023.

9. For the number registered, the number that collected their Permanent Voter Card, and the number of ballots cast, see, inter alia, International Foundation for Electoral Systems Election Guide, https://www.electionguide.org/countries/id/158; Independent National Elections Commission 2023 General Elections Update, https://www.inecnigeria.org/?page_id=11312. There was also extensive coverage in the Nigerian and international press with no significant differences in the numbers cited in each category.

10. The decision is all but inexplicable. The Buhari administration said it took the step somehow to reduce money laundering and bribery before the elections.

11. For a discussion of the shortcomings of the elections, see Michelle Gavin, "Nigeria's Elections Risk Sowing Cynicism, Distrust," March 6, 2023, Council on Foreign Relations, https://www.cfr.org/blog/nigerias-elections-risk-sowing-cynicism-mistrust.

12. https://ng.usembassy.gov/nigerias-2023-elections.

13. In November 2023, it took about 807 naira to purchase one US dollar. A year ago, it was about 443 naira to one US dollar.

CHAPTER 6

1. Kehinde Akinyemi, "ICYMI: Full Text of Obasanjo's Open Letter to Buhari," *Punch Newspapers*, July 15, 2019, https://punchng.com/full-text-of-obasanjos-open-letter-to-buhari.

2. In 2018, the chairman of the National Population Commission estimated that Nigeria's population was about 198 million. The CIA World Factbook's 2018 estimate was 203 million. The Factbook estimate is the best available. See Ifeoluwa Adeyemo, "Nigeria's Population Now 198 million—NPC," *Premium Times*, April 12, 2018, http://www.premiumtimesng.com/news/top-news/264781-nigerias-population-now-198-million-npc.html; "The World Factbook: Nigeria," Central Intelligence Agency, accessed September 11, 2019, http://www.cia.gov/library/publications/the-world-factbook/geos/print_ni.html.

3. According to the World Bank, the total fertility rate represents the number of children that would be born to a woman if she were to live to the end of her childbearing years and bear children in accordance with age-specific fertility rates of the specified year. At Nigeria's 2017 rate of 5.67, the population would double every twenty-seven years. The fertility rates in 2017 for China, India, and South Africa were 1.63, 2.30, and 2.55, respectively.

4. "Nigeria's 2004 National Policy on Population for Sustainable Development," Federal Government of Nigeria, Implementation Assessment Report, September 2015, http://www.healthpolicyplus.com/ns/pubs/7141-7252_NPPImplementationAssessmentBriefMay.pdf; Yomi Kazeem, "Nigeria's Population Problem Is the Result of Poor Policy Implementation—and It'll Only Get Worse," *Quartz Africa*, January 5, 2019, http://www.qz.com/africa/1171606/nigeria-population-growth-rising-unemployment-and-migration-suggest-things-could-get-worse.

5. "Country Comparison: Life Expectancy at Birth," Central Intelligence Agency, accessed July 18, 2019, http://www.cia.gov/library/publications/the-world-factbook/rankorder/2102rank.html.

6. In the case of surpassing India's poor population, the poverty rate was defined by those living on less than $1.90 a day. That rate, according to the World Poverty Clock, was 44 percent. But the Nigerian National Bureau of Statistics in 2013 estimated that 100 million Nigerians, or 61 percent of the population, lived on less than $1 per day, while the World Bank estimated that, in 2016, 86 percent of the population was poor or vulnerable to poverty. "Extreme Poverty in Nigeria May Increase by 2030," World Poverty Clock, accessed September 11, 2019, http://www.worldpoverty.io/blog/index.php?r=12; see "Nigerians Living in Poverty Rise to Nearly 61%," BBC News, February 13, 2012, accessed July 18, 2019, http://www.bbc.com/news/world-africa-17015873.

7. See "Nigerians Living in Poverty Rise to Nearly 61%," BBC News, February 13, 2012, accessed July 18, 2019, http://www.bbc.com/news/world-africa-17015873.

8. For comparison, according to the World Bank in 2017, South Africa's was sixty-four, India's sixty-nine, China's seventy-six, and the United States' seventy-nine. The world's highest was San Marino at almost eighty-five (though other sources peg Monaco as number one, with a life expectancy of almost ninety), and the lowest is the Central African Republic at fifty-two.

9. "Nigeria: Urbanization 2007 to 2017," Statista, 2019, http://www.statista.com/statistics/455904/urbanization-in-nigeria.

10. "Lagos Population 2019," *World Population Review*, accessed September 11, 2019, http://www.worldpopulationreview.com/world-cities/lagos-population. This discrepancy in population figures has to do with whether Lagos city or Lagos state is meant when "Lagos" is referenced.

11. "Population of Cities in Nigeria (2019)," *World Population Review*, accessed July 18, 2019, http://www.worldpopulationreview.com/countries/nigeria-population/cities.

12. "Housing Deficit Now 22 Million, Says FMBN," *Nation Online*, October 15, 2018, https://thenationonlineng.net/housing-deficit-now-22-million-says-fmbn.

13. Michael J. Watts, "Ecologies of Rule: Politics, Political Economy, and Governing the Environment in Nigeria," in *The Oxford Handbook of Nigerian Politics*, ed. A. Carl LeVan and Patrick Ukata (New York: Oxford University Press, 2018), 142.

14. Alhaji A. Aliyu and Lawal Amadu, "Urbanization, Cities, and Health: The Challenges to Nigeria—A Review," *Annals of African Medicine* 14, no. 4 (2017): 149–58.

15. Gloria Aitalohi Joseph-Raji et al. "Nigeria Biannual Economic Update: Water Supply, Sanitation & Hygiene—A Wake-Up Call," The World Bank Group (April 2019), http://documents.worldbank.org/curated/en/747151554485134566/Nigeria-Biannual-Economic-Update-Water-Supply-Sanitation-and-Hygiene-A-Wake-up-Call.

16. Somik Lall et al., *Africa's Cities: Opening Doors to the World* (Washington, DC: The World Bank, January 1, 2017), 16, http://www.openknowledge.worldbank.org/handle/10986/25896.

17. Murray Last, "The Search for Security in Muslim Northern Nigeria," *Africa: The Journal of the International African Institute* 78, no. 1 (2008): 41–63.

18. Nicola Jones, "Redrawing the Map: How the World's Climate Zones Are Shifting," *Yale Environment 360*, Yale School of Forestry and Environmental Studies, October 23, 2018, http://www.e360.yale.edu/features/redrawing-the-map-how-the-worlds-climate-zones-are-shifting.

19. Temidayo Ebenezer Olagunju, "Drought, Desertification and the Nigerian Environment: A Review," *Journal of Ecology and the Natural Environment* 7, no. 7 (2015): 196–209, doi:10.5897/jene2015.0523; "Drought Conditions and Management Strategies in Nigeria," Integrated Drought Management Programme, http://www.droughtmanagement.info/wp-content/uploads/2016/10/WS6-Nigeria_EN.pdf.

20. John Campbell, "Sea Levels along the West African Coast," *Africa in Transition* (blog), Council on Foreign Relations, October 25, 2016, http://www.cfr.org/blog/sea-levels-along-west-african-coast.

21. Matteo Fagotto, "West Africa Is Being Swallowed by the Sea," *Foreign Policy*, October 22, 2016, http://www.foreignpolicy.com/2016/10/21/west-africa-is-being-swallowed-by-the-sea-climate-change-ghana-benin.

22. "Torrential Rains Destroy Shelters for Displaced People in Northeast Nigeria," Norwegian Refugee Council, August 23, 2019, http://www.nrc.no/news/torrential-rains-destroy-shelters-for-displaced-people-in-northeast-nigeria.

23. "Nigeria's Crop Production," *AsokoInsight*, August 30, 2019, http://www.asokoinsight.com/content/market-insights/nigeria-crop-production?utm_source=Asoko%20Insight%20-%20Africa%20Business%20Week%20in%20Review&utm_campaign=76ff6204ac-2019_09_01_Newsletter&utm_medium=email&utm_term=0_7d19169446-76ff6204ac-425784753.

24. Olagunju, "Drought, Desertification and the Nigerian Environment," 196–209, doi:10.5897/jene2015.0523.

25. Aliyu and Amadu, "Urbanization, Cities, and Health," 149–58, doi:10.1107/s0108270113015370/sk3488sup1.cif; Akastair Leithead, "The City That Won't Stop Growing," BBC News, August 2017, http://www.bbc.co.uk/news/resources/idt-sh/lagos.

26. Watts, "Ecologies of Rule," 133–168.

27. Under Nigerian law, oil companies are required to pay a hefty compensation for these practices, worth billions of dollars. However, a loophole in the tax code allows these payments to be tax deductible. Christiana Okojie, *Illicit Transfers and Tax Reforms in Nigeria: Mapping of the Literature and Synthesis of the Evidence* (Nairobi: Partnership for African Social and Governance Research, May 2018), 15, http://www.pasgr.org/wp-content/uploads/2018/09/Nigeria-Illicit-Financial-Flows-Report.pdf.

28. "Nigeria's Flaring Reduction Target: 2020," The World Bank, http://www.worldbank.org/en/news/feature/2017/03/10/nigerias-flaring-reduction-target-2020.

29. Watts, "Ecologies of Rule," 135.

30. There is now a large literature on Boko Haram. For as scholarly overview, see Alexander Thurston, *Boko Haram: The History of an African Jihadist Movement* (Princeton: Princeton University Press, 2018). For the English translation of

Boko Haram documents, see Abdulbasit Kassim and Michael Nwankpa, *The Boko Haram Reader* (London: Hurst, 2018). Useful surveys are Virginia Comolli, *Boko Haram: Nigeria's Islamist Insurgency* (London: Hurst, 2015), and Brandon Kendhammer and Carmen McCain, *Boko Haram* (Athens: Ohio University Press, 2018). Jacob Zenn in *Unmasking Boko Haram* (Boulder: Lynne Rienner, 2020) argues that IS and AQIM play a much larger role in Boko Haram than Thurston, Kendhammer, and others suggest. For a weekly compilation of deaths involving Boko Haram, see John Campbell, "Nigeria Security Tracker," Council on Foreign Relations, http://www.cfr.org/nigeria/nigeria-security-tracker.

31. For an explanation of the origins of Boko Haram's moniker, see Alex Thurston, "Boko Haram: What's in a Name?," *Sahel Blog* (blog), January 7, 2013, http://www.sahelblog.wordpress.com/2013/01/07/boko-haram-whats-in-a-name; see also "Boko Haram," *Encyclopedia Britannica*, August 16, 2019, http://www.britannica.com/topic/Boko-Haram.

32. John Campbell, "Nigeria Security Tracker," Council on Foreign Relations, http://www.cfr.org/Nigeria/Nigeria-nigeria-security-tracker.

33. Joi Lee, "Northeast Nigeria Threatened by Critical Food Insecurity," Al Jazeera, June 20, 2018, http://www.aljazeera.com/indepth/inpictures/northeast-nigeria-threatened-critical-food-insecurity-180613095610940.html.

34. Audu Bulama Bukarti, "Nigeria's Child Veterans Are Still Living a Nightmare," *Foreign Policy*, August 15, 2019, http://www.foreignpolicy.com/2019/08/15/children-boko-haram-nigeria-borno-cjtf.

35. "Nigerian View of Boko Haram," Pew Research Center, June 30, 2014, http://www.pewglobal.org/2014/07/01/concerns-about-islamic-extremism-on-the-rise-in-middle-east/og-2014-07-01-islamic-extremism-04. It is highly unlikely that any Christians have a favorable view of Boko Haram.

36. Richard Wike, Katie Simmons, Margaret Vice, and Caldwell Bishop, "In Key African Nations, Widespread Discontent with Economy, Corruption," Pew Research Center, November 14, 2016, http://www.pewresearch.org/global/2016/11/14/in-key-african-nations-widespread-discontent-with-economy-corruption.

37. On the brotherhoods, see John N. Paden, *Muslim Civic Cultures and Conflict Resolution* (Washington, DC: Brookings Institution Press, 2005).

38. For an excellent examination of these roots, see Thurston, *Boko Haram*, and Kendhammer and McCain, *Boko Haram*, 25–56.

39. On the origins of Boko Haram, see Kendhammer and McCain, *Boko Haram*, 25–56.

40. See David Ehrhardt and Abdul Mustapha, "Islamic Actors and Interfaith Relations in Northern Nigeria," University of Oxford, Policy Paper no. 1 (March 2013), http://www.qeh.ox.ac.uk/sites/www.odid.ox.ac.uk/files/nrn-pp01.pdf.

41. Maitatsine comes from Marwa's nickname, "one who damns." He was actually Cameroonian.

42. Hilary Matfess, *Women and the War on Boko Haram* (London: Zed Books, 2017).

43. The other three selectively adopted sharia in those territories that are predominately Muslim.

44. An antecedent to Boko Haram was the Nigerian Taliban, modeled after that of Afghanistan. It attacked police stations in Yobe in 2002–2003. It went underground in the face of the security services.

45. Adeeb Olufemi Salaam, "The Psychological Makeup of Mohammed Yusuf," *e-International Relations*, November 4, 2013, http://www.e-ir.info/2013/11/04/the -psychological-make-up-of-mohammed-yusuf. Yusuf's sermons are translated and printed in Kassim and Nwankpa, *The Boko Haram Reader*.

46. Thurston, *Boko Haram*, 137.

47. Thurston, *Boko Haram*, 161–62. In contrast, Jacob Zenn argues that the assistance was important and transformative at various stages. See, passim, his *Unmasking Boko Haram*.

48. Kassim and Nwankpa, *The Boko Haram Reader*, 435.

49. Kassim and Nwankpa, *The Boko Haram Reader*, 432.

50. Note that they did not call it the Islamic State in Nigeria or the Islamic State in Borno State. The name explicitly ignored political borders. See Thurston, *Boko Haram*, 17–18.

51. John Campbell, "Suspected Leadership Changes to IS-Backed by Boko Haram Faction Continue," *Africa in Transition* (blog), Council on Foreign Relations, March 12, 2019, http://www.cfr.org/blog/suspected-leadership-changes-backed-boko-haram -faction-continue; "Facing the Challenge of the Islamic State in West Africa Province," International Crisis Group, May 2019, Africa Report No. 273, http://www .crisisgroup.org/africa/west-africa/nigeria/273-facing-challenge-islamic-state-west -africa-province.

52. Based on an analysis of data from the Armed Conflict Location and Event Data project (ACLED) identifying fatalities associated with each Boko Haram faction. See https://acleddata.com/#/dashboard.

53. John Campbell, "Understanding the Threat Posed by ISWA in Nigeria," *Africa in Transition* (blog), Council on Foreign Relations, August 14, 2019, http://www .cfr.org/blog/understanding-threat-posed-iswa-nigeria; John Campbell, "Notes from Yobe State on Living with ISWA," *Africa in Transition* (blog), Council on Foreign Relations, August 1, 2019, http://www.cfr.org/blog/notes-yobe-state-living-iswa.

54. Based on an analysis of ACLED data, which identified the location of JAS and ISWA attacks. See https://acleddata.com/#/dashboard.

55. Bukarti, "Nigeria's Child Veterans Are Still Living a Nightmare."

56. "Mama Boko Haram, ICRC to Partner on Leah's Release," *Vanguard* (Nigeria), July 23, 2018, http://www.vanguardngr.com/2018/07/mama-boko-haram-icrc-to -partner-on-leahs-release.

57. Karl Maier, *This House Has Fallen* (London: Penguin, 2000), 13.

58. The term "Delta" is often used imprecisely. Sometimes it is applied to the south-south region, itself without a legal justification. But Bayelsa, Delta, and Rivers are the leading oil-producing states. Unlike other parts of the region, the ethnicity of their populations is mostly non-Igbo.

59. Geopolitical zones are informal groupings of states. They have no legal basis.

60. Stephen Ellis, *This Present Darkness: A History of Nigerian Organized Crime* (New York: Oxford University Press, 2016), 100–1.

61. Notable is the rivalry between the Ijaws and the Itsikiris.

62. Production rarely has exceeded two million bpd. However, the Nigerian government calculates that there is already the capacity to produce three million bpd.

63. John Campbell, "Nigeria: Why Are Boko Haram Fighters Successful?," *Africa in Transition* (blog), Council on Foreign Relations, March 4, 2014, http://www.cfr.org /blog/sea-levels-along-west-african-coast.

64. "Country Analysis Brief: Nigeria," US Energy Information Administration, May 6, 2016, http://www.eia.gov/beta/international/analysis_includes/countries_long /Nigeria/nigeria.pdf, 5.

65. Abraham Wapner, *Downstream Beneficiation Case Study: Nigeria* (New York: Columbia Center on Sustainable Investment, March 2017), 8.

66. Based on an analysis of data from the Nigeria Security Tracker, which recorded the location of sectarian violence in the Niger Delta. John Campbell, "Nigeria Security Tracker," Council on Foreign Relations, http://www.cfr.org/nigeria/nigeria -security-tracker/p29483.

67. John Campbell, "Nigeria Continues to Buy Off Delta Militants," *Africa in Transition* (blog), Council on Foreign Relations, May 15, 2017, http://www.cfr.org/ blog/nigeria-continues-buy-delta-militants.

68. "Self-determination: Is the African Union Living Up to Its Expectations?," Radio Biafra, http://www.radiobiafra.co/self-determination-is-the-african-union -living-up-to-its-expectations.

69. "Biafran Leader Nnamdi Kanu: The Man behind Nigeria's Separatists," BBC, May 5, 2017, http://www.bbc.com/news/world-africa-39793185.

70. Emma Elekwa, "Kanu's Resounding Reception in Canada a Proof of Biafra Restoration—IPOB," *Nation* (Nigeria), June 12, 2019, http://www.thenationonlineng .net/kanus-resounding-reception-in-canada-a-proof-of-biafra-restoration-ipob.

71. "Nnamdi Kanu Didn't Escape to UK through Malaysia—IPOB," *Vanguard*, October 2, 2017, http://www.vanguardngr.com/2017/10/nnamdi-kanu-didnt-escape -uk-malyasia-ipob.

72. "Nnamdi Kanu Didn't Escape to UK through Malaysia—IPOB."

73. Christopher Isiguzo and David-Chyddy Eleke, "MASSOB: Nnamdi Kanu Remains Biafra Hero, Dead or Alive," *This Day*, October 2, 2017, http://www .thisdaylive.com/index.php/2017/10/02/massob-nnamdi-kanu-remains-biafra-hero -dead-or-alive.

74. For a typology of conflicts in the middle belt, see Laura Thaut Vinson, "Pastoralism, Ethnicity, and Subnational Conflict Resolution in the Middle Belt," in *The Oxford Handbook of Nigerian Politics*, ed. A. Carl LeVan and Patrick Ukata (New York: Oxford University Press, 2018), 679–95.

75. On the Benue and Plateau examples cited here, see Saleh B. Momale, "Violence in Nigeria's Middle Belt Region," briefing notes prepared for the All Party Parliamentary Group on International Freedom of Religion and Belief, United Kingdom Parliament, House of Commons, London, *Search for Common Ground: Forum on Farmer-Herder Relations in Nigeria*, April 1, 2019.

76. The episode in question revolves around the Plateau state governor's attempt to install his Berom brother as mayor of the Hausa-dominated LGA of Jos, sparking riots.

77. Ryan McNeill and Alexis Akwagyiram, "The Fight for Nigeria's Heartland," Reuters, December 19, 2018, http://www.graphics.reuters.com/NIGERIA -SECURITY/010081Q3332/index.html.

78. "Harvest of Death: Three Years of Bloody Clashes between Farmers and Herders in Nigeria," Amnesty International, December 17, 2018, http://www.amnesty.org/ en/documents/afr44/9503/2018/en/, 14.

79. "Global Terrorism Index 2019: Measuring the Impact of Terrorism," Institute for Economics & Peace, Sydney, November 2019, accessed May 7, 2022, http:// visionofhumanity.org/reports.

80. Off-the-record conversation in Washington, DC, in August 2019.

81. Matthias Nowak and Andre Gsell, *Handmade and Deadly: Craft Production of Small Arms in Nigeria*, Briefing Paper (Geneva: Small Arms Survey, June 2018), 3, cited in Nicolas Florquin, Sigrid Lipott, and Francis Wairagu, *Weapons Compass: Mapping Illicit Small Arms Flows in Africa* (Switzerland: Small Arms Survey, January 2019), http://www.smallarmssurvey.org/fileadmin/docs/U-Reports/SAS-AU -Weapons-Compass.pdf.

82. Momale, "Violence in Nigeria's Middle Belt Region," 2.

83. To access this data, see John Campbell, "Nigeria Security Tracker," Council on Foreign Relations, http://www.cfr.org/nigeria/nigeria-security-tracker.

84. Laila Johnson-Salami, "Nigeria's Grazing Crisis Threatens the Future of the Nation," *Financial Times*, http://www.ft.com/content/a56ccf22-a331-11e9-a282 -2df48f366f7d?

85. Katrin Gansler, "Nigeria: The Politicized Herders and Farmers Conflict," Deutsche Welle, July 16, 2019, http://www.dw.com/en/nigeria-the-politicized-herders -and-farmers-conflict/a-49598457.

86. Momale, "Violence in Nigeria's Middle Belt Region."

87. Gansler, "Nigeria: The Politicized Herders and Farmers Conflict."

CHAPTER 7

1. "201. National Intelligence Estimate, Washington, November 2, 1970," US Department of State, accessed July 31, 2019, https://history.state.gov/historicaldocuments/ frus1969-76ve05p1/d201.

2. Based on an analysis of ECOWAS funding between 2003 and 2015. The other fourteen members cover the remaining 60 percent of contributions by members. According to the same data, however, Ghana actually pays proportionally more than Nigeria relative to its GDP. "Nigeria Continues $710m to ECOWAS, More than 13 Countries," *Punch*, December 6, 2018, http://punchng.com/nigeria-contributes -710m-to-ecowas-more-than-13-countries.

3. Felix Onuah, Libby George, and Keith Weir, "Nigeria Signs Africa Free Trade Agreement: Statement," Reuters, July 7, 2019, http://www.reuters.com/

article/us-africa-trade-nigeria/nigeria-signs-africa-free-trade-agreement-statement
-idUSKCN1U20K7.

4. The US push for repeal was led by then assistant secretary for international organizations, John Bolton.

5. "Troop and Police Contributors," United Nations Peacekeeping, July 31, 2019, http://www.peacekeeping.un.org/en/troop-and-police-contributors.

6. Christof Hartmann, "ECOWAS and the Restoration of Democracy in the Gambia," *Africa Spectrum* 52, no. 1 (2017): 85–99, doi:10.1177/000203971705200104.

7. George A. Obiozor, *Uneasy Friendship: Nigeria/US Relations* (Oxford: Enugu, Fourth Dimension, 1992).

8. The only comprehensive review of US policy toward Africa is Herman J. Cohen, *US Policy Toward Africa: Eight Decades of Realpolitik* (Boulder: Lynne Rienner, 2020).

9. Portugal, the third major colonial power in Africa, was neutral during World War II.

10. Foster Rhea Dulles and Gerald E. Ridinger, "The Anti-Colonial Policies of Franklin D. Roosevelt," *Political Science Quarterly* 70, no. 1 (1955): 5–6.

11. Based on an analysis of the *Congressional Record*.

12. Judd Devermont, "The US Intelligence Community's Biases during the Nigerian Civil War," *African Affairs* 116, no. 465 (October 2017): 705–16.

13. "100. Memorandum Prepared by the Office of Current Intelligence, Central Intelligence Agency, Washington, August 5, 1969," US Department of State, http://www.history.state.gov/historicaldocuments/frus1969-76ve05p1/d100.

14. "186. Memorandum from the President's Deputy Assistant for National Security Affairs (Haig) to the President's Assistant for National Security Affairs (Kissinger), Washington, February 16, 1970," US Department of State, accessed July 31, 2019, http://www.history.state.gov/historicaldocuments/frus1969-76ve05p1/d186.

15. For the US intelligence community and the Nigerian civil war, see Devermont, "The U.S. Intelligence Community's Biases during the Nigerian Civil War," 705–16.

16. "Airgram from the Embassy in Nigeria to the Department of State," US Department of State, http://www.history.state.gov/historicaldocuments/frus1964-68v24/d395.

17. Brian McNeil, "'And Starvation Is the Grim Reaper': The American Committee to Keep Biafra Alive and the Genocide Question during the Nigerian Civil War, 1968–70," *Journal of Genocide Research* 16, no. 2–3 (2014): 317–36.

18. The Associated Press, "Late Nigerian Dictator Looted Nearly $500 Million, Swiss Say," *New York Times*, August 19, 2004, accessed February 7, 2020, https://www.nytimes.com/2004/08/19/world/late-nigerian-dictator-looted-nearly-500-million-swiss-say.html.

19. Nick Turse and Sean D. Naylor, "Revealed: The U.S. Military's 36 Code-Named Operations in Africa," YahooNews, http://news.yahoo.com/revealed-the-us-militarys-36-codenamed-operations-in-africa-090000841.html.

20. "Summary of the 2018 National Defense Strategy of the United States," Department of Defense, 2018, http://www.dod.defense.gov/Portals/1/Documents/pubs/2018-National-Defense-Strategy-Summary.pdf.

21. See Rodrigo Campos and Aaron Ross, "U.S. Pledges Up to $60 Million for Security in Sahel Region," Reuters, https://www.reuters.com/article/us-africa-security-usa/u-s-pledges-up-to-60-million-for-security-in-sahel-region-idUSKBN1CZ1OX; and Herman J. Cohen, "Trump's Africa Policy Is a Continuation of Clinton's, Bush's, and Obama's," *LobeLog*, April 23, 2018, http://lobelog.com/trumps-africa-policy-is-a-continuation-of-clintons-bushs-and-obamas.

22. Drew Hinshaw, "Hundred Killed in Jails Swelling with Islamist Suspects," *Wall Street Journal*, October 15, 2013, http://www.wsj.com/articles/hundreds-killed-in-jails-swelling-with-islamist-suspects-1381881352.

23. Timothy Obiezu, "Nigeria Marks 6th Year of Missing Chibok Girls amid Coronavirus Pandemic," Voice of America, April 14, 2020, accessed May 20, 2020, https://www.voanews.com/africa/nigeria-marks-6th-year-missing-chibok-girls-amid-coronavirus-pandemic.

24. Author's May 2018 conversation with the editorial board of a Lagos newspaper.

25. Transcript from Tim Russert interview of Vice President Dick Cheney on *Meet the Press*, NBC News, September 14, 2003, http://www.nbcnews.com/id/3080244/ns/meet_the_press/t/transcript-sept/#.Xi9DkWhKi70

26. Nina M. Serafino et al., "'Leahy Law' Human Rights Provisions and Security Assistance: Issue Overview," Congressional Research Service, January 29, 2014, http://www.fas.org/sgp/crs/row/R43361.pdf.

27. Matthew Page, "Five Reasons Washington Should Rethink Selling Warplanes to Nigeria," *War on the Rocks*, November 8, 2016, http://www.warontherocks.com/2016/11/five-reasons-washington-should-rethink-selling-warplanes-to-nigeria.

28. "Nigerian Air Force Kills More than 100 Civilians by Accident in Strike Targeting Boko Haram: Military Official," NBC News, January 17, 2019, http://www.nbcnews.com/news/world/nigerian-air-force-kills-more-100-civilians-accident-northeastern-strike-n707876.

29. The Editorial Board, "Block the Sale of Warplanes in Nigeria," *New York Times*, May 18, 2016, http://www.nytimes.com/2016/05/18/opinion/block-the-sale-of-warplanes-to-nigeria.html.

30. Fergus Kelly, "Nigeria A-29 Super Tucano Light Attack Aircraft Contract Finally Lands," *Defense Post*, November 29, 2018, http://www.thedefensepost.com/2018/11/29/nigeria-a-29-super-tucano-contract-sierra-nevada.

31. "International Military Education Training 2000–2018 West Africa," *Security Assistance Monitor*, http://www.securityassistance.org/data/country/trainee/International%20Military%20Education%20and%20Training/2000/2018/all/West%20Africa/.

32. "International Military Education Training 2000–2018 West Africa."

33. James Sheehan, "U.S. Army Trains Nigerian Infantry," March 2, 2018, http://www.army.mil/article/201415/us_army_trains_nigerian_infrantry.

34. Tomas Husted, "Gulf of Guinea: Recent Trends in Piracy and Armed Robbery," Congressional Research Service, February 26, 2019, https://fas.org/sgp/crs/row/IF11117.pdf.

35. Acha Leke and Laundry Signe, "Spotlighting Opportunities for Business in Africa and Strategies to Succeed in the World's Next Big Growth Market," Brookings

Institution, January 11, 2019, http://www.brookings.edu/research/spotlighting
-opportunities-for-business-in-africa-and-strategies-to-succeed-in-the-worlds-next
-big-growth-market; Ian Goldin, Halsey Rogers, and Nicholas Stern, "The Role and
Effectiveness of Development Assistance: Lessons from World Bank Experience,"
The World Bank, http://www.pdfs.semanticscholar.org/1ac4/304728499b2378b8614
35320a9068424b834.pdf.

36. Sam Ajiye, "Achievement of Millennium Development Goals in Nigeria: A
Critical Examination," *International Affairs and Global Strategy* 25 (2014), http://
www.pdfs.semanticscholar.org/7767/ec3ba825462626217a63ad8806e1eda687f2.pdf.

37. Cohen, "Trump's Africa Policy Is a Continuation of Clinton's, Bush's, and
Obama's." Ambassador Cohen, a career Foreign Service Officer, served in both
Democratic and Republican administrations: President Jimmy Carter (D) appointed
him US ambassador to Senegal; President Ronald Reagan (R) appointed him senior
director for Africa at the National Security Council; and President George H. W. Bush
(R) appointed him assistant secretary of state for Africa.

38. Lauren P. Blanchard and Tomas Husted, "Nigeria: Current Issues and U.S. Policy," Congressional Research Service, February 1, 2019, http://www.fas.org/sgp/crs/
row/RL33964.pdf.

39. Judd Devermont, "The Game Has Changed: Rethinking the U.S. Role in Supporting Elections in Sub-Saharan Africa," CSIS, February 15, 2019, https://www.csis
.org/analysis/game-has-changed-rethinking-us-role-supporting-elections-sub-saharan
-africa. CSIS compiled this data from USAID and Foreign Aid Explorer, http://www
.explorer.usaid.gov/#2018.

40. John Campbell, "Nigeria's Elections Do Not a Democracy Make," *American
Ambassadors Review* (Spring 2019), http://www.americanambassadorslive.org/post/
nigeria-s-elections-do-not-a-democracy-make.

41. Robert D. Kaplan, *The Return of Marco Polo's World* (New York: Random
House, 2018).

42. "So numerous and detailed are the court's findings of irregularities in the counting of votes, reconciliation of ballots, and the Malawi Electoral Commission's failure
to adhere to electoral rules, that it boggles the mind that these problems were not
picked up and amplified by the election observers. In a masterpiece of understatement,
the court observed that the widespread use of correction fluid on the return ballots was
a strong indication that the results were flawed. As were the use of duplicate sheets
and the general administrative failure to properly manage the reconciliation of votes,"
write Greg Mills and Ray Hartley in "Observers Played a Shameful Role in Malawi's
Tippex Election," *Daily Maverick*, February 4, 2020, https://www.dailymaverick.co
.za/article/2020-02-04-observers-played-a-shameful-role-in-malawi-tippex-election.

43. Formally known as the Currency and Foreign Transaction Reporting Act, 1970.

44. The first, *United States v. All Assets Held at Bank Julius Baer & Co.*, a June
2008 district court case, determined that the "district court has jurisdiction over wire
transfers of dollars between foreign countries where money passed through a New
York bank acting as intermediary." For the full decision, see: "U.S. Anti-Money Laundering Statute and Case Law," *KYC360*, February 12, 2016, http://www.riskscreen
.com/kyc360/research-papers/u-s-anti-money-laundering-statute-and-case-law. The

decision was upheld, reinforced, and broadened in the November 2012 New York Court of Appeals case *Licci v. American Express Bank Ltd. and Lebanese Canadian Bank*, the second case. "Foreign Banks Subject to the Jurisdiction of New York Courts Based on Correspondent Accounts," Crowell & Moring LLP, November 30, 2012, http://www.crowell.com/NewsEvents/AlertsNewsletters/all/Foreign-Banks-Subject -to-the-Jurisdiction-of-New-York-Courts-Based-on-Correspondent-Accounts.

45. Bukola Adebayo, "Former Nigerian Dictator's $267M Seized from Jersey Account," CNN, June 6, 2019, http://www.cnn.com/2019/06/05/africa/nigeria-abacha -stolen-loot-jersey-intl/index.html.

46. Matthew Page, "A New Taxonomy of Corruption in Nigeria," Carnegie Endowment for International Peace, July 17, 2018, http://www.carnegieendowment.org /2018/07/17/new-taxonomy-for-corruption-in-nigeria-pub-76811.

CHAPTER 8

1. Princeton N. Lyman and Patricia Dorff, eds., *Beyond Humanitarianism: What You Need to Know about Africa and Why It Matters* (New York: Council on Foreign Relations, 2007), xii.

2. Hegemon here refers to Nigeria's political, military, and economic predominance over the other states in West Africa.

3. "68% of the World Population Projected to Live in Urban Areas by 2050, Says UN," United Nations Department of Economic and Social Affairs, May 16, 2018, http://www.un.org/development/desa/en/news/population/2018-revision-of-world -urbanization-prospects.html.

4. "At Least a Million Sub-Saharan Africans Moved to Europe since 2010," Pew Research Center, March 22, 2018, http://www.pewresearch.org/global/2018/03/22/at -least-a-million-sub-saharan-africans-moved-to-europe-since-2010.

5. President Trump's December 2018 announcement that the US military presence in Africa would decrease as part of a general shift from countering terrorism to great power confrontation had not occurred as of mid-2020. US troop deployment in Africa was as high as 6,207 in 1955, reflecting US engagement during the Cold War. Tim Kane, "Global U.S. Troop Deployment, 1950–2005," The Heritage Foundation, May 24, 2006, http://www.heritage.org/defense/report/global-us-troop-deployment-1950 -2005; "Draft Congressional Resolutions: Recognizing the Strategic Importance of the African Continent and Welcoming of the Establishment of AFRICOM," US AFRICOM Public Affairs, United States Congress, March 12, 2008, http://www.africom .mil/media-room/transcript/6139/draft-congressional-resolutions-recognizing-the-st; "Mission," United States Africa Command, 2019, http://www.africom.mil/military -presence.

6. During the same time, which includes the Korean War, the Vietnam War, and the wars in Iraq and Afghanistan, sixteen US military flag officers were killed in the line of duty. https://warontherocks.com/2014/08/general-and-flag-officers-killed-in-war.

7. "Nigeria: Towards Disintegration?," *Time*, August 12, 1966, http://content.time .com/time/magazine/article/0,9171,842599,00.html.

8. See chapter 4 and Olawunmi Ojo, "Operation Amotekun: Metaphor for FG's Indecisiveness on Insecurity," *Guardian* (Nigeria), January 18, 2020, https://guardian.ng/saturday-magazine/operation-amotekun-metaphor-for-fgs-indecisiveness-on-insecurity.

9. Max Siollun, "Nigeria's Election Is Shattering Political Taboos," *Foreign Policy*, February 13, 2019, https://foreignpolicy.com/2019/02/13/nigerias-election-is-shattering-political-taboos-buhari-atiku-restructuring-federalism-oil-wealth.

10. Though even his dramatic progress is fragile. It is far from certain that the change he has ushered in will stick. See Mulugeta G. Berhe, "Ethiopia's Dramatic Political and Economic Transformation Has Left It with Deep Uncertainty," *Quartz Africa*, February 3, 2020, https://qz.com/africa/1796164/ethiopias-dramatic-change-with-abiy-leaves-it-in-deep-trouble.

11. William J. Burns, *The Back Channel: A Memoir of American Diplomacy and the Case for Its Renewal* (New York: Random House, 2019), 393.

12. For a discussion of the origins and consequences of the American recessional and its contribution to instability, see Ivo H. Daadler and James M. Lindsay, *The Empty Throne: America's Abdication of Global Leadership* (New York: Public Affairs, 2018).

13. Billy Perrico, "Top Diplomat Says U.S. Has Lost 60 percent of Its Career Ambassadors under President Trump," *Time*, November 9, 2017, http://www.time.com/5016774/trump-ambassadors-statedepartment-lost-60-percent-afsa-barbara-stephenson; "US Diplomacy Cuts 'Decapitates' [*sic*] State Department Leadership," BBC, November 9, 2017, http://www.bbc.com/news/41921907. Both references are to an interview by Ambassador Barbara Stephenson, head of the American Foreign Service Association.

14. Helms's motivation and the Clinton administration's concern to accommodate him were complex. It appears that the senator's real target was USAID—dissolving USIA would merely be a first step to that end. The Clinton administration wanted the senator's help on ratification of the chemical weapons treaty. So, it went along with dissolving USIA. However, USAID (a vastly larger operation) survived.

15. John Hughes, *Islamic Extremism and the War of Ideas: Lessons from Indonesia* (Stanford: Hoover Institution Press, 2013), 23.

16. Burns, *The Back Channel*, 389.

17. Amy Chua, *Political Tribes: Group Instinct and the Fate of Nations* (New York: Penguin, 2018), 45.

18. Chua, *Political Tribes*, 54.

19. Thomas Friedman quoted in Amy Chua, *Political Tribes*, 38. He originally wrote it here: Thomas Friedman, "ISIS and Vietnam," *New York Times*, October 28, 2014, https://www.nytimes.com/2014/10/29/opinion/thomas-friedman-isis-and-vietnam.html.

20. Quoted by Chua, *Political Tribes*, pp. 84–86.

21. General Allen is quoted in Chua, *Political Tribes*, 85. Secretary Rice is quoted on page 3 of the same book. Rice made the comment in an interview (at 22:50) with Bill Hemmer, Fox News, May 5, 2017, https://www.foxnews.com/us/2017/05/05/condolezza-rice-discusses-north-korea-russia-with-bill-hemmer.html.

22. The federal authorities perceived Peace Corps volunteers as pro-Biafra. Later, President Obasanjo blocked an effort led by Vice President Atiku Abubakar and supported by the American embassy to bring the Peace Corps back on the basis that it would take jobs away from Nigerians.

23. "About Us," Iowa Resource for International Service, http://www.iris-center.org/about-us-2.

24. Herman J. Cohen, "Pulling Troops Out of Africa Could Mean Another Endless War," *War on the Rocks*, May 13, 2020, accessed May 14, 2020, https://warontherocks.com/2020/05/pulling-troops-out-of-africa-could-mean-another-endless-war.

25. Jeremy Bender, "France's Military Is All Over Africa," *Business Insider*, January 22, 2015, http://www.businessinsider.com/frances-military-is-all-over-africa-2015-1.

26. "Nigeria Emergency," The UN Refugee Agency, May 31, 2019, http://www.unhcr.org/en-us/nigeria-emergency.html.

27. Sadeeq Garba Shehu, "Making Military Reform and Civilian Oversight a Reality in Nigeria," *Africa in Transition* (blog), http://www.cfr.org/blog/making-military-reform-and-civilian-oversight-reality-nigeria. Sadeeq Garba Shehu is a former group captain in the Nigerian Air Force and a former deputy head of safety and security in the African Union Commission.

28. Judd Devermont and Todd Moss, "Africa's Cities Are about to Boom—and Maybe Explode," Bloomberg, July 25, 2019, http://www.bloomberg.com/opinion/articles/2019-07-25/africa-s-cities-are-about-to-boom-and-maybe-explode.

29. Constitution of the Federal Republic of Nigeria (Lagos: Federal Military Government of Nigeria, 1999), http://www.constituteproject.org/constitution/Nigeria_1999.pdf.

30. See John Campbell, "Biafra Heats Up as Trials Resume, Elections Loom, and Kanu Is Still Missing," *Africa in Transition* (blog), Council on Foreign Relations, March 21, 2018, http://www.cfr.org/blog/biafra-heats-trials-resume-elections-loom-and-kanu-still-missing.

31. See Jack McCaslin, "More Shiite Processions Met with Bloodshed in Nigeria," *Africa in Transition* (blog), Council on Foreign Relations, September 19, 2019, http://www.cfr.org/blog/more-shiite-processions-met-bloodshed-nigeria; and Jack McCaslin, "Dozens Reportedly Killed as Nigerian Military Fires on Shia Protesters," *Africa in Transition* (blog), Council on Foreign Relations, November 2, 2018. http://www.cfr.org/blog/dozens-reportedly-killed-nigerian-military-fires-shia-protesters.

32. See John Campbell, "Attacks on the Media Continue Unabated in Nigeria," *Africa in Transition* (blog), Council on Foreign Relations, August 7, 2019, http://www.cfr.org/blog/attacks-media-continue-unabated-nigeria; John Campbell, "Amid Setbacks, Nigerian Security Services Raid Influential Newspaper," *Africa in Transition* (blog), Council on Foreign Relations, January 9, 2019, http://www.cfr.org/blog/amid-setbacks-nigerian-security-services-raid-influential-newspaper; and John Campbell, "Difficulties Continue for Nigerian Journalists Covering Government," *Africa in Transition* (blog), Council on Foreign Relations, June 7, 2019, http://www.cfr.org/blog/difficulties-continue-nigerian-journalists-covering-government.

33. Nic Cheeseman and Brian Klaas, "How to Rig an Election," *Constitution Unit*, July 4, 2018, accessed May 15, 2020, https://constitution-unit.com/2018/07/04/how-to-rig-an-election.

34. Burns, *The Back Channel*, 80.

CONCLUSION

1. Pilling reviews Elnathan John's book, *Becoming Nigerian* for the *Financial Times*. David Pilling, "Becoming Nigerian by Elnathan John—Rich Satire," *Financial Times*, September 13, 2019, http://www.ft.com/join/licence/e1052dcb-5092-4c0c-9143-a541afb67607/details?ft-content-uuid=26c9d350-bd20-11e9-b350-db00d509634e.

2. Daniel W. Drezner, Ronald R. Krebs, and Randall Schweller, "The End of Grand Strategy: America Must Think Small," *Foreign Affairs* 3, no. 99 (May/June 2020): 110, https://www.foreignaffairs.com/articles/world/2020-04-13/end-grand-strategy.

3. William Burns, *The Back Channel* (New York: Random House, 2019), 111.

4. Arnold Weinstein, "Closed Minds, Great Books," *New York Times*, June 21, 2015, https://www.nytimes.com/2015/06/22/opinion/closed-minds-great-books.html.

5. Ray Ekpu, "Geographical Expression: So What?," *Guardian*, August 15, 2017, http://www.guardian.ng/opinion/geographical-expression-so-what.

6. Ken Saro-Wiwa, *On a Darkling Plane: An Account of the Nigerian Civil War* (Port Harcourt: Saros International, 1989), 21.

7. Donald Duke, "A Must Read: How Governors Rig Elections," *Sahara Reporters*, July 18, 2010, http://saharareporters.com/2010/07/18/must-read-how-governors-rig-elections-donald-duke-guardian.

Selected Bibliography

BOOKS

Acemoglu, Daron, and James A. Robinson. *Why Nations Fail: The Origins of Power, Prosperity, and Poverty*. New York: Currency, 2012.

Achebe, Chinua. *There Was a Country*. New York: Penguin, 2012.

———. *The Trouble with Nigeria*. London: Heinemann, 1987.

Adebanwi, Wale, and Ebenezer Obadare, eds. *Democracy and Prebendalism in Nigeria: Critical Interpretations*. New York: Palgrave Macmillan, 2013.

Allum, Felia, and Stan Gilmour. *Routledge Handbook of Transnational Organized Crime*. London: Routledge, 2015.

Anderson, Benedict. *Imagined Communities: Reflections on the Origin and Spread of Nationalism*. London: Verso, 2016.

Awolowo, Obafemi. *The Path to Nigerian Freedom*. London: Faber and Faber, 1947.

Barclays Bank. *Nigeria*. Dominion, Colonial and Overseas, 1966.

Belloc, Hilaire. *The Modern Traveller*. London: E. Arnold, 1898.

Berlin, Ira, and Leslie Harris. *Slavery in New York*. New York: The New Press, 2005.

Burns, William J. *The Back Channel: A Memoir of American Diplomacy and the Case for Its Renewal*. New York: Random House, 2019.

Campbell, John. *Nigeria: Dancing on the Brink*, 2nd ed. Lanham, MD: Rowman & Littlefield, 2013.

Campbell, John, and Matthew T. Page. *Nigeria: What Everyone Needs to Know*. New York: Oxford University Press, 2018.

Chayes, Sarah. *Thieves of State: Why Corruption Threatens Global Security*. New York: W. W. Norton, 2015.

Cheeseman, Nic. *Democracy in Africa*. New York: Cambridge University Press, 2015.

Cheeseman, Nic, and Brian Klaas. *How to Rig an Election*. New Haven, CT: Yale University Press, 2018.

Chua, Amy. *Political Tribes: Group Instinct and the Fate of Nations*. New York: Penguin, 2018.

Clapham, Christopher. *Third World Politics: An Introduction*. London: Routledge, 1985.

Cohen, Herman J. *US Policy toward Africa: Eight Decades of Realpolitik*. Boulder, CO: Lynne Rienner, 2020.

Coleman, Isobel, and Terra Lawson-Remer, eds. *Pathways to Freedom*. New York: Council on Foreign Relations, 2013.

Coleman, James S. *Nigeria*. Berkeley: University of California Press, 1963.

Comolli, Virginia. *Boko Haram: Nigeria's Islamist Insurgency*. London: Hurst, 2015.

Curtin, Philip D. *The Atlantic Slave Trade: A Census*. Madison: University of Wisconsin Press, 1972.

Daadler, Ivo H., and James M. Lindsay. *The Empty Throne: America's Abdication of Global Leadership*. New York: Public Affairs, 2018.

Elaigwu, Jonah Isawa. *The Politics of Federalism in Nigeria*. London: Adonis & Abbey, 2007.

Ellis, Stephen. *This Present Darkness: A History of Nigerian Organized Crime*. New York: Oxford University Press, 2016.

Enwerem, Iheanyi M. *Crossing the Rubicon: A Socio-Political Analysis of Political Catholicism in Nigeria*. Ibadan: Book Builders, 2010.

Falola, Toyin, and Matthew M. Heaton. *A History of Nigeria*. Cambridge: Cambridge University Press, 2008.

Foster, Humphrey J. *Slavery in the History of Muslim Black Africa*. New York: New York University Press, 2001.

Hare, John. *Last Man In: The End of Empire in Northern Nigeria*. Kent, UK: Neville & Harding, 2013.

Hyden, Goran. *African Politics in Comparative Perspective*. Cambridge: Cambridge University Press, 2012.

John, Elnathan. *Be(coming) Nigerian: A Guide*. Abuja, Nigeria: Cassava Republic Press, 2019.

Joseph, Richard. *Democracy and Prebendal Politics in Nigeria: The Rise and Fall of the Second Republic*. Cambridge: Cambridge University Press, 1987.

Kassim, Abdulbasit, and Michael Nwankpa. *The Boko Haram Reader*. London: Hurst & Company, 2018.

Kendhammer, Brandon, and Carmen McCain. *Boko Haram*. Athens: Ohio University Press, 2018.

Konafu, Kwasi, and Clifford C. Campbell. *The Ghana Reader: History, Culture, Politics*. Durham, NC: Duke University Press, 2016.

Lall, Somik, et al. *Africa's Cities: Opening Doors to the World*. Washington, DC: The World Bank, 2017, http://www.openknowledge.worldbank.org/handle/10986/25896.

Leebaert, Derek. *Grand Improvisation: America Confronts the British Superpower, 1945–1957*. New York: Farrar, Straus and Giroux, 2016.

Lepore, Jill, *This America: The Case for the Nation*. New York: Liveright, 2019.

LeVan, A. Carl. *Contemporary Nigerian Politics: Competition in a Time of Transition and Terror*. Cambridge: Cambridge University Press, 2019.

LeVan, A. Carl, and Patrick Ukata, eds. *The Oxford Handbook of Nigerian Politics*. New York: Oxford University Press, 2018.

Lyman, Princeton N., and Patricia Dorff, eds. *Beyond Humanitarianism: What You Need to Know about Africa and Why It Matters*. New York: Council on Foreign Relations, 2007.

Matfess, Hilary. *Women and the War on Boko Haram*. London: Zed Books, 2017.

McCauley, John. *The Logic of Ethnic and Religious Conflict in Africa*. Cambridge: Cambridge University Press, 2017.

Minawi, Mostafa. *The Ottoman Scramble for Africa: Empire and Diplomacy in the Sahara and the Hijaz*. Stanford, CA: Stanford University Press, 2016.

Obadare, Ebenezer. *Pastoral Power, Clerical State: Pentecostalism, Gender, and Sexuality in Nigeria*. Notre Dame, IN: University of Notre Dame Press, 2022.

———. *Pentecostal Republic: Religion and the Struggle for State Power in Nigeria*. London: Zed Books, 2018.

Ochonu, Moses. *Colonialism by Proxy: Hausa Imperial Agents and Middle Belt Consciousness in Nigeria*. Bloomington: Indiana University Press, 2014.

Okonjo-Iweala, Ngozi. *Reforming the Unreformable: Lessons from Nigeria*. Cambridge, MA: MIT Press, 2012.

Olopade, Davo. *The Bright Continent: Breaking Rules and Making Change in Modern Africa*. Boston: Mariner Books / Houghton Mifflin Harcourt, 2015.

Olupona, Jacob. *Beyond Primitivism: Indigenous Religious Traditions and Modernity*. New York: Routledge, 2004.

Paden, John N. *Muslim Civic Cultures and Conflict Resolution*. Washington, DC: Brookings Institution Press, 2005.

Parris, Matthew, and Andrew Bryson. *Parting Shots*. London: Viking, 2010.

Sanneh, Lamin. *Translating the Message: The Missionary Impact on Culture*. Maryknoll, NY: Orbis Books, 1989.

Saro-Wiwa, Ken. *On a Darkling Plane: An Account of the Nigerian Civil War*. Port Harcourt, Nigeria: Saros International, 1989.

Siollun, Max. *Nigeria's Soldiers of Fortune: The Abacha and Obasanjo Years*. London: Hurst, 2019.

———. *Soldiers of Fortune: A History of Nigeria (1983–1993)*. Abuja, Nigeria: Cassava Republic Press, 2013.

Soyinka, Wole. *Of Africa*. New Haven: Yale University Press, 2012.

Suberu, Rotimi. *Federalism and Ethnic Conflict in Nigeria*. Washington, DC: United States Institute of Peace, 2001.

Talbott, Strobe. *The Great Experiment: The Story of Ancient Empires, Modern States, and the Quest for a Global Nation*. New York: Simon & Schuster, 2009.

Thurston, Alexander. *Boko Haram: The History of an African Jihadist Movement*. Princeton, NJ: Princeton University Press, 2018.

Zenn, Jacob. *Unmasking Boko Haram: Exploring Global Jihad in Nigeria*. Boulder, CO: Lynne Rienner, 2020).

ARTICLES AND REPORTS

"100. Memorandum Prepared by the Office of Current Intelligence, Central Intelligence Agency, Washington, August 5, 1969." US Department of State. http://www.history.state.gov/historicaldocuments/frus1969-76ve05p1/d100.

"186. Memorandum from the President's Deputy Assistant for National Security Affairs (Haig) to the President's Assistant for National Security Affairs (Kissinger), Washington, February 16, 1970." US Department of State. http://www.history.state .gov/historicaldocuments/frus1969-76ve05p1/d186.

"201. National Intelligence Estimate, Washington, November 2, 1970." US Department of State, accessed July 31, 2019. https://history.state.gov/historicaldocuments/ frus1969-76ve05p1/d201.

"2014 Oil and Gas Industry Audit Report." Nigeria Extractive Industries Transparency Initiative, December 23, 2016. http://www.eiti.org/sites/default/files/documents/ neiti-oil-gas-report-2014-full-report-301216.pdf.

Afigbo, Adiele. "The Warrant Chiefs: Indirect Rule in Southeastern Nigeria, 1891– 1929." *School of Oriental and African Studies* 36, no. 3 (1973): 725–27.

Ajayi, Rotimi. "The Anticolonial Struggle in Nigeria." In *The Oxford Handbook of Nigerian Politics*, edited by A. Carl Levan and Patrick Ukata. New York: Oxford University Press, 2018.

Ajiye, Sam. "Achievement of Millennium Development Goals in Nigeria: A Critical Examination." *International Affairs and Global Strategy* 25 (2014). http://www .pdfs.semanticscholar.org/7767/ec3ba825462626217a63ad8806e1eda687f2.pdf.

Aliyu, Alhaji A., and Lawal Amadu. "Urbanization, Cities, and Health: The Challenges to Nigeria—A Review." *Annals of African Medicine* 14, no. 4 (2017): 149–58.

Aluko, M. A. O., and O. A. Ajani. "Ethnic Nationalism and the Nigerian Democratic Experience in the Fourth Republic." *African Research Review* 3, no. 1 (2009): 483–99.

Asaju, Kayode, and Tony Egberi. "Federal Character and National Integration in Nigeria: The Need for Discretion and Interface." *Review of History and Political Science* 3, no. 1 (2015). doi:10.15640/rhps.v3n1a12.

Ashgabat, Joseph O. "The Legislatures in the First and Second Republics." In *The Oxford Handbook of Nigerian Politics*, edited by A. Carl LeVan and Patrick Ukata. New York: Oxford University Press, 2018.

Bamgbose, J. Adele. "The Place of Deities in African Political Systems, Essence." *Interdisciplinary Journal of Philosophy* 2 (2005): 231–42.

Blanchard, Lauren P., and Tomas F. Husted. "Nigeria: Current Issues and U.S. Policy." Congressional Research Service, February 1, 2019. http://www.fas.org/sgp/crs/row /RL33964.pdf.

Blommaert, Jan. "Language Policy and National Identity." In *An Introduction to Language Policy: Theory and Method*, edited by Thomas Ricento. Malden, MA: Blackwell, 2006.

Bratton, Michael. "Citizen Perceptions of Local Government Responsiveness in Sub-Saharan Africa." Afrobarometer, Working Paper no. 119 (May 2010).

Campbell, John. "Nigeria: Why Are Boko Haram Fighters Successful?" *Africa in Transition* (blog). Council on Foreign Relations. March 4, 2014. http://www.cfr.org /blog/sea-levels-along-west-african-coast.

———. "Nigeria's Elections Do Not a Democracy Make." *American Ambassadors Review* (Spring 2019). http://www.americanambassadorslive.org/post/nigeria-s -elections-do-not-a-democracy-make.

———. "What's in a Name? For the Nigerian Civil War, Everything." *Africa in Transition* (blog). Council on Foreign Relations, October 18, 2017. https://www.cfr.org/blog/whats-name-nigerian-civil-war-everything.

Cardamone, Tom. "Global Financial Integrity Releases New Study on Trade Misinvoicing in Nigeria." Global Financial Integrity, October 31, 2018. http://www.gfintegrity.org/press-release/global-financial-integrity-releases-new-study-on-trade-misinvoicing-in-nigeria.

"The Case of Hisbah: Policy Brief No. 2." In *Sharia Implementation in Northern Nigeria over 15 Years*. Kano, Nigeria: October 2016. https://www.qeh.ox.ac.uk/sites/www.odid.ox.ac.uk/files/Sharia%20-%20POLICY%20BRIEF%20TWO%20Final%20Version.pdf.

Cocks, Tim. "Special Report: Anatomy of Nigeria's $20 Billion 'Leak.'" Reuters, February 6, 2015. http://www.reuters.com/article/us-nigeria-election-banker-specialreport/special-report-anatomy-of-nigerias-20-billion-leak-idUSKBN0LA0X820150206.

"Country Analysis Brief: Nigeria." US Energy Information Administration, May 6, 2016. http://www.eia.gov/beta/international/analysis_includes/countries_long/Nigeria/nigeria.pdf.

Cousins, Alan. "The Imperial Mind in British Colonies, 1938–1947, in the Light of Indian Experience." *Social Scientist* 27, no. 7/8 (1999): 140–67.

"Criminal Politics: Violence, 'Godfathers' and Corruption in Nigeria." *Human Rights Watch Report* 10, no. 16(A) (2007). http://www.hrw.org/report/2007/10/11/criminal-politics/violence-godfathers-and-corruption-nigeria.

Devermont, Judd. "The Game Has Changed: Rethinking the U.S. Role in Supporting Elections in Sub-Saharan Africa." CSIS, February 15, 2019. https://www.csis.org/analysis/game-has-changed-rethinking-us-role-supporting-elections-sub-saharan-africa.

———. "The US Intelligence Community's Biases during the Nigerian Civil War." *African Affairs* 116, no. 465 (October 2017): 705–16.

Drezner, Daniel W., Ronald R. Krebs, and Randall Schweller. "The End of Grand Strategy: America Must Think Small." *Foreign Affairs* 99, no. 3 (May/June 2020). https://www.foreignaffairs.com/articles/world/2020-04-13/end-grand-strategy

Dulles, Foster Rhea, and Gerald E. Ridinger. "The Anti-Colonial Policies of Franklin D. Roosevelt." *Political Science Quarterly* 70, no. 1 (1955).

Ehrhardt, David, and Abdul Mustapha. "Islamic Actors and Interfaith Relations in Northern Nigeria." University of Oxford, Policy Paper no. 1 (March 2013). http://www.qeh.ox.ac.uk/sites/www.odid.ox.ac.uk/files/nrn-pp01.pdf.

Ekeh, Peter. "Colonialism and the Two Publics in Africa." *Comparative Studies in Society and History* 17, no. 1 (January 1975).

Elemo, Olufunmbi. "Fiscal Federalism, Subnational Politics, and State Creation in Contemporary Nigeria." In *The Oxford Handbook of Nigerian Politics*, edited by A. Carl LeVan and Patrick Ukata. New York: Oxford University Press, 2019.

Ellis, Stephen. "The Okija Shrine." *Journal of African History* 49, no. 3 (2008): 445–66.

Eze, Emmanuel C. "Hume, Race, and Human Nature." *Journal of the History of Ideas* 61, no. 4 (2000): 691. doi:10.2307/3654076.

"Facing the Challenge of the Islamic State in West Africa Province." International Crisis Group, May 2019. Africa Report No. 273. http://www.crisisgroup.org/africa/west-africa/nigeria/273-facing-challenge-islamic-state-west-africa-province.

Flint, John. "Planned Decolonization and Its Failure in British Africa." *African Affairs* 82, no. 328 (1983).

Frankel, Jeffrey A. "The Natural Resource Curse: A Survey of Diagnoses and Some Prescriptions." HKS Faculty Research Working Paper Series RWP12-014. John F. Kennedy School of Government, Harvard University. https://dash.harvard.edu/bitstream/handle/1/8694932/rwp12-014_frankel.pdf?sequence=1

Furlong, Patrick J. "Azikiwe and the National Church of Nigeria and the Cameroons: A Case Study of the Political Use of Religion in African Nationalism." *African Affairs* 91, no. 364 (July 1992): 433–52.

"The Future of World Religions: Population Growth Projections, 2010–2050." Pew Research Center, April 2, 2015. http://www.assets.pewresearch.org/wp-content/uploads/sites/11/2015/03/PF_15.04.02_ProjectionsFullReport.pdf.

Gale, Thomas S. "Segregation in British West Africa (La Ségrégation en Afrique Occidentale Britannique)." *Cahiers D'Études Africaines* 20, no. 80 (1980): 495–507. http://jstor.org/stable/4391717.

Gerth, H. H., and C. Wright Mills, trans. and ed. *From Max Weber: Essays in Sociology*, 77–128. New York: Oxford University Press, 1946.

"Global Terrorism Index 2019: Measuring the Impact of Terrorism." Institute for Economics & Peace, Sydney, November 2019. http://visionofhumanity.org/reports.

Goldin, Ian, Halsey Rogers, and Nicholas Stern. "The Role and Effectiveness of Development Assistance: Lessons from World Bank Experience." The World Bank. http://www.pdfs.semanticscholar.org/1ac4/304728499b2378b861435320a9068424b834.pdf.

Harries, Lyndon. "Language Policy in Tanzania." *Africa: Journal of the International African Institute* 39, no. 3 (July 1969): 275. http://www.jstor.org/stable/1157997.

Hartmann, Christof. "ECOWAS and the Restoration of Democracy in the Gambia." *Africa Spectrum* 52, no. 1 (2017): 85–99. doi:10.1177/000203971705200104.

"Harvest of Death: Three Years of Bloody Clashes between Farmers and Herders in Nigeria." Amnesty International, December 17, 2018. http://www.amnesty.org/en/documents/afr44/9503/2018/en.

Head, Keith, et al. "The Erosion of Colonial Trade Linkages after Independence." *Journal of International Economics* 81, no. 1 (2010): 1–14. doi:10.1016/j.jinteco.2010.01.002.

Hoffmann, Leena. "Fairy Godfathers and Magical Elections: Understanding the 2003 Electoral Crisis in Anambra State, Nigeria." *Journal of Modern African Studies* 48, no. 2 (2010): 285–310. http://www.jstor.org/stable/40864718.

Husted, Tomas. "Gulf of Guinea: Recent Trends in Piracy and Armed Robbery." Congressional Research Service, February 26, 2019. https://fas.org/sgp/crs/row/IF11117.pdf.

Isbell, Thomas. "Tax Compliance: Africans Affirm Civic Duty but Lack Trust in Tax Department." Afrobarometer, December 2017, 8. https://afrobarometer

.org/sites/default/files/publications/Policy%20papers/ab_r6_policypaperno43_tax
_compliance_in_africa-afrobarometer.pdf.

Isbell, Thomas, and Oluwole Ojewale. "Nigerians Support Elections and Multiparty Competition but Mistrust Electoral Commission." *Afrobarometer*, Dispatch no. 275 (February 2019). http://www.afrobarometer.org/sites/default/files/publications /D%C3%A9p%C3%AAches/ab_r7_dispatchno275_nigerian_views_on_elections .pdf.

Jackson, Robert H., and Carl G. Rosberg. "Why Africa's Weak States Persist: The Empirical and the Juridical in Statehood." *World Politics* 35, no. 1 (October 1982): 1–24. http://doi.org/ 10.2307/2010277.

Kane, Tim. "Global U.S. Troop Deployment, 1950–2005." The Heritage Foundation, May 24, 2006. http://www.heritage.org/defense/report/global-us-troop-deployment -1950-2005.

Kramer, Lloyd. "Historical Narratives and the Meaning of Nationalism." *Journal of the History of Ideas* 58, no. 3 (1997): 525–45. doi:10.2307/3653913.

Last, Murray. "The Search for Security in Muslim Northern Nigeria." *Africa: The Journal of the International African Institute* 78, no. 1 (2008): 41–63.

Legère, Karsten. "JK Nyerere of Tanzania and the Empowerment of Swahili." In *"Along the Routes to Power": Explorations of Empowerment through Language*, edited by Martin Pütz, Joshual A. Fishman, and JoAnne Neff-van Aertselaer. Berlin: Mouton de Gruyter, 2006.

Lepore, Jill. "A New Americanism." *Foreign Affairs* (March/April 2019). https:// www.foreignaffairs.com/articles/united-states/2019-02-05/new-americanism.

Lewis, Peter. "Boundaries and Bargains: Managing Nigeria's Fractious Society." In *On the Fault Line: Managing Tensions and Divisions within Societies*, edited by Jeffrey Herbst, Terence McNamee, and Greg Mills. London: Profile Press, 2012.

Mahmoud, Yahia. "Modernism in Africa." In *The Routledge Encyclopedia of Modernism*. London: Routledge, 2016.

Malden, Alexander. "Nigeria's Oil and Gas Revenues: Insights from New Company Disclosures." Natural Resource Governance Institute, December 2017. http://www .resourcegovernance.org/sites/default/files/documents/nigeria-oil-revenue.pdf.

"Mapping Sub-Saharan Africa's Future." National Intelligence Council, CR 2005-02, March 2005. http://www.dni.gov/files/documents/africa_future_2005 .pdf.

McKenna, Joseph C. "Elements of a Nigerian Peace." *Foreign Affairs* 47, no. 4 (1969): 668–80.

McNeil, Brian. "'And Starvation Is the Grim Reaper': The American Committee to Keep Biafra Alive and the Genocide Question during the Nigerian Civil War, 1968–70." *Journal of Genocide Research* 16, no. 2–3 (2014): 317–36.

Miles, William F. S., and David A. Rochefort. "Nationalism versus Ethnic Identity in Sub-Saharan Africa." *American Political Science Review* 85, no. 2 (June 1991): 393–403.

Momale, Saleh B. "Violence in Nigeria's Middle Belt Region." Search for Common Ground: Forum on Farmer-Herder Relations in Nigeria, April 1, 2019.

Morse, Yonatan L. "Presidential Power and Democratization by Elections in Africa." *Democratization* 25, no. 4 (2018).

Negedu, Isaiah, and Augustine Atabor. "Nationalism in Nigeria: A Case for Patriotic Citizenship." *American International Journal of Contemporary Research* 5, no. 3 (June 2015): 74–79.

"Nigeria's 2004 National Policy on Population for Sustainable Development." Federal Government of Nigeria, Implementation Assessment Report, September 2015. http://www.healthpolicyplus.com/ns/pubs/7141-7252_NPPImplementation AssessmentBriefMay.pdf.

Okafor, Samuel O. "Review: The Warrant Chiefs: Indirect Rule in Southeastern Nigeria, 1891–1929." *Journal of Modern African Studies* 11, no. 3 (1973): 487–89. http://jstor.org/stable/159621.

Okojie, Christiana. *Illicit Transfers and Tax Reforms in Nigeria: Mapping of the Literature and Synthesis of the Evidence.* Nairobi, Kenya: Partnership for African Social and Governance Research, May 2018, 15. http://www.pasgr.org/wp-content /uploads/2018/09/Nigeria-Illicit-Financial-Flows-Report.pdf.

Olagunju, Temidayo Ebenezer. "Drought, Desertification and the Nigerian Environment: A Review." *Journal of Ecology and the Natural Environment* 7, no. 7 (2015): 196–209. doi:10.5897/jene2015.0523.

Onwubu, Chukwuemeka. "Ethnic Identity, Political Integration, and National Development: The Igbo Diaspora in Nigeria." *Journal of Modern African Studies* 13, no. 3 (September 1975).

Osaghae, Eghosa. "The Long Shadow of Nigeria's Military Epochs." In *The Oxford Handbook of Nigerian Politics*, edited by A. Carl Levan and Patrick Ukata. New York: Oxford University Press, 2018.

Osha, Sanya. "Birth of the Ogoni Protest Movement." *Journal of Asian and African Studies* 41, no. 1/2 (2006).

Page, Matthew. "A New Taxonomy of Corruption in Nigeria." Carnegie Endowment for International Peace, July 17, 2018. http://www.carnegieendowment.org/2018 /07/17/new-taxonomy-for-corruption-in-nigeria-pub-76811.

Patterson, Frederick D. "Education in Nigeria." *Journal of Negro Education* 24, no. 2 (1955): 96–97. doi:10.2307/2293472.

Pearce, Robert. "The Colonial Office and Planned Decolonization in Africa." *African Affairs* 83, no. 330 (1984): 77–93.

Robinson, Amanda Lea. "National versus Ethnic Identity in Africa: State, Group, and Individual Level Correlates of National Identifications." Afrobarometer, Working Paper no. 122 (September 2009). http://www.afrobarometer.org/sites/default/files/ publications/Working%20paper/AfropaperNo112.pdf.

Sayne, Aaron, Alexandra Gillies, and Christina Katsouris. "Inside NNPC Oil Sales: A Case for Reform in Nigeria." Natural Resource Governance Institute, August 2015. http://www.resourcegovernance.org/sites/default/files/NRGI_ InsideNNPCOilSales_CompleteReport.pdf.

Serafino, Nina M., et al. "'Leahy Law' Human Rights Provisions and Security Assistance: Issue Overview." Congressional Research Service, January 29, 2014. http://www.fas.org/sgp/crs/row/R43361.pdf.

Sklar, Richard. "The African Frontier for Political Science." In *Africa and the Disciplines*, edited by Robert H. Bates, V. Y. Mudimber, and Jean O'Barr. Chicago: University of Chicago Press, 1993.

"Summary of the 2018 National Defense Strategy of the United States." Department of Defense, 2018. http://www.dod.defense.gov/Portals/1/Documents/pubs/2018 -National-Defense-Strategy-Summary.pdf.

Thomas, Lynn M. "Modernity's Failings, Political Claims and Intermediate Concepts." *American Historical Review* 116, no. 3 (2011): 727–40. http://jstor.org/stable /23308225.

Tipps, Dean C. "Modernization Theory and the Comparative Study of Societies: A Critical Perspective." *Studies in Society and History* 15, no. 2 (March 1973): 199– 226. http://jstor.org/stable/178351.

Vinson, Laura Thaut. "Pastoralism, Ethnicity, and Subnational Conflict Resolution in the Middle Belt." In *The Oxford Handbook of Nigerian Politics*, edited by A. Carl Levan and Patrick Ukata. New York: Oxford University Press, 2018.

Wapmuk, Sharkdam, Oluwatooni Akinkuotu, and Vincent Ibonye. "The Nigerian Diaspora and National Development: Contributions, Challenges, and Lessons from Other Countries." *Kritika Kultura*, no. 23 (August 2014): 292–342. https://journals .ateneo.edu/ojs/index.php/kk/article/view/1898/1900.

Wapner, Abraham. *Downstream Beneficiation Case Study: Nigeria*. New York: Columbia Center on Sustainable Investment, March 2017.

Watts, Michael J. "Ecologies of Rule." In *The Oxford Handbook of Nigerian Politics*, edited by A. Carl Levan and Patrick Ukata. New York: Oxford University Press, 2018.

"Weapons Compass: Mapping Illicit Small Arms Flows in Africa." Switzerland: Small Arms Survey, January 2019. http://www.smallarmssurvey.org/fileadmin/docs/U -Reports/SAS-AU-Weapons-Compass.pdf.

NEWSPAPERS, MAGAZINES, NEWS SERVICES

Agence France-Presse
Associated Press
BBC
Bloomberg
Business Insider
Council on Foreign Affairs; *Africa in Transition*
Daily Trust (Nigeria)

Deutsche Welle
Economist
Forbes
Foreign Policy
Guardian (Nigeria)

New York Times
Premium Times (Nigeria)
Pulse (Nigeria)
Punch (Nigeria)
Quartz Africa
Reuters
Sahara Reporters (New York)
This Day (Nigeria)
Vanguard (Nigeria)
Wall Street Journal

Index

Index

201n22, 215n35; of states, 196; tribal, xii, 184–85

Awolowo, Obafemi, 25, 35, 53, 106–7, 197

Azikiwe, Nnamdi, 36, 41, 55, 67, 175; Biafra secession and, 53–54

Babangida, Ibrahim, 69, 74–75, 88, 100, 138, 213n9, 214n20; administration of, 72–73, 112, 153

Balewa, Abubakar Tafawa, 67

Bello, Ahmadu, 53, 210n56

Belloc, Hilaire, 18

Biafra movements, 93, 125, 138, 190, 235n21; diaspora and, 139–41; secession and, 35–37, 53–54; US and, 156–58. *See also* civil war

Biafra region, 37, 71, 93

Biden, Joe, vii, 6, 173

"big men," 46, 89, 107, 122; politics and, 101–4, 109, 115

bin Laden, Osama, 162

Boko Haram, xiii–xiv, 7, 91–92, *126*, 170, 183, 227n44; Borno and, 122, 131, 164, 199n9; Buhari and, 152, 164; Chibok schoolgirls kidnapping and, 134, 161, 177; Christians and, 133, 226n35; governance and, 133–34; Islamic State and, 127, 129–32, 162, 173, 187, 227n50; ISWA and, 131–33, 162, 227n50; JAS, 125, 131–32; Jonathan and, 131, 152, 161, 164; leadership of, 130–32; military and, 130, 161; Shekau and, 127, 130–33, 161–62; traditional religion and, 128; US and, 160–63, 187–88; violence and, 126, 130–33, 227n52

Borno State, 15, *15*, 19, 94, 132; Boko Haram and, 122, 131, 164, 199n9; British Empire and, 16

Bourdillion, Bernard, 26–27

Brazil, slave trade and, 51, 209n46

British Colonial Office, 13, 19–20, 26–28, 30–31, 56

British Empire, 12–13, 15–16, 205n57; India and, 56–57

British governance of Nigeria, xix, 11–12, 21, 210n55; costs of, 22–24, 29, 33, 65; elites and, 24–26, 64–67, 212n4; independence and, 30–32, 34, 66–67; indirect rule and, 25–28; Islam and, 22, 24; traditional leaders and, 19–20, 23–24

British legacy, 22–23, 32–34

Buhari, Muhammadu, 70, 73, 115–17, 138, 213n9; Boko Haram and, 152, 164; elections and, 38, 100–103, 105, 178, 223n10; Fulani and, 88–89, 93, 140, 143, 146; oil industry and, 75–76, 98

Burns, William, 182–83, 192, 197

Bush, George W., viii–ix, 166, 172, 181, 186; Obasanjo and, 150, 152, 158–59, 188

Canada, 160–61; national identity and, 58–59

cannibalism, 19, 21–22, 203n16

Carter, Jimmy, 74, 232n37

Charles II (king), 56, 211n68

Chayes, Sarah, 212n3

Chibok schoolgirls kidnapping, 134, 161, 177

child soldiers, in militias, 94, 126–27, 133

China, ix, 165, 173–74, 184

Christianity, 22–23, 36–37, 91; education and, 33–34; loyalty and, 48–49. *See also* Obi, Peter

Christians, 2, 200n7; Boko Haram and, 133, 226n35; Muslims and, xiii, 17–18, 36–37, 143–44; as presidents, 100–102, 221n49; slavery and, 16, 202n8

Churchill, Winston, 30, 155

civic space, 90–91, 106, 176–77, 179–80

Civilian Joint Task Force (CJTF), 94, 126–27, 178

RWAFF. *See* Royal West African
Frontier Force

Sahara desert, 17, 51, 123, 130, 159
Sahel region, of Africa, 8, 14, 17–19,
51, 159–60, 170, 175
Sahlins, Peter, 206n8
Salafism, in Islam, 91, 108, 127–29
Saro-Wiwa, Ken, 67, 70, 136, 197
secession, Biafran, 35–37, 53–54
security, 72, 125, 175–76; Africa
and, 173; elites and, 110; French
colonialism and, 29–30; international
relations and, 155; military and, 79,
189–90, 235n26
Senghor, Léopold, 28–29, 204n39,
204n42
September 11, 2001 terror attacks, 152,
159, 186, 188
services: government and, 5, 53, 85–86,
124–25; medical, 71–72, 91–92, 105
Shagari, Shehu, 37, 70, 88, 213n9
"share the cake," elites and, 5, 62,
85–86, 97–100, 105–8, 168. *See also*
corruption
sharia, 23, 32, 72, 143, 226n43; Boko
Haram and, 129, 132; languages and,
96–97
Shekau, Abubakar, 127, 130–33, 161–62
Shia tradition, in Islam, 91, 128–29, 190
Siollun, Max, 106
slavery, 15, 60–61; Christians and, 16,
202n8; Islam and, 16–18
slave trade, 15, 19, 141–42, 202n8;
Brazil and, 51, 209n46; military and,
18; religion and, 16–18
Sokoto caliphate, *15*, 16, 19, 32, 128,
141–42, 210n56
Solzhenitzyn, Aleksandr, 78
South Africa, ix, xii–xiii, 152
Soviet Union, 31, 44, 54–56, 66, 78–79
Soyinka, Wole, 4, 54
spirituality, Nigerians and, 47–52,
210n52

stability, xiii, 107–8, 113, 171–
72; corruption and, 31–32;
detribalization and, 23–24, 33;
Federal Character and, 5
state, 43–44, 212n2; Boko Haram and,
132–33; colonialism and, 209n45;
disunity and, 4–5; dysfunction of, 11,
62–65, 111, 197; ethnic groups and,
49–50; identity and, 12; Nigerians
and, 2, 7, 9, 63–64; postcolonial,
ix–x, 2, 34, 153, 171, 195–97. *See
also* government of Nigeria
states, of Nigeria, 44; authority of, 196;
federalism and, 75; governance and,
79–80; regions and, 69
Sunni tradition, in Islam, 91, 128–29
Switzerland, 211n76; national identity
and, 58–59

Tanzania, 211n70; national identity and,
57–58
taxes, 76, 214n25, 215n33; elites
and, 90
terrorism, 132–33, 144, 159–62, 170,
186–88
Tinubu, Bola, vii, x–xi, 5–6, 38,
42, 140, 206n5; coups and, 154;
elections and, 79–80, 87, 102, 106,
111–16; governance and, 116–18
Tiv ethnic group, 49–50
trade, Africa and, 152–53
tradition: indirect rule and, 35;
modernity and, 2–3, 23
traditional leaders, xii, 3, 16, 184,
210n56; British governance and,
19–20, 23–24; elites and, 86–87,
92–93; emirate system and, 22–24,
31, 34–35, 48, 91–93, 110, 122;
ethnic groups and, 50; governance
and, 212n4; US and, 171
traditional public, 91; elites and, 92–94
traditional religion, 48; Boko Haram
and, 128; Juju and, 94–96; political
leaders and, 94–95
Trevor-Roper, H. R., 12–13

About the Author

John Campbell was the Ralph Bunche senior fellow for Africa policy studies at the Council on Foreign Relations from 2009 to 2021. He is the coauthor, along with Matthew Page, of *Nigeria: What Everyone Needs to Know*, which was published in July 2018, and he writes the blog *Africa in Transition*. From 1975 to 2007, Campbell served as a US Department of State Foreign Service officer. He served twice in Nigeria, as political counselor from 1988 to 1990 and as ambassador from 2004 to 2007. Campbell's additional overseas postings include Lyon, Paris, Geneva, and Pretoria. He also served as deputy assistant secretary for human resources, dean of the Foreign Service Institute's School of Language Studies, and director of the Office of UN Political Affairs. Campbell has also written *Morning in South Africa*, which came out in May 2016, and *Nigeria: Dancing on the Brink*, the second edition of which was released in June 2013. He is the author of numerous articles and blog posts on Africa.

From 2007 to 2008, he was a visiting professor of international relations at the University of Wisconsin–Madison. He was also a Department of State midcareer fellow at Princeton University's Woodrow Wilson School of Public and International Affairs. Prior to his career in the Foreign Service, he taught British and French history at Mary Baldwin College in Staunton, Virginia. Campbell received a BA and MA in history from the University of Virginia and a PhD in seventeenth-century English history from the University of Wisconsin–Madison.